Smart Data

Chapman & Hall/CRC Big Data Series
Series Editor: Sanjay Ranka

Big Data Computing
A Guide for Business and Technology Managers
Vivek Kale

Big Data Management and Processing
Kuan-Ching Li, Hai Jiang, Albert Y. Zomaya

Frontiers in Data Science
Matthias Dehmer, Frank Emmert-Streib

High-Performance Computing for Big Data
Methodologies and Applications
Chao Wang

Big Data Analytics
Tools and Technology for Effective Planning
Arun K. Somani, Ganesh Chandra Deka

Smart Data
State-of-the-Art Perspectives in Computing and Applications
Kuan-Ching Li, Beniamino DiMartino, Laurence T. Yang, Qingchen Zhang

For more information on this series, please visit: www.crcpress.com/Chapman–HallCRC-Big-Data-Series/book-series/CRCBIGDATSER

Smart Data

State-of-the-Art Perspectives in Computing and Applications

Edited by

Kuan-Ching Li
Beniamino DiMartino
Laurence T. Yang
Qingchen Zhang

CRC Press
Taylor & Francis Group
Boca Raton London New York

CRC Press is an imprint of the
Taylor & Francis Group, an **informa** business

A CHAPMAN & HALL BOOK

CRC Press
Taylor & Francis Group
6000 Broken Sound Parkway NW, Suite 300
Boca Raton, FL 33487-2742

First issued in paperback 2020

ISBN-13: 978-1-138-54558-8 (hbk)
ISBN-13: 978-0-367-65647-8 (pbk)

Library of Congress Cataloging-in-Publication Data

Names: Li, Kuan-Ching, editor.
Title: Smart data : state-of-the-art perspectives in computing and applications / edited by Kuan-Ching Li, Beniamino DiMartino, Laurence T. Yang, Qingchen Zhang.
Description: Boca Raton, Florida : CRC Press, [2019] | Includes bibliographical references and index.
Identifiers: LCCN 2018058459 | ISBN 9781138545588 (hardback : alk. paper) | ISBN 9780429507670 (ebook)
Subjects: LCSH: Big data. | Decision making–Data processing. | Computer network resources.
Classification: LCC QA76.9.B45 S63 2019 | DDC 005.7–dc23
LC record available at https://lccn.loc.gov/2018058459

Visit the Taylor & Francis Web site at
http://www.taylorandfrancis.com

and the CRC Press Web site at
http://www.crcpress.com

Contents

Foreword

Data volumes have continued to increase over recent years, many indicating that "data is the new oil" that drives our industry. Although the exact origin of this term remains unclear, *The Economist* magazine provided a good context in [1], suggesting that

> ... technology giants have always benefited from network effects: the more users Facebook signs up, the more attractive signing up becomes for others. With data there are extra network effects. By collecting more data, a firm has more scope to improve its products, which attracts more users, generating even more data, and so on. The more data Tesla gathers from its self-driving cars, the better it can make them at driving themselves—part of the reason the firm, which sold only 25,000 cars in the first quarter, is now worth more than GM, which sold 2.3m.

The increasing access and availability of smart phones-based apps., sensor technologies that monitor and surveil our cities, to increasing consumer communities using online ecommerce portals are reasons for this rise. The trend is global—covering both communications-infrastructure-rich regions (Europe, US, China, South East Asia) to "developing" nations where communications-infrastructure investments exceed other areas. Many developing nations are working hard to internalize communication technologies, balancing the limited allocation of their revenues, to catch up rapidly with the developed economies—seeing such investment as an enabler for other types of growth [2]. Development and access to such infrastructure also provides the basis for data generation/capture.

Google search trends over the last 5 years (normalized to a percentage on Y-axis) demonstrate how interest in "Big Data" has grown over the recent years. This can be compared with interest in Cloud Computing and Deep Learning; the latter has seen significant growth in recent years, also fueled by significant increase in data volumes.

While the generation and storage of data itself is important, making subsequent use and analysis of this is more significant and provides greater utility. The notion of "smart data" often focuses on identifying how decisions can be made using such data (both for a human-driven or an automated process). Machine learning provides an important mechanism for achieving this outcome, which is now increasingly being used across a diverse range of (often time varying) data sets. Such data may be hosted across a distributed range of potential infrastructure (cloud, IoT, and databases).

Google Search Trends (5 Years)

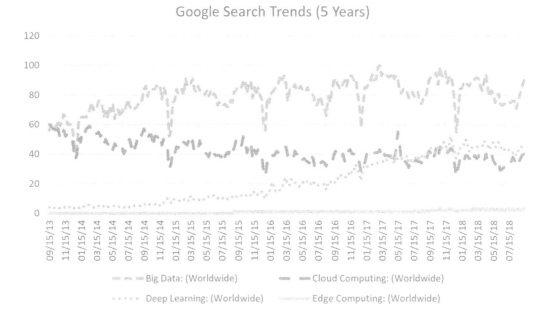

Although a large volume of data exists, many companies treat their own data in a protective manner. The Economist article [1], suggests that these "… vast pools of data can thus act as protective moats." Concerns about the ethical use of this data, and including consumers in the decision about their data use, have also become significant concerns in recent years—as evidenced by the European "General Data Protection Regulation" (GDPR) legislation. Ethical use of data to derive inferences, and informing users about how such inferences are derived, is therefore also a significant aspect of "Smart Data" research.

This book brings together chapters that cover a wide range of topics related to emergence and generation/use of such "Smart Data." The chapters cover topics such as infrastructure (Cloud computing, GPU clusters, and NoSQL databases), data analysis and its use in cybersecurity (e.g., search over encrypted data, deep learning), use of social data (e.g., human behaviour/interaction, tweets) and ethical/data protection issues.

Omer F. Rana
Professor of Performance Engineering
Cardiff University, UK

REFERENCES

1. "The world's most valuable resource is no longer oil, but data," *The Economist*, May 6, 2017. Available at: www.economist.com/leaders/2017/05/06/the-worlds-most-valuable-resource-is-no-longer-oil-but-data – last accessed: September 2018.
2. R. Pradhan, G. Mallik and T. Bagchi. Information communication technology (ICT) infrastructure and economic growth: A causality evidenced by cross-country panel data. *IIMB Management Review*, 30(1):91–103, March 2018.

Acknowledgments

First and foremost we would like to thank and acknowledge the contributors to this volume for their support and patience, and the reviewers for their useful comments and suggestions that helped in improving the earlier outline of the book and presentation of the material. We extend our deepest thanks to Randi Cohen from CRC Press (USA) for her collaboration, guidance, and most importantly, patience in finalizing this book. Finally, we would like to acknowledge the efforts of the team from CRC Press' production department for their extensive efforts during the many phases of this project and the timely fashion in which the book was produced.

Editors

Kuan-Ching Li is a Distinguished Professor of Computer Science and Engineering at Providence University, Taiwan. He is a recipient of guest and distinguished chair professorships from universities in China and other countries, and awards and funding support from a number of agencies and industrial companies. He has been actively involved in many major conferences and workshops in program/general/steering conference chairman positions, and has organized numerous conferences related to high-performance computing and computational science and engineering. He is a Fellow of IET, senior member of the IEEE and a member of the AAAS, Editor-in-Chief of International Journal of Computational Science and Engineering (IJCSE), International Journal of Embedded Systems (IJES), and International Journal of High Performance Computing and Networking (IJHPCN), published by Inderscience. Besides publication of journal and conference research papers, he is co-author/co-editor of several technical professional books published by CRC Press, Springer, McGraw-Hill and IGI Global. His research interests include GPU/many-core computing, Big Data, and Cloud.

Beniamino DiMartino is Full Professor at the University of Campania (Italy). He is author of 14 international books and more than 300 publications in international journals and conferences; has been Coordinator of EU funded FP7-ICT Project mOSAIC, and participates to various international research projects; is Editor / Associate Editor of seven international journals and EB Member of several international journals; is vice Chair of the Executive Board of the IEEE CS Technical Committee on Scalable Computing; is member of: IEEE WG for the IEEE P3203 Standard on Cloud Interoperability, IEEE Intercloud Testbed Initiative, IEEE Technical Committees on Scalable Computing (TCSC) and on Big Data (TCBD), Cloud Standards Customer Council, Cloud Computing Experts' Group of the European Commission.

Dr. Laurence T. Yang is a professor and W.F. James Research Chair at St. Francis Xavier University, Canada. His research includes parallel and distributed computing, embedded systems/internet of things, ubiquitous/pervasive computing and intelligence, and big data. He has published around 400 international journal papers in the above areas, of which half are on top IEEE/ACM Transactions and Journals, others ar mainly on Elsevier, Springer and Wiley Journals. He has been involved actively act as a steering chair for 10+ IEEE international conferences. Now he is the chair of IEEE CS Technical

Committee of Scalable Computing (2018-), the chair of IEEE SMC Technical Committee on Cybermatics (2016-) . He is also serving as an editor for many international journals (such as IEEE Systems Journal, IEEE Access, Future Generation of Computer Systems (Elsevier), Information Sciences (Elsevier), Information Fusion (Elsevier), Big Data Research (Elsevier), etc). He is an elected fellow of Canadian Academy of Engineering (CAE) and Engineering Institute of Canada (EIC).

Dr. Qingchen Zhang is an Assistant Professor at St. Francis Xavier University, Canada. His research interests include big data, machine learning, and smart medicine. He has published more than 20 top international journal papers on the above topics including papers in IEEE Transactions on Computers, IEEE Transactions on Services Computing, ACM Multimedia Computing, Communications and Applications, and so on. He got an IEEE TCSC Award for Excellence in Scalable Computing for Early Career Researchers in 2018. He served as vice chair of IEEE Canada Atlantic Section CIS/SMC joint chapter (2018-2019). He served as a program chair of IEEE 14th International Conference on Pervasive, Intelligence and Computing (PICom 2016) and IEEE 11th International Conference on Internet of Things (iThings 2018). In addition, he is one of the guest editors of several international journals such as Future Generation Computer Systems, IEEE Access and Wireless Communication and Mobile Computing.

Contributors

Mohammad Saad Alam
Aligarh Muslim University
Aligarh, India

Jeff Anderson
The George Washington University
Washington, USA

Paolo Balboni
Professor
Privacy, Cybersecurity, and IT Contract
Law at the European Centre on Privacy
   and Cybersecurity (ECPC)
Maastricht University Faculty of Law
   Maastricht, Netherlands

Founding Partner
ICT Legal Consulting
Milan, Italy

President
European Privacy Association
Brussels, Belgium

Yixin Bao
Department of Computer Science
The University of Hong Kong
Hong Kong, China

I. Barranco-Chamorro
Department of Statistics and Operations
   Research
University of Sevilla
Sevilla, Spain

Elizabeth Bautista
Lawrence Berkeley National Labs
Berkeley, CA

M.M. Sufyan Beg
Aligarh Muslim University
Aligarh, India

Rajkumar Buyya
School of Computing and Information
Systems
The University of Melbourne
Melbourne, Australia

Liliana Carvalho
COPELABS,
Universidade Lusófona
Lisboa, Portugal

Theodora Chaspari
College Station, Texas
TX, USA

Edward T. Chen
University of Massachusetts Lowell
Lowell, Massachusetts

David Dampier
The University of Texas at San Antonio
San Antonio, Texas

Daniel Dunea
Valahia University of Targoviste
Targoviste, Romania

Tarek El-Ghazawi
The George Washington University
Washington, D.C.

Yupeng Hu
College of Computer Science and
    Electronic Engineering
Hunan University
Changsha, China

Md. Muzakkir Hussain
Aligarh Muslim University
Aligarh, India

Shashikant Ilager
School of Computing and Information
    Systems
The University of Melbourne
Melbourne, Australia

Kenichi Ito
School of Human Sciences
Waseda University
Tokyo, Japan

Qun Jin
Faculty of Human Sciences
Waseda University
Tokyo, Japan

Raghavendra Kune
Advanced Data Processing Research
    Institute
Department of Space
Secunderabad, India

Keqin Li
College of Computer Science and
    Electronic Engineering
Hunan University
Changsha, China

Department of Computer Science
State University of New York
Albany, New York

Wenjia Li
Department of Computer Science
New York Institute of Technology
Long Island, NY

Yonghe Liu
Department of Computer Science and
    Engineering
University of Texas
Arlington, Texas

Emil Lungu
Valahia University of Targoviste
Targoviste, Romania

Gayla Margolin
University of Southern California
Los Angeles, California

Armin Mehrabian
The George Washington University
Washington, D.C.

Melody Moh
Department of Computer Science
San Jose State University
San Jose, California

Teng-Sheng Moh
Department of Computer
    Science
San Jose State University
San Jose, California

S. Muñoz-Armayones
Datrik Intelligence
Sevilla, Spain

Jiaxin Peng
The George Washington University
Washington, D.C.

Francisco M. Pereira
COPELABS
Universidade Lusófona
Lisboa, Portugal

Alin Pohoata
Valahia University of Targoviste
Targoviste, Romania

Zheng Qin
College of Computer Science and
    Electronic Engineering
Hunan University
Changsha, China

Robinson Raju
Department of Computer Science
San Jose State University
San Jose, California

F. Romero-Campero
Department of Computer Science and
    Artificial Intelligence
University of Sevilla
Sevilla, Spain

Plant Development Unit Institute
    for Plant
Biochemistry and Photosynthesis
Sevilla, Spain

A. Romero-Losada
Department of Computer Science and
    Artificial Intelligence
University of Sevilla
Sevilla, Spain

Plant Development Unit Institute
    for Plant
Biochemistry and Photosynthesis
Sevilla, Spain

Sonny Sevin
Slippery Rock University of Pennsylvania
Slippery Rock, Pennsylvania

S. M. Shariff
Department of Electrical Engineering
Taibah University
Madinah, Saudi Arabia

Rute C. Sofia
COPELABS
Universidade Lusófona
Lisboa, Portugal

Kiichi Tago
Graduate School of Human Sciences
Waseda University
Tokyo, Japan

Christophe Thovex
France French-Mexican Laboratory
    on Computer Science and Control
LAFMIA
Universidad de Las Americas
Puebla, Mexico

Adela C. Timmons
Florida International University
Miami, Florida

Rajeev Wankar
School of Computer and Information
    Sciences
University of Hyderabad
Hyderabad, India

Chuan Wu
Department of Computer Science
The University of Hong Kong
Hong Kong, China

Linjun Wu
College of Computer Science and
  Electronic Engineering
Hunan University
Changsha, China

CHAPTER 1

Extreme Heterogeneity in Deep Learning Architectures

Jeff Anderson, Armin Mehrabian, Jiaxin Peng, and
Tarek El-Ghazawi

The George Washington University

CONTENTS

1 INTRODUCTION

Within the past few years, electronic devices that process voice commands have become ubiquitous in society. Some of these devices, such as the Amazon Echo and the Google Home, provide information to users and control their homes, while other devices, such as cellular phones, are more mobile in nature but perform similar functions.

The recent success of voice-activated electronics can be attributed to the field of Machine Learning (ML), and more specifically to the development of Convolutional Neural Networks (CNNs) and Deep Learning (DL). Due to the development of these advanced techniques, neural networks (NNs) can now successfully perform classification tasks such as far-field voice recognition, speech-to-text translation, natural language processing, and computer vision [1].

Researchers are now turning NN-based systems to other application areas, such as identification of radio frequency (RF) wave modulation [2–4]. These functions are building blocks for higher level functionality, such as cognitive radio and cognitive radar, where efficiency is gained through automatic adjustments made in response to the system's knowledge of its current RF environment [3].

Current research in ML focuses on different application areas and efficient training methods, but the bulk of research has been on NNs implemented in server-based computing clusters [1–8]. This does not match well with cognitive radio and cognitive radar, which are implemented as small, embedded systems, where real-time performance is expected and power and energy consumption is watched very closely [9,10]. These systems are characterized by constraints on compute resources, size, weight, and power, and follow a different model than a server-based model [11]; instead of increasing efficiency by servicing multiple users in a batch-processing fashion, one task at a time must be executed quickly and efficiently.

Before implementing NNs in embedded computer platforms, it is worth reviewing state-of-the-art hardware architectures implementing NNs for various applications. The remainder of this section will review Deep Neural Networks (DNNs) and advances in ML. Section 2 summarizes hardware architectures that are likely to be useful for NN implementations in embedded systems. Following the review of hardware architectures, field-programmable gate arrays in DL are summarized in Section 3 and then a discussion on the future of heterogeneous embedded systems in DL in Section 4.

1.1 Deep Learning

Machine Learning is the practice of enabling computers to learn how to perform a task through exposure to data, as opposed to simply executing routines explicitly coded to accomplish specific tasks. During their learning phase, machines go through exhaustive iterations of a training procedure; and over the course of the training, they try to minimize errors generated from the mismatch between what they understand to be true and the ground truth.

Since their introduction by McCulloch and Pitts in 1943 [12], NNs have become the primary architecture used for machine learning applications. These networks comprise multiple layers of neurons, where the connections between layers are selected to maximize the likelihood of a correct classification. Initially an academic curiosity, NNs have recently gained mainstream acceptance due to their successes in solving many complex artificial intelligence (AI) problems. In 2006, Hinton et al. [13] proposed a method to train an NN with many layers (Deep), which was not feasible beforehand. The field, Deep Learning, put NNs back in the spotlight and has become the mainstream solution to many AI problems including, but not limited to, voice and speech recognition [1], image classification/segmentation [5,6], natural language processing (NLP) [14,15], gaming AI [10], and analysis of particle physics data [16].

Almost all types of ML (including DL) go through two phases of operation, namely training and inference. During the training phase, NNs are trained to perform particular tasks by taking input vectors and checking the output of the network. Incorrect outputs are used to train the network through back-propagation from the output layer to the input layer, where parameters (weights) of each input layer are adjusted until the output of the NN reaches the desired result. This is repeated for a large training data set until the NN reaches an acceptable probability of classification. Then, the trained NNs are used to perform the designated task during the inference phase.

Different types of NNs, called NN models, such as CNNs, Recurrent Neural Networks (RNNs), and Long Short-Term Memory (LSTM) Neural Networks, have been shown to be efficient for specific classifications and have their own sets of operations with diverse computational and communication requirements. For instance, CNNs are widely used to solve image classification problems in DL as described by Champlin et al. [17]. The input of a CNN is typically an image, and the CNN uses several filters, comprising multiple neurons, to derive the feature maps, which are considered distinguished components for image classification tasks. There are hundreds of filters in each convolutional layer, and each CNN has several convolutional layers. In fact, 2D convolution, implemented as multiply-accumulate (MAC) operations inside of a neuron, occupies more than 90% of the CNN computation time [18]. After flowing through several convolutional layers, the feature maps are sent to several fully connected layers, where the CNN produces classification categories.

RNN and LSTM, while similar to a CNN from the standpoint of network architecture, introduce a time dependency to the network, where a neuron's output is stored and then fed back into the neuron during subsequent calculations. Time-dependent networks such as these have proven useful for natural language processing tasks [2].

While the focus of the DL community has primarily been on functionality and the introduction of novel DL approaches, hardware and software performance optimizations of the existing NN models are now receiving more attention. Each new implementation attempts to optimize specific facets of performance, from specific network architectures designed to reduce latency and increase throughput, to computation accelerators designed to increase the performance of specific calculations. Prior to elaborating on specific architectures, it is beneficial to understand which facets of DL can benefit most from optimization.

1.2 Deep Learning Operations

The most obvious facet of DL which can benefit from optimization is the weighted summation function, usually implemented as a MAC. Each neuron in each layer is required to perform a weighted summation of all inputs from the prior layer, as shown below:

$$Y_j = \sum_{i=1}^{s} in_{i,j-1} \times w_{i,j} \qquad (1)$$

For an NN with millions of neurons, this represents an opportunity to optimize a large operation which occupies the majority of the NN's computation time in both training and inference phases. Alternative NN accelerator architectures which use exotic technologies, such as memristors [19], charge-trap devices [20], and photonics [21], target this operation, specifically. NNs implemented in a traditional digital architecture optimize this operation for either performance [22] or hardware footprint [23]. Binarized Neural Networks (BNN) were developed to minimize the MAC footprint by constraining the multiply operation to weights of $-1, 0$, or 1.

The output of a neuron's MAC is then sent through an activation function before exiting the neuron. This applies a transfer function to the output of a weighted summation, and can range from a simple linear function, such as a step or ramp, to a nonlinear function such as a sigmoid or Rectified Linear Unit (ReLU). While great in number, the simplest of these functions (ReLU and step) consist of only a comparator, limiting the types of optimizations that can be done and increasing the importance of selecting an efficient function.

Pooling and normalization operations are among the most common types of operations found in CNNs. Pooling layers in CNNs act as digital filters in both phases, making the network insensitive to small variations of values by performing Average or Max operations, as shown below:

$$Y_{i,j} = max/average(X_{i+l_i,j+l_j}) \qquad (2)$$

Pooling functions are implemented through the replacement of a neuron's accumulator with a function which selects the maximum or average value out of a group of multipliers. Usually implemented as a parallel comparator or serial comparator with feedback, this function can be viewed, from a resource or performance perspective, as approximately equivalent to the accumulator that it replaces.

Normalization conducts a form of lateral inhibition by normalizing over local input regions [24]. Also called Local Response Normalization (LRN), two modes exist: across neighboring features and within the same feature, as calculated with Equations (3) and (4), respectively.

$$Y_{i,j}^t = X_{i,j}^t \div (u + \alpha \sum_{l=max(0,t-\frac{s}{2})}^{min(n-1,t+\frac{s}{2})} (X_{i,j}^l)^2)^\beta \tag{3}$$

$$Y_{i,j}^t = X_{i,j}^t \div (u + \alpha \sum_{l_i=i-\frac{s}{2}}^{i+\frac{s}{2}} \sum_{l_j=j-\frac{s}{2}}^{j+\frac{s}{2}} (X_{i+l_i,j+l_j})^2)^\beta \tag{4}$$

1.3 Deep Learning Network Communications

The complex and varied communication structure within an NN places an equal importance on an efficient network structure as it does efficient neuron architectures. For instance, different types of layers in an NN impose their own set of connection demands. Fully Connected (FC) layers have all-to-all connections from neurons in one layer to the adjoining layer. Convolutional layers also use the all-to-all connection network; however, weights are shared between neurons, thus requiring less memory in a shared-memory architecture and increasing the importance of locality of neurons in a Nonuniform Memory Access (NUMA) architecture.

Gradient Descent is used in the NN training phase to tune input weights. Upon completion of an incorrect classification, back-propagation occurs through the network where neuron weights are adjusted until the classification is correct. Adjustment of weights is done iteratively, where small adjustments are made, minimizing the absolute error (the squared difference of the predicted value and the required value) of the neuron's output. The direction of weight adjustment is based on a history of past adjustments, which is stored in memory during the training phase. This places importance on efficient inter-chip communications during the back-propagation of results, making array-based architectures (multiple cores on a single chip) the preferred architecture for efficient operation. Stochastic Gradient Descent (SGD) is a method of optimizing the Gradient Descent algorithm, where only a subset of weights is adjusted, decreasing the amount of traffic between memory and specific neurons.

1.3.1 Data and Model Parallelism

NNs, in general, enjoy two types of parallelism, namely data parallelism and model parallelism (shown in Figure 1.1). In data parallelism, the input data is broken into segments of mutually exclusive sets. Each data segment, or shard, is then trained on a full local copy of the NN. Afterwards, all trained models are combined to return a full global model. In model parallelism, the model is broken into multiple model segments, each being trained with full copy of the dataset. Augmenting all of these sub-models will result in a full global model. In practice, the two approaches can be combined to take advantage of the best of both worlds.

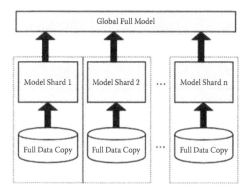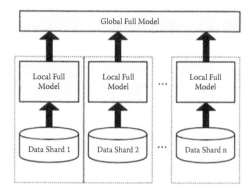

FIGURE 1.1   Model parallelism (left) and data parallelism (right). These optimizations enable an NN to be distributed over a large system, reducing the time needed for training.

With DL models becoming larger and more complicated, the need for hardware platforms that can fulfill the computational requirements of DNNs, while maintaining efficiency, has become obvious. Despite the success of Graphics Processing Unit (GPU)-based coprocessing during the training and inference phases of DL, many recent hardware platforms have incorporated application-specific hardware for DNN processing in the form of special features [25] or accelerators for specific DNN processing subtasks [26]. These new hardware architectures have a complex network and memory hierarchy which require software optimizations to achieve peak performance for DL computation kernels. Recent DL algorithms [27,28] have shown that using lower precision data types can give similar performance with higher power-efficiency.

2 HARDWARE ARCHITECTURES FOR DEEP LEARNING

2.1 Microprocessors

Microprocessor-based, or Central Processing Unit (CPU), DL systems are the most flexible, enabling CPU-based execution of any neuron function. This flexibility comes at a cost; CPU-based DL systems generally cannot, by themselves, quickly execute complex DL classifications. High-performance implementations of large NNs typically require more parallelism than can be provided by single CPU [29], thus requiring a complex network of CPUs, which subjects them to penalties associated with network performance. Multicore architectures contain clusters of CPUs which, typically, access a shared memory. This shared memory can increase the NN's performance over that of traditionally-networked CPUs through reduced latencies during data fetch and store cycles.

Manycore processor architectures, such as Intel Xeon Phi Knights Landing (KNL), provide the advantage of CPU-based flexibility with the performance advantages of an on-chip, high-speed network (shown in Figure 1.2), also called a Network-on-a-Chip (NoC). Neurons are mapped over several CPU cores, with each core executing a subset of calculations required by the neuron, and intermediate results are passed between

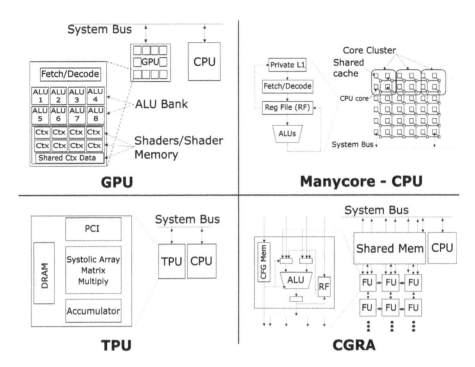

FIGURE 1.2 CGRA, GPU, TPU and Manycore computer architectures. These architectures enable the natural flow of data from one processing unit to another, enabling accelerated NN computations. The TPU differs from all other architectures, as it is a domain-specific accelerator designed for NN coprocessing.

cores within a neuron's cluster until they are reduced to a single value output from one core. For CPU-intensive operations, the Manycore architecture enables efficient passing of intermediate values from one processor to another without saturating the memory bus [30]. High-bandwidth communications between processors and memory in the KNL accelerate the training phase, where large amounts of data are frequently moved between memory and execution units [31].

Advances in computer architecture have increased the number of neuron operations which can be successfully implemented in a single microprocessor. CPUs whose execution units contain wide vector processing units or Single Instruction Multiple Data (SIMD) units are capable of DL processing through support of temporal parallelism or data parallelism, respectively [30].

2.2 Digital Signal Processors

Digital Signal Processor (DSP)-based DL systems are similar to CPU-based systems in terms of their flexibility. As such, they can be treated as CPU-based architectures, where the DSP contains specialized hardware to accelerate MAC functions. Driver assistance research has made extensive use of DSPs in DL systems and gains in efficiency have been made by using the DSP's natively-accelerated MAC, fixed-point conversion, and lookup tables [32]. It should be noted that recent research has shown that the feed-forward inference phase of NNs only requires limited numerical precision, making DSPs which support fixed-point arithmetic an attractive choice [24,32].

2.3 Graphics Processing Units

The mainstreaming of General Purpose Graphics Processing Unit (GPGPU)-assisted computing has enabled the successful implementation of nontrivial DL systems. With each CPU core acting as a neuron, MAC operations required by a multi-input neuron are accelerated using the massive SIMD operations enabled by a GPU, under CPU coordination (shown in Figure 1.2). The flow of data within a GPU becomes problematic, as GPU cores cannot communicate in the most efficient manner possible. The difficulties arise when mapping neuron operations, which require parallelism and efficient reductions, to a GPU architecture which is designed to accelerate highly parallel, streaming operations. Research has shown that for the multiplication of small matrices, the overhead associated with GPU data duplication results in poor efficiency and decreases its performance to that of many other, more generic, parallel architectures [10].

2.4 Coarse Grained Reconfigurable Architectures

Coarse Grained Reconfigurable Architectures (CGRAs) reside somewhere in between a GPU and Manycore architecture and are primarily used in embedded applications. A CGRA (shown in Figure 1.2) can be tightly coupled (integrated with the CPU) or loosely coupled (a coprocessor architecture) with a larger processor and is simply an array of Issue Slots (IS), or Functional Units (FU), connected by a network. An IS is simply a module containing an Arithmetic Logic Unit (ALU), or multiple ALUs, and a Register File for storing temporary computations and instructions awaiting execution. The great benefit of the CGRA is its support for single-cycle reconfiguration. Recent research has targeted both inference [10,33] and training [10] by focusing on specialized FUs capable of efficient MAC operations and communication reduction using efficient and highly scalable interconnects.

2.5 Tensor Processing Units

Tensor Processing Units (TPUs) are specifically designed to accelerate high-overhead neuron operations, and are used as accelerators in CPU-based DL architectures [7,8]. In general, TPUs are designed to efficiently execute MAC operations before sending results to a local CPU for decision-making. MAC operations are efficiently accelerated using a systolic array and results are passed to a CPU over a high-bandwidth communication bus [7,34]. Recent research has shown that TPU coprocessors outperform GPU-based coprocessor systems in terms of operations and power dissipation [7].

2.6 Mapping Deep Learning to an Architecture

Mapping a DL architecture onto a particular hardware architecture requires that trades be made regarding neuron functions within a node (or, conversely, the spreading of

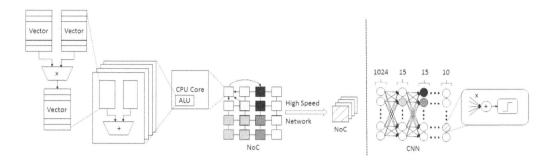

FIGURE 1.3 Convolutional Neural Network (right) and its mapping onto a Manycore distributed architecture (left). Note the decline in traffic as the neural network goes from left to right, due to a reduction of inputs from previous layers. Also note that temporal parallelism is gained by vectorizing weight multiplication and spatial parallelism is gained by SIMD execution of addition and multiplication. Cores in neuron-mapped clusters (comprising adjacent cores) send intermediate results to the cluster's biasing neuron, which completes the accumulation and determines the neuron's output.

neuron functions among several nodes), and the network connecting the nodes (shown in Figure 1.3). As data flows from the input layer to the output layer, a critical path can be drawn through the paths with the highest latency. For fully connected neural networks, the total network latency is the sum of maximum delays for all layers.

Due to the system's dependence on network latencies, the principles of data locality should be adhered to when assigning tasks to nodes. Multi-node neuron calculations should be kept as physically close together as possible to keep the timing of all nodes consistent, thus reducing the calculation's dependence on network latency. While same-layer neurons do not need to be physically co-located, their distance to the next-layer neurons should be kept consistent in order to minimize the critical path. Ideally, the NN mapping should be structured such that large movements of data are confined to nearest-neighbor cores, and fully connected neuron-to-neuron messages contain a reduced dataset. This should yield optimal network traffic and reduce the parasitic effects of network distance.

Locality was optimally exploited by Tanomoto and Fan, and they achieve comparable performance to high-performance parallel processing architectures for small, streaming datasets [10,33]. Locality can also be exploited in CNN layers, due to weight-sharing among neurons. For any cluster-based architecture, such as multicore architectures, processors executing neuron operations within a layer should be chosen such that they have affinity to the memory where weights reside.

Additionally, advanced features native to processors can be used to accelerate NN functionality. While the BNN was developed for efficient implementation in a Field Programmable Gate Array (FPGA), it can also be mapped to a processor's vector engine, where the neuron weights are used as mask bits for vector addition. Negative weights arc used to reverse the sign bit of the neuron's input data, and are then subsequently used as mask bits during the accumulation.

Combining MAC coprocessors and multicore microprocessors gives an additional degree of freedom to designers of DL systems. Each core can be mapped to a neuron and share coprocessor resources until resources are unavailable or the CPU-coprocessor network fabric becomes saturated. Due to CPU-coprocessor network overhead, multiple partial MAC reductions can be sent from a coprocessor to a microprocessor core, where the final reduction can be accelerated by the core's SIMD or vector operations and take advantage of low-latency local cache.

3 FPGAS IN DEEP LEARNING

FPGAs have been used to implement the aforementioned architectures in both prototype and production systems [8,34,35] and are used where high performance per watt is required, such as high-performance systems and resource-constrained embedded systems [33,36]. In fact, due to their usefulness in NN implementation, many FPGA frameworks have been introduced which take, as input, NN descriptions such as Caffe and produce Register Transfer Language (RTL) which can then be synthesized and converted into an FPGA bitstream [37]. These frameworks, at a minimum, allow the designer to specify the NNs data type and select from a library of components designed to provide efficiencies in footprint or performance.

Due to an FPGA's internal architecture containing DSP blocks and localized memory, highly efficient implementations of NNs can be realized [34,38]. The focus of FPGA-based NN optimizations centers around two areas: communications reduction [24,38,39] and processing element optimizations [8,24,39,40].

3.1 FPGA Optimizations for NN Operations

3.1.1 Communications Path Optimizations

In [24] and [39], a reduction in communications is achieved through a reduction in memory accesses. Local memory shared between multiple neighboring processing elements in a single layer serves as a cache for data stored in main memory. Additionally, intermediate results are moved from one layer to another via a bus between local memories. Latency is reduced to the time needed to transfer weights from main memory to the local memory of the initial layer, as computations for one layer are executed while the next layer's weights are being transferred to local memory. Zhang et al. also promote reuse of weight data between different processing elements in an attempt to compress the data requiring transfer. Kamel exploited data locality by using neighboring DSPs as processing elements for adjacent layers in [38], reducing the need for long-distance data transfers.

3.1.2 Processing Element Optimizations

Processing element optimizations are shown in [8,24,39,40]. Zhang et al. and Ma et al. use loop unrolling and loop pipelining to accelerate MAC operations [39,40]. Liu et al. explored custom blocks for convolution, fully connected, pooling, and normalization layers using DSPs internal to the FPGA [24]. Nurvitadhi explored the use of an FPGA framework to accelerate known bottlenecks in NN computation: matrix multiplications for both sparse and dense matrices, binarized matrix operations, and weight-sharing using lookup tables [8].

3.1.3 NN Model Optimizations

FPGAs are especially well suited for the execution of BNNs [41]. A BNN reduces the footprint of a neuron through constraining all weight multiplicands to values of −1, 0, or 1. This effectively reduces the multiplication hardware to an exclusive-OR gate for the sign bit, followed by a pass-gate for the entire register. This structure can be emulated using the mask bit of a vector engine in a CPU, but requires unnatural data movements, reducing performance. An FPGA can simply be configured to implement a BNN and reap the benefits of a reduced hardware footprint directly.

3.2 FPGA Reconfigurability for NNs

3.2.1 FPGA Reconfigurability in Inference Processing

While FPGAs are used when a high performance per watt is required, their true strength lies in their ability to be tailored for a specific application. State-of-the-art FPGAs support partial reconfiguration, which can be used to optimize a fielded system for high efficiency at low cost [42]. For cognitive systems implemented in an embedded computer, an NN can be used as an AI system [10], where a final reconfiguration decision is made after analyzing initial readings from the environment. This allows resource-constrained systems to implement a variety of NN architectures.

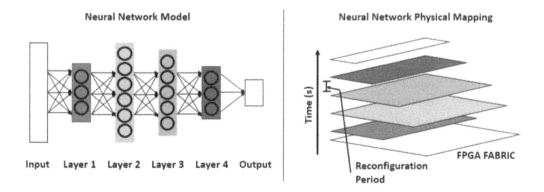

FIGURE 1.4   Time-sharing of an FPGA (right) by segments of a distributed DNN (left). Relaxing the requirement for the batch processing of requests from multiple users enables a distributed DNN to share FPGA resources among multiple segments in a pipeline fashion. The time required for layer reconfiguration is negligible when compared with the time required for NN layer execution, and enabled by modern FPGA support for high-speed partial reconfiguration.

As the performance of DNNs in the acoustic and image domains is limited by network depth [2], larger and deeper networks could be required to achieve required classification accuracies. To combat the inevitable situation where an NN model overwhelms the resources available through its host system, a method for distributed deep learning has been proposed in [43], where model parallelism is achieved by splitting the NN model temporally over the FPGA, as shown in Figure 1.4. This allows a large NN to be implemented on a small FPGA, thereby reducing cost and power budget, at the expense of batch processing. This technique can also be used in large NN systems, where multiple NN architectures are daisy-chained to execute complex inferences [2].

3.2.2 FPGA Reconfigurability in NN Training

The reconfigurability of FPGAs also enables optimized training and inference processing on the same system. Current NNs are trained offline, usually on a server-based system, and then ported to embedded architectures for the inference phase. This is a less-than-desirable situation, as inference performance cannot be adequately gauged until the embedded system has been built [10]. This situation must be addressed as embedded implementations of NNs reach maturity.

To this end, reconfigurability can help bridge the gap between NNs configured for training and inference. Recent findings have shown that the NN training phase only requires 16-bit precision [34], but the inference phase can successfully be executed with only 8 bits of precision [7]. Additionally, the back-propagation requirement of NN training consumes resources that are never used during inference processing. Static systems designed for training cannot easily be tailored for inference processing, causing inefficiencies in the NN after the training phase completes. An FPGA-based embedded system could be reconfigured from training-optimized to inference-optimized, and any unused resources could be reconfigured for general-purpose use by the system.

4 DISCUSSION

Heterogeneous computer systems comprise many different accelerators, and possibly reconfigurable components, and have been shown to be effective architectures for high-performance computing. Recent research has attempted to address heterogeneity in NN computing, but as standard NN models are constructed with a single data type, distribution of the NN is limited to modules with like precisions [44,45]. This leaves much of a heterogeneous system wasted, as floating point units cannot take part in computation of a fixed-point NN operation. For advanced nodes, where static power draw of transistors consumes as much as half of the power of an ASIC [46], idle hardware cannot be tolerated.

4.1 Neural Network Models for Heterogeneous Systems

A heterogeneous NN model (Figure 1.5) would allow for an NN comprising layers, each of which being a different precision data type. This enables additional compute

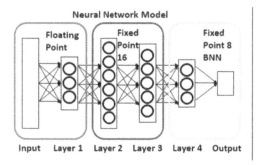
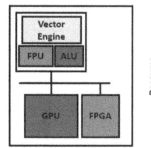
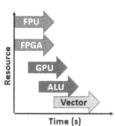

FIGURE 1.5   A heterogeneous NN model enables the use of more resources within a heterogeneous computer than standard NN models, which contain neurons of a single data type. This NN model supports the parallelization of operations within a heterogeneous system, thereby supporting high-efficiency operation.

units in a heterogeneous system to participate in the classification task, reducing the power consumed during a single classification. Batch processing schedulers of NN classifications could then take advantage of idle hardware during an NN classification task and start preprocessing the next NN task with the idle hardware. Additionally, more power savings could be achieved through the assignment of NN data type based on the operation being performed. It was shown in [47] that the efficiency with which specific NN operations are executed varies depending on the data type involved in the operation. Thus, for specific layers within a heterogeneous NN architecture, the most appropriate hardware could be selected for a given network configuration.

Heterogeneity within an NN model has the ability to increase the classification accuracy of NN models which have historically low classification accuracies. While current research shows that appropriate levels of classification accuracies are maintained when using NN models of lower precision [34], it cannot be denied that classification accuracies decline as precision of the NN data type is reduced [45]. This is due to error propagation through the NN hidden layers (Figure 1.6), governed by

FIGURE 1.6   Error propagation through the hidden layers reduces the classification accuracy of an NN for a given precision. Replacement of neurons within select layers in a heterogeneous NN reduces the total error propagated through the system, resulting in increased classification accuracy.

Equation (5). Note the recursive nature of the error function, as it is expanded throughout the network. This best illustrates the natural error imparted on the system by an individual NN layer, *i*, with an associated error function, Err_i, which is then absorbed by the next layer.

$$error_i = Err_i(Err_{i-1}(Input_{i-1})) \tag{5}$$

Replacement of select low-precision neurons within the hidden layers would reduce error propagation, thereby increasing the classification accuracy of a low-precision homogeneous NN. Analysis of Equation (5) shows that best results require the use of high-precision data types early in the NN to minimize the reduction in classification accuracy associated with long-term error propagation through the network.

This observation also shows that a heterogeneous NN model would enable energy-quality (EQ) scaling within the system, where a scheduler could assign resources of different precisions based on the energy required to achieve an accuracy objective. As low-power computer operation has recently begun to draw widespread attention, EQ scaling has proven to be an important technique to be adopted by future computing systems [48]. Maximum likelihood classifiers, such as NN-based systems, naturally take advantage of EQ scaling through their theory of operation, and the use of a heterogeneous NN model would serve to increase the granularity of EQ scaling supported by these systems.

5 CONCLUSION

As more everyday uses are found for NNs, it is inevitable that more use cases will arise that do not match with the current server-based NN implementation model. For these use cases, an embedded system may be expected to host the NN locally with little performance degradation. FPGAs create an avenue by which NNs can be efficiently implemented in embedded systems and optimized for either training or inference. This flexibility allows the NN to be designed and tested directly on the system, affording designers the opportunity to gauge performance early in the design cycle.

As FPGAs are offered with ML frameworks and native ML functionality, further advances in DL platforms will likely come from taking advantage of NN-specific resources and time-sharing of the FPGA for distributed NNs. Time-sharing of FPGA resources is made possible by FPGA support of dynamic partial reconfiguration, and the realization that embedded systems do not need to support the batching of user requests in the name of efficiency. This diversion from the common use model opens up degrees of freedom in the NN design space.

Finally, combinations of microprocessors and hardware accelerators can take the form of a heterogeneous system. These systems, while able to execute a large number of simultaneous operations, cannot be maximally exploited for NN processing due to inconsistencies in the data types being handled. A heterogeneous NN would improve this situation, maximizing resource usage during NN execution. Additionally, portions of the NN could be assigned to different data types for reduced-power implementations of specific NN configurations.

FURTHER READING

Ardakani, A., Condo, C., Ahmadi, M. and Gross, W.J. (2018). An architecture to accelerate convolution in deep neural networks. *IEEE Transactions on Circuits and Systems I: Regular Papers.*

Fox, P. (2013). Massively parallel neural computation. *University of Cambridge Computer Laboratory Technical Report: Number 830.*

Guo, K., Zeng, S., Yu, J., Wang, Y. and Yang, H. (2017). A survey of FPGA based neural network accelerator. *arXiv*, 1712.08934.

Venieris, S.I., Kouris, A. and Bouganis, C. (2018). Toolflows for mapping convolutional neural networks on FPGAs: A survey and future directions. *ACM Computing Surveys*, 51.

Hennessey, J. and Patterson, D. (2017). *Computer Architecture: A Quantitive Approach*, 6th ed. Morgan Kaufmann. Chap. 7.

West, N. and OShea, T. (2017). Deep architectures for modulation recognition. *IEEE International Symposium on Dynamic Spectrum Access Networks (DySPAN).*

Giefers, H., Staar, P., Bekas, C. and Hagleitner, C. (2016). Analyzing the energy-efficiency of sparse matrix multiplication on heterogeneous systems: A comparative study of GPU, Xeon Phi and FPGA. *IEEE International Symposium on Performance Analysis of Systems and Software (ISPASS).*

REFERENCES

1. Li Deng, Jinyu Li, Jui-Ting Huang, Kaisheng Yao, Dong Yu et al. Recent advances in deep learning for speech research at Microsoft. In *2013 IEEE International Conference on Acoustics, Speech and Signal Processing (ICASSP)*, pp. 8604–8608. IEEE, 2013.
2. Nathan E. West and Tim O'Shea. Deep architectures for modulation recognition. In *IEEE International Symposium on Dynamic Spectrum Access Networks*. IEEE, 2017.
3. Timothy J. O'Shea, Johnathan Corgan, and T. Charles Clancy. Convolutional radio modulation recognition networks. In *International Conference of Engineering Applications of Neural Networks*. February 2016.
4. Krishna Karra, Scott Kuzdeba, and Josh Peterson. Modulation recognition using hierarchical deep neural networks. In *IEEE International Symposium on Dynamic Spectrum Access Networks*. IEEE, 2017.
5. Christian Szegedy, Sergey Ioffe, Vincent Vanhoucke, and Alexander A Alemi. Inception-v4, inception-resnet and the impact of residual connections on learning. In *AAAI Conference on Artificial Intelligence*. 2017.
6. Liang-Chieh Chen, George Papandreou, Iasonas Kokkinos, Kevin Murphy, and Alan L Yuille. Deeplab: Semantic image segmentation with deep convolutional nets, atrous convolution, and fully connected CRFs. *arXiv preprint arXiv:1606.00915*, 2016.
7. Norman P. Jouppi, Cliff Young, Nishant Patil, David Patterson, Gaurav Agrawal et al. In-datacenter analysis of tensor processing unit. In *Proceedings of the International Symposium on Computer Architecture (ISCA)*, 2017.
8. Eriko Nurvitadhi. Can FPGAs beat GPUs in accelerating next-generation deep neural networks? In *Proceedings of the ACM/SIGDA International Symposium on Field-Programmable Gate Arrays (FPGA17)*, 2017.

9. Marilyn Wold. *High-Performance Embedded Computing: Applications in Cyber-Physical Systems*. Elsevier, 2014.

10. Masakazu Tanomoto, Shinya Takamaeda-Yamazaki, Jun Yao, Yasuhiko Nakashima. A CGRA-based approach for accelerating convolutional neural networks. In *Proceedings of the IEEE 9th International Symposium on Embedded Multicore/Many-core Systems on a Chip (MCSOC2015)*, 2015.

11. Li Du, Yuan Du, Yilei Li, Junjie Su, Yen-Cheng Kuan, Chun-Chen Liu, and Mau-Chung Frank Chang. A reconfigurable streaming deep convolutional neural network accelerator for internet of things. In *IEEE Transactions on Circuits and Systems I: Regular Papers*, (99):1–11, 2017.

12. Warren McCullogh and Walter Pitts. A logical calculus of ideas immanent in nervous activity. *Bulletin of Mathematical Biophysics*, 5, (4):115–133, December 1943.

13. Geoffrey E Hinton, Simon Osindero, and Yee-Whye Teh. A fast learning algorithm for deep belief nets. *Neural Computation*, 18(7):1527–1554, 2006.

14. Ilya Sutskever, Oriol Vinyals, and Quoc V Le. Sequence to sequence learning with neural networks. In *Advances in Neural Information Processing Systems*, pages 3104–3112, 2014.

15. Dzmitry Bahdanau, Kyunghyun Cho, and Yoshua Bengio. Neural machine translation by jointly learning to align and translate. *arXiv preprint arXiv:1409.0473*, 2014.

16. Pierre Baldi, Peter Sadowski, and Daniel Whiteson. Searching for exotic particles in high-energy physics with deep learning. *arXiv preprint arXiv:1402.4735*, 2014.

17. Cary Champlin, David Bell, and Celina Schocken. AI medicine comes to Africa's rural clinics. *IEEE Spectrum*, 54(5):42–48, 2017.

18. Jason Cong and Bingjun Xiao. Minimizing computation in convolutional neural networks. In *International Conference on Artificial Neural Networks*, pages 281–290. Springer, 2014.

19. Miao Hu, John Paul Strachan, Zhiyong Li, Emmanuelle M. Grafals, Noraica Davila et al. Dot product engine (DPE) for neuromorphic computing: Programming 1T1M crossbar to accelerate matrix-vector multiplication. In *The 53rd Annual Design Automation Conference*. ACM, 2016.

20. Suma George, Sihwan Kim, Sahil Shah, Jennifer Hasler, Michelle Collins et al. A programmable and configurable mixed-mode FPAA SoC. *IEEE Transactions on Very Large Scale Integration (VLSI) Systems*, 24(6), 2015.

21. Armin Mehrabian, Yousra Alkabani, Volker Sorger, and Tarek El-Ghazawi. PCNNA: A photonic convolutional neural network accelerator. *arXiv:1807.08792*, 2018.

22. Paul J. Fox. Massively parallel neural computation. *Technical Report: Number 830*, 2013.

23. Arash Ardakani, Carlo Condo, Mehdi Ahmadi, and Warren J. Gross. An architecture to accelerate convolution in deep neural networks. *IEEE Transactions on Circuits and Systems I: Regular Papers*, 65:1349–1362, 2018.

24. Zhiqiang Liu, Yong Dou, Jingfei Jiang, Jinwei Xu, Shijie Li et al. Throughput-optimized FPGA accelerator for deep convolutional neural networks. *ACM Transactions on Reconfigurable Technology and Systems (TRETS)*, 103, 2017.

25. James Jeffers, James Reinders, and Avinash Sodani. *Intel Xeon Phi Processor High Performance Programming: Knights Landing Edition*. Morgan Kaufmann, 2016.

26. Tianshi Chen, Zidong Du, Ninghui Sun, Jia Wang, Chengyong Wu et al. Diannao: A small-footprint high-throughput accelerator for ubiquitous machine-learning. In *ACM SIGPLAN Notices*, volume 49, pages 269–284. ACM, 2014.

27. Matthieu Courbariaux, Itay Hubara, Daniel Soudry, Ran El-Yaniv, and Yoshua Bengio. Binarized neural networks: Training deep neural networks with weights and activations constrained to+ 1 or-1. *arXiv preprint arXiv:1602.02830*, 2016.

28. Ganesh Venkatesh, Eriko Nurvitadhi, and Debbie Marr. Accelerating deep convolutional networks using low-precision and sparsity. In *2017 IEEE International Conference on Acoustics, Speech and Signal Processing (ICASSP)*, pages 2861–2865. IEEE, 2017.

29. Jimmy SJ. Ren and Li Xu. On vectorization of deep convolutional neural networks for vision tasks. In *Proceedings of the 29th AAAI Conference in Artificial Intelligence (AAAI-15)*, 2015.

30. Chansup Byun, Jeremy Kepner, William Arcand, David Bestor, Bill Bergeron et al. Benchmarking data analysis and machine learning applications on the Intel KNL many-core processor. In *IEEE High Performance Extreme Computing Conference*. IEEE, 2017.

31. Yang You, Aydin Buluc, and James Demmell. Scaling deep learning on GPU and knights landing clusters, August 2017.

32. Shyam Jagannathan, Mihir Mody, and Manu Mathew. Optimizing convolutional neural network on DSP. In *IEEE International Conference on Consumer Electronics*. IEEE, 2016.

33. Xitian Fan, Huimin Li, and Lingli Wang. DT-CGRA: Dual-track coarse-grained reconfigurable architecture for stream applications. In *IEEE International Conference on Field Programmable Logic and Applications*. IEEE, 2016.

34. Ankur Agrawal, Suyog Gupta and Kailash Gopalakrishnan. Deep learning with limited numerical precision. *Proceedings of the 32nd International Conference on International Conference on Machine Learning (ICML'15)*, 37: 1737–1746, 2015.

35. Andrew Putnam, Adrian M. Caulfield, Eric S. Chung, Derek Chiou, Kypros Constantinides et al. A reconfigurable fabric for accelerating large-scale datacenter services. In *41st Annual International Symposium on Computer Architecture*, pages 13–24. IEEE, ACM, 2014.

36. Griffin Lacey, Graham W. Taylor, and Shawki Areibi. Deep learning on FPGAs: Past, present, and future, February 2016.

37. Stylianos I. Venieris, Alexandros Kouris, and Christos-Savvas Bouganis. Toolflows for mapping convolutional neural networks on fpgas: A survey and future directions. *ACM Computing Surveys (CSUR)*, 51(3), 2018.

38. Kamel Abdelouahab, Cedric Bourrasset, Maxime Pelcat, Francois Berry, Jean-Charles Quinton, and Jocelyn Serot. A holistic approach for optimizing DSP block utilization of a CNN implementation on FPGA, March 2017.

39. Chen Zhang, Peng Li, Guangyu Sun, Yijin Guan, Bingjun Xiao, and Jason Cong. Optimizing FPGA-based accelerator design for deep convolutional neural networks. In *ACM/SIGDA International Symposium on Field-Programmable Gate Arrays*. ACM, 2015.

40. Yufei Ma, Yu Cao, Sarma Vrudhula, and Jae-sun Seo. Optimizing loop operation and dataflow in FPGA acceleration of deep convolutional neural networks. In *Proceedings of the 2017 ACM/ SIGDA International Symposium on Field-Programmable Gate Arrays*. ACM, 2017.

41. Eriko Nurvitadhi, David Sheffield, Jaewoong Sim, Asit Mishra, Ganesh Venkatesh, and Debbie Marr. Accelerating binarized neural networks: Comparison of FPGA, CPU, GPU, and ASIC. In *International Conference on Field-Programmable Technology (FPT)*. IEEE, 2016.

42. Amor Nafkha and Yves Louet. Accurate measurement of power consumption overhead during FPGA dynamic partial reconfiguration. In *2016 International Symposium on Wireless Communication Systems (ISWCS)*. September 2016.

43. Stylianos I. Venieris and Christos-Savvas Bouganis. FPGA convnet: A framework for mapping convolutional neural networks on FPGAs. In *24th Annual International Symposium on Field-Programmable Custom Computing Machines (FCCM)*. IEEE, 2016.

44. Guanwen Zhong, Akshat Dubey, Tan Cheng, and Tulika Mitra. Synergy: AHW/SW framework for high throughput CNNs on embedded heterogeneous SOC. *arXiv:1804.00706*, 2018.

45. Sam Amiri, Mohammad Hosseinabady, Simon McIntosh-Smith, and Jose Nunez-Yanez. Multi-precision convolutional neural networks on heterogeneous hardware. In *Design, Automation & Test in Europe Conference & Exhibition (DATE)*. IEEE, 2018.

46. Hooman Farkhani, Ali Peiravi, Jens Madsen Kargaard, and Farshad Moradi. Comparative study of finFETs versus 22nm bulk CMOS technologies: SRAM design perspective. In *27th IEEE International System-on-Chip Conference (SOCC)*. IEEE, 2014.

47. Heiner Giefers, Peter Staar, Costas Bekas, and Christoph Hagleitner. Analyzing the energy-efficiency of sparse matrix multiplication on heterogeneous systems: A comparative study of GPU, xeon phi and FPGA. In *IEEE International Symposium on Performance Analysis of Systems and Software (ISPASS)*. IEEE, 2016.

48. Massimo Alioto. Energy-quality scalable adaptive VLSI circuits and systems beyond approximate computing. In *Design, Automation & Test in Europe Conference & Exhibition (DATE)*. IEEE, 2017.

CHAPTER 2

GPU PaaS Computation Model in Aneka Cloud Computing Environments

Shashikant Ilager

Cloud Computing and Distributed Systems (CLOUDS) Laboratory, School of Computing and Information Systems, The University of Melbourne, Melbourne, Australia

Rajeev Wankar

School of Computer and Information Sciences, University of Hyderabad, Hyderabad, India

Raghavendra Kune

Advanced Data Processing Research Institute, Department of Space, Secunderabad, India

Rajkumar Buyya

Cloud Computing and Distributed Systems (CLOUDS) Laboratory, School of Computing and Information Systems, The University of Melbourne, Melbourne, Australia

CONTENTS

1 INTRODUCTION

The cloud computing has revolutionized the computing paradigm in recent years. It provides on-demand convenient access to a shared pool of configurable computing resources through the Internet [1]. Platform as a Service (PaaS) is a cloud service delivery model that provides tools for rapid development and deployment of applications in the cloud. Presently, most PaaS frameworks target to build cloud applications that use only CPU computing resources. Aneka [2] is one such PaaS framework, which helps to perform the aforementioned functionalities. Aneka provides Application Programming Interfaces (APIs) to build the distributed cloud applications using Task, Thread, and MapReduce programming models. The application can be deployed over private, public, and hybrid clouds.

Due to recent advancements and breakthroughs in AI technology, many of the software applications are using these advanced AI techniques to boost their performance and the quality of their decision-making in real time. Most of these applications have at least one or more module that makes use of machine learning algorithms or such available techniques for problem-solving. Meanwhile, GPUs have become the standard computing platform for machine learning algorithms due to its abundant computing cores which yield high throughput. GPUs usage has been driven by multiple use cases like autonomous vehicles, scientific computing, finance, healthcare, and computational biology domains [3]. In addition, real-time applications like online gaming, video streaming, and Blockchain applications such as Bitcoin mining demand high-end GPUs for their performance boost. To that end, applications have to be designed to use both the CPU and GPU resources together to cater the diverse user needs. The specific part of applications that are computationally intensive is delegated to the GPU to leverage the massive parallel capabilities of GPU while the CPU handles other imperative functionalities of the applications.

However, having GPU accelerators on every machine of the physical/virtual cluster would increase cost and energy usage during processing [4]. Moreover, the throughput of cluster reduces since the majority of their GPUs are in the idle state for most of the time. One way to address this issue is by acquiring a minimum number of GPU instances and sharing the GPU workload across machines. This can be achieved through techniques like remote GPU access and proper scheduling mechanisms.

Public cloud service providers like Amazon AWS[1] and Microsoft Azure[2] offer GPU instances for the end-users. However, these offerings do not have platform support for distributed GPU computing that uses both CPU and GPU resources. The GPU clusters are managed (scheduling, provisioning, etc.) by using either platform-specific schedulers like Apache Spark or standard cluster resource management systems (RMSs) like SLURM or TORQUE (Linux based). Nevertheless, these platforms are application-specific and are not prudent for many generic applications, and also managing these platforms on the cloud is an onus on users. In addition, most of the frameworks are targeted for Linux environment only, which cannot be used for heterogeneous resource usage applications that are developed and deployed in a Windows operating system environment.

To overcome the aforementioned limitations, the PaaS frameworks are needed which automatically manage the underlying resources with different scheduling policies in a seamless manner. Developers can leverage the standard APIs provided by the PaaS platform to develop and deploy the application rapidly. Therefore, to achieve this, the extension should be made to the Aneka PaaS scheduling interfaces and task programming model to support the GPU computing, specifically, CUDA programming model. In the proposed model in this chapter, applications are built using .NET-supported programming languages targeting windows operating system environment. The advantages of these frameworks are as follows: 1) Cost reduction; 2) Provide transparent APIs to access the remote GPUs; 3) Enable distributed GPU programming by extending the existing Aneka scheduler for GPU-aware resources.

The problem that is addressed in this chapter is "How to effectively provide programming support for building the cloud applications that can use GPUs in the cluster where only some of the nodes in the cluster have GPU units?" To solve this, a framework is required that supports resource management, including provisioning, monitoring, and scheduling services integrated. To that end, the Aneka provides all these integrated services to manage the CPU-based resources, and thus current Aneka architecture is extended to support for GPU resources as well.

The rest of the chapter is organized as follows: Section 2 describes the background topics that are relevant to this context such as Cloud computing, GPU computing, and Aneka. Section 3 briefly details the motivation for this study. Section 4 explains the related work as well as current practices in public clouds regarding GPU computing. Section 5 presents a proposed methodology to incorporate GPU model in Aneka and show the extended Aneka architecture and scheduling mechanism. The feasibility of the system is demonstrated in Section 6 with an

[1] https://aws.amazon.com/
[2] https://azure.microsoft.com

image processing application for edge detection along with performance results that are carried out on a desktop-based private cluster. The open challenges and future directions are explained in Section 7, and finally, the chapter is summarized in Section 8.

2 BACKGROUND

This section briefly discusses Cloud computing and GPU computing, and concisely explains about Aneka and its architectural elements.

2.1 Cloud Computing

Cloud computing offers access to shared pool of dynamically reconfigurable computing resources as on-demand pay-as-you-go computing basis. The virtualization technology in the cloud has enabled much-needed elasticity and allows to dynamically (de)provision the resources. The vast amount of such advantages has attracted many of the enterprises to move their IT infrastructure to the cloud. Besides, it offers a wide range of services at different levels of abstractions based on the user requirements. Accordingly, cloud services are broadly categorized into three types as follows:

1. **Infrastructure as a Service (IaaS):** This service model provides compute, network, and storage services for end-users. Most of the resources are virtualized and they can be scaled quickly both horizontally and vertically. Examples include Amazon AWS EC2, Microsoft Azure, and Google Cloud.

2. **Platform as a Service (PaaS):** This service model provides frameworks, tools, and SDKs to manage resources, and build and deploy the applications rapidly. Users are relieved from procuring and managing the computing infrastructure. Examples include Google App Engine and Aneka.

3. **Software as a Service (SaaS):** This service model provides direct access to the software system. Users are relieved from both managing infrastructure and developing and maintaining the software applications. Examples include Gmail, Facebook, and Microsoft Office 365.

2.2 GPU Computing

Graphical Processing Units (GPUs) have been extensively used as a fixed-function processor, built around the graphics pipeline, for processing images or videos [5]. With the advent of technology breakthroughs, GPUs have broadened their horizon and are also now used for general-purpose computation and hence also called as General-Purpose Graphic Processing Unit (GPGPU) [5].

The GPUs follow SIMD stream architecture and are efficient in processing parallel computing applications. They are connected to CPU though high-speed Peripheral Component Interconnect Express (PCIe) bus and are also known as co-processors or accelerators. In addition, a GPU follows multi-core architectures with low clock speed focused on high throughput, a contrast to CPU which focuses on low latency instruction

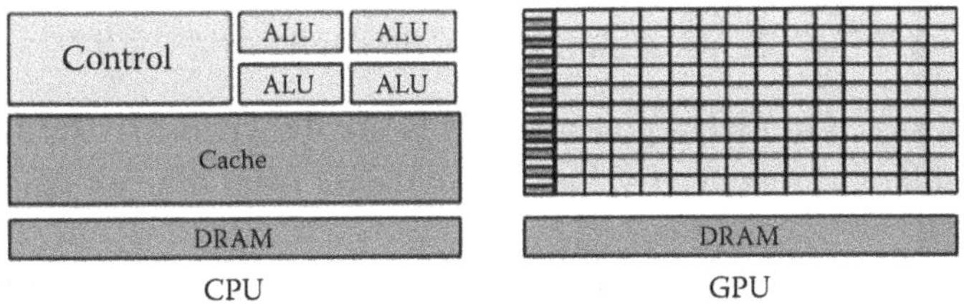

FIGURE 2.1   The architecture of CPU vs. GPU.

execution with sophisticated branch prediction techniques. Each GPU core is less powerful than CPU core; however, the number of cores in GPU is much higher than CPU which makes it a computing powerhouse compared with the latter.

GPUs have evolved in its architecture to support the general-purpose computation that now includes new memory hierarchy that has Double Data Rate (DDR) memory, shared memory, cache memory, and registers which are essential elements in reprogrammable computing devices. With this, the user can arbitrarily read and write to memory which was not possible in older GPUs. As shown in Figure 2.1, a CPU has a limited number of cores and large cache memory, whereas GPU has a large number of cores with smaller caches that are suitable for parallel applications.

To easily develop the GPGPU applications, new programming models have been introduced. CUDA [6] is a one such GPU programming model developed by NVIDIA; it provides simple-to-use APIs with multiple programming languages support. OpenCL [7] is another opensource library targeted for multiple GPGPU vendors agnostic architectures.

2.3 Aneka: Cloud Application Platform

Aneka [2] is a complete PaaS framework supporting multiple programming models for the rapid development of applications and their deployment on distributed heterogeneous computing resources.

Aneka provides a rich set of .NET based APIs to developers for exploiting resources transparently that are available in cloud infrastructure and expressing the business logic of applications by using the preferred programming abstractions. Moreover, system administrators can leverage on a collection of tools to monitor and control the deployed infrastructure. The infrastructure can be built upon a public cloud available to anyone through the Internet, or a private cloud constituted by a set of nodes with restricted access. More importantly, the Aneka can also be used to set up a hybrid cloud that includes computing nodes from both private and public cloud. It supports multiple programming models and hence developers can choose a suitable model to build the cloud-native applications according to the application needs. The four programming models that are supported by the Aneka are:

- **Task model:** Applications are built with a set of independent bag-of-tasks;

- **Thread model:** Applications are composed with a set of distributed threads;

- **MapReduce model:** Applications that demand a large amount of data processing and follow MapReduce programming model; and

- **Parameter sweep model:** Applications that are designed for execution of the same task over different ranges of values and datasets from a given parameter set.

The Aneka framework has been designed based on Service-Oriented Architecture (SOA). Services are the basic elements of Aneka platform that allows to incorporate new functionalities or replace the existing one by overriding the current implementation. The abstract description of these services is as follows: *Scheduling*–the job of scheduling is to map the tasks to the available resources. *Provisioning*–this service can be used to acquire the resources (computing elements in terms of virtual or physical machines).

The network architecture of Aneka follows the master and worker nodes; the former orchestrates and manages all the resources viz. monitoring, scheduling, pricing, etc. while the latter acts as computing elements which are responsible for executing the jobs assigned by its master.

Different services of Aneka are managed with layered architecture. Fabric layer of Aneka provides automated services such as high availability, resource provisioning, and hardware profiling. Foundation layer provides services such as billing, storage, resource reservation, and license and policing while Application service layer provides a set of programming models. The detailed architecture of Aneka is shown in Figure 2.4 and discussed in Section 5.2.

3 MOTIVATION

The important aspect of any computing infrastructure is to attain high resource utilization and reduce operational cost, which is obvious in the case of the economically driven clouds. To achieve high resource utilization, resources must be carefully shared among multiple applications or users. The following are the benefits of providing GPGPU as Platform service in the cloud through remote GPU sharing:

- **Cost**: GPUs are expensive. Having GPU installed on every machine in the cluster is infeasible and economically unsustainable. Moreover, GPUs are not a primary component of a computer system; consequently, CPUs are a primary component that is designated to run both system software like operating system and the user applications. Contrary to GPU, this makes CPUs an integral part of every machine.

- **Utilization**: GPU sharing in the cluster increases the resource utilization of the computing system.

- **Energy Efficiency**: GPUs are power-hungry devices; efficient resource utilization saves a huge amount of energy that would have been spent unnecessarily.

Although the benefits of GPU remote sharing for cloud applications are manifold, it has many challenges and shortfalls to provide GPGPU as PaaS in the cloud.

3.1 Challenges for GPU Programming in Cloud

The following are the issues that inhibit the usage of GPUs in the cloud.

- **Non-Transparent Remote Access**: GPU devices across a network provide an indirect non-transparent remote access. Resource requests must be wrapped with remote APIs and data should be serialized, marshaled, and deserialized; this introduces performance overhead.

- **Virtualization**: Virtualization technology in cloud data center injects another level of complexity for GPU usage. Unlike CPU, GPU cannot be easily virtualized either by time-sharing or space-sharing using existing hypervisor technologies. There are some recent efforts to virtualize some of the NVIDIA cards [8]; however, most of them are restricted to graphics-rendering purpose and very few support general-purpose computations.

- **Lack of Programming Supports for Cloud-Native Applications:** The cloud-native application development process needs advanced tools and APIs to efficiently build the systems. However, lack of such tools for incorporating the GPUs hinders GPU usage in the cloud.

- **Lack of Support for Windows Platform:** Most of the customized frameworks that support GPU sharing are targeted for Linux platforms. There have been very few efforts for GPGPU regarding Windows environment where most of the today's desktop applications are built on top of the .NET framework.

- **Dynamic Resource Provisioning and Scheduling for GPGPUs.** Traditionally, clouds are used to adapt to the varying resource demand by dynamically provisioning and de-provisioning resources at runtime. Despite GPU resource provisioning at the cloud, GPUs lack this critical future of dynamic provisioning and scheduling to benefit from adaptive resource usage that reduces huge amount cost.

The GPU remote sharing in the context of providing it as a platform service is the focus of this study. To achieve this, Aneka is extended which acts as the middleware that provides integral resource management services.

4 RELATED WORK

Using the GPUs in the cloud or virtualizing in a cluster has been a challenging work that many researchers have tried to solve in recent years. There are many approaches followed to virtualize or remotely access the GPU. Figure 2.2 shows the brief taxonomy of existing solutions, and the relevant works are described in this section.

4.1 GPU Virtualization Through API Remoting

Several methods have been proposed to use GPUs in shared or virtualized environment. The most widely used technique is to intercept CUDA API calls at local machine and

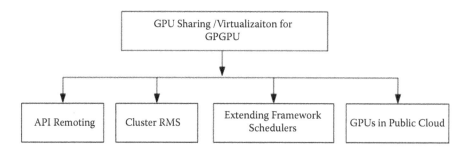

FIGURE 2.2   Taxonomy of shared GPGPU programming.

redirect it to a remote machine that has GPU access. The computation is done on a remote machine and the result is sent back to the requested machine.

4.1.1 vCUDA

vCUDA [9] elucidates GPUs access in a virtualized cloud environment for CUDA programming, and it is built upon a client–server architecture. The CUDA API calls are bundled and marshaled with the necessary parameters and required information and further redirected to the remote host that has direct GPU access. It uses XML-based Remote Procedure Call (RPC) to transfer the intercepted call to host (remote) machine. A special stub is used at the host, which handles request from the guest OS and unmarshals the messages and calls underlying CUDA device driver to execute.

Figure 2.3 illustrates the generic architecture of the API remoting technique. In this architecture, every invocation to CUDA API from guest OS is intercepted and forwarded to the remote host machine. Note that, this method is useful for GPU sharing among virtual machines (VMs)within a host or within the cluster.

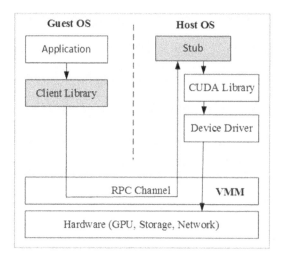

FIGURE 2.3   The schematic overview of remote intercept method [9].

4.1.2 gVirtus

gVirtus [10] is another library that relies on API remoting method. Like vCUDA, it also intercepts CUDA API calls; however, it utilizes efficient communication techniques by using communicators provided by different hypervisors that depend on TCP/IP protocol. gVirtus encompasses the virtualization layer and communicates directly to host OS. Therefore, it is efficient but highly dependent on the communicators provided by hypervisors, like XENLoop, vmSocket, VMware Communicator Interface, etc.

4.1.3 rCUDA

rCUDA [4], also called remote CUDA, is designed for GPU clusters. Initially built for physical clusters, rCUDA is later extended for VM. This framework offers GPU-sharing solution for HPC clusters, a way of reducing the total number of GPUs in the cluster by utilizing the GPUs in remote machines, which are regarded as GPU servers in this framework. This framework mainly consists of two software components, a client module, and a GPU server module. It uses several optimization technologies like RDMA and it is by far the most robust GPU-sharing technology among the many existing solutions. In the case of VMs, client module software is installed on guest OS and server module is installed in the host OS.

These standalone libraries provide a way to perform GPU programming in virtualized or physical cluster. However, these solutions lack several capabilities of PaaS framework, such as resource provisioning and monitoring. In addition, the remote API wrappers must be written for every CUDA API and signatures of these APIs change rapidly, and new APIs and functionalities are included with their frequent new software updates, which make developers to continuously update the APIs which is a cumbersome process.

4.2 Using Resource Management Systems

The other prominent approach employed for distributed GPU programming or GPU sharing is extending the schedulers of popular cluster RMSs. Some of the works have explored using the RMS like TORQUE [11], SLURM [12], and HTCondor [13]. In such workaround solutions, jobs can specify their request for the GPUs but it is left up to the user to ensure that the job is executed properly on the GPU. Jobs are tagged to indicate GPU and non-GPU jobs and RMSs scheduling policies have extended to be aware of GPU nodes and the respective jobs are scheduled from the job queue. For example, Netflix has extended celery system, a distributed task queue system for their distributed machine learning application that was deployed on Amazon AWS with GPU instances. Nevertheless, this approach is application-specific and mostly restricted for the HPC cluster setup and does not suit for generic application developments.

4.3 Using Framework Schedulers

Cluster programming languages like MPI and data processing frameworks like Spark and Hadoop have been extensively used for the distributed GPU programming. Coates et al. [14] have demonstrated performing deep learning tasks using GPU-enabled HPC systems. They have built system using Commodity Off-The-Shelf High-Performance Computing Technology: a cluster of GPU servers with InfiniBand interconnection. The application has been built using C++ with MVAPICH2 [15], an implementation of MPI. MVAPICH2 handles all the low-level communication using InfiniBand including the GPU support.

SparkGPU [16] is an extension of the in-memory MapReduce framework Spark for GPU. It transforms a generic data processing system and enables applications to exploit the GPU resources in the cluster. It addresses several challenges like reducing the internal and external communication data by efficient data format and optimal batching modes for GPU execution. It also provides task scheduling capacity among CPU and GPU.

Integration of GPU in Hadoop Cluster has been explored in GPU-in-Hadoop [17]. The default Hadoop scheduler is used to schedule the jobs on nodes of the cluster. The JCuda, JNI, Hadoop streaming, and Hadoop pipelines technology have been used to achieve this. However, this approach assumes all the nodes in the cluster have access to GPU. Consequently, this approach is not economically feasible. In a similar way, Xin and Li [18] demonstrated the implementation of Hadoop framework with the OpenCL.

The framework-coupled extensions provide an alternative solution for remote GPU access; however, the applications will be restricted to specific frameworks which are designed for a specific set of tasks. Moreover, managing these platforms adds more complexity to application development and logic which is not suitable for cloud-native applications.

4.4 GPUs in Cloud

The inherent virtualization characteristics of cloud introduce additional complexity in GPU access among VMs. The elementary problem is that GPUs are not designed to be shared or virtualized. Unlike CPU, a single GPU cannot be time-shared or space-shared using hypervisor softwares due to its technological constraints. However, a GPU can be dedicatedly attached to a VM using GPU passthrough technology [19]; most of the hypervisor software support this passthrough technology. Hence, one can have multiple GPUs in a machine that are dedicated to different VMs or devise a virtualization-independent technique to share a GPU among the VMs. However, GPU passthrough is limited to provide access to the single VM within its host node and cannot be encompassed across multiple nodes.

Amazon Offers EC2 P3[3] instances that have up to eight NVIDIA Tesla V100 GPUs. These machines are powerful, yet do not offer any mechanisms to share the GPU among multiple nodes. Similarly, Google offers GPU machines in their accelerated cloud computing arena; they have the flexibility to attach multiple types of GPUs to any type of instances and can be pre-empted based on the load to save the cost.

NVIDIA virtual GPUs (vGPUs) have made possible to virtualize the GPU among VMs to accelerate remote virtual desktop interface (VDI) performance. These are

---

[3] www.nvidia.com/en-us/data-center/gpu-cloud-computing/amazon-web-services/

designed to accelerate video encoding, decoding, and also other graphics-rendering operations and do not support the GPGPU on most of the GPU cards [8]. For example, vGPU has CUDA support for only GRID M60-8Q, M6-8Q cards.

Considering the limitations of remote GPU access in the cloud, it is imperative that existing solutions are not designed to support GPU sharing for GPGPU on the cloud. Here, the focus is on providing PaaS support for GPGPU application development for cloud-native applications.

5 METHODOLOGY FOR ANEKA GPU COMPUTING

In this section, the methodology for integrating GPU computing paradigm in the Aneka is presented and also shown how to effectively share the GPUs in the cluster. The base entities that have extended and scheduling policies that are used for GPU sharing in the cloud are briefly discussed.

5.1 Methodology

The current Aneka PaaS framework is extended to support GPU programming in Aneka Cloud. To achieve this, first, the master node should be aware of the worker nodes that have direct GPU access (connected through the PCIe bus in the physical cluster, or through passthrough technology in the virtual cluster). Second, scheduling policy must be capable of mapping GPU tasks to the nodes that have GPU access. Finally, the GPU programming or tasks must be programmed with .NET-supported programming languages.

As the default CUDA programming language does not have support for the .NET environment, there have been multiple efforts from the community to overcome this limitation and develop the coherent wrappers that provide simple APIs to program the GPU applications with .NET-supported programming languages. These wrappers including CUDAfy,[4] managed CUDA,[5] and Alea GPU[6] are some of those that are currently available to program the GPU-based applications in the .NET environment. In this chapter, CUDAfy and Alea GPU have been tested with the Aneka SDKs. The Alea GPU library is actively updated and supports a vast number of prevailing CUDA libraries like cuBLAS [20] and cuRAND [21], and it is also available on standard .NET package manager NuGet. Therefore, this library is used for the case-study experiments.

Our proposed methodology aims to achieve the following objectives:

- **Programmability**: The integrated high-level APIs of Aneka SDKs along with .NET-supported CUDA programming language manifest the efficient way of developing an application to utilize heterogeneous resources.

---

[4] www.codeproject.com/Articles/202792/Using-Cudafy-for-GPGPU-Programming-in-NET
[5] https://github.com/kunzmi/managedCuda
[6] www.aleagpu.com/release/3_0_4/doc/

- **Ease of Use:** The low-level communication, message (de)serialization, and network aspects are automatically managed by integral management services of Aneka. Users can unreservedly focus on the actual business logic of the applications.

- **Cost Reduction:** The reduction in the number of GPUs in cluster benefits economically by reducing excess amount of resource acquisition and operational costs.

5.2 Extended Aneka Architecture

The extended architecture of Aneka is shown in Figure 2.4. The new GPU-related components that are included in its architectural framework are highlighted. They include:

- Including GPU resources in IaaS

- Extending task programming model for GPU

- Providing easy-to-use SDKs for GPGPU on Aneka Cloud

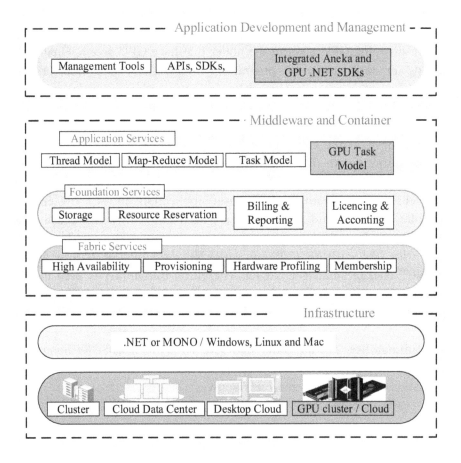

FIGURE 2.4   Extended Aneka architecture for GPU programming.

5.2.1 GPU Resources in IaaS

The present architecture of Aneka allows to develop and deploy applications which target CPU as a computing resource. Previously, at the infrastructure layer, all resources included were consisting of CPU computing resources only. In this architecture, GPU resources are also included in the IaaS. The computing infrastructure can be a standard physical cluster, virtualized cloud cluster, or desktop-based private cluster. In this aspect, it is assumed that one or more nodes in the cluster have direct GPU access.

5.2.2 Task Programming Model for GPU

The bag of tasks programming model is extended for GPGPU in which tasks are independent work units which can be executed or scheduled in any order. This feature can be effectively leveraged to execute the GPU tasks. In this regard, the current Aneka Task model is extended for GPU programming. Each CUDA kernel is wrapped as an independent task and it can be executed independently. This can be contemplated as a new application model from Aneka.

5.2.3 APIs and SDKs for GPGPU on Aneka Cloud

At the application development layer, extended Aneka SDKs along with .NET wrappers for CUDA programming can be leveraged to develop the GPGPU applications. The required entities of the Aneka that are responsible to profile GPU-enabled worker nodes and schedule accordingly are extended and built. Further explanations can be found in the next section.

5.3 GPU-Aware Scheduling of Tasks

The important feature of any cloud PaaS platform is to efficiently schedule the user tasks/jobs on cloud infrastructure in a user-transparent way. To this aspect, Aneka has separate Runtime scheduling service that transparently schedules user tasks on available resources. It is also responsible for interacting with several other services like active worker node membership catalog, dynamic resource provisioning services, heartbeat services, etc. The default task-scheduling policy is to map tasks to the resources in a First Come First Serve (FCFS) round-robin fashion. The resource capacity of each node is unified based on CPU capacity (MegaHertz) and tasks are assigned accordingly. The default scheduling interfaces in Aneka can be extended and new advanced policies can be incorporated to improve the performance and cost benefits based on application demand [22,23].

A schematic overview of GPU-aware scheduling in Aneka is illustrated in Figure 2.5. It is assumed that the applications are constituted with multiple independent tasks where some tasks are CPU-bound and some others are GPU-bound.

To accomplish the GPU-aware scheduling, Aneka Runtime Scheduling service has been redesigned. First, the tasks are differentiated into GPU tasks and non-GPU tasks; this is achieved by introducing a simple parameter into Aneka Task entity that tags an attribute to note GPU and non-GPU tasks, respectively. Second, the worker nodes are also segregated into two categories based on their ability to have direct GPU access.

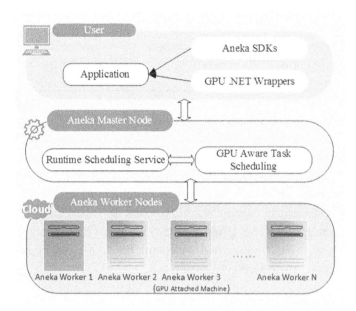

FIGURE 2.5   An overview of GPU-aware scheduling of tasks in Aneka.

Finally, the Runtime Scheduling entity maps GPU tasks to only those nodes that have direct GPU access, and remaining CPU-based tasks are mapped to the rest of the machines based on CPU capabilities.

CPU-bound tasks follow existing Aneka policy and GPU-bound tasks are scheduled in a round-robin fashion on GPU-enabled nodes. In the present system, the capabilities of a GPU (number of cores and memory) and current load are not considered for scheduling decision. This can be considered in the future as a performance improvement.

5.4 Template for Aneka GPU Task Programming

In this section, a sample template is outlined that shows how to write GPU program using extended Aneka task programming model. Aneka task programming model provides the flexibility to create a number of tasks and add it into the task pool. Once the task pool is submitted for execution, the master node distributes the tasks across worker nodes based on selected scheduling policies. By default, *Execute()* method of the task class is invoked that initiates the task execution. The following template of .NET class shows a sample schema for writing the Aneka GPU tasks.

<summary>
    // Every Aneka class implements interface called ITask, and this class is serializable
    // Public data members or public class members. The output of the GPU task must
    be written to these data members or shared file systems of Aneka containers.

// Only these data members can be accessed by master node once the task is complete
</summary>

public class Aneka GPU Task: ITask {
<summary>
// constructor to initialize the data members
<parameters, all the input data members or class members can be initialized by through these parameters>
</summary>

public Aneka GPU Task() {
// initialize the data members of the object
}
<summary>
//This is a start method and can be used to create a GPU handler and also for launching the kernel
//<parameters, it can take any parameters and returns void always>
</summary>

public void Execute() {
//Initialize the CUDAfy/ Alea GPU object or module
// Set the GPU handler
//Perform GPU memory allocation and copy the input data
//Set the appropriate blocks and threads; this decides total number of threads we generate
// Launch the kernel or GPU Method Invocation
//Copy back the result from GPU to public data members of Aneka Task class using APIs
}

<summary>
// This method acts as a GPU method that executes on GPU; all the threads work in parallel in a SIMD manner.
//<Parameters, all the input data, output data members or variables>
</summary>

public void Kernel Method() {
//Map the thread id to the data index and define actual compute logic
}
}

This template precisely presents how to write the GPU tasks in Aneka; other required necessary functionalities like how to create tasks, submit tasks, access the result once the tasks are finished and handling other events remains the same as before. The only difference would be to set the flag *is GPU Task* to the true value which is part of extended Aneka Task object. For more detailed information about building and executing Aneka applications, readers are advised to refer the Aneka programming documents [24].

6 IMAGE EDGE DETECTION ON ANEKA CLOUD USING GPU: A CASE STUDY

An image processing application built for edge detection of objects in an image has been chosen to evaluate the feasibility and performance of modified Aneka system. Both sequential and parallel algorithm and its GPU version of Aneka have been implemented. The experiments were carried out on a private desktop cluster. The implementation details, results and outcomes are discussed below.

6.1 Edge Detection Algorithm

Detecting edges of an object in a digital image is one of the essential applications of image processing. It requires a high amount of computational resources and time. There exist several methods to perform this operation using different operators or filters. Here, the commonly adopted Sobel operator [25] is used.

To find the edges of objects in an image, one needs to compute the new value for every pixel based on the certain operation. In the Sobel filter, the output value of pixels is calculated based on the Equation 1. The value of S_x and S_y in Equation 1 can be derived based on the Equation 2.

$$P = \sqrt{S^2_x} + \sqrt{S^2_y} \tag{1}$$

$$S_x = \begin{bmatrix} -1 & -2 & -1 \\ 0 & 0 & 0 \\ 1 & 2 & 1 \end{bmatrix} * M_i \quad S_y = \begin{bmatrix} 1 & 0 & -1 \\ 2 & 0 & -2 \\ 1 & 0 & -1 \end{bmatrix} * M_i \tag{2}$$

In Equation 2, S_x and S_y are resultant value produced by the product of 3×3 filter matrices with M_i, where the matrices represent horizontal, and derivative approximations. M_i is a 3×3 matrix for pixel i that is constituted by including its all eight neighbor pixels from the matrix, where i = 1 to m*n, m is the width of the image, and n is the height.

It is important to note that finding the value of P for each pixel is independent of other pixels. Hence, this embarrassingly parallel property can be exploited using GPU architecture which supports such inherent data-parallel applications.

In sequential computation on CPU, all the pixels values are calculated in a sequential manner. However, this increases the execution time of applications because the complex image may have millions of pixels. To reduce this computational time, this application is adapted for GPU architecture which runs faster than the only CPU versions by using abundant GPU cores and running parallel with GPU threads.

6.2 Parallel Implementation of Sobel Edge Detection on GPUs

In the parallel implementation of edge-detection application, the value of each pixel is calculated in parallel with a dedicated separate GPU thread. At first, the image matrix is converted into a byte array, and then the byte array is transformed into integer array to perform the matrix operations.

The CUDA kernel takes the array of pixels as input and returns the output array. Each pixel value is calculated by separate CUDA thread where all the threads run in parallel. The output pixels are written into a separate output array. This output array is later copied to CPU memory using the CUDA APIs.

In the GPU version implementation, K (K = image width × image height) number of CUDA threads are generated. Inside CUDA kernel, each thread index is mapped to corresponding data (pixel) index based on the thread id and pixel number.

Parallel version uses Aneka Cloud where its scheduling service is responsible to schedule the GPU tasks on appropriate nodes. The image read, deserialization (converting to a byte array) and serialization (converting output byte array into image matrix), is done by Master thread which runs on Master node and edge detection operation is wrapped into Aneka GPU task that runs on a GPU-equipped worker node.

In Aneka GPU implementation, the *Execute()* method of Aneka task class, which is the default method to begin task execution, is responsible for querying the GPU device and setting up the handler for the GPU device. Furthermore, another method is invoked with the GPU handler to perform the main application logic. The output image is written to the Aneka container file system; alternatively, if the shared file repository has been set up, the output can be stored in the repository from where all nodes in the cloud can access the data.

6.3 Results and Analysis

The experiments are conducted on a 4-node desktop-based cluster. Aneka PaaS framework has been installed on all the four nodes. One node is designated as Aneka Master and three nodes were assigned worker roles. All the nodes have preinstalled with Windows 7 as their operating system.

In this setup, one machine from worker nodes is equipped with NVIDIA QUADRO K620 GPU Card (consumer grade card). This GPU has 384 computing cores and 2 GB of GPU memory; CUDA driver 9.1 is installed on this machine. The application has been built using C# console on .NET framework 4.0 with Visual Studio 2015.

The access to the input image is given to the worker node directly from the local storage. In a real public cloud setup, data is stored in some shared storage servers and these storage servers are usually mounted on all the worker machines or have high-speed network access. The local access to input image overcomes large overhead that would have been introduced by network transfer of the input data.

To evaluate the performance of the implementation, different dimensions of images are considered. The following sample image shown in Figure 2.6 has a dimension of

FIGURE 2.6   Edge detection sample input and output images.

1024×768 (width and height). Here, the CUDA kernel is launched with 1024×768 threads. All the threads calculate the resultant pixel value using formula explained in Equation 1. To analyse the effect on execution time, several other images with different dimension have been used. Table 2.1 shows the detailed timing analysis with a different dimension of images.

As shown in Table 2.1, for the larger images, GPU implementation performs better. The timing includes local GPU computation time at worker nodes. The Aneka framework has overhead which includes all the network serialization and deserialization of code and other necessary functionalities. It is almost a constant (around 2000 ms, empirically calculated) time as it is independent of input size and the size of the code remains the same. So, to get the clear performance benefit, our input should be large enough to absorb this overhead. In this experiment, it is only possible to consider maximum dimension image of 5184 × 3456. This is because of the limited memory on GPU (2GB) in our consumer-grade GPU card. If the experiments are run with enterprise-level GPUs such as NVIDIA Tesla [26] cards and with images of higher dimension which is a usual case in today's digital platforms (for example, video rendering/streaming or online gaming), performance benefit will be clearly visible. This evaluation can be considered in the future.

To conclude, this case study demonstrates how to develop cloud-native GPU applications with remote GPU sharing. The results have demonstrated performance benefit and feasibility of Aneka platform with GPU computing model.

TABLE 2.1   Results of Sobel edge detection algorithm.

Image Size	Sequential (time in ms)	Aneka GPU Task (time in ms)
512 × 512	60	75
1024 × 586	185	115
5184 × 3456	5437	887

7 FUTURE DIRECTIONS

The elementary principal of cloud computing is elasticity to provide resource provisioning based on application demand to reduce the cost and meet Service-Level Agreements (SLA). Towards this, Aneka can be extended to dynamically provision and deprovision the GPU instances on public cloud based on the application demands. This can be achieved by extending Aneka provisioning service and utilizing the public cloud REST APIs and further considering application-specific profiles and load. For example, the deadline-driven provisioning for scientific application for Aneka is studied in [23]. In a similar way, application-specific dynamic provisioning of integrated CPU- and GPU-based instances can be investigated.

Another useful avenue to explore is fine-grained resource capacity-aware scheduling policies. The GPU capabilities differ with different types of cards. The scheduling policy can consider the number of cores, the memory capacity of GPU instance for scheduling decision. In a similar way, another key area to evaluate is the parameter sweep model with existing GPU applications. Instead of redeveloping GPU applications with Aneka SDKs and GPU wrappers, the executables can be used with different input data range to directly execute on Aneka cloud. In a similar line, GPU computing support can be extended to thread and MapReduce model-based applications.

8 SUMMARY AND CONCLUSIONS

The GPU computing is gaining popularity for executing many scientific and business applications. In addition, cloud computing has become a mainstream paradigm to deliver subscription-oriented computing services. Consequently, having GPU on every machine in a cluster is expensive and infeasible. Therefore, it is important to have useful tools and frameworks to easily develop and deploy the applications and share the underlying resources effectively to reduce the cost.

In this chapter, the GPGPU PaaS model is presented with Aneka and also identified the challenges in realizing the GPU sharing in a cloud scenario. The relevant works have been studied and categorized them into a taxonomy. The methodology adopted for integrating GPGPU model into Aneka framework is described. The feasibility of the proposed solution is demonstrated through a case study with an image processing application that performs edge detection of objects in an image. This chapter also identifies important future directions in this domain.

The support for GPUs as part of Aneka PaaS environments enables rapid creation and deployment of big data applications on clouds, and at the same time harnessing GPU capabilities for performance and energy-efficient computing.

REFERENCES

1. R. Buyya, C. S. Yeo, S. Venugopal, J. Broberg, and I. Brandic. "Cloud computing and emerging IT platforms: Vision, hype, and reality for delivering computing as the 5th utility." *Future Generation Computer Systems*, 25(6):599–616, 2009.
2. C. Vecchiola, X. Chu, and R. Buyya. "Aneka: A software platform for. NET-based cloud computing." In *High Speed and Large Scale Scientific Computing*, W. Gentzsch, L. Grandinetti, G. Joubert (Eds.), ISBN: 978-1-60750-073-5, pp. 267–295, 2009.

3. J. Dowens, D. Luebke, N. Govindaraju, M. Harris, J. Krüger, et al. "A survey of general-purpose computation on graphics hardware." *Computer Graphics Forum*, Oxford, UK: Blackwell Publishing Ltd, 26(1):80–113, 2007.

4. J. Duato, A. J. Pena, F. Silla, R. Mayo, and E. S. Quintana-Ortí. "rCUDA: Reducing the number of GPU-based accelerators in high performance clusters." In *International Conference on High Performance Computing and Simulation (HPCS)*, IEEE, pp. 224–231, 2010.

5. J. D. Owens, M. Houston, D. Luebke, S. Green, J. E. Stone, and J. C. Phillips. "GPU computing." *Proceedings of the IEEE*, 96:879–899, 2008.

6. J. Sanders and E. Kandrot. "CUDA by example: An introduction to general-purpose GPU programming" *Concurrency Computation Practice and Experience*, 21:312, 2010.

7. J. E. Stone, D. Gohara, and G. Shi. "OpenCL: A parallel programming standard for heterogeneous computing systems." *Computing in Science and Engineering*, 12(3):66–72, 2010.

8. A. Herrera. "NVIDIA GRID: Graphics accelerated VDI with the visual performance of a work station." Nvidia Corp, May, pp. 1–18, 2014.

9. L. Shi, S. Member, H. Chen, J. Sun, and K. Li. "vCUDA: GPU-accelerated high-performance computing in virtual machines." *IEEE Transactions on Computers*, 61(6), 804–816, 2012.

10. G. Giunta, R. Montella, G. Agrillo, G. Coviello. "A GPGPU transparent virtualization component for high performance computing clouds." In *European Conference on Parallel Processing*, Springer, Berlin, Heidelberg, pp. 379–391, 2010.

11. R. Phull, C.-H. Li, K. Rao, H. Cadambi, and S. Chakradhar. "Interference-driven resource management for GPU-based heterogeneous clusters." In *Proceedings of the 21st International Symposium on High-Performance Parallel and Distributed Computing – HPDC'12*, p. 109, 2012.

12. S. Soner and C. Özturan. "Integer programming based heterogeneous CPU-GPU cluster schedulers for SLURM resource manager." *Journal of Computer and System Sciences*, 81 (1)):38–56, 2015.

13. M. Burtscher and H. Rabeti. "A scalable heterogeneous parallelization framework for iterative local searches." *Proceedings – IEEE 27th International Parallel and Distributed Processing Symposium, IPDPS2013*, pp. 1289–1298, 2013.

14. A. Coates, B. Huval, T. Wang, D. Wu, and A. Y. Ng, "Deep learning with COTS HPC systems." *Proceedings- 30th International Conference of Machine Learning*, pp. 1337–1345, 2013.

15. H. Wang, S. Potluri, M. Luo, A. K. Singh, S. Sur, and D. K. Panda "MVAPICH2-GPU: Optimized GPU to GPU communication for InfiniBand clusters." *Computer Science – Research and Development*, 26(3–4):257–266, 2011.

16. Y. Yuan, M. F. Salmi, Y. Huai, K. Wang, R. Lee, and X. Zhang. "Spark-GPU: An accelerated in-memory data processing engine on clusters." In *Proceedings– 2016IEEE International Conference on Big Data, Big Data 2016*, pp. 273–283, 2016.

17. J. Zhu, J. Li, E. Hardesty, H. Jiang, and K. C. Li. "GPU-in-Hadoop: Enabling MapReduce across distributed heterogeneous platforms." In *2014 IEEE/ACIS 13th International Conference on Computer and Information Science, ICIS 2014 – Proceedings*, pp. 321–326, 2014.

18. M. Xin and H. Li. "An implementation of GPU accelerated MapReduce: Using Hadoop with OpenCL for data- and compute-intensive jobs." In *Proceedings – 2012International Joint Conference on Service Sciences, Service Innovation in Emerging Economy: Cross-Disciplinary and Cross-Cultural Perspective, IJCSS 2012*, pp. 6–11, 2012.

19. J. P. Walters, A. J. Younge, D. I. Kang, K. T. Yao, M. Kang, et al. "GPU passthrough performance: A comparison of KVM, Xen, VMWare ESXi, and LXC for CUDA and OpenCL applications." In *7th International Conference on Cloud Computing (CLOUD)*, IEEE, pp. 636–643, 2014.

20. C. Nvidia. "Cublas library." *NVIDIA Corporation, Santa Clara, California*, 15(27):31, 2008.
21. C. Nvidia. *CURAND Library*. Santa Clara, CA: NVIDIA Corporation, 2010.
22. A. Nadjaran Toosi, R. O. Sinnott, and R. Buyya. "Resource provisioning for data-intensive applications with deadline constraints on hybrid clouds using Aneka." *Future Generation Computer Systems*, 79:765–775, 2018.
23. C. Vecchiola, R. N. Calheiros, D. Karunamoorthy, and R. Buyya. "Deadline-driven provisioning of resources for scientific applications in hybrid clouds with Aneka." *Future Generation Computer Systems*, 28(1):58–65, 2012.
24. R. Buyya, C. Vecchiola, and S. T. Selvi. *Mastering Cloud Computing: Foundations and Applications Programming*. Waltham, MA: Morgan Kaufmann, 2013.
25. I. Sobel and G. Feldman. "A 3x3 isotropic gradient operator for image processing." In *A talk at the Stanford Artificial Project*, pp. 271–272, 1968.
26. E. Lindholm and J. Nickolls. "Nvidia Tesla: Aunified graphics and computing architecture." *Micro, IEEE*, 28(0272-1732):39–55, 2008.

CHAPTER 3

Toward Complex Search for Encrypted Mobile Cloud Data via Index Blind Storage

Yupeng Hu and Linjun Wu

College of Computer Science and Electronic Engineering, Hunan University, Changsha, China

Wenjia Li

Department of Computer Science, New York Institute of Technology, New York, USA

Keqin Li

College of Computer Science and Electronic Engineering, Hunan University, Changsha, China

Department of Computer Science, State University of New York, New Paltz, USA

Yonghe Liu

Department of Computer Science and Engineering, University of Texas at Arlington, Arlington, TX, USA

Zheng Qin

College of Computer Science and Electronic Engineering, Hunan University, Changsha, China

CONTENTS

1 BACKGROUND

With the rapid development of mobile cloud storage systems in recent years [1], mobile users or institutions are more willing to outsource the data to external cloud servers for better scalability and usability [2]. Cloud storage users can access data with no limits of time and space using different terminals, like computers and smartphones since cloud storage provides the most suitable solution for sharing data between these devices [3,4]. In cloud storage mode, the user's data are completely managed and stored by the Cloud Service Provider (CSP) which can obtain and search sensitive data stored by the user in the cloud [5]. However, the CSP may lose the user's data due to unexpected system failures. On top of that, some potential attackers may obtain data illegally by attacking the CSP server which eventually leads to information leakage. The hidden security troubles caused by the separation of data ownership and management rights make cloud storage security a problem that cannot be ignored.

Encrypting the data before uploading it to the CSP appears as a natural solution to overcome such an information leakage since it can safeguard users' data privacy. One traditional way to do this is to download and decrypt all the data locally, but an unavoidable reality is that it has not been developed a real sense to put into practical operation due to the huge bandwidth costs. In addition, the resources stored in the cloud are not aware of any significance to users if the data resources cannot be retrievable, used, and shared quickly and easily. Therefore, finding a searchable encryption scheme for efficiently searching encrypted data in the cloud platform becomes a pressing problem.

2 SEARCHABLE SYMMETRIC ENCRYPTION (SSE) AND SEARCHABLE ASYMMETRIC ENCRYPTION (SAE)

As a general rule, outsourced data are encrypted with various cryptographic algorithms, then secure indexes are generated by executing some searchable encryption schemes. Searchable encryption makes search service on encrypted data possible. The searchable encryption technology can be divided into two categories according to the cryptographic strategies: Searchable Symmetric Encryption (SSE) [6–14] and Searchable Asymmetric Encryption (SAE) [15–18].

2.1 Searchable Symmetric Encryption

The basic idea of SSE scheme is sharing the keys between data owners and the users who access the data. It usually uses pseudo-random functions, pseudo-random permutation, and hash algorithms to process keywords. The search model is shown in Fig. 3.1.

The data owner conducts a symmetric encryption algorithm (F) and a key (K) to generate a ciphertext data (C) from a plaintext data (M), $C \leftarrow F_K(M)$, then uploads the ciphertext (C) data to the CSP. When trying to access the stored ciphertext data (C), the user needs to request the trapdoor and key from the data owner, and then send the trapdoor to the CSP. The CSP executes a search algorithm based on the trapdoor and returns the searching result to the user. Finally, the user restores the ciphertext(C) and obtains the plaintext data (M), $M \leftarrow F_K(C)$. The symmetric key encryption algorithms commonly include AES, DES, Triple DES, RC2, and RC4.

2.2 Searchable Asymmetric Encryption

On the contrary, SAE schemes can be applied to the multi-user cloud model. Only authorized users possessing the corresponding secret key can access the data since the data owner encrypts the outsourced data with a public key.

Normally, keys of SAE schemes are built on Bilinear Paring. Anyone holding a public key can store data in the CSP, but only authorized users can use the key to perform the search. The search model is shown in Fig. 3.2. Asymmetric encryption algorithms require a pair of keys (PK, SK) to encryption and decryption.

The data owner employs an asymmetric encryption algorithm (F) and a public key (PK) to generate a ciphertext data (C) from a plaintext data (P), $C \leftarrow F_{PK}(M)$, and then uploads the ciphertext (C) data to the CSP. When attempting to search encrypted data in the cloud, the authorized user does not need to establish communication with the data owner, since it can

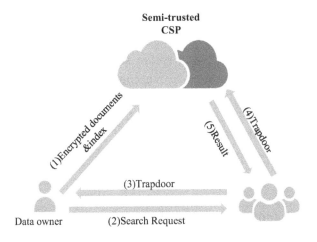

FIGURE 3.1 Searchable symmetric encryption.

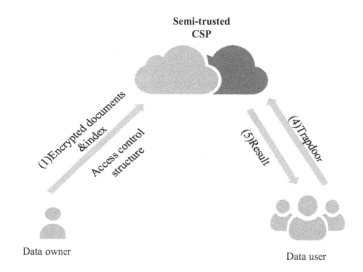

FIGURE 3.2   Searchable asymmetric encryption.

generate trapdoors and send trapdoors to the CSP directly. The CSP executes a search algorithm based on the trapdoor, and then returns the searching result to the user. Finally, the user restores the ciphertext (C) and obtains the plaintext data (M), $M \leftarrow F_{SK}(C)$. The symmetric key encryption algorithms commonly include RSA, ElGamal, D-H, and ECC.

2.3 Trapdoor

In 1976, Diffie and Hellman proposed a method of constructing a public key cryptosystem with trapdoor one-way function. The trapdoor function is a special one-way function: $f : \{0,1\}^* \rightarrow \{0,1\}^*$. If x is known, it is easy to obtain $f(x)$. On the contrary, it is hard to derive x from $f(x)$. For example, given two large prime numbers (p,q), we can derive its product $n \leftarrow p \cdot q$ easily, but it is difficult to divide n into p and q in the effective period time, especially if n is large enough. The public key cryptosystem means that in the case of the encryption algorithm, the decryption algorithm and the public key are all disclosed, and it is still infeasible to derive the private key from the public key. In the existing categories of searchable encryption schemes, the trapdoor is equivalent to a secure search credential. It expresses search conditions and query capabilities of the search demand side to the search execution party in an encrypted manner. According to different data-sharing application scenarios, the trapdoor may be generated by the data owner, an authorized user locally, or a trusted third-party authority.

3 INDEX BLIND STORAGE SCHEME OVERVIEW

3.1 System Model

As shown in Figs. 3.3 and 3.4, the index blind storage (IBS) scheme consists of four parts: data owner, search user, central authority (CA), and the CSP consisting of blind storage (BS) and IBS. It is worth noting that the BS in our model denotes a simple data

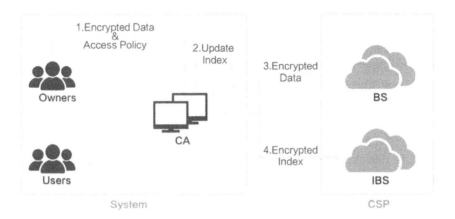

FIGURE 3.3   The data uploading process in IBS.

blind storage rather than the complete blind storage scheme as shown in [13]. All files in the original blind storage are represented by a fixed-size array of blocks. These blocks are indexed by a set of numbers randomly generated by a file-related seed. In our model, the IBS is responsible for storing and returning the encrypted index. In contrast to blind storage discussed in [13], IBS significantly improves the performance and focuses on the index so as to support a more complex search. The value of the proposed IBS scheme lies in its co-existence with blind storage system as an efficient search interface.

The Central Authority: Prior searchable encryption systems do not contain a CA, which usually plays a key facilitating role in practical secure storage systems. From the

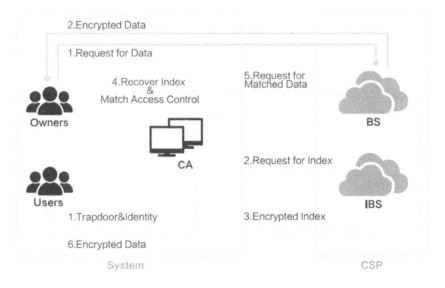

FIGURE 3.4   The data access process in IBS (light gray lines describe how users search for shared data; dark gray lines describe how owners access their own data).

standpoint of secure management of enterprise, a CA is necessary to strengthen the data privacy policy and handle the unexpected emergencies such as medical accidents. In our model, the CA is an administrative and intermediary agent of an institution, which is in charge of integrating data from owners, generating/updating indexes, and performing search and access control policy. As depicted in Fig. 3.3, on receiving a new file from the owner, the CA would update the index and encrypt the data according to the specific access control policy of the owner. Afterwards, it forwards the encrypted index and data to IBS and BS, respectively. In addition, there is no bottleneck concern on the CA; our experimental results show that a common PC is able to afford CA's all tasks.

The Search Process: As Fig. 3.4 shows, first, a search request that consists of a trapdoor and the user's ID will be delivered to CA. The CA then browses a local look-up table to find out the address of the corresponding index in IBS and then sends them out to CSP for encrypted index data. The IBS in CSP will return the encrypted index data to CA, and thus the CA can decrypt them and obtain the original IDs of the requested files. Instead of searching all requested files, the CA only retrieves the authorized files stored in BS for the users who can then access according to an access control policy. Finally, the BS returns the authorized data as query results to the CA according to the file IDs, and the CA forwards them to the users. On the other hand, the data owners themselves can directly search and acquire the data from BS with any regular blind storage technique.

3.2 Security Guarantees

In our system, the CA should be absolutely trusted. It is responsible for encryption/decryption operations, the establishment and update of index, and also most of the computation services. The CSP is honest-but-curious, i.e., it will complete the missions assigned by users honestly but it wants to learn additional information such as trapdoor as much as possible, so as to learn more about data, data owners, and the search users. Therefore, our system provides the following key security guarantees:

Confidentiality of Data and Index: The data and index will be encrypted before uploading. Especially, we hide the associations between the files and the indexes from CSP.

Concealing of Access Pattern: We also hide the access pattern, where a search or access pattern is defined as a sequence of search results, in this paper. Since the trapdoor is submitted to CA, we just need to ensure the CSP is unable to derive any more information from the search results, such as the kind of operation or keywords. Moreover, CSP learns nothing about the data and indexes to be searched on, including the number and the size of them.

3.3 Data Structures

Figure 3.5 illustrates the difference between BS and IBS scheme. Unlike the original BS scheme, the IBS allows the CA rather than the data owner to execute all algorithms of index search, so that IBS can be adapted to the multi-owner multi-user circumstance. To support complex search including arbitrary multi-dimensional keyword and range query over encrypted data, this paper studies the first IBS scheme which relies on the following key data structures.

Document: In our model, a document $F = \left(\vec{A}, f \right)$ is composed of the body content f as well as an attribute vector $\vec{A}$ that can be searched on. The vector

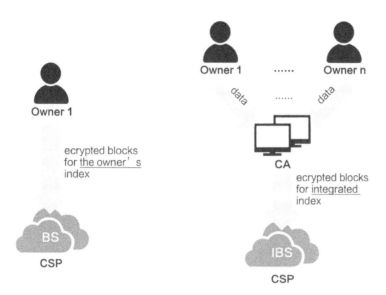

FIGURE 3.5   Blind storage vs. IBS.

$\vec{A} = (r_1, r_2 \cdots r_n, w_1, w_2 \cdots w_m)$ consists of $= n + m$ attribute values. r_i stands for a specific value of a range attribute R_i, i.e., a numerical attribute that could be arranged in order, such as age and date. w_j stands for a specific value of a keyword attribute W_j, i.e., a textual attribute such as gender and position. $|R_j|$ and $|W_j|$ denote the number of all possible values that can be assigned to R_i and W_j respectively. For a document set FILE, let A be the set of all possible attribute values of $\vec{A}$ then we have $|A| = \prod_{i=1}^{n} |R_I| \cdot \prod_{j=1}^{m} |W_j|$. As for the Electronic Medical Record (EMR) management prototype system that we develop below, which is shown in Table 3.1, in addition to the file identifier FID, the EMR document's major structure is defined as $F = (\dot{F}, \ddot{F})$ where $\dot{F} = (\vec{A}, f)$ in which $\vec{A}$ is the attribute set and f is the medical data content that could be shared in treatments, medical researches, medical data collations, public health reports, and so on. $\ddot{F}$ represents the binary access control vector for this file, which can be used by CA to inform the authorized users under a secure mechanism. Note that the F is actually stored in BS that exploits the blind storage [13] to keep the secrets, whereas the IBS merely stores the generated index file.

TABLE 3.1   The typical data structure of a file F

File identifier	$\dot{F}$							$\ddot{F}$
	$\vec{A}$						f	Access control vector
	R_1	...	R_n	W_1	...	W_m	Content	
FID (random value)	r_1	...	r_n	w_1	...	w_m	...	011..

Index File: First, the index is an integrated file for all related documents for the multi-owner scenario as shown in Fig. 3.5. The set of index file in IBS is defined as $IND = \{I_i\}_{I=1}^{|A|}$, consisting of $|A|$ index files generated for the document set FILE. An index file $I_i = (IID_i, data_i)$ is generated according to a specific attribute vector $\vec{A}_i = (r_1, r_2 \cdots r_n, w_1, w_2 \cdots w_m)$. The $IID_i = E_{r1}||E_{r2}|| \cdots E_{rn}||E_{w1}||E_{w2}|| \cdots E_{wm}$ is the encrypted attribute string that can be used to identify I_i, where E_r and E_w represent the encrypted value of a range attribute and a keyword attribute, respectively. $data_i$ is a list of FID for all correlated F that could be searched with I_i. The FID in $data_i$ indicates that its corresponding document F has the same attribute vector as $\vec{A}_i$. This integrated index structure will save the communication rounds in a multi-keyword search.

Look-up Table: We define $T = \{T_j\}_{j=1}^{n}$ as a set of n look-up table which is composed of three columns and $|A|$ rows. Each table T_j is used to depict a range attribute R_j. Each row of T_j is a tuple $\left(IID_i, E_{r_j}, addr_i\right)$, where IID_i corresponds to an index I_i, and $addr_i$ is the address of I_i in IBS. Generally, the rows are arranged according to r_j in an ascending order.

Trapdoor: The data access trapdoor $Q = ED_{\vec{A}}||UID$ describes the data format of a search request that a user should follow. The set $ED_{\vec{A}} = (ED_{R1}, \cdots ED_{Rn}, ED_{W1}, \cdots ED_{Wm})$ denotes the encrypted format for each $D_i = (1 \leq i \leq n+m)$ which is a specific value or numerical range of an attribute in the request. The UID is the user's identity that will be exploited in the access control by CA. Specifically, if the user wants to search the documents according to the attribute R ranging from r_{x1} to r_{x2} the trapdoor has the ciphertext $ED_{R_x} = [X(r_{x1}), X(r_{x2})](X(r_{x1}) \leq X(r_{x2}))$ via some order-preserving transformation function X. Similarly, the keyword attribute values $\{w_{x1}, w_{x2}, \cdots\}$ which correspond to the $DW_x = \{w_{x1}, w_{x2}, \cdots\}$ have the encrypted form $ED_{W_x} = \{\Psi_{K_\Psi}(w_{x1}), \Psi_{K_\Psi}(w_{x2}), \cdots\}$ with the full-domain pseudorandom function Ψ.

Request Freight Station: A request station denoted by FS is a list that is used to cache the updating requests for index that have not been processed. A node in FS is a tuple $(IID_i, op, request)$ that represents an updating request on I_i. If $op = write$, the request is $data_{new}$ which needs to be written in the related index file. If $op = alter$, the request is $data_{alt}$ which represents the data to be altered. If $op = delete$, the request could be null. Actually, the FS works as a lazy updating method for index files so as to reduce the communication cost significantly. Upon receiving an updating request for an index file, the CA would first cache the request temporarily in FS, and passively executes the updating operations when the right file is returned via other requests. To avoid the FS overflow, the CA periodically checks the FS to clear the remaining requests by performing them actively.

Access Control Vector: Our access control vector $\vec{P}$ stored in $\ddot{F}$ is a binary vector generated by Bloom Filter based on user identity types. Assume that the set of user identity type is $L = \{l_1, l_2, \cdots\}$ for a cloud storage system, such as doctor, patient, and nurse. A user at least belongs to one type $l_i(1 \leq i \leq |L|)$. Given F, if there are x types of identity, $\hat{L} = \{l_i\}_{1 \leq i \leq |L|}^{x} \subseteq L$ that can access it, then the $\vec{P}$ for F would be generated through $HASH = \{H_1, H_2, ..., H_h\}$ of the Bloom Filter. The detailed generation and matching algorithms for $\vec{P}$ are described in next section. Notice that the $\vec{P}$ stored in $\ddot{F}$ is cached in CA so that CA can only retrieve the authorized data for the corresponding users by performing matching algorithms.

3.4 Index Blind Storage Operations

Based on the structures introduced above, we use three operations to implement our IBS scheme, i.e., **IBS.KeyGen, IBS.Initial**, and **IBS.Access**.

IBS.KeyGen(λ): Based on a security factor λ, the IBS.KeyGen generates a key with the PRF and a key K_Ψ, with the FD-PRF, respectively. Then, the key for the index cryptographic KIBS is (K_Ψ, K_Φ) that is stored in CA.

IBS.Initial(*IND, T, KIBS*): This operation is used to generate the index file set *IND* and the query table set T. Each I_i in *IND* is divided into $size_i$ blocks of equal size. Note that the last block might be padded with 0s. There are two headers in a block, one of them records IID_i and the other records the version number v_i. Initially, all blocks have version number 0, and when re-encrypting a block, its version number is incremented. Let B be an array of n_B blocks and initialize each block to 0s. For each I_i in *IND*:

1. By using $\sigma = IID_i$ as a seed, IBS.Initial generates a sufficiently long integer sequence $S \leftarrow \Gamma(\sigma)$. We can then choose $size_i$ different integers in S from the beginning and make sure that the blocks in B indexed by these integers are all free. Let $\Lambda[\sigma, l]$ represent the first ℓ different integers generated through σ and Γ. Then, we can create a pseudorandom subset $S_i \subseteq [n_B]$, where $S_i = \Lambda[\sigma, size_i]$.

2. Put the $size_i$ blocks divided from I_i into the blocks in B indexed by S_i in ascending order and mark these blocks as non-free.

3. Write S_i into the field *addr* of I_i in T.

4. Then, the CA encrypts each block in B with Φ and K_Φ, and outsources the encrypted B to IBS. The *i*th block in B is $B[i] = B[i] \oplus \Phi_{K_\Phi}(v_i\| i)$.

IBS.Access(Q, *op*, T, K_{IBS}): This operation takes the query trapdoor Q, the operations on files *op*, the query table set T, and K_{IBS} as input parameters. Unlike the original blind storage scheme, we leverage Q and T to achieve the complex search. As for all file operations $op \in \{read, write, alter, delete\}$, the *write, alter*, and *delete* are carried out after the *read* via the lazy updating method mentioned in the request freight station so as to improve the performance, as we illustrate in our evaluations. The implementation of IBS.Access is as follows:

1. Upon receiving trapdoor Q, CA looks for the qualified *IID*s in T based on the *UID* in Q. In this way, CA can obtain the corresponding *addr*s and the integer sequence $S_Q \subseteq \{n_B\}$. Let $size_Q$ be the number of blocks indexed by S_Q. Specifically, when the set of all range attributes $(ED_{R_1}, \cdots, ED_{R_n})$ in Q is not empty, then we pick out the

attribute $R_{\min}(1 \leq \min \leq n)$ that has the minimal value range. Owing to the ascending order of T, CA could quickly locate the corresponding tuples in $T_{\min}$ according to the numerical range $r_{\min}$. Afterwards, CA can compare the other attributes with $ED_{\bar{A}}$ according to the remaining tuples in T. If $(ED_{R_1}, \cdots ED_{R_n})$ in Q is empty, CA could directly use $(ED_{W_1}, \cdots, ED_{W_m})$ to implement search operation.

2. Given the S_Q, CA chooses a random number τ to generate a long integer sequence $V \leftarrow \Gamma(\tau)$. Then, CA constructs a pseudorandom sequence $V_Q \subseteq \{n_B\}$ as the confusion blocks while assuring the first $\beta \cdot size_Q$ integers are different from V. The introduction of confusion parameter β assures that the number of confusion blocks correlated to an index file is different from the size of requested index in a search. By this means, the more index files are requested, the lower the probability of finding out the correlations between downloaded blocks.

3. CA downloads the mixed blocks indexed by S_Q and V_Q simultaneously, and then decrypts the blocks indexed by S_Q and recovers the requested index files using $B[i] = B[i] \oplus \Phi_{K_\Phi}(v_i\|i)$. In this way, the CA can request multiple index files for one or more users per search, while the original blind storage scheme needs one or two communication rounds to fetch an index file.

4. Upon recovering the index files, CA checks the FS to perform updating if there are updating requests for them, and then the requests in FS that have been processed will be cleared. There are two cases which need to be handled for the write operation on I_i.

   a. If the $size'_i$ of updated I'_i is the same as that of the unmodified version, CA just needs to update the last block belonging to I_i, and set the version of I''_i's blocks as $v_i = v_i + 1$.

   b. If the $size'_i$ is bigger than $size_i$, CA has to compute a subset $S_{new} = \Lambda\left[IID_i, \left(size_i - size'_i\right)\right] \subseteq n_B$ and then fetches the free blocks indexed by S_{new} and $\beta \cdot \left(size'_i - size_i\right)$ confusion blocks from B. Afterwards, CA combines the S_{new} and S_i together to get $S'_i = S_i \vee S_{new}$ and updates the new blocks indexed with S'_i. Finally, the system updates the corresponding $add\ r_i$ fields in T to S'_I.

Additionally, the implementation of *alter* operations and *delete* operations is similar to *write* operations, except for the updated content. In the *delete* operations, the IBS will replace the blocks with 0s, indicating that they are free.

4 THE ALGORITHMS IMPLEMENTATIONS FOR IBS-SSE

In this section, we describe the implementations for IBS in detail with a symmetric encryption in our prototype system, i.e., IBS-SSE, which mainly relies on the following polynomial time operations: IBS-SSE.Setup → IBS-SSE.IndexGen → IBS-SSE.Enc → IBS-SSE. Trapdoor → IBS-SSE.Search → IBS-SSE.Dec. Table 3.2 summarizes the major cryptographic primitives and notations in this paper.

TABLE 3.2 Notations

Notation	Illustration
H	a full-domain collision resistant hash function CRHF
Φ	a pseudorandom function PRF
Γ	a pseudorandom generator PRG
Ψ	a full-domain pseudorandom function FD-PRF
X	an order-preserving transformation function OPTF
A	an integer $\alpha > 1$ defining the expansion factor
B	an integer $\beta > 1$ defining the confusion factor
Λ	a security factor
FILE	a collection of EMR files, $FILE = \{F_i\}_{i=1}^{\lvert FILE \rvert}$
A	the collection of all attribute sets in FILE, $A = \{\vec{A}_i\}_{i=1}^{\lvert A \rvert}$
$\vec{A}$	an attribute set, $\vec{A} = (r_1, \cdots r_n, w_1, \cdots w_m)$
IND	a set of index files
I	an index file, $IND = \{I_i\}_{i=1}^{\lvert A \rvert}$
D_i	the specific value of an attribute in the request
$length_i$	the total byte length of index file I_i
T	a look-up table realized by MySQL
Q	the trapdoor for data access

4.1 The Implementation Flow

IBS-SSE.Setup: The CA first conducts the following setup operations by inputting the security factor λ:

First, it generates the key $K_{SSE} = K_{IBS}$ for the cryptographic primitives to be used later. Then, it creates a user list (UL) of length $\lvert UL \rvert$. The ith node in UL for the user U_i is $(UID_i, UN_i, BI_i, TS_i, \varepsilon_i)$, where the UID_i is set to the user ID of U_i, the UN_i represents the user name, BI_i contains U_i's basic information (gender, age, address, etc.), TS_i is the treatment schedule which updates after a treatment, and ε_i is a random factor of U_i. While $UID_i = (s_i \| l)$, where the $s_i \leftarrow H(id_i)$, id_i is the unique identity number of U_i and s_i is an r-length string transformed from id_i. The $l \in L$ is a character indicating U_i's user identity types. The UID_i is used to encrypt privacy data $\ddot{F}$, and can only be accessed by U_i and CA.

IBS-SSE.IndexGen(FILE, A): By taking the file set $FEIL = \{F_j\}_{j=1}^{\lvert FILE \rvert}$ and the set of attributes $A = \{\vec{A}_i\}_{i=1}^{\lvert A \rvert}$ as input, this operation works as follows:

(1) CA assigns a file identifier $FID_j \leftarrow H(UID \| t) \oplus \varepsilon$ to each $F_j \in FILE$. The UID is the user ID of the file owner, t is the visit time of F_j, and ε is the random factor that is associated with the owner. By using the identity-based access control method introduced above, IBS-SSE. IndexGen generates the access policy P_j according to the rules specified by the owner of F_j.

(2) IBS-SSE.IndexGen initializes a collection of index files named IND and a query table T for FILE. Algorithm 1 illustrates the construction process of them. Each index file I_i in IND is created for an attribute vector $\vec{A}_i \in A$. The $\vec{A}_i : \{FID\}$ represents the set that contains all IDs of the files which satisfy $\vec{A}_i$. The query table T is used in the search for index files. Each tuple in T is composed of a name field recording the identifier of I_i,

a range field indicating the transformed range value E_r in $\vec{A}_i$, along with an empty address field which would be used to store the address of blocks belonging to I_i.

(3) Then, CA initializes an IBS by IBS.Initial(IND, T, $KIBS$).

(4) Finally, the CA outsources all index files IND into CSP and store T.

IBS-SSE.Enc(FILE): This operation takes *FILE* as input and performs encryption for each file F in *FILE*, i.e., $\dot{C} = SE_{FID}(\dot{F})$, $\ddot{C} = SE_{UID}(\ddot{F})$. Then, CA uploads $C = \dot{C}||\ddot{C}$ to CSP. The separated encryption for privacy data and shared data provides the basis of fulfilling the data access for different users. Moreover, we use typical symmetric cryptography algorithm here to encrypt the files, while it also can easily be changed to some more complicated methods to enhance the security in practical applications. According to the identity of visitor and the purpose of data access, there are two cases in the phases of IBS-SSE.Trapdoor and IBS-SSE.Search. We omit the detail of IBS-SSE. Trapdoor due to the page limit of the paper. The process of IBS-SSE.Search is shown as follows.

IBS-SSE.Search(Q, T, KIBS): In Case 1, the CA would execute IBS.Access when it receives Q from U_i. Once recovering the index files that match the search criteria, the CA then executes the access control matching between UID_i and each $(FID, \vec{P})$ contained in index files. Finally, CA returns back the ciphertext blocks in CSP according to the (FID)s that match user's request. In Case 2, U_i just needs to request the encrypted blocks belonging to the target files from BS directly by using (FID)s.

IBS-SSE.Dec(C): The user U_i carries out $\dot{F} \leftarrow DE_{FID}(\dot{C})$ locally to obtain the shared data in F. Only the owner or the authorized users who have the owner's UID can run $\ddot{F} \leftarrow DE_{FID}(\ddot{C})$ to acquire the private data. In addition, there are two key add operations in our scheme.

IBS-SSE.AddUser (s', l', UN', BI', TS'): Upon receiving the request about adding a user, CA first checks if the user already exists in the user list *UL* according to s'. If not, then CA assigns a $UID_{|UL|+1} = \langle s'||l' \rangle$ to the new user and appends $U_{|UL|+1} = \langle UID_{|UL|+1}, UN', BI', TS', \varepsilon' \rangle$ to *UL*. $UL = |UL|+1$. Finally, CA sends $\langle UID_{|UL|+1}, TS', \varepsilon' \rangle$ to the new user.

IBS-SSE.AddDoc(F_{new}): The user carries out IBSSSE.Enc and then uploads the encrypted F_{new} to CSP. Meanwhile, the identifier of F_{new}, the trapdoor describing the attribute groups of F_{new}, and the access policy of F_{new} would be sent to CA as a tuple $(FID_{new}, Q_{\dot{A}_{new}}, \vec{P}_{new})$. Afterwards, the CA checks whether the owner of F_{new} exists in UL or not. If not, CA implements IBS-SSE.AddUser first. CA then calls IBS.Access $(Q_{\vec{A}_{new}}, write, T, K_{IBS})$ to finish index updating.

4.2 Access Control Algorithms

In general, the $\ddot{F}$ of the file $F = ((\dot{F}), \ddot{F})$ is not allowed to be shared and accessed. As for the shared part $\dot{F}$ the owner is able to specify different access control policies for it to ensure that the unauthorized users cannot access them. To facilitate this, we use an identity-based access control method that employs a Bloom Filter to realize the authorization.

Algorithm 1 The generation of access policy $\vec{P}$

1:        new a vector $\vec{P} = \overbrace{(0, 0, ...)}$ of $q - $ bit

2:        *for each* $l_i \in \hat{L} = \{l_i\}_{1 \leq i \leq |L|}^{x}$ *do*

3:          *for each* $H_y \in HASH = \{H_1, H_2, \cdots H_h\}$ *do*

4:            compute $H_y(l_i)$

5:            $\vec{P}\big[H_y(l_i)\big] = 1$

6:          *end for*

7:        *end for*

8:        return $\vec{P}$

The generation of access policy $\vec{P}$ and the implementation of access control matching are presented in Algorithm 1 and Algorithm 2. The owner of F can tell the identity types of authorized users based on the set $\hat{L} = \{l_i\}_{1 < i \leq |L|}^{x} \subseteq L$ of x elements. As shown in Algorithm 1, the h hash functions in $HASH = \{H_1, H_2, ...H_h\}$ of the Bloom Filter could map the x elements in $\hat{L}$ to a binary vector $\vec{P}$ of q bits. We use the SHA-256 as the full-domain collision-resistant hash function H in our prototype system. Thus, the $\vec{P}$ is exactly the access policy correlated to F. As shown in Algorithm 2, when a user requests to access F according to $\vec{P}$, CA can judge whether the identity l of this user belongs to the authorized set $\hat{L}$ of F through Bloom Filter. If so, the user can access $\dot{F}$ in F; otherwise, the user will be denied access.

Algorithm 2 The access control for a file **F**

1:   a new integer *flag* = **0**

2:    for each $H_y \in HASH = \{H_1, H_2, \cdots H_h\}$ do

3:      compute $H_y(l)$

4:       if $\vec{P}\big[H_y(l)\big] = 0$ then

5:         return false

6:         Break

7:       Else

8:          flag+=1

9:       end if

10:    end for

11:   if flag = h then

12:    return true

13:   end if

---

5 SECURITY ANALYSIS

This section provides the security analysis and emphasizes the choice of parameters for IBS.

5.1 Confidentiality of Data and Index

All data and index files will be encrypted through the traditional symmetric encryption method before uploading. In particular, the index files are shredded into pieces and stored with the IBS mechanism. Both data and index are just encrypted blocks stored regularly from the viewpoint of cloud server. In addition, when files are accessed, in Case 1, the index files are decrypted and recovered in CA, which can be absolutely trusted. Then CA would follow the access policy P and ensures that no unauthorized user can access the files. When the encrypted data arrive at the client side, unauthorized users can only recover the shared part, while the private part can only be seen by the authorized one. As for Case 2, a data owner can conveniently compute the address of requested file with known information, and retrieve the file by himself without the CA. The crucial key to decrypt the most private part $\ddot{F}$ is set to *UID* which usually is a pseudorandom string kept by the owner.

5.2 Trapdoor Security

The trapdoor Q will be generated only in Case 1 when a user has to submit his/her search along with his/her *UID* to CA. In our scheme, CSP is supposed to be a carrier rather than a conductor. In other words, it is only responsible for data downloading in a search operation. Since CA works as an intermediate agent, we definitely do not need to worry about the trapdoor leakage by CSP because it is unable to access the trapdoor. In addition, although the transmission channel between the search users and the CA is supposed to be safe, we still encrypt the trapdoor Q so as to further secure the search command.

5.3 Complete Concealing of Access Pattern

The access pattern denotes the sequence of search results, which indicates the association between the searches and the files. Most of the previous schemes leak the access pattern to CSP because the search users can obtain the files directly from CSP. Because we use IBS in our approach, the access pattern is completely hidden from the cloud server. Since each file is divided into encrypted pieces that are deployed in the cloud server in a random way, except for the occurrence of blocks uploading and downloading, the cloud server knows nothing about the relations among blocks, and consequently cannot tell the number of files stored on it and the size of each file.

In addition, the CA helps conceal the user from CSP as an intermediary by returning index blocks back along with varying numbers of confusion blocks based on the factor β. Unlike the original blind storage which shuffles the data blocks with fixed number of confusion blocks, the number of confusion blocks attached to each search varies, which helps completely conceal the access pattern. The CSP would be undoubtedly confused so that it fails to carry out a known plaintext attack. Moreover, it is worth noting that CA can acquire blocks for multiple index files in one search round for multiple users. This way, the number of communication rounds is greatly reduced.

5.4 The Probability of Aborting

Let p_{err} be the probability of operation aborting when the error occurs, i.e., the empty blocks indexed by the integers in sequence S are not enough in our model. To measure p_{err}, we take n_B, b, and α into account, where n_B is the length of array B, b is the total number of blocks of all the index files stored on the cloud server, and $\frac{1}{\alpha}$ is the ratio of the number of blocks belonging to an index file to the number of blocks in the pseudorandom set that needs to be downloaded when the file is added. For simplicity, we define $\theta = \frac{n_B}{b}$.

Suppose that there is a new index file I_i of $size_i$ blocks that needs to be added into the system (or an existing index file I_i which needs to update $size_i$ blocks). While b out of n_B blocks in array B have already been filled (i.e., not free).

When I_i has been added, we pick a random set S of size $|S| = size_i \cdot \alpha$. Based on a standard application of Chernoff bound, the probability that more than $\frac{2b}{n_B} |S|$ blocks are filled is $2^{-\Omega(|S|)}$, so that the upper limit of $\frac{1}{n_B}$ is less than 1. $|S| \geq \alpha$ the probability p_{err} which is negligible when compared to k, as α is super-logarithmic in k (e.g., $\log_2 k$). Thus, at least $|S|\left(1 - \frac{2b}{n_B}\right) \geq \alpha \cdot size_i \cdot \left(1 - \frac{2b}{n_B}\right)$ blocks out of the $|S|$ blocks are empty. Now we have p_{err} in Equation (1), which indicates that p_{err} can be fixed at 2^{-60} orso. Thus, the CA will not abort when adding I_i if the above condition holds.

$$P_{err}(\theta, \alpha) \leq \max_{n \geq \alpha} \sum_{i=0}^{n-1} \binom{\left|\frac{1}{\alpha}n\right|}{i} \left(\frac{\theta - 1}{\theta}\right)^i (\theta)^{\frac{1}{\alpha}(n-i)} \tag{1}$$

6 PERFORMANCE EVALUATION

We implemented the prototype EMR management system based on IBS-SSE on a server running Windows 7, with IntelCore i5-3210M processor and 4GB memory. The Crypto++ library is employed to implement the block cipher (AES)and the collision-resistant hash function (SHA256). We evaluate our scheme in terms of functionality, computation cost, and communication cost.

We set $\alpha = \beta = 4$ to make sure that $p_{err} \leq 2^{-40}$ when at most $\frac{1}{4}$ blocks of the total blocks in B are occupied. We set $n_B = 2 \times 10^4$. The number of hash functions in $HASH$ is $h = 7$ so as to minimize the error probability of Bloom filter when $|L| = 3$ and the length is 32-bit. The experiments are based on three kinds of real datasets that have attribute dimensions of $Dim = 3$, 6, and 9, respectively. We choose datasubsets of 128MB, 256MB, 512MB, 1G, and 2G from the three datasets to evaluate the performance.

6.1 Functionality

As shown in Table 3.3, we compare the functionalities of the IBS-SSE scheme in EMR management system, the BSTORE-SSE scheme in blind storage [13], and the EMRS scheme proposed in [14].

6.2 Computation Costs

The experimental results demonstrate that our scheme is scalable in terms of index generation, search, and document adding with the increasing size of file.

(1) Index Generation: Generally, the index generation is the most expensive part in regard to the computation cost in prior encryption schemes. We evaluate all related operations involved in the index generation. The IBS.Initial operation generally incurs most of the computation

TABLE 3.3 Comparisons of functionalities

	BSTORE-SSE	EMRS	Our scheme
Single-keyword Search	√	√	√
Multi-keyword Search		√	√
Range Search			√
Ranked Search		√	
Multi-owner Multi-user			√
Access Control		√	√

cost in index generation with complexity $O(|A| + n_B)$ that is not correlated with the size of dataset. For IBS-SSE.IndexGen, the complexity of our index naming operations is $O(|A|)$, indicating a linear correlation to the number of attribute sets, i.e., the number of index file. As Fig. 3.6 shows, the time cost for index building grows almost linearly with the increase of $|A|$ under different attribute dimension. As we can see, it only takes 13 s–15 s to finish the index generation even when $Dim = 6$. Therefore, our scheme can complete the index generation in a stable and short time period for varying size of datasets.

(2) Index Search: Search phase mainly involves index access and access control operations. Here we only consider Case 1. Index access operation involves two phases: the trapdoor generation, and the search and recovery of index files (including the updating). The former is implemented via IBS-SSE.Trapdoor with complexity $O(Dim)$, while the latter is accomplished using IBS.Access(Q, op, T, K_{IBS}). Figure 3.7 depicts that the computation cost of index access is irrelevant to the size of datasets when launching search requests with a trapdoor Q including multi-keyword and range values. In addition, the attribute dimensions show little impact on the computation cost. Compared to the prior schemes, such as [13] and APKS in [19], our scheme is more efficient which only takes 0.5s to execute the search operation, whereas APKS takes about 42 s to

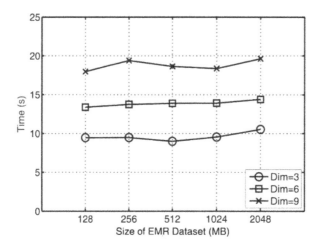

FIGURE 3.6   Computation cost of index generation.

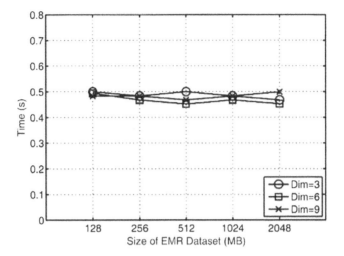

FIGURE 3.7   Computation cost of index search.

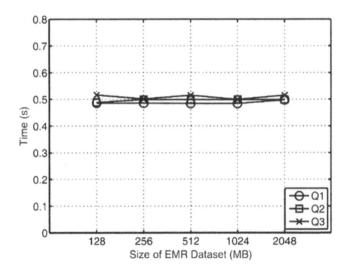

FIGURE 3.8   Computation costs of index search with varying Q values.

accomplish the same operation. Figure 3.8 shows the computation costs for datasets of $Dim = 9$ under varioustrapdoors Q_1, Q_2, and Q_3. As we can see, the computation cost of index search basically remains the same as the size of datasets increases.

The access control operation for EMR files is performed after recovering index files; Fig. 3.9 shows the overhead for an access control matching, which is equal to $\frac{total\ overhead}{the\ number\ of\ natched\ files}$. Thus, the computation overhead is near to 0. Besides, the error probability of Bloom Filter is negligible according to the experiment results.

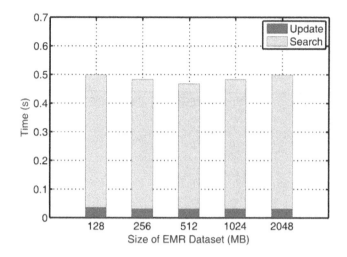

FIGURE 3.9   Computation costs: index with varying Q values.

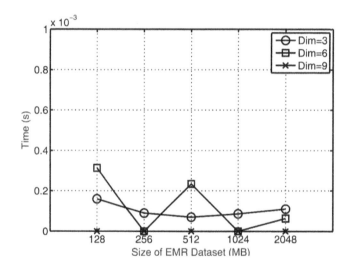

FIGURE 3.10   Computational cost of access control.

(3) Updating: We use a lazy update strategy in IBS. Therefore, the overhead of update is only related to the number of updating requests to be processed and is irrelevant to the size of datasets. As shown in Fig. 3.10, when $Dim = 9$, the overhead for update is quite small compared with the computation cost of search.

6.3 Communication Cost

(1) We measure the communication cost of index uploading during initialization. The communication overhead of index uploading relies on the size of array B. There is

a tradeoff between the communication cost and aborting rate. In our experiments, the array B consists of 2×10^4 file blocks of 1K bytes or less. The size of B is almost 20M bytes. Actually, the amount of index files for a 2G bytes EMR dataset that consists of about 2×10^4 "document-attribute group" pairs is about 1366K bytes. However, to assure the probability of aborting p_{err} below 2^{-40}, we need to set (θ, α) = (4, 4). We actually only need about 6M bytes to store the 1366K bytes index. Hence, B = 20M is sufficient for more documents under an affordable communication cost.

(2) The communication overhead of index search is composed of two parts: the size of trapdoor Q sent from the user, and the index data along with confusion blocks returned from IBS. (a) The size of Q relies on $D_{\vec{A}}$, which grows linearly with the increase of query conditions. In our experiment, when $Dim = 9$, the length of $D_{\vec{A}}$ is $length\ _{D_{\vec{A}}} = 2|X(r)| + |\Psi_{K_{\Psi}}(w)| \cdot \sum(|W_i|)_{i=1}^{8} = 2$ where $|X(r)|$ and $|\Psi_{K_{\Psi}}(w)|$ are fixed at 2-bit and 32-bit, respectively. Consider the worst case, i.e., when the query value for each attribute field covers the whole range of that field, if $\sum(|W_i|)_{i=1}^{8} = 2$, then the maximum length of $D_{\vec{A}}$ is only 0.5K bytes. Actually, when the query value for an attribute field covers the whole range of it, the value would be set null, implying there is no query for that field. (b) With regard to the communication cost of index data, we have to download more index data than we actually need due to the utilization of IBS for stronger security. As shown in Fig. 3.11, for the EMR dataset, the communication overhead of index is negligible compared with the size of EMR documents retrieved, which clearly indicates that the communication overhead is also not a concern in our system.

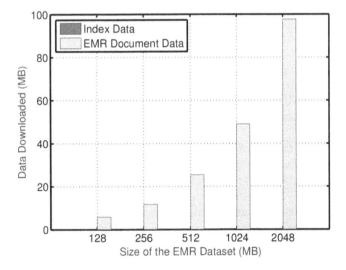

FIGURE3.11   Communication cost of index search.

7 CONCLUSION

In this chapter, we propose a searchable encryption scheme that relies on an attribute vector-based IBS technique so as to support multi-key and range search for multi-owner multi-user application. First, our index structure integrates multiple search results into one communication round so as to significantly reduce the communication cost. Second, our scheme further eliminates the correlation of blocks and obtains higher privacy preserving through a confusion factor that ensures the confusion blocks correlated to an index file are variable in a search. Moreover, the Bloom Filter-based access control policy in our scheme can fit into multi-owner multi-user scenario. The extensive experiments demonstrate that our scheme is more scalable and achieve much better search efficiency.

REFERENCES

1. H. T. Dinh, C. Lee, D. Niyato, and P. Wang. "A survey of mobile cloud computing: Architecture, applications, and approaches." *Wireless Communications and Mobile Computing*, 13(18):1587–1611, 2013.
2. C. Liu, F. Lin, D. Chiang, T. Chen, et al. "Secure PHR access control scheme for healthcare application clouds." In *Proceedings of 42nd International Conference on Parallel Processing (ICPP)*, 2013, pp. 1067–1076.
3. R. Canetti, U. Feige, O. Goldreich, and M. Naor. "Adaptively secure multi-party computation." In *28th ACM Symposium on Theory of Computing*, 1996, pp. 639–648.
4. C. Wang, N. Cao, J. Li, K. Ren, and W. Lou. "Secure ranked keyword search over encrypted cloud data." In *Proceedings of IEEE 30th International Conference on Distributed Computing Systems (ICDCS '10)*, 2010, pp. 253–262.
5. D. X. Song, D. Wagner, and A. Perrig. "Practical techniques for searches on encrypted data." In *Proceedings of S&P*. IEEE, 2000, pp. 44–55.
6. S. Kamara, C. Papamanthou, and T. Roeder. "Dynamic searchable symmetric encryption." In *ACM CCS*, 2012, pp. 965–976.
7. C. Wang, N. Cao, K. Ren, and W. Lou. "Enabling secure and efficient ranked keyword search over outsourced cloud data." *IEEE Transactions on Parallel and Distributed Systems*, 23 (8):1467–1479, 2012.
8. W. Sun, B. Wang, N. Cao, M. Li, W. Lou et al. "Verifiable privacy-preserving multi-keyword text search in the cloud supporting similarity-based ranking." *IEEE Transactions on Parallel and Distributed Systems*, 25(11):3025–3035, 2014.
9. N. Cao, C. Wang, M. Li, K. Ren et al. "Privacy-preserving multikeyword ranked search over encrypted cloud data." *IEEE Transactions on Parallel and Distributed Systems*, 25(1):222–233, 2014.
10. B. Wang, S. Yu, W. Lou, and Y. T. Hou. "Privacy-preserving multikeyword fuzzy search over encrypted data in the cloud." In *IEEE INFOCOM*, 2014, pp. 2112–2120.
11. R. Li, A. X. Liu, A. L. Wang, and B. Bruhadeshwar. "Fast and scalable range query processing with strong privacy protection for cloud computing." In *IEEE/ACM Transactions on Networking*, pp. 2305–2318, 2016.
12. J. H. Park. "Efficient hidden vector encryption for conjunctive queries on encrypted data." *IEEE Transactions on Knowledge and Data Engineering*, 23(10):1483–1497, 2011.
13. M. Naveed, M. Prabhakaran, and C. A. Gunter. "Dynamic searchable encryption via blind storage." In *IEEE Symposium on Security and Privacy*, 2014, pp. 639–654.

14. H. Li, D. Liu, Y. Dai, T. Luan et al. "Enabling efficient multi-keyword ranked search over encrypted mobile cloud data through blind storage." *IEEE Transactions on Emerging Topics in Computing*, 3(1):127–138, 2015.
15. D. Boneh, G. D. Crescenzo, R. Ostrovsky, and G. Persiano. "Public key encryption with keyword search. Advances in cryptology." In *EUROCRYPT*. Springer, Berlin Heidelberg, 2004, pp. 506–522.
16. A. Lewko and B. Waters. "New proof methods for attribute-based encryption: Achieving full security through selective techniques." In *CRYPTO*, 2012, pp. 180–198.
17. K. Yang and X. Jia. "Expressive, efficient, and revocable data access control for multi-authority cloud storage." *IEEE Transactions on Parallel and Distributed Systems*, 25 (7):1735–1744, 2014.
18. W. Sun, S. Yu, W. Lou, Y. T. Hou et al. "Protecting your right: Attribute-based keyword search with fine-grained owner-enforced search authorization in the cloud." *IEEE Transactions on Parallel and Distributed Systems*, 27(4):1187–1198, 2016.
19. M. Li, S. Yu, N. Cao, and W. Lou. "Authorized private keyword search over encrypted data in cloud computing." In *31st International Conference on Distributed Computing Systems*, 2011, pp. 383–392.

CHAPTER 4

Encrypted Big Data Deduplication in Cloud Storage

Zheng Yan and Xueqin Liang

The State Key Laboratory of ISN, School of Cyber Engineering, Xidian University, Xi'an, China
Department of Communications and Networking, Aalto University, Espoo, Finland

Wenxiu Ding and Xixun Yu

The State Key Laboratory of ISN, School of Cyber Engineering, Xidian University, Xi'an, China

Mingjun Wang

The State Key Laboratory of ISN, School of Telecommunications Engineering, Xidian University, Xi'an, China

Robert H. Deng

The School of Information Systems, Singapore Management University, Singapore

CONTENTS

1 INTRODUCTION

Cloud computing is an Internet-based service infrastructure, through which shared hardware and software resources and information can be provided to various terminals and devices based on the demands of cloud users. Its unique characteristics, such as virtualization, reliability, versatility, scalability, pay-per-use, and low price, provide cloud computing a wide range of application prospects.

Cloud storage is one of the typical services of cloud computing, which provides cloud users with an efficient way to save storage space, back data up online, and access data from any place and at any time via the Internet. However, this service brings some problems for both cloud users and Cloud Service Providers (CSPs). For data users, uploading data to the cloud makes them lose the direct control of their data. Especially when the data is related to their personal and sensitive information, data privacy leakages could happen. With the increasing concern about security and data privacy, data users prefer to upload their data to the cloud in an encrypted form. Moreover, different cloud users may have different preferences for the management of data based on the sensitivity of their data. It is obvious that the access control of popular data, like music or movies, is not as strict as that of sensitive data. Considering the risk of privacy leakage in the cloud, some cloud users prefer to control the access to data on their own. Some cloud users entrust a third party to take over the access control of their data when they are not convenient to do such a task or when they cannot be always online. Consequently, flexible data access control becomes critical for cloud storage service concerning different data security requirements and user demands. From the perspective of CSPs, repeatedly storing the same data by the same user or different users causes serious waste of cloud storage resources, especially in a big data scenario. Even if the storage capability of CSPs is large, they still need a lot of energy to manage those data. Therefore, it is urgent for the CSP to adopt some efficient resource management schemes, for example, deduplication, which is very useful for saving storage consumption and can finally benefit cloud users.

A recent survey [1] shows that deduplication in standard file systems can save as much as 68% of its original required storage space. Therefore, a CSP-deployed deduplication will definitely save many network resources and storage costs. However, as we stated before, the services provided by CSP should also support data encryption and flexible data access control. Cloud data encryption causes new challenges to data deduplication since different cloud users encrypt the same data with different secret keys, which makes it difficult to identify duplicate data. Traditional schemes cannot manage encrypted data deduplication with flexible access control in a practical way. The big data paradigm makes deduplication on encrypted cloud data a rather tough issue.

In this chapter, we propose three deduplication schemes that suit different application scenarios. The first one can be deployed into such a situation that the data owners cannot be always online by applying two technologies: data ownership challenge and Proxy Re-Encryption (PRE). The second one is suitable for the situation that the data owners want to control data access entirely by themselves with the support of Attribute-Based Encryption (ABE) for secure data access control. The last scheme is a heterogeneous deduplication scheme with flexible access control. In this scheme, either data owner or CSP, or both of them or none of them can control deduplication and data access. One advantage of the proposed three schemes is the data size does not influence their performance. Therefore, they are scalable to big data scenarios. Specifically, the contributions of this chapter are summarized as below:

- We propose three deduplication schemes on encrypted data to save cloud storage across multiple CSPs and achieve data security and privacy preservation. These schemes can support different application scenarios with different security requirements.

- We integrate flexible data access control into encrypted data deduplication in our proposed schemes. All these schemes are secure and can support big data storage.

- We analyze the security of our schemes and evaluate their performance in terms of operation time and computation cost.

- We compare and discuss the application scenarios and practical deployment limitations of the three schemes. Some future research trends are also proposed at the end of this chapter.

The rest of this chapter is organized as follows. Section 2 briefly overviews the related work about access control on encrypted data, encrypted data deduplication, and proof of ownership. We summarize notations and introduce some algorithms in cryptography, like PRE, ABE, and symmetric encryption in Section 3. Section 4 gives the detailed presentations of three encrypted data deduplication schemes in cloud storage. We analyze their security and evaluate their performance in Section 5 and compare their usage scenarios and deployment limitations, along with some future research directions in Section 6. The last section concludes the whole chapter.

2 RELATED WORK REVIEW AND OPEN RESEARCH ISSUES

2.1 Access Control on Encrypted Data

With the concern about privacy issues, cloud users upload their data to the cloud in an encrypted form. An efficient way to achieve the access control of encrypted data is to issue only the decryption keys to corresponding eligible cloud users. However, it is difficult to achieve flexible access control when access permission changes and data deletion happens.

Access Control Lists (ACLs) in a file system is a data structure that gives a clear statement about each file's authorized users and these users' access rights and operations allowed. Applying ACLs in a system with a distrusted or semi-trusted party can guarantee the safety of data to some extent.

Goh et al. [2] proposed a secure file system called SiRiUS, which can be layered over insecure networks and P2P file systems. Each data uploaded to the file server is split into two parts. One part contains the ACLs and the other part contains the file encrypted with a File Encryption Key (FEK). Each entry of the ACLs is the FEK encrypted by the public key of the authorized user. However, this scheme is not scalable. Once the owner of a file revokes one authorized user's access to the file, the owner needs to generate a new FEK and perform the new FEK encryption for all authorized users. The authors then extended the SiRiUS to SiRiUS-NNL, which use the Naor–Naor–Lotspiech (NNL) [3] construction for key revocation, to solve this inherent shortcoming of ACLs. In this new system, FEK is encrypted by a broadcast encryption algorithm instead of each authorized user's public key. Because the complexity of user revocation in NNL increases linearly with the number of revoked users, the scheme does not achieve the desired scalability even if it is better than SiRiUS.

ABE is another commonly used method to achieve encrypted data access control. ABE is one kind of public-key encryption algorithm. It takes identities as a series of attributes. Only when the attribute set of a user's key matches the attributes of the ciphertext, can he/

she decrypt the ciphertext. There are two types of ABE schemes. The first type is called key-policy ABE (KP-ABE) [4], in which an access tree is used to generate secret keys for users and data is encrypted with attribute sets. The other type is called ciphertext-policy ABE (CP-ABE) [5], which encrypts data with an access tree and generates secret keys for users through attribute sets. The difference between KP-ABE and CP-ABE is how data is encrypted and how secret keys are generated.

ABE has been widely used in encrypted data storage systems to support fine-grained access control with security [6,7]. Yu et al. [6] combined KP-ABE with PRE [8] and lazy re-encryption [9] to achieve fine-grained access control with scalability and data confidentiality at the same time. Yu et al. also proposed a practical scheme [10] to revoke attribute based on CP-ABE and PRE, which is proved to resist chosen ciphertext attacks. Moreover, this method is also applicable to KP-ABE. Other similar applications in cloud computing can be found in [11–13].

2.2 Encrypted Data Deduplication

Deduplication is a technique in cloud storage to eliminate duplicated data and only store one copy of data. A CSP can save a large number of storage costs by deduplication significantly, especially in big-data era. As more and more people begin to take data security and privacy into consideration, the need for encrypted data deduplication is urgent. However, encrypted data deduplication has not been applied in practical CSPs, like Dropbox [14] and Google Driver [15].

The entities involved in a data deduplication scheme are the clients (cloud users) who hold the data to be stored, and the CSPs who provide cloud data storage services. Existing deduplication schemes can be divided into client-side deduplication and server-side deduplication based on whether the cloud user always needs to upload data to the CSP. In a server-side deduplication, CSPs perform duplication check on the outsourced data, while this check is based on the hash value of the outsourced data in a client-side deduplication. Therefore, a client-side deduplication is more practical than a server-side deduplication because it can reduce more network bandwidth consumptions [16]. Considering this, we only discuss client-side deduplication in the following aspects.

Bellare et al. [17] first introduced Message-Locked Encryption (MLE) [18] to secure deduplication. MLE is a symmetric encryption scheme where the encryption key and decryption key are derived from the message. Convergent Encryption (CE) [18], which is also known as content hash keying, is one typical MLE. CE has been deployed in some CSPs, for example, Bitcasa (shut down in 2017). In a deduplication scheme deployed CE, a cloud user derives a key based on the hash code of its data (we call it the convergent key) and then encrypts its data with this convergent key. Another cloud user with the same data will derive the same information thus a CSP can find data duplication. There are some shortcomings of CE-based deduplication schemes. First, CE cannot resist offline brute-force attacks (i.e., dictionary attacks) on predictable message spaces to achieve semantic security. Second, a cloud user can learn whether a data has been uploaded to the cloud by requesting to upload this data. Third, the number of convergent keys will increase with the increasing number of users. Therefore, the key management cost is too high to support fine-grained access control.

To overcome the first problem we listed above, Bellare et al. [19] proposed DupLESS, in which the keys cloud users used to encrypt their data are obtained from an additional Key Server (KS) via an oblivious Pseudo Random Function (PRF) protocol [20]. The independent KS limits the number of queries for each cloud users. Through this protocol, KS cannot obtain any information about the data of cloud users and the cloud users cannot obtain the key of KS. Unfortunately, if the KS colludes with CSPs, DupLESS cannot be more secure than any other MLE-based schemes. Adding more KSs like Miao et al. proposed in [21] can reduce this risk to some degree. In [21], each cloud user should communicate with all the KSs to obtain the desired keys. It is insecure only when all the KSs are malicious. However, it definitely adds more communication overhead to the cloud users.

Liu et al. [22] proposed a secure deduplication scheme without additional independent servers based on Password Authenticated Key Exchange (PAKE), which can solve the first and second problems of CE. In this scheme, randomized threshold strategy is applied to prevent a later cloud user to learn information about the data of the former cloud user. Moreover, instead of sending the hash of the whole data to CSPs, a cloud user just sends a short hash. As the short hash has high collision rate, a malicious CSP cannot guess the real data easily. Therefore, offline brute-force attacks are resisted in this scheme. Nevertheless, it incurs additional computation overhead for previously outsourced cloud users.

Li et al. [23] addressed the third shortcoming of CE with an efficient and reliable convergent key management scheme called *Dekey*. The basic idea of *Dekey* is to split the convergent key into many shares and distribute them to multiple servers. Only a cloud user that really holds this whole data can recover the convergent key.

Ding et al. [24] applied an additive homomorphic re-encryption algorithm for effective public ownership verification and flexible access control. It does not introduce great communication costs to cloud users and CSPs for verifying ownership but its computation cost is relative high than some existing work.

2.3 Proof of Ownership (PoW)

PoW is an effective way to prevent unauthorized cloud users to access data. It usually happens between a cloud user and a CSP at a client-side deduplication scheme. Only when a cloud user passes data ownership verification, can he/she prove that he/she really possesses the data rather than only the hash value of the data he/she requests to upload.

The first commonly used PoW in deduplication is based on Merkle tree. Halevi et al. [25] applied erasure coding or hash function to encode the content of a particular data and then used the encode data to build a Merkle tree. The verifier (i.e., CSP) randomly chooses some number of leaf indexes to challenge a prover (i.e., cloud user). After receiving the leaf indexes, the prover calculates the corresponding sibling paths of these leaves and sends the response back to the verifier. The verifier only admits the prover pass the ownership challenge when all these sibling paths are valid. However, the CSP is assumed trustful because the data is not encrypted in [25], which is not practical, especially in public cloud scenarios. Ng et al. [26] first attempted to address PoW with encrypted data on the basis of [25]. In their solution, the value of each leaf of the Merkle tree is a commitment of a block. When a prover (i.e., cloud user) receives some leaf indexes as a challenge from the verifier (i.e., CSP), it calculates the corresponding sibling path and the commitments of these indexes. Only when all these values are valid, can the prover prove its ownership. However, this scheme incurs heavy computation overhead to cloud users and requires high Input/Output (I/O).

The second kind of PoW in deduplication is based on spot checking. Instead of calculating a Merkle tree in a Merkle tree-based PoW, a prover (i.e., cloud user) just needs to respond with a proof of some portions of a data file that are randomly selected by the verifier (i.e., CSP) [27]. Therefore, this kind of PoW can save computation costs and I/O operations of the prover. Unfortunately, the verification process incurs more I/O costs to the verifier. To address this problem, Blasco et al. [28] introduced Bloom filter, which is a space-efficient way to test membership, into PoW. In [28], the verifier (i.e., CSP) builds a Bloom filter for each data by dividing the data into many blocks of the same size and generating the token (e.g., hash) for each block. The challenge information is the indexes of some blocks randomly chosen. Upon receiving a challenge, the prover (i.e., cloud user) calculates corresponding tokens and sends them as the response to the verifier (i.e., CSP). Only when all the tokens are valid, can the prover pass the challenge. The I/O costs of CSPs are reduced since a CSP do not need to load the whole data to check the validity of responses. By combining spot-checking PoW with CE technique, González-Manzano and Orfil [29] proposed a novel PoW that can ensure the confidentiality of cloud users' data.

The third kind of PoW in existing literature of deduplication is with data integrity auditing. In the deduplication scheme proposed by Zheng and Xu [30], each cloud user generates a key pair and an authentication tag, and uploads data with the authentication tag to the CSP. With the cloud user's public key and this authentication tag, the CSP can perform PoW. However, this scheme suffers from high computation and communication costs. Yuan and Yu [31] applied polynomial-based authentication tags and homomorphic linear authenticators to address this problem. The authors proved their scheme efficient in keeping the auditing time and auditing communication cost at the client side constant. However, they did not take the CSP-side performance evaluation and big data scenarios into consideration.

2.4 Summary of Open Research Issues

Many access control schemes on encrypted data are proposed recently to prevent data privacy from malicious CSPs. Data access is controlled either by CSPs or by cloud users. However, a CSP-controlled deduplication scheme cannot satisfy the demand of the cloud users who want to control their data on their own. There will always be a delay in a client-controlled deduplication scheme, since it is impractical to ask cloud users to always be online for processing access requests. Moreover, the performance of most existing deduplication schemes will be influenced by the size of data and the number of cloud users, which seriously affect their applications in the big-data storage scenario. Therefore, it is still an open problem to design a holistic and comprehensive access control scheme to address the above concerns.

3 NOTATIONS AND PRELIMINARIES

3.1 Notations

We conclude all the notations in this chapter in Table 4.1 for clear reference and easy presentation.

3.2 Preliminaries

3.2.1 Elliptic-Curve Cryptography (ECC)

ECC is a typical public-key cryptography and has been widely applied for key arrangement, digital signatures, and pseudo-random generators.

There is an elliptic curve $Eq(a, b)$ over a field $GF(q)$, and a base point P which is on the curve $Eq(a, b)$. $Eq(a, b)$ and P are public in the network. With a security parameter σ, a user i randomly chooses an integer $s_i \in \{0, \ldots, 2^\sigma - 1\}$ as its secret key and then the corresponding public key V_i can be derived by $V_i = -s_i P$. It is hard to obtain s_i from V_i and P (Elliptic Curve Discrete Logarithm Problem, ECDLP). The key pair (V_i, s_i) is bound to a unique identifier of user i, which can be applied to verify the user identity.

3.2.2 Symmetric Encryption

Symmetric encryption is a simple cryptographic algorithm that the key used to perform decryption is just the key to perform encryption.

- $E(DEK, M)$: this algorithm takes the plaintext M and the symmetric key DEK as inputs and then outputs the ciphertext CT.

TABLE 4.1 Notations

Notation	Description
M	Raw data to be stored with deduplication;
$H(M)$	The hash value of data M;
$HC(M)$	The hash code of data M;
CT_i	The ciphertext of cloud user h_i's data;
CK_i	The cipher-key of cloud user h_i's data;
PK_i	The public key of cloud user h_i used for Public-Key Cryptography (PKC) encryption and signature verification;
SK_i	The secret key of cloud user h_i used for PKC decryption and signature generation;
pk_i	The public key of cloud user h_i about ABE used for attribute verification and personalized secret attribute key generation;
sk_i	The secret key of cloud user h_i about ABE used for decryption;
pk_i'	The public key of cloud user h_i about PRE used for re-encryption key generation;
sk_i'	The secret key of cloud user h_i about PRE used for decryption;
ID	The identity attribute of cloud users;
DEK_i	The symmetric key of cloud user h_i used to encrypt data M;
DEK_i^1	The partial key 1 of the symmetric key DEK_i;
DEK_i^2	The partial key 2 of the symmetric key DEK_i;
$PKID_i$	The public key of cloud user h_i concerning the attribute ID used to encrypt DEK_i^2;
$SKID_{i,j}$	The secret key cloud user h_i issued to h_j concerning the attribute ID, which h_j can use to access DEK_i^2 with decryption.

- $D(DEK, CT)$: this algorithm takes the ciphertext CT and the symmetric key DEK as inputs and then outputs the plaintext M.

3.2.3 PRE

Image a scenario that there is an entity i who wants to share its plain text M with an entity j by PRE. There are five algorithms in PRE, which are represented as $(KG; RG; En; R; De)$.

- $KG(1^{k_i})$ is the key generation algorithm of PRE. It can output a pair of public and secret key (pk'_i, sk'_i) for every entity i with the input of security parameter 1^{k_i};

- $En(pk'_i, M)$ is the encryption algorithm of PRE. It can output a ciphertext C_i with the input of the public key pk'_i and a plain text M;

- $RG(sk'_i, pk'_j)$ is the re-encryption key generation algorithm, which outputs the re-encryption $rk_{i \rightarrow j}$ for a third entity j;

- $R(rk_{i \rightarrow j}, C_i)$ is the re-encryption algorithm of PRE, which can output a ciphertext C_j that can only be decrypted by sk'_j;

- $De(sk'_j, C_j)$ is the decryption algorithm. It can output a plain text M with the input of the secret key sk'_j and ciphertext C_j;

3.2.4 ABE

An entity i wants to grant its data access control to another entity j who satisfies the access policy λ.

- $MKG(1^{k_i})$ is the key generation algorithm of ABE. It generates two key pairs (PK_i, SK_i) and (pk_i, sk_i) for every entity i. The first key pair is for PKC encryption and signature verification while the other one is for attribute key generation and attribute verification.

- $CreateIDPK(ID, sk_i)$ is a public attribute key generation algorithm of ABE. It outputs a public attribute key $IDPK_i$ based on attribute ID for the user i;

- $IssueIDSK(ID, sk_i, pk_j)$ is a secret attribute key issuance algorithm of ABE. It outputs a key $IDSK_{i,j}$ for the eligible entity j;

- $EK(DEK_i, \lambda, IDPK_i)$ outputs cipher-key CK_i that can only be decrypted by a user who satisfies the access policy λ;

- $DK(CK_i, \lambda, sk_j, IDSK_{i,j})$ is performed by the entity j. It can derive DEK_i from inputting $CK_i, IDSK_{i,j}$ and its secret key sk_j.

Since most of data access over the cloud is based on user identity, we can simplify our presentation by setting user identity as an example attribute rather than complex attribute herein. For a data to be accessed by cloud users with $ID = PK_j$ $(j = 1, 2, ..., J)$, the kcy DEK_t is encrypted with policy $\lambda : PK_1 \vee PK_2 \vee ... \vee PK_J$ and the cipher-key $CK_i = \langle CK_{i_1}, CK_{i_2}, ..., CK_{i_j} \rangle$.

3.2.5 Symmetric Key Management
$SeparateKey(DEK_i)$ can randomly separate the input DEK_i into several partial keys, for example, DEK_i^1 and DEK_i^2, while the algorithm $CombineKey(DEK_i^1, DEK_i^2)$ can output DEK_i by combining all the partial keys.

4 ENCRYPTED DATA DEDUPLICATION SCHEMES
We introduce three client-side deduplication schemes that are applicable to different application scenarios. The data access is controlled at the client side and the cloud side in Scheme 1 and Scheme 2, respectively. The access control in Scheme 3 is more flexible than the first two schemes because data access can be controlled at any side in Scheme 3.

4.1 Scheme 1: Cloud-Controlled Deduplication Based on PRE and Ownership Challenge
In this scheme [32,33], we apply PRE to issue keys to the cloud users who can pass data ownership challenge. Data access is controlled at the cloud side, so it is suitable for the application scenario that data holders cannot be online all the time.

There are four entities in Scheme 1. Key Generation Center (KGC) is a trusted entity who generates system parameters and certificates the other entities. Cloud User is the one who wants to upload data to the cloud. We call the one who first uploads data as data owner and the other cloud users as data holders. CSP is the one who provides various cloud services (e.g., data storage) to cloud users. It is possible for all data owner and data holders of the same data are the subscribers of different CSPs. Authorized Party (AP) is a trusted third party that will not collude with CSPs. CSP and AP cooperate to work as the proxy to perform data deduplication for data owners.

We assume CSPs will not collude with ineligible cloud users. This is easy to understand. Collusion makes CSPs and cloud users lose reputation so that CSPs cannot attract users and cloud users may be blocked to access data [34]. We also assume data holders to be honest that they will not send the information that is not calculated by the algorithms in Scheme 1 to CSPs. All data holders agree to grant delegation for data access management and ownership verification. Multiple CSPs can cooperate with each other to perform deduplication together under the incentive of saving storage spaces. All entities communicate with each other through a secure channel (e.g., Secure Socket Layer, SSL). As the number of AP will not influence the performance of our scheme, we simplify our system with one AP.

We present the detailed procedure of Scheme 1 as shown in Fig. 1, in the following subsections.

4.1.1 System Setup
P is a base point and σ is a security parameter. The two parameters are shared in public for data token generation and data ownership challenge. Each cloud user $h_i(i = 1, 2, ...)$

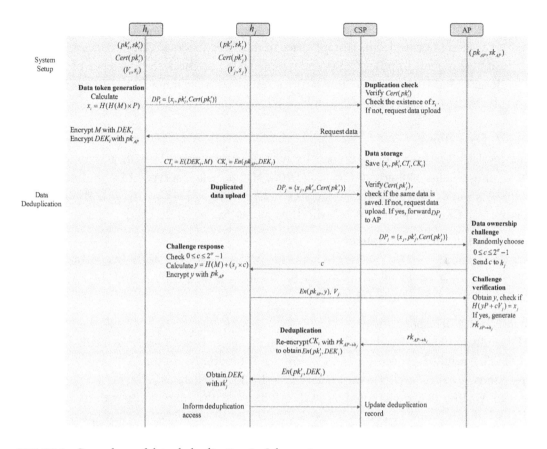

FIGURE 1   Procedure of data deduplication in Scheme 1.

generated a key pair (pk'_i, sk'_i), where $a_i \in Z_p$ and $sk'_i = a_i, pk'_i = g^{a_i}$, and (V_i, s_i) based on ECC. KGC generates a certificate $Cert(pk'_i)$ of h_i's public key. During system setup, AP also generates a pair of public key and secret key (pk_{AP}, sk_{AP}) for itself.

4.1.2 Data Deduplication

We try to introduce Scheme 1 by taking the following situation as an example. A cloud user h_i uploads a data M, which has not been stored before, to a CSP. Then, CSP receives another cloud user h_j's storage request of data M. Therefore, h_i is the data owner of data M and h_j is the data holder of data M. After system setup, h_i and h_j obtain $\left\{(pk'_i, sk'_i), Cert(pk'_i), (V_i, s_i)\right\}$ and $\left\{(pk'_j, sk'_j), Cert(pk'_j), (V_j, s_j)\right\}$, respectively. The procedure of Scheme 1 is presented as follows:

Step 1. Data token generation

First, h_i generates a token $x_i = H(H(M) \times P)$. Then, it sends its data package $DP_i = \left\{x_i, pk'_i, Cert(pk'_i)\right\}$ to its local CSP.

Step 2. Duplication check

The local CSP verifies $Cert(pk'_i)$ and checks the existence of x_i in its local space.

a) If the check result is positive, the local CSP forwards DP_i to AP. Move to Step 5.

b) If x_i does not exist in the storage space of this CSP, the local CSP broadcasts the data storage request to other CSPs (i.e., remote CSPs) to check the existence of x_i. If the local CSP does not receive any positive responses from other CSPs, it conducts Step 3. Otherwise, the remote CSP with positive feedback executes Step 5.

Step 3. Data storage

The local CSP requests h_i to upload its data M. h_i encrypts M with a symmetric key DEK_i and obtains ciphertext $CT_i = E(DEK_i, M)$. h_i also encrypts this symmetric key with AP's public key pk_{AP} and obtains cipher-key $CK_i = En(pk_{AP}, DEK_i)$. Afterward, it sends $\{CT_i, CK_i\}$ to the local CSP who then stores $\{x_i, pk'_i, CT_i, CK_i\}$.

Step 4. Duplicated data upload

Another cloud user h_j wants to upload M as well. It sends its data package $DP_j = \{x_j, pk'_j, Cert(pk'_j)\}$ to its local CSP. There will be a CSP to find the existence of x_j, then that CSP forwards DP_j to AP.

Step 5. Data deduplication

AP conducts data ownership challenge to verify if h_j really possess data M based on ECC. The detailed procedure is as follows. AP randomly chooses $c \in_R \{0, \ldots, 2^\sigma - 1\}$ and sends it to h_j. h_j checks if $0 \leq c \leq 2^\sigma - 1$ and calculates $y = H(M) + (s_j \times c)$. y is sent to AP after being encrypted by pk_{AP}. AP decrypts the encrypted y with its secret key sk_{AP} to obtain y and calculates $H(yP + cV_j)$. If $H(yP + cV_j) = x_j$, it can prove that h_j really occupies x_j. Then, AP generates a re-encryption key $rk_{AP \to h_j} = RG(pk_{AP}, sk_{AP}, pk'_j)$ and sends it to the CSP.

CSP uses this re-encryption key to re-encrypt CK_i by calling $R(rk_{AP \to h_j}, CK_i) = En(pk'_j, DEK_i)$ and sends it to h_j. h_j decrypts $En(pk'_j, DEK_i)$ with its secret key sk'_j and obtains DEK_i, with which it can decrypt CT_i and access data M. If h_j can access M successfully, it sends a notification to CSP and then CSP records this deduplication information.

4.1.3 Data Deletion

If a cloud user h_j wants to delete its data M, stored at the cloud, it sends $\{Cert(pk'_j), x_j\}$ as deletion request to its local CSP, who will then check if such a request is valid. If yes, the CSP deletes the deduplication record of h_j and blocks h_j's access to M.

If the data M is locally stored by this local CSP and the deduplication record of data M is empty after this deletion, the CSP deletes all stored data related to M. Otherwise, it contacts the data owner to perform DEK update.

If the data M is not locally stored by this local CSP, the local CSP will contact the remote CSP that really stores data M. The remote CSP checks if the deduplication record of data M is empty after this deletion. If yes, the remote CSP deletes all stored information related to M. Otherwise, it contacts the data owner to perform DEK update.

4.1.4 DEK Update

Updating *DEK* after data deletion can ensure that those cloud users who have deleted data M cannot access M again. It is also an essential way of guaranteeing system security.

The data owner h_i generates a new DEK_i', with which it encrypts data M as CT_i'. DEK_i' is encrypted with pk_{AP} as CK_i'. h_i sends $\{x_1, CT_i', CK_i', update\ CT_i\}$ to its local CSP as an update request. When the CSP receives this request, it contacts AP to generate re-encryption keys (e.g., $rk_{AP \to h_j}$) for some eligible data holders (e.g., h_j) whose re-encryption keys have never been generated before. Then, the CSP uses the re-encryption keys of all eligible data holders to re-encrypt CK_i' and generates re-encrypted keys (e.g., $En(pk_j, DEK_i')$). After that, all eligible data holders can access the updated data M.

4.2 Scheme 2: Client-Controlled Deduplication Based on ABE

In this scheme [35], the data access is totally controlled at the client side by applying ABE, so that the data owner is requested to be online all the time.

There are three entities in Scheme 2. KGC is a trusted entity which generates system parameters and provides certifications for the other entities. Cloud User is the one who wants to upload data to the cloud. We call the one who first uploads data as data owner and the other cloud users as data holders. It is possible for all data owner and data holders of the same data to be the subscribers of different CSPs. CSP is the one who provides various cloud services (e.g., data storage) to cloud users.

We hold the same assumptions as those in Scheme 1. CSPs will not collude with ineligible cloud users based on the game theoretical analysis in [34]. All data holders are honest that they will not send the information that is not calculated by the algorithms in Scheme 2 to CSPs. All entities (cloud users and CSPs) communicate with each other through a secure channel (e.g., SSL). Fig 2 shows the detailed procedure of Scheme 2.

4.2.1 System Setup

Each cloud user $h_i (i = 1, 2, \dots)$ generates two pairs of keys (PK_i, SK_i), (pk_i, sk_i) and a public key $IDPK_i$ by calling $CreateIDPK(ID, sk_i)$. KGC generates the certificate of h_i's public keys: $Cert(PK_i)$, $Cert(pk_i)$. Therefore, h_i and h_j can get $\{(PK_i, SK_i), (pk_i, sk_i), Cert(PK_i), Cert(pk_i), IDPK_i\}$ and $\{(PK_j, SK_j), (pk_j, sk_j), Cert(PK_j), Cert(pk_j), IDPK_j\}$, respectively, after system setup.

4.2.2 Data Deduplication

We try to illustrate Scheme 2 by taking the following situation as an example. A cloud user h_i uploads a data M, which has not been stored before, to a CSP. Then, CSP receives another cloud user h_j's storage request of data M. Therefore, h_i is the data owner of data M and h_j is the data holder.

Step 1. Data token generation

First, h_i calculates $H(M)$ and signs it with sk_i. It then encrypts its data with a symmetric key DEK_i and obtains $CT_i = E(DEK_i, M)$. This symmetric key is then

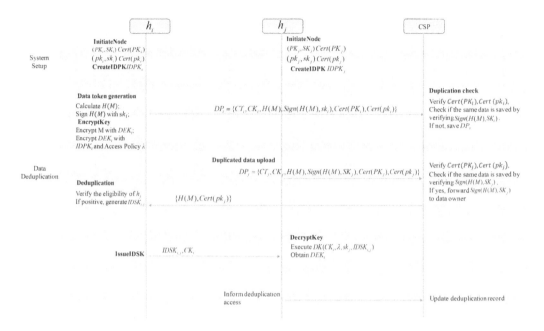

FIGURE 2   Procedure of data deduplication in Scheme 2.

encrypted with $IDPK_i$ and obtains $EK(DEK_i, \lambda, IDPK_i)$. It sends $DP_i = \{CT_i, CK_i, H(M),$ $Sign(H(M), sk_i), Cert(PK_i), Cert(pk_i)\}$ to its local CSP.

Step 2. Duplication check

The local CSP first verifies $Cert(PK_i)$ and $Cert(pk_i)$. If the results are positive, it continues to check the existence of the same data in its local space by verifying $Sign(H(M), SK_i)$.

a) If the check result is positive, this CSP forwards $\{H(M), Cert(pk_i)\}$ to the data owner of this data to conduct deduplication. Move to Step 5.

b) If this data does not exist in the storage space of this CSP, the local CSP broadcasts the data storage request to other CSPs to check the existence of such a data. If the local CSP does not receive any positive responses from other CSPs, it conducts Step 3. Otherwise, the CSP with positive feedback executes Step 5.

Step 3. Data storage

The local CSP saves DP_i in its storage space. h_i is the data owner of data M.

Step 4. Duplicated data upload

Another cloud user h_j wants to upload M as well. It sends its data package $DP_j = \{CT_j, CK_j, H(M), Sign(H(M), SK_j), Cert(PK_j), Cert(pk_j)\}$ to its local CSP. There will be a CSP to find this data has been stored already, then that CSP forwards $\{H(M), Cert(pk_j)\}$ to the data owner of this data for data deduplication.

Step 5. Data deduplication

The data owner h_i first verifies the eligibility of h_j. If the result is positive, h_i conducts $IssueIDSK(ID, sk_i, pk_j)$ to generate $IDSK_{i,j}$, with which h_j can get access to h_i's data. $IDSK_{i,j}$ and CK_i are issued to h_j by h_i. After h_j receiving $IDSK_{i,j}$ and CK_i, it executes $DK(CK_i, \lambda, sk_j, IDSK_{i,j})$ to obtain DEK_i, with which it can decrypt CT_i to access data M.

4.2.3 Data Deletion

If a cloud user h_j wants to delete its data M stored at CSP, it sends $\{Cert(pk_j), H(M)\}$ as the deletion request to its local CSP, which will then check if such a request is valid. If yes, this CSP deletes the deduplication record of h_j and blocks h_j's access to M.

If the data M is locally stored by this local CSP, it checks if the deduplication record of data M is empty after this deletion. If yes, the CSP deletes all stored information related to M. Otherwise, it contacts the data owner to perform DEK update.

If the data M is not locally stored by this local CSP, it contacts the remote CSP that really stores data M. The remote CSP checks if the deduplication record of data M is empty after this deletion. If yes, the remote CSP deletes all stored information related to M. Otherwise, it contacts the data owner to perform DEK update.

4.2.4 DEK Update

The data owner h_i generates a new DEK'_i to encrypt data M. The DEK'_i is then encrypted with pk_{AP}. h_i then sends the new data package $DP'_i = \{CT'_i, CK'_i, H(M), Sign(H(M), SK_i)\}$ to its local CSP. The CSP stores DP'_i if h_i is eligible.

If there exists a current eligible data holder h_j, whose attribute-based secret key $IDSK_{i,j}$ has never been generated, h_i issues $IDSK_{i,j}$ to h_j along with CK'_i. After h_j receiving $IDSK_{i,j}$ and CK'_i, it executes $DK(CK'_i, \lambda, sk_j, IDSK_{i,j})$ to obtain DEK'_i, with which it can decrypt the newly encrypted data CT'_i to access data M.

4.3 Scheme 3: Heterogeneous Data Deduplication with Flexibility

Scheme 3 is a deduplication scheme that supports heterogeneous data storage management [36]. It can support different application scenarios with different security requirements. The procedure of this scheme is shown in Fig 3.

There are four entities in Scheme 3. KGC generates system parameters and issue certifications for the other entities. It is a fully trusted entity. Cloud User is the one who wants to upload data to the cloud. We call the one who first uploads data as data owner and the other cloud users as data holders. CSP is the one who provides various cloud services (e.g., data storage) to cloud users. CSPs can perform deduplication with each other to save storage. The cloud users of the same data do not need to choose the same CSP. AP is a fully trusted third party and it will not collude with any CSP.

We hold the same assumptions as those in Scheme 1 and Scheme 3. CSPs will not collude with ineligible cloud users based on the game theoretical analysis in [34]. Even though CSPs are curious about the content of the data stored at their storage spaces, they will strictly follow the deduplication scheme. All data holders are honest that they will

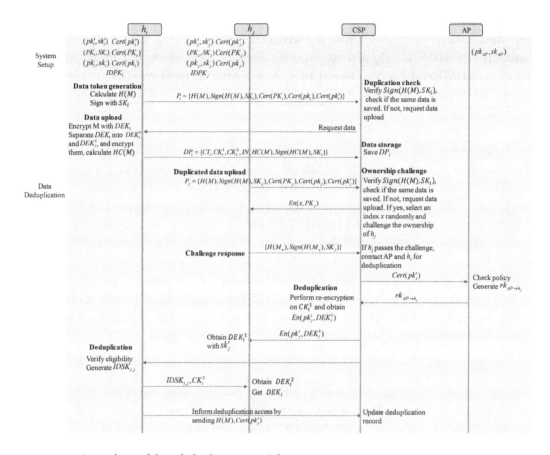

FIGURE 3   Procedure of data deduplication in Scheme 3.

not send the information that is not calculated by the algorithms to CSPs. We assume all data holders agree to grant delegation for data access management and ownership verification. There may exist multiple APs in a cloud storage system, but we assume there is only one AP for simplification. All entities (cloud users, CSPs, and AP) communicate with each other through a secure channel (e.g., SSL).

4.3.1 System Setup
Each data holder $h_i(i = 1, 2, ...)$ generates three pairs of keys (pk_i', sk_i'), (PK_i, SK_i), and (pk_i, sk_i), along with a public key $IDPK_i$ by calling $CreateIDPK(ID, sk_i)$.

KGC generates the certificate of all h_i's public keys: $Cert(pk_i')$, $Cert(PK_i)$, and $Cert(pk_i)$.

AP also generates a pair of public key and secret key (pk_{AP}, sk_{AP}).

4.3.2 Data Deduplication
Imaging the following data storage scenario. A cloud user h_i uploads a data M, which has not been stored before, to a CSP. Then, CSP receives another cloud user h_j's storage request of data M. We introduce the detail of Scheme 3 under this scenario.

Step 1. Data token generation

First, h_i calculates $H(M)$ and signs it with SK_i. It sends a data package $P_i = \{H(M), Sign(H(M), SK_i), Cert(PK_i), Cert(pk_i), Cert(pk'_i)\}$ to its local CSP.

Step 2. Duplication check

The CSP verifies the signature and checking the existing of $H(M)$ to evaluate whether the same data has been stored already.

a) If the check result is positive, move to Step 5.

b) If this data does not exist in the storage space of this local CSP, it broadcasts the data storage request to other CSPs to check the existence of this data. If the local CSP does not receive any positive responses from other CSPs, it conducts Step 3 (i.e., data storage). Otherwise, the CSP with positive feedback executes Step 5.

Step 3. Data storage

This local CSP requests h_i to upload data M. h_i encrypts M with DEK_i to get ciphertext $CT_i = E(DEK_i, M)$. It then separates DEK_i into two random parts, DEK_i^1 and DEK_i^2, by the algorithm $SeparateKey(DEK_i)$. h_i encrypts DEK_i^1 and DEK_i^2 with pk_{AP} and $IDPK_i$ by calling $CK_i^1 = En(pk_{AP}, DEK_i^1)$ and $CK_i^2 = EK(DEK_i^2, \lambda, IDPK_i)$, respectively. h_i randomly chooses a set of k indexes, $IN = \{In_1, In_2, ..., In_k\}$, to represent the special parts of data M and calculates the hash code of M according to IN. We use $HC(M) = \{H(M_1), H(M_2), ..., H(M_k)\}$ to indicate the hash code of data M, h_i signs $HC(M)$ as $Sign(HC(M), SK_i)$. The data package sent to the local CSP to store is $DP_i = \{CT_i, CK_i^1, CK_i^2, IN, HC(M), Sign(HC(M), SK_i)\}$.

Step 4. Duplicated data upload

h_j sends $P_j = \{H(M), Sign(H(M), SK_j), Cert(PK_j), Cert(pk_j), Cert(pk'_j)\}$ to its local CSP for cloud storage. The local CSP executes the duplication check as in Step 2 and finds this data exists in the cloud. Then comes to Step 5.

Step 5. Data deduplication

The CSP where the data exists randomly selects an index x in IN and encrypts x with PK_j to challenge h_j. If h_j is able to calculate $H(M_x)$ and send it back to CSP along with $Sign(H(M_x), SK_j)$, CSP performs data deduplication as follows:

- If $DEK_i^1 = DEK_i$ and $DEK_i^2 = null$, data deduplication is controlled by AP. CSP sends $Cert(pk'_j)$ to AP. AP checks the storage policy of data M to verify whether h_j is eligible to access M. If the verification is positive, AP generates $rk_{AP \rightarrow h_j}$ and sends it to CSP who uses it to re-encrypt CK_i^1. CSP issues this re-encrypted CK_i^1, which is in the form of $En(pk'_j, DEK_i^1)$. h_j performs decryption with sk'_j to obtain DEK_i^1, with which it can access data M.

- If $DEK_i^1 = null$ and $DEK_i^2 = DEK_i$, data deduplication is controlled by the data owner h_i. CSP contacts h_i to perform deduplication by sending $H(M)$ and

$Cert(pk_j)$. When h_i makes sure that h_j is an eligible data holder of M, it conducts $IssueIDSK(ID, sk_i, pk_j)$ to generate $IDSK_{i,j}$ and sends it to h_j with CK_i^2. h_j executes $DK(CK_i^2, \lambda, sk_j, IDSK_{i,j})$ to obtain DEK_i^2, with which it can decrypt CT_i to access data M.

- If $DEK_i^1 \| DEK_i^2 = DEK_i$, $DEK_i^1 \neq null$, and $DEK_i^2 \neq null$, data deduplication is controlled by both h_i and AP. CSP contacts h_i and AP to perform deduplication. h_j obtains DEK_i^1 and DEK_i^2 from h_i and AP separately. It can obtain DEK_i by combining DEK_i^1 and DEK_i^2 together with the algorithm $CombineKey(DEK_i^1, DEK_i^2)$. h_j can access data M by decrypting CT_i with DEK_i.

4.3.3 Data Deletion

If a data holder h_j wants to delete its data M, it sends $\{H(M), sign(H(M), SK_j)\}$ as the deletion request to its local CSP. The CSP randomly chooses an index x in IN to challenge the ownership of h_j. If h_j passes this challenge, the CSP deletes the deduplication record of h_j and blocks its access to data M.

If the data M is locally stored by this local CSP, it checks if the deduplication record of data M is empty after this deletion. If yes, the CSP deletes all stored information related to M. Otherwise, it contacts the data owner to perform DEK update (refer to Section 4.3.4).

If the data M is not locally stored by this local CSP, it contacts the remote CSP that really stores data M. The remote CSP checks if the deduplication record of data M is empty after this deletion. If yes, the remote CSP deletes all stored information related to M. Otherwise, it contacts the data owner to perform DEK update (refer to Section 4.3.4).

4.3.4 DEK Update

The data owner h_i generates a new DEK_i' to encrypt data M. DEK_i' is separated as $DEK_i'^1$ and $DEK_i'^2$, which are encrypted with pk_{AP} and $IDPK_i$ separately. h_i then sends the new data package $DP_i' = \{CT_i', CK_i'^1, CK_i'^2, HC(M), Sign(HC(M), SK_i)\}$ to its local CSP. The CSP stores DP_i' if h_i is eligible.

If there exists a current eligible data holder h_j, whose re-encryption key $(rk_{AP \to h_j})$ has never been generated, the CSP contacts AP to generate the re-encryption key $rk_{AP \to h_j}$ for h_j. Then, the CSP generates a re-encrypted key $En(pk_j, DEK_i'^1)$ by encrypting $CK_i'^1$ with $rk_{AP \to h_j}$. At the same time, h_i issues $IDSK_{i,j}$ to h_j.

From now on, h_j can obtain $DEK_i'^1$ by decrypting $En(pk_j', DEK_i'^1)$ with sk_j, and get $DEK_i'^2$ by performing $DK(CK_i'^2, \lambda, sk_j, IDSK_{i,j})$. When combining $DEK_i'^1$ with $DEK_i'^2$, h_j can obtain and decrypt the newly encrypted data CT_i' to access data M.

5 PERFORMANCE ANALYSIS AND EVALUATION

5.1 Performance Analysis

5.1.1 Security Analysis

The security of these three schemes relies on PRE, ABE, PKC and symmetric key encryption. The proof of the security of PRE and ABE can be found in [37]. As for the other two theories, we assume that the key sizes applied in them are long enough to support the security of our system. We analyze the security of our proposed schemes from the perspective of data ownership verification and data deduplication.

Proposition 1. *Data M is deduplicated securely. Only eligible data holders can access data M when data owner, CSP, and AP cooperate with each other without collusion.*

Proof. In all these deduplication schemes, the data confidentiality is guaranteed by the algorithms of symmetric key encryption, PRE, and ABE.

There are two methods to obtain data M. The first one is to obtain it from $H(M)$, which is impossible because the hash function can resist collision attacks. The other one is to break the ciphertext $CT_i = E(DEK_i, M)$, which is obtained by the symmetric encryption algorithm.

In Scheme 1, data confidentiality is ensured because DEK_i is encrypted with pk_{AP} based on PRE. CSP cannot access DEK_i even though it stores the re-encrypted DEK_i, namely, CK_i, as long as AP does not provide sk_{AP} to it. Meanwhile, when CSP does not collude with AP, CSP will always block AP's access to data M. DEK_i is re-encrypted to a form that can only be decrypted with data holder h_j's secret key sk_j. Therefore, only eligible data holders can access data M.

In Scheme 2, DEK_i is encrypted with $IDPK_i$ based on ABE. This can keep data confidential. Data deduplication is performed by data owner in this scheme; only eligible data owner h_j can receive the secret key based on attribute issued by the data owner h_i. There is no incentive for data owner and data holders to collude with CSP considering their personal data profits; CSP cannot obtain DEK_i and $IDSK_i$ from them. Therefore, only eligible data holders can access data M.

In Scheme 3, DEK_i is separated as DEK_i^1 and DEK_i^2, which are encrypted with pk_{AP} and $IDPK_i$, respectively. According to the above analysis, CSP cannot obtain DEK_i^1 and DEK_i^2 when at least one of the AP and the data owner refuses to collude with it.

Based on the above explanation, all these deduplication schemes can ensure the security of data M stored and only the eligible data holders can access data M through these schemes.

Proposition 2. *In Scheme 1 and Scheme 3, only the data holder that really has data M can pass the data ownership verification.*

Proof. In Scheme 1, AP performs the data ownership verification. If a data holder h_i really holds data M, it generates correct $H(M)$ and $y = H(M) + (s_i \times c)$ based on AP's challenge. AP can find $H(yP + cV_i)$ is exactly the same as x_i. Thus, h_i passes the ownership verification of AP.

In Scheme 3, even if an ineligible data holder steals the correct $H(M)$ by some ways, it is still difficult for it to send the correct $H(M_x)$ since the randomness of x and the hash function is a one-way function. The eligible data holder that really holds data M can easily generate correct M_x and compute $H(M_x)$ to pass the ownership verification.

5.1.2 Computation Complexity

There are four entities in our schemes: data owner, data holder, CSP, and AP. In this section, we compare the computation complexities of these three schemes and the results are presented in Table 4.2. The algorithms we used in this chapter are Advanced Encryption Standard (AES) for symmetric encryption, ECC, and PRE proposed in [38]. We can see that these three schemes have the similar computation complexity.

5.2 Performance Evaluation

We implemented all of these three schemes and tested their performance. We used AES for symmetric encryption, Rivest-Shamir-Adleman (RSA) for PKC, and Secure Hash Algorithm-1 (SHA-1) for hashing. We used PRE with JHU-MIT Proxy Re-cryptography Library (http://isi.jhu.edu/~mgreen/prl/index.html), CP-ABE with the pairing-based cryptography (PBC) library (http://crypto.standford.edu/pbc), MIRACL Crypto Library (http://info.certivox.com/docs/miracl), OpenSSL Cryptography, and SSL/TLS Toolkit (www.openssl.org). We built a database based on MySQL v5.5.41. We mainly evaluated the performance of deduplication without considering the procedures of data uploading and data downloading.

We applied AES with different sizes of the key (128/196/256 bits) to test the operation time of data encryption and decryption. The size of the tested file varies from 0 to 600 MB. The results are plotted in Fig. 4. We can obtain from Fig. 4 that the time spent for not only AES encryption but also AES decryption is linearly related to the size of files. The larger the file, the longer the time, which cannot be avoided in any encryption and decryption algorithms. Even if the file size is as large as 600 MB, the time to decrypt it is less than 13,000 ms, which is the longest time among all these operations. As a very efficient encryption and decryption algorithm, AES is a practical and reasonable algorithm for operating big data.

5.2.1 Performance Evaluation of Scheme 1
Test 1: Efficiency of PRE
PRE is one of the main algorithms in Scheme 1. It cannot be applied widely if it is not efficient. In our tests, we evaluated the execution time of every operation in PRE. These operations include PRE key pair generation (KeyGen), re-encryption key generation (ReKeyGen), encryption (Enc), re-encryption (ReEnc), and decryption (Dec). The PRE that we applied is of 1024-bit with different sizes of AES symmetric

TABLE 4.2 Comparison of Computation Complexity

Entity	Scheme 1	Scheme 2	Scheme 3
Data owner	$O(1)$	$O(n)$	$O(n)$
Data holder	$O(1)$	$O(1)$	$O(1)$
CSP	$O(n)$	$O(n)$	$O(n)$
AP	$O(n)$	-	$O(n)$

n: the number of data holders

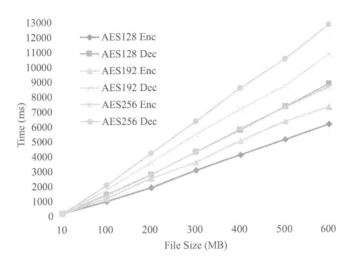

FIGURE 4   Operation time of data encryption and decryption.

keys (128/196/256 bits). The test results shown in Fig. 5 are the average results of 500 tests.

First, we can see that the size of AES symmetric keys will not influence the time needed to execute all these operations. From this perspective, our scheme is suitable for different application scenarios with different security requirements. Second, the time for encryption is less than 5 ms and the time for decryption is less than 1 ms. Therefore, data owners or data holders can encrypt and access cloud data very quickly. Finally, these operations are not related to the size of data. Scheme 1 can easily support big data deduplication.

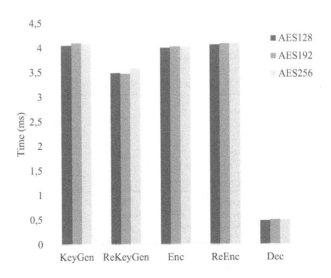

FIGURE 5   Operation time of PRE in Scheme 1.

Test 2: Data ownership challenge

The algorithm applied to challenge data ownership in Scheme 1 is ECC. In our test, we chose 192-bit field of an elliptic curve, along with 1024-bit PRE with 256-bit AES. The size of the tested file was 10 MB. We tested the operation time for generating (V_i, s_i) at the step of system setup, generating data token, uploading data, responding to ownership challenge, and verifying challenge. We conclude the results in Table 4.3 as follows.

Among these five operations in Table 4.4, uploading data takes most of the time, while this happens in all schemes. In Scheme 1, only the data owner needs to upload data. Therefore, it can save much operation time and computation costs for data holders. Moreover, the total time in data ownership challenge for data owner/holder and AP is slight, which makes Scheme 1 to be very efficient especially in the scenario with big data.

5.2.2 Performance Evaluation of Scheme 2

Test 1: Efficiency of CP-ABE

We tested the operation time of the following steps (refer to Fig. 2): InitiateNode, Create-IDSK, EncryptKey, IssueIDSK, and DecryptKey, and provided the results in Table 4.4. Under our test environments, the operation times of all steps are constant except for EncryptKey.

We plotted how the encryption time varies with the number of IDs in access policy in Fig. 6. We can see that the trend is not obvious and the average operation time is about 54 ms. The reason may lie in that there is only one type of attribute ID in the access policy. Based on our tested results, we can easily conclude that Scheme 2 is efficient and can be widely applied because the number of data holders will not influence the operation time significantly.

TABLE 4.3 Operation Time of Each Step in Data Ownership Challenge

	Operation	Time (ms)
Cloud user	System setup	0.5
	Data token generation	0.6
	Data upload (10 MB data)	149.8
	Challenge response	4.31
AP	Ownership challenge verification	1.2

TABLE 4.4 Operation Time of Each Step in CP-ABE

Operation	Time (ms)
InitiateNode	69.2
CreateIDPK	4.3
EncryptKey	Fig. 6
IssueIDSK	3.9
DecryptKey	12.7

5.2.3 Performance Evaluation of Scheme 3

Test 1: Efficiency of PRE

In Scheme 3, all data owner/holders in PRE share a common set of public parameters, which just need to be generated only once. In our tests, these public parameters generation takes about 34.79 ms. Besides that, all data owners and data holders should personally generate a PRE key pair, which takes 6.5 ms under our test environments in Scheme 3. The execution time for PRE operations, PRE key pair generation (KeyGen), re-encryption key generation (ReEncKeyGen), encryption (Enc), re-encryption (ReEnc), and decryption (Dec), are plotted in Fig. 7(a). All these five operations are very efficient that can finish in less than 7 ms. Therefore, PRE in Scheme 3 is an efficient and practical way to protect data encryption key.

Test 2: Efficiency of RSA sign and verification

We applied RSA for PKC to check duplication and sign hash code. The performance of RSA in Scheme 3 is tested in this section. We tested the operation time to sign an SHA-1 hash code and verify a signature generated by RSA with different sizes of RSA key (512/1024/2048/4096 bits) and plotted the results in Fig. 7(b). The result shows RSA is very efficient in both signature and verification. Signing takes more time than verification with the same RSA key size. The operation time of signing and verifying increases with the increase of RSA key size. However, the longest time that a test takes is the one to sign with a 4096-bit RSA key, which is only 10 ms. Therefore, applying RSA is practical and reasonable in Scheme 3.

Test 3: Efficiency of CP-ABE

The execution times of all CP-ABE operations are shown in Fig. 7(c). In this test, the number of IDs (e.g., eligible data holders) is set as 5 for simplification. Setup means to

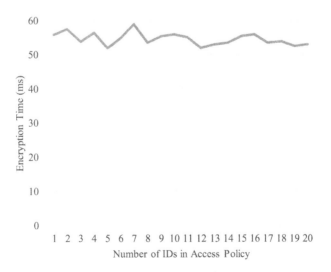

FIGURE 6   Operation time of EncryptKey in Scheme 2.

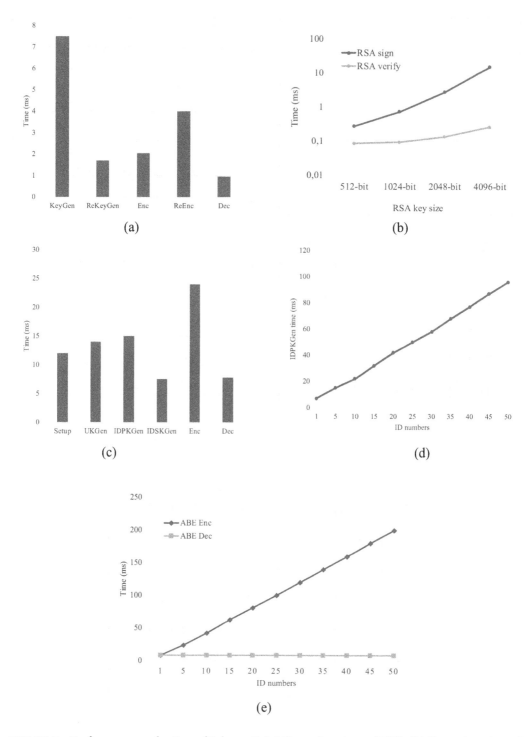

FIGURE 7   Performance evaluation of Scheme 3: (a) Operation time of PRE; (b) Operation time of RSA sign and verification; (c) Operation time of CP-ABE; (d) ID public key generation time with different number of IDs; (e) Operation time of CP-ABE encryption and decryption with different number of IDs.

generate a global key pair, which only happens once. It takes about 12 ms. UKGen in Fig. 7(c) is the representation of user key pair generation. All data owner and data holders need to generate this key pair when registering for the first time and the execution time is about 14 ms. IDPKGen represents an ID-based public key generation. The time for IDPKGen is influenced by the number of IDs and the detailed variation is presented in Fig. 7(d). IDSKGen, Enc, and Dec stand for ID secret key generation, ABE encryption, and ABE decryption, respectively. We plot the relationship between the number of IDs and the execution times of Enc and Dec in Fig. 7(e). We found that the ABE decryption time is constant, which is about 7.8 ms. The ABE encryption time increases as the number of IDs increases, due to the reason that the encryption algorithm iterates over all IDs and a data owner should generate ciphertext for all eligible data holders.

6 DISCUSSIONS AND FUTURE RESEARCH DIRECTIONS

6.1 Usage Scenarios and Limitations for Practical Deployment

After introducing the data deduplication schemes and performance evaluation, we now discuss their usage scenarios and deployment restrictions in practice. A brief comparison of these three schemes is shown in Table 4.5.

Scheme 1 can definitely save a large number of storage spaces for CSPs since CSPs only store one copy of duplicated data and deduplication records. The deduplication record for each cloud user h_i contains the cloud user's public key pk_i and data token x_i. The storage cost of a deduplication record is about 1184 (i.e., 1024 + 160) bits, which is trivial when compared with the sizes of duplication data. The advantage of this scheme when storing big data lies in the following two aspects. First, CSPs only need to store pk_i and x_i for data holders with duplicated data. Second, when CSPs perform duplication check and contact AP to verify data ownership, the communication and computation cost is not related to the size of data. Scheme 1 is also flexible to support data updating without introducing too many overheads and it does not require data owners to be online all the time. However, Scheme 1 cannot support fine-grained access control.

Scheme 2 makes up for the shortcoming of Scheme 1. It achieves fine-grained access control through ABE and can support flexible data update without much operation cost. It saves a large amount of storage space, especially in big-data scenario. However, since the data access control is totally at the client side, Scheme 2 requires data owners to be

TABLE 4.5 Comparison of All Proposed Schemes

Property	Scheme 1	Scheme 2	Scheme 3
Basic algorithm	ABE	PRE, ECC	PRE, ABE
Fine-grained access control	✓	✗	✓
Possession proof	✗	✓	✓
Offline access control	✗	✓	✓

online all the time and have enough resources to process the deduplication procedures. Moreover, data ownership verification is out of consideration in this scheme.

We use hash code set to verify data ownership in Scheme 3 instead of using ECC as in Scheme 2. If the challenged part of the hash code is significantly small, e.g., within 1 kilobyte, the performance of Scheme 3 will be much better than that of Scheme 2 because of the fast operation time of the hash function. Scheme 3 is more flexible than Scheme 1 and Scheme 2 because it can support fine-grained access control without requiring data owners to be online all the time. Big data deduplication and flexible data update are also supported in this scheme.

6.2 Challenges and Future Research Directions

All these deduplication schemes are proposed to support encrypted data. Therefore, they can ensure data privacy. However, identity privacy is beyond consideration. In order to add identity privacy preservation into our schemes, we can apply pseudonyms in KGC. A pseudonym is related to a real identity and is verified and certified by KGC.

Scheme 2 and Scheme 3 have relatively high requirements on data owners' hardware. In the future, we can optimize our schemes with hardware acceleration at the client side to make them more practical.

We assume CSPs will strictly abide by the process of our schemes. However, if there is no enough incentive, this assumption may be impractical. We can try to figure out how to apply verifiable computing in our schemes to ensure that CSPs behave as expected. Meanwhile, it is worthy to study practical incentive mechanisms in order to propose a proper business model to support real deployment of the three schemes.

Our schemes are still at the theoretical stage. At present, deduplication schemes on encrypted data are not widely deployed in practice. Next, we intend to conduct game theoretical analysis on these schemes to verify their rationality and security.

7 CONCLUSIONS

Encrypted data deduplication plays a significant role in cloud storage services, especially in the scenarios with big data. In this chapter, we presented three deduplication schemes. The first one is a cloud-controlled scheme based on PRE in which the data deduplication is controlled by a proxy (CSP and AP). The second one is a client-controlled scheme based on ABE in which the data deduplication is controlled by data owners. The third one is an integrated solution of the first two schemes in which the data deduplication can be controlled by either data owners or the cloud, or controlled by both of them or none of them. Data deletion, data update, and cross-CSP deduplication are also supported. The proposed three schemes can satisfy different demands of cloud users and different security requirements. We conduct a number of tests to evaluate their performance with regard to security, efficiency, and practicability. We also conclude their pros and cons and limitations in terms of practical applications.

ACKNOWLEDGEMENTS

This work is sponsored by the NSFC (grants 61672410, 61802293 and U1536202), Academy of Finland (grant No. 308087), the Project Supported by Natural Science Basic Research Plan in Shaanxi Province of China (Program No. 2016ZDJC-06), the National Key Research and Development Program of China (grant 2016YFB0800704), National Postdoctoral Program for Innovative Talents (grant BX20180238), the Project funded by China Postdoctoral Science Foundation (grant 2018M633461), and the 111 project (grants B08038 and B16037).

REFERENCES

1. Meyer, D.T., Bolosky, W.J.: A study of practical deduplication. *ACM Transactions on Storage (TOS)*, 7(4):14. ACM, Jan 2012. ISSN: 1553-3077.
2. Goh, E.J., Shacham, H., Modadugu, N., Boneh, D.: SiRiUS: Securing remote untrusted storage. In *Proc. NDSS*, pp. 131–145. Feb 2003.
3. Naor, D., Naor, M., Lotspiech, J.: Revocation and tracing schemes for stateless receivers. In *Annual International Cryptology Conference*, pp. 41–62. Springer, Aug 2001.
4. Goyal, V., Pandey, O., Sahai, A., Waters, B.: Attribute-based encryption for fine-grained access control of encrypted data. In *Proceedings of 13th ACM Conference on Computer and Communications Security*, pp. 89–98. ACM, Oct 2006.
5. Bethencourt, J., Sahai, A., Waters, B.: Ciphertext-policy attribute-based encryption. In *2007 SP'07. IEEE Symposium on Security and Privacy*, p. 321.IEEE, May2007.ISBN 0-7695-2848-1.
6. Yu, S., Wang, C., Ren, K., Lou, W.: Achieving secure, scalable, and fine-grained data access control in cloud computing. In *2010 Proc. IEEE INFOCOM*, pp. 1–9. IEEE, Mar 2010.
7. Wang, G., Liu, Q., Wu, J., Guo, M.: Hierarchical attribute-based encryption and scalable user revocation for sharing data in cloud servers. *Computers & Security*, 30(5):320–331. Elsevier, Jul 2011. ISSN: 0167-4048
8. Blaze, M., Bleumer, G., Strauss, M.: Divertible protocols and atomic proxy cryptography. In *International Conference on the Theory and Applications of Cryptographic Techniques*, pp. 127–144.Springer, May1998.
9. Kallahalla, M., Riedel, E., Swaminathan, R., Wang, Q., Fu, K.: Plutus: Scalable secure file sharing on untrusted storage. In *FAST'03. USENIX Conference on File and Storage Technologies*, pp. 29–42.USENIX, Mar 2003.
10. Yu, S., Wang, C., Ren, K., and Lou, W.: Attribute based data sharing with attribute revocation. In *Proceedings of the 5th ACM Symposium on Information, Computer and Communications Security*, pp. 261–270. ACM, Apr 2010.
11. Zhou, M., Mu, Y., Susilo, W., Au, M.H., Yan, J.: Privacy-preserved access control for cloud computing. In *TrustCom. 2011 IEEE 10th International Conference on Trust, Security and Privacy in Computing and Communications*, pp. 83–90.IEEE, Nov.2011.
12. Wan, Z., Liu, J.E., Deng, R.H.: HASBE: A hierarchical attribute-based solution for flexible and scalable access control in cloud computing. *IEEE Transactions on Information Forensics and Security (TIFS)*, 7(2):743–754. IEEE, Apr 2012. ISSN: 1556-6013
13. Tang, Y., Lee, P.P., Lui, J.C., Perlman, R.: Secure overlay cloud storage with access control and assured deletion. *IEEE Transactions on Dependable and Secure Computing (TDSC)*, 9 (6):903–916. IEEE, Nov.–Dec 2012.ISSN: 1545-5971
14. www.dropbox.com
15. www.google.com/drive/

16. Bobbarjung, D.R., Jagannathan, S., Dubnicki, C. Improving duplicate elimination in storage systems. *ACM Transactions on Storage (TOS)*, 2(4), 424–448. ACM, Nov 2006.

17. Bellare, M., Keelveedhi, S., Ristenpart, T.: Message-locked encryption and secure deduplication. In *Annual International Conference on the Theory and Applications of Cryptographic Techniques*, pp.296–312. Springer, May2013.

18. Douceur, J.R., Adya, A., Bolosky, W.J., Simon, P., Theimer, M. Reclaiming space from duplicate files in a serverless distributed file system. In *Proceedings of 22nd International Conference on Distributed Computing Systems*, pp. 617–624. IEEE, Jul.2002.

19. Bellare, M., Keelveedhi, S., Ristenpart, T. DupLESS: Server-aided encryption for deduplicated storage. In *Proceedings of 22nd USENIX Security Symposium*, pp. 179–194. USENIX, Aug.2013.

20. Naor, M., Reingold, O.: Number-theoretic constructions of efficient pseudo-random functions. *Journal of the ACM (JACM)*, 51(2):231–262. 2004.ISSN: 0004-5411

21. Miao, M., Wang, J., Li, H., Chen, X.: Secure multi-server-aided data deduplication in cloud computing. *Pervasive and Mobile Computing*, 24:129–137. Elsevier, Dec 2015. ISSN: 1574-1192

22. Liu, J., Asokan, N., Pinkas, B.: Secure deduplication of encrypted data without additional independent servers. In *CCS'15. Proceedings of the 22nd ACM SIGSAC Conference on Computer and Communications Security*, pp. 874–885. ACM, Oct 2015.

23. Li, J., Chen, X., Li, M., Li, J., Lee, P.P., Lou, W.: Secure deduplication with efficient and reliable convergent key management. *IEEE Transactions on Parallel and Distributed Systems (TPDS)*, 25(6), 1615–1625. IEEE, Jun 2014.ISSN: 1045-9219

24. Ding, W., Yan, Z., Deng, R.H.: Secure encrypted data deduplication with ownership proof and user revocation. In *ICA3PP'17. International Conference on Algorithms and Architectures for Parallel Processing*, pp. 297–312.Springer, Aug 2017.

25. Halevi, S., Harnik, D., Pinkas, B., Shulman-Peleg, A.: Proofs of ownership in remote storage systems. In *CCS'11. Proceedings of the 18th ACM conference on Computer and Communications Security*, pp. 491–500. ACM, Oct 2011.

26. Ng, W.K., Wen, Y., Zhu, H.: Private data deduplication protocols in cloud storage. In *SAC'12. Proceedings of the 27th Annual ACM Symposium on Applied Computing*, pp. 441–446.ACM, Mar, 2012.

27. Di Pietro, R., Sorniotti, A.: Boosting efficiency and security in proof of ownership for deduplication. In *Proceedings of the 7th ACM Symposium on Information, Computer and Communications Security*, pp. 81–82. ACM, May 2012.

28. Blasco, J., Di Pietro, R., Orfila, A., Sorniotti, A.: A tunable proof of ownership scheme for deduplication using bloom filters. In *CNS'14. 2014 IEEE Conference on Communications and Network Security*, pp.481–489. IEEE, Oct 2014.

29. González-Manzano, L., Orfila, A.: An efficient confidentiality-preserving proof of ownership for deduplication. *Journal of Network and Computer Applications (JNCA)*, 50:49–59. Elsevier Apr. 2015.

30. Zheng, Q., Xu, S.: Secure and efficient proof of storage with deduplication. In *Proceedings of the second ACM conference on Data and Application Security and Privacy*, pp. 1–12. ACM, Feb 2012.

31. Yuan, J., Yu, S.: Secure and constant cost public cloud storage auditing with deduplication. In *CNS'13. 2013 IEEE Conference on Communications and Network Security*, pp. 145–153. IEEE, Oct 2013.

32. Yan, Z., Ding, W., Yu, X., Zhu, H., Deng, R.H.: Deduplication on encrypted big data in cloud. *IEEE Transactions on Big Data*, 2(2):138–150. IEEE, Jun 2016.

33. Yan, Z., Ding, W., Zhu, H.: A scheme to manage encrypted data storage with deduplication in cloud. In *ICA3PP'17. International Conference on Algorithms and Architectures for Parallel Processing*, pp. 547–561, Springer, Nov 2015.

34. Gao, L., Yan, Z., Yang, L.T.: Game theoretical analysis on acceptance of a cloud data access control system based on reputation. *IEEE Transactions on Cloud Computing* 2016. (Early Access)

35. Yan, Z., Wang, M., Li, Y., Vasilakos, A.V.: Encrypted data management with deduplication in cloud computing. *IEEE Cloud Computing*, 3(2):28–35. IEEE, Mar. –Apr 2016.

36. Yan, Z., Zhang, L., Ding, W., Zheng, Q.: Heterogeneous data storage management with deduplication in cloud computing. In *IEEE Transactions on Big Data*. IEEE, 2017. (Early Access)

37. Yan, Z., Li, X., Wang, M., Vasilakos, A.V.: Flexible data access control based on trust and reputation in cloud computing. *IEEE Transactions on Cloud Computing*, 5(3):485–498. IEEE, Jul. –Sept 2017.

38. Ateniese, G., Fu, K., Green, M., Hohenberger, S.: Improved proxy re-encryption schemes with applications to secure distributed storage. *ACM Transactions on Information and System Security (TISSEC)*, 9(1):1–30. ACM, Feb 2006.

CHAPTER 5

The Role of NonSQL Databases in Big Data

Antonio Sarasa Cabezuelo

Complutense University of Madrid, Madrid, Spain

CONTENTS

1 INTRODUCTION

In most computer systems, it is necessary to persistently store the information that is processed. In recent decades, the persistence systems that have dominated the market have been relational databases. This has been due, among other reasons, to the efficiency to process information through the use of ACID transactions, the solidity of the formal model on which they are based (the relational model) or the existence of a standard language for data manipulation (the SQL language). In addition, conceptually, it is a simple and intuitive model (it is based on tables where information is stored).

However, in recent years, this situation has changed, due to the appearance of Big Data. It is a phenomenon that has occurred due to the availability of huge amounts of data and the need to process them. The main objective is to obtain information from the data with economic purposes. To implement this objective, a set of technologies has been developed that allow for the collection, storage, management, analysis, and visualization, potentially under real-time conditions, of large data sets with heterogeneous characteristics. In the specific case of Big Data storage needs, there are three problems [1]:

- The quick and constant growth of data makes that it is necessary to have storage systems with greater processing capacity. In this sense, processing needs to grow exponentially, and in order to acheive this, horizontal scaling is required, resulting in distributed solutions. This point is conflicting with the relational databases, which are designed for execution in centralized systems, not being possible in most cases their execution in a distributed environment.

- Heterogeneity of the data. In this context, the data can be of very different types (structured, semi-structured, or without structure); they can have erroneous data, empty data, etc. This condition clashes with the type of data managed by a relational database, where information that has a predefined structure is efficiently processed. For this reason, it is necessary to have more flexible information structures.

- Variability of data models. Due to the wide variety of information sources available with different information models, it will be necessary to dynamically adapt the persistence systems to the different models. Flexibility is required so that data models can evolve and adapt to new situations.

Relational databases have been the most widespread persistence model used in information systems. However, it is not an adequate model to respond optimally to the problems described in [2]:

- The solution to achieve more processing capacity is to use more powerful machines (vertical scaling).

- The solution to the evolution of the data models consists of modifying the schemas of the database. This causes problems of maintenance and consistency of previously stored information.

- The solution to the heterogeneity of the data is to perform transformations of the information to be able to store complex data in basic data types (the only ones that manage the relational databases).

These reasons and others created the need to look for persistence systems more in line with the new context. In this sense, some companies such as Google or Amazon created new database models that solve the needs raised in the context of Big Data. These new models are the origin of the so-called NonSQL Databases. Their common characteristic is that they are all based on conceptual models that are different from the relational model, and that conform to most of the data persistence needs that have arisen in the Big Data field.

The goal of this chapter is to show the role that NonSQL databases play in the Big Data. Specifically:

- To show the processing and persistence needs of information in the Big Data.

- To describe the limitations of relational databases to be used in Big Data solutions.

- To describe the main characteristics of the NonSQL databases, and how they solve the storage and information processing needs that arise in the Big Data.

The structure of the chapter would be the following. First, the Big Data phenomenon and the technological consequences of it are presented. The limitations of relational databases to cover the persistence needs of Big Data are described below. In the following section, the NoSQL databases are presented: their main characteristics, existing types, distribution models, and the CAP theorem. Next, a couple of cases of successful application of the NoSQL databases are described. Finally, a set of conclusions and lines of future work are presented.

2 THE BIG DATA PHENOMENON

Big Data can be defined as a set of technologies that allow the collection, storage, management, analysis, and visualization, potentially under real-time conditions, of large datasets with heterogeneous characteristics [3]. In this sense, there are five characteristics known as the "5 vs" (velocity, volume, variety, verity, and value) that define the type and nature of the data that is processed and the purposes that are sought with the processing thereof [4].

- Volume. It refers to the large volume of information handled (magnitudes of the order of petabytes or exabytes of information are considered). In addition, the data that needs to be managed increase with an exponential growth, which forces continuous extensions of the storage capacity of the machines.

- Velocity. It refers to the enormous speed at which information data are generated, collected, and processed. In this sense, it is necessary to be able to store and process millions of data in real time that are generated in seconds. Many of these data come from information sources such as sensors, social networks, environmental control systems, and other information-gathering devices. Observe that it is the processing speed that allows obtaining a profit from the exploitation, before the data becomes obsolete.

- Variety. This characteristic refers to the need to be able to manage information that comes from very heterogeneous information sources in which the data have different levels of structuring, different types of data, etc. So, to be able to add all the data and be able to manage them as a unit, you need information storage that is flexible enough to host heterogeneous data. In this sense, relational databases do not constitute an adequate solution, given that the expected data type is homogeneous, regular, and with a previously defined structure in the database schema.

- Value. This aspect refers to the ability to exploit stored information in order to take advantage of it for different purposes such as obtaining an economic return, optimizing production, improving the corporate image, better approaching the needs and preferences of customers, or predicting how an advertising or sales campaign for a specific product can be developed well. This feature is basic so that a company or entity may be interested in investing in processing such amounts of information.

- Verity. This characteristic refers to the need to adequately process the large volumes of information, so that the information obtained is true, and allows to make appropriate decisions based on the results of its processing. This aspect together with the previous one constitutes two important reasons that give meaning to the massive processing of the information.

On the other hand, from a technological point of view, there is a set of new needs that did not exist before [5]:

- Need for a decentralized and flexible data architecture.

- Need to use distributed computing models that allow managing and processing the type of data specific to these environments (semi-structured or non-structured data).

- The need to analyze large amounts of data in real time in distributed execution environments (it will be required to carry out very intensive processing tasks in a massive way).

In order to describe the technological developments that have occurred in the field of Big Data, one can speak of Big Data Operational and Analytical Big Data [6].

The Big Data Operational refers to the set of tools that have been developed to solve some of the technological problems that have arisen and have been commented. In a schematic way by areas, we have the following tools [7]:

- Algorithms for processing information from the area of statistics and the area of artificial intelligence that work very efficiently when used on a large amount of data. For example, machine learning algorithms or deep learning algorithms.

- Mass processing systems to be able to work with huge amounts of data in real time. These systems require being able to work in parallel to obtain sufficient computing power and use new computing paradigms such as the map-reduce algorithm. Some examples of these processing systems are Spark or Hadoop.

- Data visualization tools that aim to help interpret the results of the processed data through visual representations that intuitively and simply show the data. In this way, the analysts can make decisions and take advantage of the information obtained from the processing of the data. Some examples of these tools are Tableau or Qlikview.

- Specific programming languages to perform data analysis and process information. Data structures are required to facilitate the manipulation of data and operations on them. Some examples are the R programming language, a specific language for data analysis, or the scientific libraries of the general purpose Python programming language.

- New systems of persistence of the information more adapted to the new needs of storage and data processing. This is the case of the so-called NoSQL databases.

Observe that in order to take advantage of the benefits that the described technologies can bring, it is necessary to know the characteristics of the information sources, to know the nature of the data that will be obtained, to know the type of questions to which they want to answer, and to know the characteristics of the available tools so that they can select the most appropriate to be able to answer the questions posed. In this sense, choosing the right tool is a critical step in the application of Big Data to a specific problem and domain.

On the other hand, the Big Data Analytical refers to the types of analysis and processing of the information that you want to perform. In general, these are predictive processing models that aim to answer questions about the future behavior of a process, an individual, or a human group based on the known behaviors of the past and other related complementary data available [8]. Thus, in this type of models, it is sought to achieve objectives of the following style:

- To predict certain behaviors from the data generated by an individual. For this, the probability that an individual has to show a specific behavior in the future is evaluated based on the previous behaviors, as well as other adjacent data.

- To look for regularities in the information. In this sense, information is processed in order to find repetitive patterns that allow information to be discriminated. These patterns can be used to answer questions that arise about the behavior of an individual, human group, or institution.

- To determine a risk or opportunity. To do this, real-time calculations are carried out on the data collected with the aim of being able to evaluate a certain risk or opportunity, which will guide in taking an appropriate decision. For this, some factors are important, such as the speed at which it is processed, the amount of data that is processed, and the quality of the data regarding its generation and processing time.

- To discover relationships between the data in order to classify individuals in groups. This type of analysis is often very useful in business areas to distinguish business segments, so, for example, the type of product that can be offered to a young person is not the same as to an elderly person or adult. In this way, you can know common information of each group and be able to make specific decisions for each segment.

- To identify relationships between different individuals. This allows predicting the consequences that a decision can have on a group of individuals, as well as planning different types of actions and effects on the related individuals or being able to infer information implicitly from existing relationships. A typical example may be the search for relationships and information from people who are in contact through a social network.

- To describe the relationship that may exist between all the elements that must be taken into account in order to make a decision, be able to obtain the decision to be taken that is the most optimal of the possible ones based on the known information, and know the variables and values that determine the decision itself. All in order to predict the results by analyzing many variables. This type of analysis has an especially important application in the decision-making of a company where there are many variables to be taken into account, there is an economic risk, and certain results are expected to be obtained.

Therefore, the Big Data phenomenon appears due to the business opportunities that arise from having huge amounts of data to be processed and exploited. This is why new information processing needs arise that lead to a technological change with the appearance of a set of new technologies, algorithms, programming languages, and computing paradigms.

This chapter will focus on one of the aspects of Big Data discussed, specifically in the new information persistence needs. In this sense, it will be analyzed what are the requirements that arise around the storage of information, what limitations the relational databases present to cover these needs, and what NoSQL databases provide to cover them.

3 THE LIMITATIONS OF THE RELATIONAL MODEL IN THE BIG DATA

In the previous section, we have presented the needs regarding the persistence of information that arise in the context of Big Data. In this sense, relational databases present three important limitations to cover these needs that affect cost and efficiency.

The first problem refers to the difference presented by the data structures that are used in the field of relational databases and those that are used in the programs that exploit the data of these storage systems [9]. In the case of relational databases, the stored data corresponds to simple data such as numbers, strings, or Booleans. They do not support any type of complex structured data such as a list or record. Likewise, the unit of storage and exchange of information are the rows of the tables that serve as storage. However, programming languages manipulate data with greater richness and structural complexity such as stacks, tails, and lists. This supposes a problem of communication of the information between the databases and the programs, since it forces to implement a translation process between both contexts. Thus, every time information is retrieved from a relational database for use in a program, it is necessary to decompose it and transform it into the data structures that are being used in it. And likewise, when a program needs to store information in a relational database, it requires another process of transforming the information stored in the data structures managed by the program into simple data and grouped into sequences that constitute rows, which is what which supports storing a relational database. These transformations constitute an additional computational cost to the information processing that is carried out in the programs, which can have a significant impact on both code lines with execution time, depending on the amount of data and transformations that are necessary to carry out the task. This problem has been called the problem of "impedance" or the difference in the nature of the data managed by a relational database and by programming languages [10]. To alleviate this problem, some solutions have been created such as object-oriented databases or frameworks that map the information stored in the database to an object-oriented model such as Hibernate. However, these solutions are not entirely effective because, although they solve part of the problem of impedance, they introduce other problems such as a reduction in the performance of the database due, among other reasons, to the implementation of operations and queries that obviate the existence of a database below the object-oriented model.

The second problem refers to the distributed execution of the relational databases [11]. At present, we need to process huge amounts of data that grow exponentially and with a very fast generation speed, since in many cases, they come from sensors or vital signs control devices, nature phenomena, etc. In this sense, machines with an important processing capacity are required. To meet these requirements, there are two alternatives. On the one hand, vertical scaling solutions and, on the other hand, horizontal scaling solutions are found [12]. The first type of solution consists in having a machine with high performance that covers the required processing needs. From the point of view of the relational databases, it is an ideal solution, since these are designed to run in centralized environments on a single machine. However, from the economic and strategic point of view, it is a bad solution given that the exponential growth of the data and its speed of generation means that, in a relatively short time, the machines become obsolete and small with respect to the processing needs required, making it necessary to purchase a new machine. Likewise, we must unite the fact of the strategic weakness of a centralized solution, given that a failure in the machine that contains the storage system will have as a consequence a loss of information and therefore of all the applications that exploit the stored data. (It is true that normally there are security copies that are made periodically so that the impact of an event of this nature has limited effects). The second type of solution consists of using a set of machines that work collaboratively in parallel with the processing of information called machine cluster [13]. In this way, the joint work of all of them allows to reach the required processing capacity. In addition, when you need to increase the processing capacity at a given time, just increase the number of machines that make up the cluster. Likewise, the type of machines used in the clusters is usually of inferior quality in terms of performance and cheaper than the machines used in a vertical scaling solution. A requirement in this type of solution is that the data that is being managed is distributed among the machines in the cluster. This requirement, in certain conditions, constitutes an advantage with respect to a vertical solution since, if any machine in the cluster fails, the system does not have to stop working as the rest of the machines will continue to work (and if they have also replicated data in several machines, it will be enough to redirect the system to the replicated machine). However, this feature conflicts with the natural scope of execution of a relational database that is centralized in a single machine. Thus, in general, relational databases are not designed or prepared for execution in distributed environments [12]. Problems of the type such as knowing how to decompose the tables of a relational database and deciding which tables are stored in one machine and which in another, or how to execute the queries on the tables, in case of being distributed, are considered. You would have to know where each table is located. Other problems also occur about the type of queries that are possible to perform in a distributed environment, referential integrity, transaction management, or concurrency control. On the other hand, there is an economic factor that must also be taken into account if a relational database is distributed, and this is due to the fact that this type of executions would require the execution of several different instances of the databases, which would increase its economic cost. To solve these limitations, solutions have emerged within the scope of relational databases that have tried to add some of the necessary requirements for their distributed execution [14]. These solutions are generically called NewSQL databases. They maintain the main characteristics of a relational database, as well as the use of the standard SQL language. However, none of them has achieved sufficient implantation to become a distributed solution of the relational model [15]. Thus, the relational databases are still used for the areas for which they were created.

The third problem refers to the fixed data schema used by the relational databases [16]. In the relational model, a task prior to the storage of the data consists of creating a schema of the type of information to be stored. In this way, they fix the types of data that are admitted. If you want to store other types of data, you will have to make changes to the scheme. However, these changes often introduce anomalies in the stored data (for example, in terms of the relational model, there will probably be rows with many columns with null values). In this sense, it is said that the information stored in a relational database is structured because it follows a previously defined scheme. In the field of Big Data, the information that needs to be stored can be very diverse, from structured, semi-structured data, to even data without structure. In addition, in general, it is not known a priori how the type of data will be. For these reasons, you cannot fix a fixed structure for the information you want to store. Thus, the characteristics of the data that needs to be stored in a Big Data environment are incompatible with the need to set a previous scheme in the relational model, since its use would make it necessary to make changes in the schema for each new type of data that is stored. This would introduce anomalies in the database or it would be necessary to make changes in the tables or in the defined relationships.

4 NOSQL DATABASES. A SOLUTION TO THE STORAGE NEEDS IN BIG DATA

a. General characteristics

Given the limitations present in the relational databases to cover the needs arising in the field of Big Data, some companies such as Amazon and Google began to develop alternative persistence systems that fit better than these requirements (Google's Big Tables and Dynamo's Amazon). These databases have the common characteristic of being able to manage and process huge amounts of data through a distributed system. From that moment, other databases emerged with the same objective of solving the problems and limitations that the relational databases were not able to cover. The databases that emerged in this process were called NoSQL Databases [17], and share some characteristics such as:

- They do not use the SQL language to make queries (there are some databases that use languages with a very similar syntax as is the case of the Cassandra database with the CQL language). However, they all have query languages with a similar purpose.

- Most NoSQL databases include among its features the possibility of running in distributed environments, thus responding to the needs of distributed processing. It is a success factor since it allows to process large amounts of data in a cheaper and more efficient way by running the databases in distributed solutions of cluster-type machines that allow to scale the systems by adding new machines to the cluster. This feature influences the underlying data models of how to manage data consistency or concurrency. Not all NoSQL databases comply with this characteristic, as is the case of graph-oriented databases that are not designed for execution in a distributed environment.

- They do not use pre-defined information structuring schemes [10]. One of the characteristics of the NoSQL databases that represents a major change with respect to the relational databases is their lack of need to define a schema or the structure of the information that will be stored in it. The origin of this characteristic is found in the conditions of information processing that occur in the Big Data field. In this context, the type of data generated can be semi-structured or unstructured; it is necessary to aggregate together data that are heterogeneous; in many cases, the data that needs to be stored may have errors or there may be empty information fields; the data is generated at a great speed and in huge quantities. Therefore, no schemas are used in the NoSQL databases, the information to be stored is simply added, and there is no verification process about the structure and types of data used. The only requirement is that the data be compatible with the data model underlying the type of NoSQL database being used. These conditions are incompatible with the type of information for which a relational database is designed, given that data is expected that responds to a structure of previously fixed information, homogeneous data will be added, the expected amounts of data are not so enormous, and its inclusion in the tables is generally done in a planned manner. Note that in relational databases, the first thing to do is to define a schema of the information to be stored, indicating how the information will be structured and what type of data will be used. In this way, the information that is stored must comply with this definition (not admitting data that does not comply with it). It is true that relational databases could be used for these situations; however, the implications would be that tables with many fields would be needed to store any type of information, and that the resulting tables after storing the information would have many empty fields (specifically the rows of heterogeneous data). That is why it is not a good idea. This dissonance with the relational model gave rise to this characteristic that is present in the NoSQL databases, and that represents the need to have unlimited flexibility to be able to store what is necessary, since we cannot predict what the information will be like. It must be managed. However, this feature has precisely the advantage of being able to store any information element without being subject to any type of restrictions, being able to adapt to different situations, which is very useful in the context of Big Data (which is by nature dynamic), as previously argued. Likewise, it represents a solution to the problem of impedance. The possibility of storing data with any type of structure eliminates the need for information transformations to adapt the information managed by the applications that process the information in the database and the data structures used by the databases to store it. As already mentioned, this involved a cost to be taken into account, since part of the application code had to be dedicated to this task.

- In most cases, NoSQL databases are open-source projects.

Note that the NoSQL databases also present some disadvantages that are summarized in the transfer of responsibilities that were previously carried out by the database management systems to the programmer [18]. Thus, some operations that were done in a transparent manner, such as maintaining the consistency of the data when they are updated or deleted, ensuring that the data entered are of the expected types, managing the concurrency of data access, as well as others, must now be made directly from the programs that process the information. This also has as a problem that, in order to access the data, it is necessary for the programmer to know what type of information and how it is structured in the database. Likewise, this situation has another direct consequence that is the implicit representation of the information scheme in the code of the programs that process the information (with the difference that this scheme in the relational world is automatically managed by the management system of databases, while in the world of NoSQL must be managed manually by the programmer with the negative implications that this situation has). Some consequences of this situation are, for example, that changes in the content of the database will produce changes in the code (that is, a strong dependence between the code and persistence system is created). This dependence with respect to the code has a negative effect on the quality of the code, given that the degree of reuse of the programming codes decreases because they are particularized to a specific situation. In addition, when you want to know what information is stored and how it is related, you need to consult the code of the application. Consistent erasure is another major problem that occurs, since the execution of an operation of this nature erases related information between which there is a dependency with which the consistency of the information is reduced. In this way, successive deletions may leave isolated information that cannot be accessed (garbage), thus requiring a database cleanup to eliminate these information elements that are no longer useful. Other consequences are the impossibility of creating scheduled procedures to check restrictions of the information that is stored.

b. Types of NoSQL databases

Although the NoSQL databases share the general characteristics mentioned, there are other characteristics that allow to differentiate them and use them to make a classification. Although there is no single classification, however, it is possible to differentiate them according to the underlying data model. So we can talk about the following types of families [19]:

- Key-value data bases: Riak, Redis, Dynamo, Voldemort.

- Document-oriented databases: MongoDB, CouchDB.

- Database based on columns: Cassandra, Hypertable, HBase, SimpleDB.

- Graph databases: Neo4J, Infinite Graph.

It should be noted that this classification is artificial because many of the databases that are classified into different families, however, share common characteristics, so that it would have been just as well that they were classified into one family [20]. For example, MongoDB is a documentary-type database; however, one of the ways to access information is through the key of the information fields, so it would be correct to classify it as a key-value database.

Families of NoSQL documentary, key-value, and column-oriented databases are said to be aggregate-oriented [21]. In this context, an aggregate represents a complex data structure that maintains a set of data related to each other. This structure can correspond to typical data structures of programming languages such as lists and nested data records. Aggregates are treated as a non-decomposable unit for the purpose of processing or consistency management. Thus, the operations carried out on an aggregate are considered atomic, and from the operational point of view, the operations take aggregates and give as aggregate results.

This organization of information has some advantages such as the management of the clusters where the aggregates are used as a unit of replication and distribution of the data, or the manipulation of the information from the programs since, being structures similar to those used in programming languages, they are easier to manipulate and manage from the programs.

Regarding the management of the consistency of the information, it should be noted that, although this type of databases does not support ACID-style transactions on a set of aggregates [22], nevertheless, the operations on individual aggregates are performed in atomic form one aggregate at a time [23]. In this sense, if you want to perform atomic operations on a set of aggregates, it would be necessary to implement it from the programs that manage them.

From a semantic point of view, when you have a complex information element, if a relational database is used, then it is necessary to decompose that information into simpler information elements with basic types, in order to be stored in a relational database. And in the same way, to return the information, it will be necessary to reconstruct the existing relations in the information. However, in an aggregate-oriented model, this process of decomposition of information will not be necessary, given that aggregates are directly managed, that is, aggregates are recovered, aggregates are processed, and aggregates are returned. However, it must be borne in mind that the use of aggregates makes it difficult to define aggregates that can be used in different contexts.

c. Distribution models in NoSQL databases

With respect to the distribution of the data, two models can be found to manage the data in a distributed way:

- Sharding

In some cases, the databases are very busy since there are many users who are accessing different parts of the data set. In these circumstances, you can think of performing a horizontal scaling by putting the different parts of the data on different servers. This technique is called sharding [24]. In the ideal case, there would be different users that would consult different server-nodes. In this way, when each user interacts with a different server, then quick responses could be obtained from each server and the workload would be balanced between the servers. In order to implement it, it is necessary to guarantee that the data that will be accessed together is grouped in the same node and that these groups are arranged in the nodes to provide the best access to the data. The first problem that arises is how the data can be agglutinated so that the user retrieves their data from a single server. To organize the data in the nodes, certain factors must be taken into account such as:

1. If it is known that most access to information is made based on a physical location, then the data should be stored near where you are accessing.

2. Another factor to keep in mind is to maintain the workload. In this sense, you must store the information so that it is distributed evenly across the nodes, getting equal amounts of load. This organization could vary with time if, for example, it is observed that certain data tend to be more visited on certain days, for which specific rules of the domain can be defined to be used in these cases.

3. In some cases, it may be useful to keep certain data together if it is expected that they will be read in sequence.

The sharding can be implemented at the level of the logic of the application by dividing the data into the fragments that are necessary. However, this complicates the programming model since the code must ensure that queries are distributed across the different fragments, and any re-balancing of the sharding will require changes in the application code and data migrations. To solve this problem, many NoSQL databases offer autosharding where it is the database itself that has the responsibility to assign the data to different fragments, and ensure that access to the data is carried out in the correct fragment. The sharding technique is particularly valuable with respect to performance, since it improves performance in both reading and writing. In this sense, sharding provides a way to horizontally scale the scriptures. With respect to failure recovery, sharding does not achieve significant improvements when used alone. Thus, if the data is in different nodes and a failure occurs in a node, the impossibility of accessing the data to the corresponding fragment will affect only the users of the data of that fragment since they will not be able to access their data. However, it is not a good solution to have a part of the database not accessible. Note that sharding tends to decrease the ability to recover from failures, since in the clusters, there is a tendency to use less reliable machines, which increases the probability of failures in the nodes.

- Replication

There are two types of replication: master-slave and peer-to-peer [24]. The master-slave distribution consists in replicating the data through multiple nodes, so that there is a node that acts as a primary or master node, which represents the valid source of the data and is responsible for processing any modification thereof. The rest of the nodes are slaves or secondary, existing as a process that synchronizes them with the primary node. The main advantages of this model are:

1. It is very useful for scaling when you have to perform intensive readings on the data. This can be scaled horizontally to maintain many read requests, adding more secondary nodes and ensuring that all requests are directed to the secondary nodes. The only limitation is the ability of the primary node to process the updates and move them to the slave nodes. In this sense, it is not a good scheme in situations where there is a large writing traffic, although the downloading of the reading traffic helps to handle the writing load.

2. Another advantage is the ability to recover from failures. If the primary node fails, then at least the slave nodes can handle the read requests. This situation is useful when most of the accesses are readings. When the primary node fails, it is not possible to write scripts until the node is recovered or a new primary node is chosen from among the secondary ones (this situation is fast in this case, since there are secondary nodes that are replicas of the primary node). Note that this possibility of being able to replace the primary node with a secondary one is not only useful when you want to scale, it can also be useful in other situations. For example, you can design a single-server solution with a large recovery capacity before failures, so that all read-and-write traffic goes to the primary node while the secondary nodes act as backup copies.

The primary node can be chosen manually or automatically. Manual selection means that when the cluster of nodes is configured, there is a node that is chosen as primary. In the automatic election, the cluster of nodes is created and it is the nodes themselves that choose between them the primary node. This option is simpler and also allows the cluster to choose a new primary node when a failure occurs, reducing the downtime. In order to achieve a recovery in the event of failures in the readings, it is necessary to ensure that the paths of the readings and the writings are different, so that a fault in the writing can be handled and readings can still be made. This means that readings and writings have to be made in separate connections to the database. The main disadvantage of this model is inconsistency. There is a danger that different clients will read different secondary nodes and the data will be different because certain changes have not yet been propagated to the secondary nodes. In the worst case, it means that a client cannot read a script he/she has just made. Even this can be a problem in a single-server configuration with nodes that are backup copies, because if the primary node fails, some updates will be lost by not passing to the secondary nodes.

The master–slave model facilitates scalability at the reading level, but not at the writing level. In addition, it provides failover recovery for a secondary node, but not for the primary node. However, the primary node is still the only point of failure. In this sense, peer-to-peer replication eliminates this problem, eliminating the figure of the primary node. All replicas are equally important and can accept scripts, and if any of the replicas fail, it does not prevent access to the database. In addition, it is possible to add new nodes to improve performance. The biggest problem with this model is consistency. So when you can write in two different places, then there is a risk that two processes are trying to update the same record at the same time, producing a writing–writing conflict. In this sense, to observe that inconsistencies in the reading will lead to transitory problems, however, inconsistencies in the scriptures are permanent. To avoid these problems we have two approaches:

1. Each time data is written, replicas are coordinated to avoid conflicts. The main disadvantage is the cost of network traffic to coordinate writes. Observe that it is not necessary that all the replicas reach an agreement, but the majority. In this approach, consistency over availability is valued.

2. Another option is to consider an inconsistent writing. There are situations in which a policy of merging inconsistent writes can be followed. The maximum performance of the writing on any replica is obtained as a benefit. In this case, the availability on the consistency is valued.

- Combination Sharding and Replication

Replication and sharding are strategies that can be combined [25]. If both techniques are used, then there will be multiple primary nodes, but for each data item, there will be only one primary node. Depending on the configuration, you can choose that a node is primary for some data and secondary for others, or have dedicated primary or secondary nodes for certain jobs. The combination of techniques is a common strategy in column-type NoSQL databases. In this context, you could have tens or hundreds of nodes in a cluster with fragmented data about them.

d. The CAP theorem

The CAP theorem formalizes some properties that are met in a distributed system running in a cluster of machines. In this sense, it establishes in [26], given a system in the previous conditions, only two of the following possible properties can be fulfilled at the same time: consistency of the managed data, and availability of access to the stored data in the machines that form the cluster and tolerance to the partitioning of the system. The theorem can be analyzed in several cases [26]:

1. If the system consists of a single machine. In this case, if the machine works correctly, the information will be available and the consistency of the stored information can be guaranteed. In addition, it is not possible for partitioning of the system to occur.

2. If the system consists of more than one machine. In this case, if a partitioning of the system occurs, it is interpreted that availability is maintained whenever a request is made to a machine that is in operation, a response is received. Thus, the partitions have as a consequence a compensation between the consistency and the availability of the system, that is, some inconsistencies of the system will be maintained in exchange for increasing the availability of the system. Note that this balance between consistency and availability is directly related to the latency of a system. So, the more machines exist in a system, the better the consistency, but the availability is worse since the latency of the system increases.

In relation to consistency, we must observe that the more machines are involved in a request, the greater the possibility of avoiding an inconsistency.

In this context, the concepts of "writing quorum" and "reading quorum" are defined [27]. The "writing quorum" indicates that the number of machines participating in the writing must be greater than half the number of machines involved in a replication. The number of replicas is often known by the replication factor. Similarly, the reading quorum is defined as the number of machines that need to be contacted in order to be sure that the most up-to-date data is available. This case is more complicated because it depends on how many machines are needed to confirm a writing.

Note that it is easy to confuse the number of machines in the cluster with the replication factor, and these values are often different. In fact, it is generally suggested that a replication factor of 3 is sufficient, since it allows a single node to fail while still maintaining the quorum for readings and writes. If you have automatic rebalancing, it will not take long to create a third replica, and the chances of losing the second replica before being replaced are very small.

The number of machines involved in an operation may vary with the operation. When writing, quorum might be required for some types of updates, but not for others depending on how much the consistency and availability are valued. Similarly, a reading needs speed, but it can tolerate lack of updating if it contacts fewer machines.

It is often necessary to take both aspects into account. If rapidity is needed, strongly consistent readings, then the writings may be required to be recognized by all the machines, allowing the readings to contact only one machine. That would mean that the writings are slow, since they have to contact all the machines and they would not be tolerant of the loss of a machine.

5 PRACTICAL APPLICATION OF NOSQL DATABASES IN BIG DATA PROBLEMS

In this section, we will analyze two examples of application of the NoSQL databases in problem

a) The investigations were carried out with respect to the "Panama papers" or the "Paradise papers" [28]. The information that had to be analyzed consisted of different document formats with different structures referring to entities and persons with assets in tax havens. A relational model was not adequate due to the following reasons:

- The information presents a great heterogeneity since not all documents have the same fields despite being similar, nor are they as complete. This would result in tables with many of the empty fields, and efficiency in storage and retrieval will decrease.

- Each time you want to add a new type of document, you should define your scheme, and it will probably be subject to various changes, since different attributes will be known as the investigation proceeds.

- A relational database would be less efficient in detecting local relationships, and would result in very complex queries (several JOINs between tables).

- The visualization of the results is less efficient, since a graph is directly interpretable and visualizable. In fact, queries produce subsets of graphs.

- The only advantage that a relational model could offer would be greater consistency; however, in this case, it is not necessary since the published data have been contrasted, and will be subject to infrequent and massive updates.

However, a model in graph presents interesting advantages:

- First of all, there is great heterogeneity in the data that appear in the documents, so a flexible data model is required, both for the data that may exist in similar documents and for admitting future typologies of documents: mail, money flows, etc. Each entity can have a variable number of associated metadata.

- A graph model also allows adding new types of nodes that are discovered, and that would be easily added to the existing network: financial entities, family ties, etc. Four types of nodes were found: customers, companies, addresses, and managers.

- Being an investigation, a graph allows a direct interpretation of the relationships between the entities that appear in the documents, especially the close relationships of specific companies/individuals. Several types of relationships were found between managers and companies, between managers and addresses, between clients and companies, and between managers and addresses.

- It is the most appropriate model to perform local operations of the proximity type, or the calculation of minimum length to another node. The graph is optimized to perform this type of operations, which are the ones that have the greatest interest in research.

b) Design of the personalized and real-time content service of the BBC [29]. The company sought to offer interactive content in real time to its customers and adapt to the preferences of each user. To do this, they had to access the preferences of each user at a given time, process the information, and consult and access the contents that fit the requirements of preferences and offer them. If you take into account that these operations are for each user, this supposes a huge amount of data and it requires a great efficiency and speed in the realization of the queries and answers so that the contents can be offered in real time. In this sense, to implement the personalized content service and in real time, a documentary model was chosen for the following reasons:

- The requirements in terms of storage and processing require a distributed approach based on the use of a cluster. This solution is not possible with a relational database, since they are not designed to work efficiently in clusters.

- Likewise, a very flexible and content-rich data structure would be necessary. However, the relational model would require defining the schema initially, before adding any data to the system (or its modification and subsequent use), unlike what happens with NoSQL, that there is no predefined schema, which makes much more easy to update the data and adapt the requirements.

- Regarding the data structure, in this case, very different types of data had to be integrated (from multimedia files to statistical data) and they had to present high availability in a synchronized way. In this sense, NoSQL databases are optimal for managing and processing in a distributed way large amounts of semi-structured and unstructured data. It has benefited the company in the face of the offer to the client. In this sense, the BBC was able to make up to 25,000 transactions per second and a total of 45,000 million requests, having been the system capable of managing them, and in real time.

- Regarding scalability, it is preferable to perform a horizontal scaling of a NoSQL database due to the economic implications of having to expand a relational database. In this sense, the implemented NoSQL solution allowed the management of more than 2.8 petabytes of data of large audience in a single day, without having dropped the server.

On the other hand, among the different NoSQL databases, the documentary model was chosen given that it allows queries based on any field of a document, which contributed great wealth, unlike key-value models, which are necessary access through the cave. This would allow, for example, transactions based on a certain preference or attribute within a user's document, or certain attributes associated with the client, for example. The documentary model simplifies access to data, reducing the need for complex transactions. In addition, the outlook of the scheme is dynamic and each document can have different fields, easily allowing fields to be added and, therefore, segmentation according to the client's offer to them and, finally, flexibility and scalability.

This solution has meant an improvement of the company in terms of the quality of its service and content offer to its customer, an increase in user satisfaction, and a reduction in costs and optimization of the investment. In this sense, the profitability of the changes has resulted in an increase in productivity and income.

6 CONCLUSIONS

In this chapter, we have described the Big Data phenomenon and some of the new technological needs that are required. In the particular case of storage and processing of information, it is necessary to process almost in real time large amounts of information without a regular structure that may change over time. These conditions make necessary systems that run distributed in a cluster of machines that are very flexible to the type of data that is to be stored and that are easily adaptable to new types of data that may arise. Relational databases pose limitations with respect to these aspects because they are not designed to run in distributed environments, and the type of data they are able to manage are structured and according to previously defined information schemes. In this sense, the NoSQL databases are developed as an alternative to relational databases and with the aim of covering the needs of Big Data.

Likewise, the main characteristics of the NoSQL databases, the types of existing databases, the distribution models they implement, and a set of application cases have been presented.

ACKNOWLEDGMENTS

The authors thank the financial support of the Santander-UCM GR3/14 (group 962022) and eLITE-CM S2015/HUM-3426 projects.

REFERENCES

1. Pokorný, J. (2015, June). Database technologies in the world of big data. In *Proceedings of the 16th International Conference on Computer Systems and Technologies* (pp. 1–12). ACM.
2. Stonebraker, M. (2010). SQL databases v. NoSQL databases. *Communications of the ACM*, 53(4):10–11.
3. Chen, M., Mao, S. and Liu, Y. (2014). Big data: A survey. *Mobile Networks and Applications*, 19(2):171–209.
4. Jacobs, A. (2009). The pathologies of Big Data. *Communications of the ACM*, 52 (8):36–44.
5. Assunção, M. D., Calheiros, R. N., Bianchi, S., Netto, M. A., and Buyya, R. (2015). Big Data computing and clouds: Trends and future directions. *Journal of Parallel and Distributed Computing*, 79:3–15.

6. Chen, C. P. and Zhang, C. Y. (2014). Data-intensive applications, challenges, techniques and technologies: A survey on Big Data. *Information Sciences*, 275:314–347.
7. Warden, P. (2011). *Big Data Glossary*. O'Reilly Media, Inc.
8. Khan, N., Yaqoob, I., Hashem, I. A. T., Inayat, Z., Ali, M., Kamaleldin, W., … Gani, A. (2014). *Big data: Survey, Technologies, Opportunities, and Challenges*. The Scientific World Journal, 2014:1–18.
9. Elmasri, R. and Navathe, S. (2010). *Fundamentals of Database Systems*. Addison-Wesley Publishing Company.
10. Li, Y. and Manoharan, S. (2013, August). A performance comparison of SQL and NoSQL databases. In *2013 IEEE Pacific Rim Conference on Communications, Computers and Signal Processing (PACRIM)* (pp. 15–19). IEEE.
11. Jatana, N., Puri, S., Ahuja, M., Kathuria, I., and Gosain, D. (2012). A Survey and Comparison of Relational and Non-relational Database. *International Journal of Engineering Research & Technology*, 1(6): 1–5.
12. Melton, J. and Simon, A. R. (1993). *Understanding the New SQL: A Complete Guide*. Morgan Kaufmann.
13. Coronel, C. and Morris, S. (2016). *Database Systems: Design, Implementation, & Management*. Cengage Learning.
14. Stonebraker, M. (2012). Newsql: An Alternative to NOSQL and Old SQL for New OLTP Apps. *Communications of the ACM*. Retrieved 22-12-2018. https://cacm.acm.org/blogs/blog-cacm/109710-new-sql-an-alternative-to-nosql-and-old-sql-for-new-oltp-apps/fulltext
15. Kumar, R., Gupta, N., Maharwal, H., Charu, S., and Yadav, K. (2014). Critical analysis of Database Management UsingNewSQL. *International Journal of Computer Science and Mobile Computing*, 3:434–438.
16. Zhao, G., Lin, Q., Li, L., and Li, Z. (2014, November). Schema conversion model of SQL database to NOSQL. In *2014 Ninth International Conference on P2P, Parallel, Grid, Cloud and Internet Computing (3PGCIC)* (pp. 355–362). IEEE.
17. Pavlo, A. and Aslett, M. (2016). What's Really New with NewSQL? *ACM Sigmod Record*, 45 (2):45–55.
18. Vaish, G. (2013). *Getting Started with NoSQL*. Packt Publishing Ltd.
19. Tiwari, S. (2011). *Professional NoSQL*. John Wiley & Sons.
20. Perkins, L., Redmond, E., and Wilson, J. (2018). *Seven Databases in Seven Weeks: A Guide to Modern Databases and the NoSQL Movement*. Pragmatic Bookshelf.
21. Nayak, A., Poriya, A., and Poojary, D. (2013). Type of NOSQL Databases and Its Comparison with Relational Databases. *International Journal of Applied Information Systems*, 5 (4):16–19.
22. Han, J., Haihong, E., Le, G., and Du, J. (2011, October). Survey on NoSQL Database. In *2011 6th International Conference on Pervasive Computing and Applications (ICPCA)* (pp. 363–366). IEEE.
23. Niazi, S., Ismail, M., Haridi, S., Dowling, J., Grohsschmiedt, S., and Ronström, M. (2017, February). HopsFS: Scaling Hierarchical File System Metadata Using NewSQL Databases. In *FAST* (pp. 89–104).
24. Sadalage, P. J. and Fowler, M. (2013). *NoSQL Distilled: A Brief Guide to the Emerging World of Polyglot Persistence*. Pearson Education.
25. Hecht, R. and Jablonski, S. (2011, December). NoSQL Evaluation: A Use Case Oriented Survey. In *2011 International Conference on Cloud and Service Computing (CSC)* (pp. 336–341). IEEE.
26. Pokorny, J. (2013). NoSQL Databases: A Step to Database Scalability in Web Environment. *International Journal of Web Information Systems*, 9(1):69–82.

27. Pethuru, R., Ganesh, C. (2018). *A Deep Dive into NoSQL Databases: The Use Cases and Applications*. Academic Press.
28. Panama Papers. (2017). Retrieved 07-05-2018. https://neo4j.com/blog/analyzing-panama-papers-neo4j/
29. BBC NoSQL. (2016). Retrieved 10-05-2018. www.marklogic.com/customers/bbc/

CHAPTER 6

Prescriptive and Predictive Analytics Techniques for Enabling Cybersecurity

Nitin Sukhija and Sonny Sevin

Slippery Rock University of Pennsylvania, Slippery Rock, USA

Elizabeth Bautista

Lawrence Berkeley National Labs, Berkeley, USA

David Dampier

The University of Texas at San Antonio, San Antonio, USA

CONTENTS

O ver the last few decades, significant research and development efforts have been explored and implemented in the area of cyber-attack tolerant and survivable systems. Such efforts have led to an ever-increasing growth in development of defensive technologies, such as smarter intrusion detection devices, and sensors to make systems robust and secure against the unintended events and targeted attacks. Furthermore, these surveillance and monitoring devices capture large amount of real-time streams of complex structured or unstructured datasets that can be further analyzed and utilized to mitigate cyber-attacks and achieve cyber resilience in real time. However, gathering, storing, exploring, and processing such unprecedented amount of data is challenging both methodologically and practically for cybersecurity research community. For instance, learning the network structure of a large data set represented as graph is computationally demanding, and dynamically monitoring the network over time for any real-time changes in structure threatens to be more challenging. To address this problem, big data analytic techniques, explicitly predictive and prescriptive analytics, have been proposed and applied to cybersecurity by various scientists and analytics [1]. The prescriptive analytics comprises a predictive model with two additional components: actionable data and a feedback system that tracks the outcome produced by the action taken. In general, various machine learning techniques catalyze the speed of predictive and prescriptive analytics and the breadth of data that can be incorporated to not only predict the outcomes but also to construct automated plans based on learning agents which perform actions autonomously based on intelligent learning. Consequently, a comprehensive study of the state-of-the-art machine learning techniques used in predictive and prescriptive analytics is of paramount importance, especially for researchers from both academic and industrial domains dealing with cybersecurity applications involving big data [2]. This chapter highlights significant research and challenges pertaining to the applicability of emerging predictive and prescriptive analytics solutions to achieve cyber resilience.

1 INTRODUCTION

Securing High-Performance Computing (HPC) systems from internal and external threats is a challenging task due to the number and the heterogeneous nature of their components and due to the complex interactions among them. Such systems are usually shared by a number of internal and external users that, even unintentionally, could introduce malicious software. Given the HPC systems encompass large amount of available resources, such as CPU, memory, and network, these systems are of particular interest to prospective adversaries who could potentially exploit these systems in order to launch further attacks towards other resources in the HPC environments. In general, these computing systems achieve a very high aggregated network throughput which could be in the order of tens of Tbps for the internal message exchanges. Furthermore, the heterogeneity of this network throughput, mainly due to different applications running concurrently in the same environment, makes it very difficult to effectively monitor and protect the HPC clusters in real time with traditional security products like firewalls, IDSs, and event loggers. Moreover, storing data generated by monitoring tools and security products for offline analysis has become unfeasible as well. Thus, protecting HPC systems has become extremely challenging for the scientists given the complex and heterogeneous nature of these infrastructures and the typical issues related to 4 Vs of Big Data [3] which are as following:

1. **Huge Volume**: An enormous amount of data is being produced and collected by sensors, monitors, machines, networks, and human interaction on systems such as social media, and storing and managing such immense amount of data could be infeasible for enabling security for even smaller systems.

2. **High Velocity**: The pace at which data flows HPC operations, machines, networks, and human interaction is massive and continuous. For example, the aggregate network throughput can be in the order of tens of Tera bytes per second, and thus to detect and avoid a potential attack, this immense data must be monitored, processed, and analyzed in real time.

3. **Vast Variety**: HPC environments involve execution of diverse and complex applications with unpredictable fluctuations on highly heterogeneous computing systems. Thus, it involves varied applications and platform data from the networks, monitors, sensors, logs, and media, resulting in development of multifaceted view of the HPC environments. Therefore, it requires developing customer resources maps and plans to engage more with variety data for enabling cybersecurity.

4. **High Veracity**: The immense amount of data collected does not ensure the correctness and validity of the data. The major challenge for data analysis in cybersecurity is to consolidate, clean, and process the amassed structured and unstructured data to avoid biases, noise, and abnormality in data to make the right decisions for detecting and responding to cyberattacks on the mission-critical systems in the given time-frame.

In recent years, there have been some development and integration efforts by some commercial players in the development of Security Information and Event Management Systems (SIEM) products. These holistic solutions facilitate organizations' IT security by integrating several monitoring and analysis features, such as collecting data from multiple sources, cleansing of data, correlation of alerts and events, and profiling, automating, and analyzing data for avoiding potential threats. Some of the most important SIEM products include Micro Focus ArcSight, Splunk Enterprise Security (ES), and IBM Security QRadar [4,5]. However, most of the proposed solutions are proprietary and have integration limitations with the components from different vendors. Furthermore, they are usually built on a classic relational database, which limits their scalability and their ability to process huge flows of data. Moreover, they limit their operations to the strict analysis of the data produced by the sensors and to the eventual generation of alerts. Finally, all the research and development pertaining to the existing SIEM products is based on defensive technologies, which thus limits their functionality and ability to plan a pro-active response policy in order to automatically respond to the ongoing threat/attack.

Effectively protecting the distributed cyberinfrastructure (CI) supporting scientific research workflow is a challenging task due to the complex and heterogeneous nature of these infrastructures. The scope of a scientific research workflow encompasses various hardware and software elements (such as instruments, processing software, analysis tools, computing and storage resources, as well as information repositories and data archives) connected through communication networks. Multi-tenancy and the sharing of resource pools on the same physical platforms could introduce serious vulnerabilities. Also, the variety of network protocols and interfaces that characterize cyber infrastructures introduce the potential for illicit cyber penetration of such infrastructure and the underlying services. Additionally, intruders can exploit the massive computation resources to launch sophisticated and damaging attacks. As CIs grow in complexity, responding to threats in realtime manually is not just tedious and error-prone, but infeasible. Traditional security management systems have addressed the detection of some attacks, but have not provided effective techniques to protect against them.

This chapter covers significant predictive and prescriptive analytics solutions for protecting the CI supporting scientific research. There is considerable ongoing research into intrusion detection and identification; research on automatic intrusion response based on predictive and prescriptive analytics is still in its early stages. The chapter especially involves surveying the integration of data analytics, vulnerability and risk assessment, autonomic computing, predictive control, and stochastic optimization techniques and models for:

1. detection and monitoring of cyberattacks at an early stage by correlating and aggregating the flows of events produced by different types of threat detection tools and sensors;

2. identification and analysis of near-optimal defense plans based on the data aggregated by monitors and sensors, and user-defined multi-criteria objective functions;

3. execution of the defense plans by employing and deploying the necessary remedial actions, and system modules; and

4. prescription and modification of the defense plans against the cyberattacks based on feedback from the defense system and detected changes in the attack strategy.

2 PREDICTIVE ANALYTICS FOR CYBERSECURITY

Securing the systems used in scientific computing is a challenging task considering the nature of the systems, with HPC systems being especially vulnerable. The systems used to execute the scientific applications have unique cyber defense needs compared to those of desktops and servers due to the vastly different use cases and simulations encompassing these applications. Scientific computing systems deal with a much larger user pool, and process much more data than desktops and servers, thus opening more avenues of cyberattack. The users of these systems may also have largely different workflows with diverse resource needs that make monitoring these systems extremely difficult as there is no common pattern of use among various users. Thus, the monitoring tools must be much more sophisticated in predicting cyberattack by distinguishing between malicious activity and that of an actual user.

Cybersecurity demands an even more proactive approach. The cybersecurity data analytics requires an agile approach based on predictive analytics that employs various techniques and algorithms to process and analyze the enormous pools of data gathered by monitors and sensors to automatically identify patterns and detect anomalies in near-real time so that the computing systems can be prepared for the next upcoming attack by cybercriminals.

2.1 System Monitoring and Detection

The detection of cyberattacks is extremely important so that the data cannot be stolen, altered, or damaged at the initial stages of application runs on HPC systems. However, it becomes extremely difficult to detect these attacks due to the sheer number of and diversity of jobs that maybe running on HPC systems. The traditional anti-virus and anti-malware tools match executing processes to a predefined list of malicious activities to detect cyberattacks, but work only for the more common use cases, personal computers, and servers [6]. However, the systems that support scientific research are not a typical use case, and thus require specialized methods to sift through all these processes. Moreover, matching events through traditional means is not feasible for several reasons. First, the attacks on scientific computing resources are vastly different than the attacks on personal computers and servers, so making a match becomes almost impossible. Second, given the complexity of the scientific environments, the attacks can change rapidly, and therefore a computing system must be able to learn which processes are potential attacks, and which are of normal use. Apparently, the ultimate goal is to stop all attacks from penetrating through the computing environments, but when they inevitably do, it is important to monitor, detect, and stop these attacks early.

There have been many research and development efforts for implementing strategies/ algorithms to identify malicious activities/actors focusing mainly on either misuse detection or anomaly detection. In misuse detection technique, a cyber defense algorithm is employed to search and identify the events that have similar signatures to the malicious events. The algorithm employed monitors the network, file access, and job creation of any activity that would constitute potential misuse of the system. While detecting anomalies that are potential cyberattacks, the anomaly detection algorithm looks for behaviors that do not match with the typical use of the computing systems. For instance, malicious occurrences include behaviors such as users accessing files that they normally would not edit, network signals that do not match with the services on the system, and starting jobs that are not typical to the system [7]. The detection of either type of malicious events implies that there is a potential threat to the system and the threat needs to be dealt at an early stage before it leads to failure of the computing system. There are many ways to detect these events, and to distinguish them from the benign use of the system. The following paragraphs give an overview of the different methods, and algorithms applied in real systems to predict the cyberattacks based on the data collected by various monitoring and analysis mechanisms.

The signature of the attacks changes rapidly, and thus mandates detection methods to evolve as new attacks are encountered. Various machine learning techniques can be utilized to analyze the patterns of the events occurring on a system where a malware detection system learns which signatures are malicious by matching similar sequences together. One such concept is borrowed from the world of biology, specifically how DNA sequences are represented and matched [8]. Therefore, representing system events as string encodings, as DNA is represented by ATCG, allows for a detection system to match events against each other. Furthermore, like DNA signatures, system event signatures can also vary, and by matching similar events to each other, the algorithm can determine if an event is malicious [8]. Thus, by adding signatures to its repertoire, the detection algorithm continually evolves and learns in response to an ever-changing environment. One other machine learning technique developed to defend and remove cyberattacks uses monotonicity models to learn the difference between malicious and actual user events. In the monotonicity model, data is only added to the model if it does not contradict what the model has already learned. The idea is that attackers only change the signature of their attack in one direction, that is, to make their attacks look less suspicious, not the other way around. By analyzing the inexpensive parts of the signature, hacker changes to appear less suspicious; the model can identify malicious activity even if the hacker has changed parts of its program to look more like a legitimate process [6].

One of the many issues with mining data for cybersecurity is identifying rare use case intrusions [8,9]. The PNrule algorithm is a highly precise tool that can be used to classify rare events as malicious. It is composed of two distinct rule sets: P-rules and N-rules [10]. The P-rules establish whether a target class is present or not. The P-rules are made up of a set of rules that can define a substantial portion of the training set. The issue with the P-rules is that many false-negatives can be produced because the rule set is too general or broad. Many other algorithms used in rare-case learning suffer from this same dysfunction (CN2, AQ algorithms, and RAMP are examples of such) [9], but the N-rules of the PNrule algorithm help to solve this issue [10]. By including a set of rules that define an absence of the target class, the PNrule algorithm removes many of the false-negatives that can crop up from being overly general in the N-rules. The combination of these rulesets helps to eliminate both false-positives and false-negatives, while still ensuring a high rate of detection of malicious intrusions. The main drawback in using PNrule algorithm is that it is a supervised training model that requires human interaction to train, which requires an analyst to label and feed data into the algorithm [11,12].

In recent years, deep learning algorithms have become an attractive option for detecting intrusions in realtime with many different algorithms being developed [11,12]. A properly trained neural network is a valuable tool in helping to detect threats in real time. These algorithms have gained attention due to the fact that they do not require supervision while learning, whereas other machine learning algorithms require pretraining and continued supervision. Deep Neural Networks (DNN) have shown promise in furthering research and discovery in several other fields, such as image, text, and voice processing [13], and have been applied successfully to intrusion detection. The Restricted Boltzmann Machine (RBM) and AutoEncoder algorithms are some of the more promising algorithms applied to intrusion detection; when they are properly applied, they produce highly accurate results with great performance. Furthermore, combining these algorithms with each other, and other supervised training models, produces greater accuracy and performance [12,14].

Deep Belief Networks (DBN), a variety of DNN, are made up of layers of hidden and visible layers. The most common way of constructing a DBN is stacking RBMs [15]. DBNs can be used to monitor network and user activity for threats by analyzing and flagging behavior that is out of the norm in real time [15]. The Boltzmann Machines come in several different flavors, but in general, they are a network of stochastic neurons that make decisions based on weighted connections. The RBMs are named so because the connections in a layer are not connected to each other but rather only to the layers before and after. Each layer in a RBM is trained sequentially and then stacked on top of each other using unlabeled training data and a selected training algorithm [16]. This allows for each layer to be finely tuned and increases efficiency over training all the layers at the same time [16–18]. The main challenge in using DBNs is balancing accuracy, training times, and efficiency [18].

Autoencoders are another promising class of algorithms employed to build DNNs. In general, Autoencoders consist of two or three parts depending on implementation; there is an encoder, a decoder, and sometimes a hidden layer [19]. The objective of an autoencoder is to reduce the dimensionality of the data that is inputted into the neural network [19]. Most dataset have a large number of attributes termed as "dimensions", and this can have a large impact on analyzing the data for useful information since not every attribute will be needed [20]. Typically, a series of autoencoders are stacked on each other to form a DNN. These DNNs can be used to monitor and detect malicious activity by flagging abnormal behavior, like the DBNs [19,20], but can also be used in more novel ways like detecting application layer DDoS (Distributed Denial of Service) attacks [21].

2.2 Threat Identification and Event Analysis

It is not enough to simply identify what the potential threats are; after threats are identified, there must be a defense plan in place to stop the threats. A good defense plan must address the needs of the system, include which underlying systems are involved, and allow for the ability to change the plan as needs change. Scientific research systems process huge amount of computationally complex data and an optimal defense plan must ensure that the jobs on the system are not bogging down the system unnecessarily. The defense plan must identify which underlying systems are necessary to complete the stated goals. Moreover, a defense plan must exhibit a degree of flexibility to deal with the rapidly changing world of computing. A compressive, flexible defense plan is key to protecting systems against malicious users.

First, when designing a defense plan, one must decide on the potential avenues of attack that are possible. An attack and defense tree method can be employed for identifying the possible attacks and avenues that a hacker may use to get into the system [22]. An attack/defense graph is a representation of the possible target of an attacker, the avenues an attacker could use to reach his or her target, and the potential counter measures that could be taken by a system. By analyzing these trees, one can develop a plan to thwart the attackers. Furthermore, while choosing the countermeasures necessary to disrupt an attack, close attention to the resources that these defenses use should be given to avoid the performance degradation of the existing computing system.

Scientific computing systems are almost always made up of a set of distributed computing resources and this unique feature must be given special attention while designing defense plans. The heterogeneous mix of hardware and software makes it difficult to have one large blanket solution to the whole system, especially while considering the Internet of Things (IoT) devices that will be attached to the system (in the form of sensors and monitoring devices). Securing the system with IOT devices is especially difficult due to the nature of these devices, given IOT devices have limited processing and storage capabilities due to their size and energy constraints [23]. These limitations make it difficult to install security features on the IOT devices. It is extremely difficult for an IOT device to both run the security software and perform its designed function given there is simply no room in the devices memory for additional software. IOT devices are a popular avenue of attack for hackers and all computing systems with attached IOT devices need an extra layer of security. The following paragraphs give an overview of the different methods, algorithms, and tools developed and implemented for threat identification and event analysis to predict the cyberattacks.

One of the tools used for event analysis is Bayesian Networks (BN) [22,24]. BNs are directed acyclic graphs that can be used as probabilistic models [25]. In a BN, the nodes represent events and the connections represent the dependencies between them. That is, an event can only occur if one of the conditions preceding is true, and these connections can then be weighted and used to determine the probability of an event occurring and the possible avenues that cause it. Using BNs, it is possible not only to determine the probabilities of an outcome occurring by following events but also to see the possible routes that caused an event to occur [22]. BNs can be constructed from attack and defense graphs to model attacks and determine affected files and services [26].

Researchers have implemented BN in several tools and systems to detect and analyze intrusions. Kruegel et al. developed a system to detect and identify attacks against a system by analyzing operating system calls [27]. Herein, the system call behavior is fed into the detection system and features are compared against different models to determine if the calls are malicious or of normal use, with each model represented as a node in the BN. The BN in the developed detection system was built using the C++ library Smile [27], where Smile is a closed-source library that requires a commercial license for deployment in a production environment [28].

Another area of research focused on identifying cyber threats against a system are Petri nets [29]. A Petri net is a system modeling tool that is based on graphs and mathematics [29–31]. Petri nets are particularly suited for cyber threat analysis in a computing system because they can model distributed and parallel systems [30]. In a Petri net, the system is modeled by the changes in states and transitions between states of the system, being described both graphically and with mathematic equations. By comparing the transitions and state changes of the system with normal operation, cyber threats can be identified, and appropriate countermeasures can then be taken [29]. The colored Petri nets are the most used class of Petri nets in cybersecurity systems, extending the general Petri net by allowing data types to be assigned to nodes [32].

The Multi-Agents Intrusion Detection System (MAIDS) is an example of a system that utilizes colored Petri nets [33,34]. The MAIDS system has three main components: the data collection agents that gather and convert necessary data from logs and system events, agents that monitor and classify ongoing (real time) system events, and the machine learning agents that provide the predictive rules learned from processing logs and system events. The machine learning agents adjust the underlying Petri net to reflect the system as it evolves.

Researchers have also utilized Markov Chains in cybersecurity threat identification and analysis [35]. Markov Chains resemble Petri nets in modeling states and probabilities of a system, but in a Markov Chain, nodes represent states rather than entities. Markov Models also model a sequential series of events rather than modeling the probabilities of different series of events occurring [36]. Most cybersecurity applications have focused on the use of Hidden Markov Models (HMMs), in which some of the states are not directly observable. HMMs can be trained on a real data set and then used to detect attacks by signaling when an unlikely series of events have occurred.

Hidden Markov Chains have been used in many different cybersecurity applications. Sperotto et al. implemented a model to detect brute-force SSH attacks by analyzing network flow [35]. Herein, the developed model had mixed results but showed how HMMs could be used to model network flow and be implemented in an Intrusion Detection System (IDS). Ariu et al. proposed HMMPayl to detect attacks against web applications, where the analysis is done by an underlying HMM [37]. In HMMPayl, first, a training phase using normal traffic pattern is completed to determine the most effective probability matrices for each of the HMMs used in the IDS. This allows the system to detect abnormal traffic patterns (HTTP payloads) that are indicative of an attack.

3 PRESCRIPTIVE ANALYTICS FOR CYBERSECURITY

Cybersecurity analytics involves two categories of advanced analytics, which are predictive and prescriptive; each implements big data and different levels of human involvement for producing different outcomes. As discussed in previous sections, the predictive analytics enables the defense system to be more effective at detecting cyberattacks by analyzing the current and historical data generated by various sensors and monitors. However, using predictive analytics will only help in predicting attack but will not aid in choosing an action plan in a state where the system is under cyberattack. Prescriptive analytics not only aids a defense system in predicting cyberattack events but also analyses all the possible outcomes to suggest the action plans during each particular use case. Prescriptive analytics uses the predictive analytics model to identify potential outcomes and then formulates a set of recommended actions that answer: what and when to do? Prescriptive analytics is relatively complex to administer but enables defense systems to go a step further by suggesting actions that can produce the desired results.

3.1 Defense Response Planning and Execution

Simply detecting system intrusions is not enough; remedial actions must be planned and executed to stop the attack and mitigate damage done to the system. There exist various diverse classifications of cyberattacks and it is extremely important to have defense plans for as many cyberattacks as possible. In general, the attackers aim to accomplish at least one of the three goals: 1) disruption; 2) access and alter data that attackers do not have regular access to; and 3) to take control of a system to use it for malicious purposes [38]. DDoS attacks are used to disrupt cyber systems and intrusions are used to access a system for data or system control [39,40].

Intrusion Response Systems (IRSs) are systems designed to select an appropriate response to detected intrusion. The traditional IRSs needed human feedback in order to select an appropriate action for an intrusion [41]. This approach, however, is cumbersome, error-prone, and does not hold up against modern-day attacks. Most of the current sophisticated attacks are automated, happen in multiple stages, and involve multiple security vulnerabilities, thus making it almost impossible for a human analyst to defend against it manually [42]. This limitation mandates the need for IRSs that automatically select and deploy an appropriate response. The main objective of an effective IRS is to contain the attack, resume normal system services, and reconfigure the system to defend against future attacks of a similar nature.

IRSs can be divided into two broad categories: static and dynamic systems [40,41]. The static IRS systems focus on mapping a response to a specific type of attack. These systems have many downsides, such as the inability to factor in previous defense measures and the inability to take in to account the possible side effects of a response. Another limitation of the static IRSs is that their responses are hard coded into the system, and thus responses are updated by administrators to defend against new attacks or to improve responses to existing attacks. The static IRSs have limited usability and most research and development is focused more on dynamic systems.

Dynamic IRSs are more useful in comparison to the static IRSs described above. One of the main advantages to using a dynamic IRS is its ability to choose the most effective countermeasure among the multiple countermeasures depending on multiple criteria. Since there are generally side effects to a selected response, the dynamic IRS must select the one with the least negative consequences. The criteria taken into consideration by IRS can include, but are not limited to, computational costs, service downtime, terminating useful interdependent resources, and user disconnection. Moreover, there are also the chances of selecting a failing response where another, typically escalated response is necessary. The dynamic IRSs are equipped with the ability to learn and adapt response strategies based on the former feedback, allowing them to respond both more successfully and with less damage to the system [39,40].

Existing works on dynamic IRS can be classified based on the following aspects: (i) multi-objective: optimal response action (or plan) is selected according to a set of weighted criteria; (ii) IDS uncertainty: the ability to deal with stochastic IDS alerts; (iii) long-term plan: provides long-term protection plan rather than immediate optimal response; (iv) system model: the IRS is based on a system model describing its dynamics under normal and attack conditions; (v) attacker model: the IRS considers a model describing the attacker behavior and the potential graph of achievable targets.

In [43], the authors introduce a network model to choose the response action able to avert certain threats and to minimize the overall impact on the system and users. ADEPTS [44] focuses on restricting the effect of the intrusion to a subset of the services by maximizing the availability of the system at the expenses of the features compromised by the attack, which are isolated from the rest of the system. An attack-centric model, based on intrusion graphs, is used to represent attack propagation. The Compromised Confidence Index (CCI) is used to compute the confidence of the detected alert and the confidence of a particular system breach. The response action is selected from a response repository by evaluating the effectiveness and the potential disruptiveness of all the available responses. In [45], the authors propose an IRS that takes into consideration the stochastic nature of the detections made by the IDS and the response action is only triggered if the confidence level of the detected attack is greater than a specified threshold. Response actions are manually mapped to known attack patterns and the best response action is chosen based on its impact on the system. In [46], an optimal response selection is proposed based on financial cost, reputation loss, and processing resource. A modified version of the classical genetic algorithm is used to represent the association between each response action and the system resources affected by the execution of the action.

A long-term response planning is presented in [47]. The work uses a Hierarchical Task Network (HTN) to model the IRS goal, the high-level response actions, and the mechanisms to enable response actions. This work uses a fixed set of goals and statically maps each goal to a sequence of high-level response actions. The latter are mapped at run-time to the actual actions, according to their effectiveness in countering the attack. The presented approach, however, has a fixed high-level structure of the response plan for a given specific IRS goal. Also, updating IRS goals requires a careful planning of the high-level response actions. A Partially Observable MDP (POMDP) is used in [48] to model an IRS able to plan optimal response policies. Since the POMDP is subject to an exponential growth of the states according to the number of the considered attributes, the authors propose a hierarchical decomposition to reduce the computational complexity. This work, however, does not fully exploit the potentialities offered by the MDP framework; the response actions rewards are statically defined (therefore simulating a static attack–response mapping) and long-term plans are not considered.

The authors of [49] use a Bayesian Direct Acyclic Graph (DAG) to model attacker behavior. The DAG nodes describe system assets and their dependencies, while edges represent possible exploitation paths. Herein, the system assets are represented as binary attributes that characterize them as active or disabled. The authors propose binary response actions that can deactivate or activate a certain service or asset. Responses are evaluated according to the Confidentiality–Integrity–Availability (CIA) triad, but since all the considered actions deal with services or machines deactivation, their evaluation always increase confidentiality and integrity and always penalize the overall system availability. The response selection problem is formulated by building a POMDP from the DAG and by selecting the optimal single-response action according to an evaluation with infinite look-ahead, aimed at minimizing the overall execution cost.

The DDoS attacks can also be used to disrupt user services or to completely take offline a cyber entity [50]. Not only are these attacks difficult to detect because of their ability to mimic legitimate traffic but also they are increasingly easier to orchestrate due to the wide availability of toolkits used to perform these attacks. The machine learning algorithms have become a popular tool to defend against these attacks because of their ability to pick out patterns of use and to determine which traffic is legitimate and which traffic is part of a DDoS attack. Since there are diverse types of DDoS attacks that operate at different levels of the Open System Interconnection (OSI) model using different attack vectors, it is important that the computing system selects the most appropriate defense strategy [51,52].

Seufert and O'Brien proposed and built a system that featured machine learning for detection and defense against DDoS attack [50]. They implemented probes throughout the system that monitored not only network traffic but also resource utilization attached to available services. The data gathered from the probes is fed through the machine learning layer, and when an attack is detected, it drops the malicious packets. The authors used a backpropagation algorithm as the basis for their ANN but other algorithms could be implemented just as well [53]. Linear Vector Quantization (LVQ) ANNs are another promising method used in DDoS defense that shows even more accuracy than the backpropagation models. Similar to the system in [50], after an attack is detected, the system then drops the identified malicious packets [53].

3.2 Defense Response Modification, Learning, and Knowledge

The defense plan, and by extension the defense system deployed, needs to be able to evolve with the feedback from the system as it is produced. It is critical that the defense system must be able to react to the unpredictable fluctuations as adversaries use more advances and varied attacks on the system. As technology is rapidly advancing, it is imperative that the defense systems protecting scientific computing outpace those who wish to do harm.

A flexible defense system itself should be able to react to both changes in the defense plan and in the responses to the actual attacks. More importantly, the defense system should be able to react to and evolve automatically as the threats occur to the system. It is essential that the defense system can process its own feedback in order to adapt to the ever-changing landscape of cyberattacks. The system should be provided feedback on variety of actions, such as network behaviors, user behavior, system behavior, attacks, and defenses employed. This information can be obtained from a variety of locations, such as log files, user input, system files, and network monitoring. The feedback provided can be utilized by the defense system to learn to distinguish between malicious and normal behaviors, and to automatically create models for detecting attacks [13]. The models created from the feedback produced have two distinct advantages: first, the models can deal with novel, previously unknown attacks and, second, the defense system can be molded to fit the specific use of the computing system. However, to maintain the accuracy of the system, it is advisable to include some sort of supervision with respect to the continued learning of the system. It is unlikely that the system will be 100% accurate, especially after its first deployment. Thus, allowing the system to request clarification and feedback from administrators increases the chances that the models will be able to accurately learn to differentiate between normal and abnormal behavior at an increased rate [54].

Autonomic computing is a rapidly developing concept in computing, with a large body of research focusing on perfecting and implementing the idea of self-configurable, self-healing, self-optimizing, and self-protecting computing systems and environments [55]. In domain of cybersecurity, this involves building systems that have situational awareness [56]. A situation-aware system is able to detect and identify attacks, deal with the attacks in real time, analyze the effects of the attack on the system, and be able to adapt its defense mechanisms against future attacks. Situational awareness is the key to achieving autonomic computing; without it, a defense system is unaware of the state of the computing system it is trying to protect. This awareness allows for the defense system to not only react but also to adapt [55,56].

There are several different models used in designing systems based on autonomic computing, such as IBMs MAPE-K, Possibilistic Self-adaptation (POISED), and Mechatronic UML [57–59]. The IBMs MAPE-K is the most popular reference model used and has several derivations. In general, the MAPE-K feedback loop is composed of five components: Monitor, Analyze, Plan, Execute, and System Knowledge. A system built on the MAPE-K reference model uses data from sensors and probes in the computing system to monitor the state of the system. When there are changes detected, the data is analyzed and a plan is formulated based on the knowledge that the system has garnered. After a plan is formulated and executed, the system's knowledge base is updated based on feedback from the computing system and the loop starts over again. POISED is a similar model but focuses on the underlying uncertainty of the underlying system [60].

There are many implementations of the MAPE-K loop. Some of the earliest implementations were IBMs Autonomic ToolKit [61], IBMs Agent Building and Learning Environment (ABLE) toolkit, and KinestheticseXtreme [62]. The IBMs Autonomic ToolKit and ABLE toolkit are written in Java and can be used to construct autonomous agents from subcomponents that can communicate with each other. These individual agents use a combination of machine learning techniques and rule-based inference in their decision-making to give them a well-rounded decision-making skill set [61,62]. While no longer used, these toolkits were the foundation for later works in autonomic computing.

In past decades, there has been much research into the field of autonomic computing and the algorithms that can be used for developing self-x systems. The genetic algorithms are one such group of algorithms that have been successfully applied in this area [63,64]. The genetic algorithms mirror natural selection in both how they operate and the end goal, that is, an optimal solution to a problem [65]. The genetic algorithms start with a work space of possible solutions to a problem, then select the most fit of these solutions according to a cost function [66]. These most fit solutions are then combined according to a combination function, crossing traits from each solution to create new solutions. Eventually, the best "fit" solution will arise from the convergence of the selected traits of the solutions. Note that genetic algorithms do not generally find the best solution but instead find a solution that is acceptable and will perform adequately for the problem being solved.

The genetic algorithms can be used in the reinforcement learning portion of autonomic systems, the K in the MAPE-K loop [67]. The reinforcement learning is highly desirable for autonomic systems because it is unsupervised, which means that no labeled data is needed to produce a model. Instead, the system learns by evolving through past experience, that is what produced a desirable state versus what produced undesirable states [67]. Thus, combining genetic algorithms with another form of machine learning, for example neural networks, generally increases the performance and accuracy of the system [68]. For example, a genetic algorithm can be used to update the model used in the system that detects and counters against cyberattacks.

Recent research has shown that reinforcement learning, particularly deep learning, does not have to involve massive computing power or specialized GPUs [69]. In [69], the researchers tested several asynchronous methods for reinforcement learning on a single, multi-core processor and showed that they performed as fast, or faster, than running them on a large distributed computing system or GPU clusters. The researchers tested two versions of the Q-learning algorithms, a variant of Sarsa, and asynchronous advantage actor-critic (A3C) algorithm [69]. In Q-learning, agents learn by trying an action and then evaluating that decision based on the reward or penalty incurred [70,71]. The Q-learning algorithm is Markovian based, so the algorithm compares the state it exists in currently with the possible state that an action will produce to determine the possible reward or penalty. The Sarsa algorithm is similar to the Q-leaning algorithm except that it is an on-policy method [72]. The A3C algorithm is based on the actor-critic algorithm, which is an on-policy algorithm that consists of two parts: a critic that evaluates the state that an action produces and the "actor" that maps these values to parameters of the problem being solved [73].

An important part of the implementing reinforcement learning that can be used for prescriptive analytics for cybersecurity applications is the optimization function. There are large variety of optimizers to choose from, such as ADADELTA, ADAGRAD, RMSProp, Adam, SGD, and Bayesian [74–77]. The goal of an optimizer is to find the minimum or maximum of an objective function by updating its parameters. The Bayesian optimization is based on Bayes theorem, where the probability of a future state can be calculated with the knowledge of the prior probability of a state. The ADADELTA is an optimizing function based on stochastic gradient descent, derived from ADAGRAD. ADADELTA works by finding the steepest change in gradient from sampling of local samples, then stepping in that direction, and repeating until the parameters of the function are at optimal values. A big advantage of ADADELTA method is that one does not have to manually tune the learning rate, rather it is computed dynamically for each dimension. The RMSProp function works by following the sign of a gradient, rather than looking at both magnitude and sign, and allows for adjusting step size of weights independently. This helps to avoid getting stuck in plateaus in the gradient and allows for finer and more flexible tuning of the weights.

In recent years, there has been an evolution of many machine learning libraries and frameworks, many of which are free and open-source, that can be used to implement the algorithms described in this chapter. For instance, TensorFlow is a popular library developed by Google with APIs for Python, C++, Java, Go, and even JavaScript [78], which includes both high-level APIs, like Keras, and low-level APIs for advanced uses. Moreover, Python is one of the most popular languages for writing machine leaning systems with many mature libraries available [72]. Some of the more popular libraries are Scikit-learn [79], PyBrain [80], and Pylearn2 [81]. The C++ language, which has more performance capacity than python at the trade-off of having higher development time, has libraries like Shark and dlib-ml for writing machine-learning code [82]. For Java users, there also exists libraries, such as Java-ML [7], Encog [83], and MULAN [84]. Furthermore, the Apache Spark is a widely used data analytic platform that includes the MLlib library for distributed machine learning [85]. The MLlib provides APIs for several popular languages, like Java, Python, and Scala, and provides excellent performance for analyzing large datasets on distributed systems.

The machine learning and optimization tools discussed above can be combined together to build a defense system suitable for securing the HPC environments. Thus, by combining model-based machine learning techniques for monitoring and reacting with reinforcement learning algorithms, the system will be able to not only detect and defend against attacks (predict the attacks) but also improve its performance by learning which actions produce desirable results (prescribe the response actions). With the recent advances in learning algorithms, it is possible to build a system that does not require massive amounts of processing power or specialized equipment [69], which implies that the defense system will not negatively impact the performance of the computing system. This leaves more computing resources for the intended purpose of the system.

4 SUMMARY

Over the last few decades, significant research and development efforts have been explored and implemented in the area of cyberattack tolerant and survivable systems. In general, the efforts in mitigating cyberattacks can be broadly categorized into two categories: to make systems secure against the unintended events and targeted attacks, and to make systems more responsive to initial and subsequent compromise. The current state-of-the-art security solutions majorly fall under the first category focusing on the detection of malicious software before it can execute, which is desirable, but has a less-than-perfect success rate. Furthermore, when security solutions fail to stop the cyberattack, the systems are subject to significant downtime as they are reinstalled, reimaged, or fixed manually. Consequently, when the cyberattacks target the most mission-critical systems, the current cyberdefense systems are generally ineffective at achieving full protection and providing alternative means of continuity of critical operation execution.

With the goal of reducing the downtime of mission-critical HPC systems in presence of cyberattacks, this chapter discusses various predictive and prescriptive analytics techniques/algorithms that when combined effectively will aid in proactively re-architecting the computing system to impede or neutralize malicious attacks and diminish their impact and consequences.

REFERENCES

1. Tariq Mahmood and Uzma Afzal. Security analytics: Big data analytics for cybersecurity: A review of trends, techniques and tools. In *20132nd National Conference on Information Assurance (NCIA)*, pp. 129–134. IEEE, 2013.
2. Hsinchun Chen, Roger HL Chiang, and Veda C Storey. Business intelligence and analytics: From big data to big impact. *MIS Quarterly*, 36(4):1165–1188, 2012.
3. Brad Brown, Michael Chui, and James Manyika. Are you ready for the era of big data. *McKinsey Quarterly*, 4(1):24–35, 2011.
4. David R. Miller, Shon Harris, Allen Harper, Stephen VanDyke, and Chris Blask. *Security Information and Event Management (SIEM) Implementation (Network Pro Library)*. McGraw Hill, 2010.
5. Top 10 SIEM Products, 2018. Accessed = 2018-08-06.
6. Inigo Incer, Michael Theodorides, Sadia Afroz, and David Wagner. Adversarially robust malware detection using monotonic classification. In *Proceedings of the Fourth ACM International Workshop on Security and Privacy Analytics*, pp. 54–63. ACM, 2018.
7. Thomas Abeel, Yves Van de Peer, and Yvan Saeys. Java-ml: A machine learning library. *Journal of Machine Learning Research*, 10(Apr):931–934, 2009.
8. Christopher Oehmen, Elena Peterson, and Scott Dowson. An organic model for detecting cyber-events. In *Proceedings of the Sixth Annual Workshop on Cyber Security and Information Intelligence Research*, p. 66. ACM, 2010.
9. Paul Dokas, Levent Ertoz, Vipin Kumar, Aleksandar Lazarevic, Jaideep Srivastava, and Pang-Ning Tan. Data mining for network intrusion detection. In *Proceedings of NSF Workshop on Next Generation Data Mining*, pp. 21–30, 2002.
10. Ramesh Agarwal and Mahesh V Joshi. Pnrule: A new framework for learning classifier models in data mining (a case-study in network intrusion detection). In *Proceedings of the2001SIAM International Conference on Data Mining*, pp. 1–17. SIAM, 2001.
11. Khaled Alrawashdeh and Carla Purdy. Toward an online anomaly intrusion detection system based on deep learning. In *201615th IEEE International Conference on Machine Learning and Applications (ICMLA)*, pp. 195–200, IEEE, 2016.
12. Simone A. Ludwig. Intrusion detection of multiple attack classes using a deep neural net ensemble. In *2017IEEE Symposium Series on Computational Intelligence (SSCI)*, pp. 1–7. IEEE, 2017.
13. Mohammad A. Faysel and Syed S. Haque. Towards cyber defense: Research in intrusion detection and intrusion prevention systems. *IJCSNS International Journal of Computer Science and Network Security*, 10(7):316–325, 2010.
14. Animesh Patcha and Jung-Min Park. An overview of anomaly detection techniques: Existing solutions and latest technological trends. *Computer Networks*, 51(12):3448–3470, 2007.
15. Jyoti Haweliya and Bhawna Nigam. Network intrusion detection using semi supervised support vector machine. *International Journal of Computer Applications*, 85(9):27–31, 2014.
16. Ugo Fiore, Francesco Palmieri, Aniello Castiglione, and Alfredo De Santis. Network anomaly detection with the restricted boltzmann machine. *Neurocomputing*, 122:13–23, 2013.

17. Adam Coates, Andrew Ng, and Honglak Lee. An analysis of single-layer networks in unsupervised feature learning. In *Proceedings of the Fourteenth International Conference on Artificial Intelligence and Statistics*, pp. 215–223, 2011.

18. Ruslan Salakhutdinov and Hugo Larochelle. Efficient learning of deep boltzmann machines. In *Proceedings of the Thirteenth International Conference on Artificial Intelligence and Statistics*, pp. 693–700, 2010.

19. Wei Wang, Yan Huang, Yizhou Wang, and Liang Wang. Generalized autoencoder: A neural network framework for dimensionality reduction. In *Proceedings of the IEEE Conference on Computer Vision and Pattern Recognition Workshops*, pp. 490–497, 2014.

20. Mahmood Yousefi-Azar, Vijay Varadharajan, Len Hamey, and Uday Tupakula. Autoencoder-based feature learning for cyber security applications. In *2017 International Joint Conference on Neural Networks (IJCNN)*, pp. 3854–3861.IEEE, 2017.

21. Satyajit Yadav and Selvakumar Subramanian. Detection of application layer ddos attack by feature learning using stacked autoencoder. In *2016International Conference on Computational Techniques in Information andCommunicationTechnologies(ICCTICT)*, pp. 361–366. IEEE, 2016.

22. Teodor Sommestad, Mathias Ekstedt, and Pontus Johnson. Cyber security risks assessment with Bayesian defense graphs and architectural models. In *HICSS*, pp. 1–10. IEEE, 1899.

23. Teng Xu, James B. Wendt, and Miodrag Potkonjak. Security of iot systems: Design challenges and opportunities. In *Proceedings of the 2014 IEEE/ACM International Conference on Computer-Aided Design*, pp. 417–423. IEEE Press, 2014.

24. Peng Xie, Jason H. Li, Xinming Ou, Peng Liu, and Renato Levy. Using Bayesian networks for cyber security analysis. In *IEEE/IFIP international conference on Dependable Systems and Networks (DSN), 2010*, pp. 211–220. IEEE, 2010.

25. Judea Pearl. Bayesian networks. 2011.

26. Anna L. Buczak and Erhan Guven. A survey of data mining and machine learning methods for cyber security intrusion detection. *IEEE Communications Surveys & Tutorials*, 18 (2):1153–1176, 2016.

27. Christopher Kruegel, Darren Mutz, William Robertson, and Fredrik Valeur. Bayesian event classification for intrusion detection. In *null*, p. 14. IEEE, 2003.

28. Marek J. Druzdzel. Smile: Structural modeling, inference, and learning engine and genie: A development environment for graphical decision-theoretic models. In *AAAI/IAAI*, pp. 902–903, 1999.

29. Bartosz Jasiul, Marcin Szpyrka, and Joanna Liwa. Detection and modeling of cyber attacks with petri nets. *Entropy*, 16(12):6602–6623, 2014.

30. Tadao Murata. Petri nets: Properties, analysis and applications. *Proceedings of the IEEE*, 77 (4):541–580, 1989.

31. Michael K. Molloy. Performance analysis using stochastic petri nets. *IEEE Transactions on Computers*, 31(9):913–917, 1982.

32. Guy Helmer, Johnny Wong, Mark Slagell, Vasant Honavar, Les Miller, Yanxin Wang, Xia Wang, and Natalia Stakhanova. Software fault tree and coloured petri net–based specification, design and implementation of agent-based intrusion detection systems. *International Journal of Information and Computer Security*, 1(1–2):109–142, 2007.

33. Guy Helmer, Johnny SK Wong, Vasant Honavar, and Les Miller. Automated discovery of concise predictive rules for intrusion detection. *Journal of Systems and Software*, 60 (3):165–175, 2002.

34. Guy Helmer, Johnny SK Wong, Vasant Honavar, Les Miller, and Yanxin Wang. Lightweight agents for intrusion detection. *Journal of systems and Software*, 67(2):109–122, 2003.

35. Anna Sperotto, Ramin Sadre, Pieter-Tjerk de Boer, and Aiko Pras. Hidden markov model modeling of SSH brute-force attacks. In *International Workshop on Distributed Systems: Operations and Management*, pp. 164–176. Springer, 2009.

36. Yoshua Bengio. Markovian models for sequential data. *Neural Computing Surveys*, 2 (199):129–162, 1999.

37. Davide Ariu, Roberto Tronci, and Giorgio Giacinto. Hmmpayl: An intrusion detection system based on hidden Markov models. *Computers &Security*, 30(4):221–241, 2011.

38. Shailendra Singh and Sanjay Silakari. A survey of cyber attack detection systems. *International Journal of Computer Science and Network Security*, 9(5):1–10, 2009.

39. Saman Taghavi Zargar, James Joshi, and David Tipper. A survey of defense mechanisms against distributed denial of service (DDoS) flooding attacks. *IEEE Communications Surveys & Tutorials*, 15(4):2046–2069, 2013.

40. Bingrui Foo, Matthew W. Glause, Gaspar M. Howard, Yu-Sung Wu, Saurabh Bagchi, and Eugene H. Spafford. Intrusion response systems: A survey. *Information Assurance: Dependability and Security in Networked Systems. Morgan Kaufmann, Burlington*, pp. 377–412, Elsevier, 2008.

41. Erik Miehling, Mohammad Rasouli, and Demosthenis Teneketzis. A pomdp approach to the dynamic defense of large-scale cyber networks. *IEEE Transactions on Information Forensics and Security*, 13(10):2490–2505, 2018.

42. Ivan Balepin, Sergei Maltsev, Jeff Rowe, and Karl Levitt. Using specification-based intrusion detection for automated response. In *International Workshop on Recent Advances in Intrusion Detection*, pp. 136–154. Springer, 2003.

43. Thomas Toth and Christopher Kruegel. Evaluating the impact of automated intrusion response mechanisms. In *Proceedings of the 18th Annual Computer Security Applications Conference, 2002*, pp. 301–310. IEEE, 2002.

44. Bingrui Foo, Yu-Sung Wu, Yu-Chun Mao, Saurabh Bagchi, and Eugene Spafford. ADEPTS: Adaptive intrusion response using attack graphs in an e-commerce environment. In *International Conference on Dependable Systems and Networks, 2005. DSN 2005. Proceedings.*pp. 508–517. IEEE, 2005.

45. Natalia Stakhanova, Samik Basu, and Johnny Wong. A cost-sensitive model for preemptive intrusion response systems. *AINA*, 7:428–435, 2007.

46. Boutheina A. Fessi, Salah Benabdallah, Noureddine Boudriga, and Mohamed Hamdi. A multi-attribute decision model for intrusion response system. *Information Sciences*, 270:237–254, 2014.

47. Chengpo Mu and Yingjiu Li.An intrusion response decision-making model based on hierarchical task network planning. *Expert Systems with Applications*, 37(3):2465–2472, 2010.

48. Xin Zan, Feng Gao, Jiuqiang Han, Xiaoyong Liu, and Jiaping Zhou. A hierarchical and factored POMDP based automated intrusion response framework. In *20102nd International Conference on Software Technology and Engineering (ICSTE)*, volume 2, pp. V2–410. IEEE, 2010.

49. Erik Miehling, Mohammad Rasouli, and Demosthenis Teneketzis. Optimal defense policies for partially observable spreading processes on Bayesian attack graphs. In *Proceedings of the Second ACM Workshop on Moving Target Defense*, pp. 67–76. ACM, 2015.

50. Stefan Seufert and Darragh O'Brien. Machine learning for automatic defence against distributed denial of service attacks. In *IEEE International Conference on Communications, 2007. ICC'07*, pp. 1217–1222. IEEE, 2007.

51. Josep L. Berral, Nicolas Poggi, Javier Alonso, Ricard Gavalda, Jordi Torres, and Manish Parashar. Adaptive distributed mechanism against flooding network attacks based

on machine learning. In *Proceedings of the 1st ACM Workshop on Workshop on AISec*, pp. 43–50. ACM, 2008.

52. Manjula Suresh and R Anitha. Evaluating machine learning algorithms for detecting ddos attacks. In *International Conference on Network Security and Applications*, pp. 441–452. Springer, 2011.

53. Muhammad Aamir and Mustafa Ali Zaidi. A survey on DDoS attack and defense strategies: From traditional schemes to current techniques. *Interdisciplinary Information Sciences*, 19(2):173–200, 2013.

54. Hema Raghavan, Omid Madani, and Rosie Jones. Active learning with feedback on features and instances. *Journal of Machine Learning Research*, 7(Aug):1655–1686, 2006.

55. Markus C. Huebscher and Julie A McCann. A survey of autonomic computingdegrees, models, and applications. *ACM Computing Surveys (CSUR)*, 40(3):7, 2008.

56. Paul Barford, Marc Dacier, Thomas G. Dietterich, Matt Fredrikson, Jon Giffin, Sushil Jajodia, Somesh Jha, Jason Li, Peng Liu, Peng Ning, et al. Cyber sa: Situational awareness for cyber defense. In *Cyber Situational Awareness*, pp. 3–13. Springer, 2010.

57. Didac Gil De La Iglesia and Danny Weyns. Mape-k formal templates to rigorously design behaviors for self-adaptive systems. *ACM Transactions on Autonomous and Adaptive Systems (TAAS)*, 10(3):15, 2015.

58. Paolo Arcaini, Elvinia Riccobene, and Patrizia Scandurra. Modeling and analyzing mape-k feedback loops for self-adaptation. In *Proceedings of the 10th international Symposium on Software Engineering for Adaptive and Self-managing Systems*, pp. 13–23. IEEE Press, 2015.

59. Eric Rutten, Nicolas Marchand, and Daniel Simon. Feedback control as mape-k loop in autonomic computing. In *Software Engineering for Self-Adaptive Systems III. Assurances*, pp. 349–373. Springer, 2017.

60. Naeem Esfahani, Ehsan Kouroshfar, and Sam Malek. Taming uncertainty in self-adaptive software. In *Proceedings of the 19th ACM SIGSOFT Symposium and the 13th European Conference on Foundations of Software Engineering*, pp. 234–244. ACM, 2011.

61. Edson Manoel, Morten Jul Nielson, Abdi Salahshour, Sai Sampath Kvl, and Sanjeev Sudarshanan. *Problem Determination UsingSelf-Managing Autonomic Technology*. IBM International Technical Support Organization, 2005.

62. Joseph P. Bigus, Don A. Schlosnagle, Jeff R. Pilgrim, WNathaniel Mills III, and Yixin Diao. Able: A toolkit for building multiagent autonomic systems. *IBM Systems Journal*, 41(3):350–371, 2002.

63. Andres J. Ramirez, David B. Knoester, Betty HC. Cheng, and Philip K. McKinley. Plato: A genetic algorithm approach to run-time reconfiguration in autonomic computing systems. *Cluster Computing*, 14(3):229–244, 2011.

64. Martina Maggio, Henry Hoffmann, Alessandro V. Papadopoulos, Jacopo Panerati, Marco D. Santambrogio, Anant Agarwal, and Alberto Leva. Comparison of decision-making strategies for self-optimization in autonomic computing systems. *ACM Transactions on Autonomous and Adaptive Systems (TAAS)*, 7(4):36, 2012.

65. Christine M. Anderson-Cook. Practical genetic algorithms, 2005.

66. John E. Galletly. An overview of genetic algorithms. *Kybernetes*, 21(6):26–30, 1992.

67. David E. Moriarty, Alan C. Schultz, and John J. Grefenstette. Evolutionary algorithms for reinforcement learning. *Journal of Artificial Intelligence Research*, 11:241–276, 1999.

68. Marco A. Wiering and Hado Van Hasselt. Ensemble algorithms in reinforcement learning. *IEEE Transactions on Systems, Man, and Cybernetics, Part B (Cybernetics)*, 38(4):930–936, 2008.

69. Volodymyr Mnih, Adria Puigdomenech Badia, Mehdi Mirza, Alex Graves, Timothy Lillicrap, Tim Harley, David Silver, and Koray Kavukcuoglu. Asynchronous methods for deep reinforcement learning. In *International Conference on Machine Learning*, pp. 1928–1937, 2016.

70. Christopher JCH Watkins and Peter Dayan. Q-learning. *Machine Learning*, 8(3–4):279–292, 1992.

71. Hado Van Hasselt, Arthur Guez, and David Silver. Deep reinforcement learning with double q-learning. In *AAAI*, volume 2, p. 5. Phoenix, AZ, 2016.

72. Marco A. Wiering and Hado Van Hasselt. Two novel on-policy reinforcement learning algorithms based on td ()-methods. In *IEEE International Symposium on Approximate Dynamic Programming and Reinforcement Learning, 2007.ADPRL 2007*, pp. 280–287. IEEE, 2007.

73. Vijay R. Konda and John N. Tsitsiklis. Actor-critic algorithms. In *Advances in Neural Information Processing Systems*, pp. 1008–1014, 2000.

74. Matthew D. Zeiler. Adadelta: An adaptive learning rate method. *arXiv preprint arXiv:1212.5701*, 2012.

75. Mahesh Chandra Mukkamala and Matthias Hein. Variants of rmsprop and adagrad with logarithmic regret bounds. *arXiv preprint arXiv:1706.05507*, 2017.

76. Diederik P. Kingma and Jimmy Ba. Adam: A method for stochastic optimization. *arXiv preprint arXiv:1412.6980*, 2014.

77. Eric Brochu, Vlad M. Cora, and Nando De Freitas. A tutorial on bayesian optimization of expensive cost functions, with application to active user modeling and hierarchical reinforcement learning. *arXiv preprint arXiv:1012.2599*, 2010.

78. Martn Abadi, Paul Barham, Jianmin Chen, Zhifeng Chen, Andy Davis, Jeffrey Dean, Matthieu Devin, Sanjay Ghemawat, Geoffrey Irving, Michael Isard, et al. Tensorflow: A system for large-scale machine learning. *OSDI*, 16:265–283, 2016.

79. Fabian Pedregosa, Gaël Varoquaux, Alexandre Gramfort, Vincent Michel, Bertrand Thirion, Olivier Grisel, Mathieu Blondel, Peter Prettenhofer, Ron Weiss, Vincent Dubourg, et al. Scikit-learn: Machine learning in python. *Journal of Machine Learning Research*, 12(Oct):2825–2830, 2011.

80. Tom Schaul, Justin Bayer, Daan Wierstra, Yi Sun, Martin Felder, Frank Sehnke, Thomas Rckstie, and Jrgen Schmidhuber. Pybrain. *Journal of Machine Learning Research*, 11(Feb):743–746, 2010.

81. Ian J. Goodfellow, David Warde-Farley, Pascal Lamblin, Vincent Dumoulin, Mehdi Mirza, Razvan Pascanu, James Bergstra, Frédéric Bastien, and Yoshua Bengio. Pylearn2: A machine learning research library. *arXiv preprint arXiv:1308.4214*, 2013.

82. Davis E. King. Dlib-ml: A machine learning toolkit. *Journal of Machine Learning Research*, 10(Jul):1755–1758, 2009.

83. Jeff Heaton. Encog: Library of interchangeable machine learning models for java and c#. *Journal of Machine Learning Research*, 16:1243–1247, 2015.

84. Grigorios Tsoumakas, Eleftherios Spyromitros-Xioufis, Jozef Vilcek, and Ioannis Vlahavas. Mulan: A java library for multi-label learning. *Journal of Machine Learning Research*, 12(Jul):2411–2414, 2011.

85. Xiangrui Meng, Joseph Bradley, Burak Yavuz, Evan Sparks, Shivaram Venkataraman, Davies Liu, Jeremy Freeman, DB Tsai, Manish Amde, Sean Owen, et al. Mllib: Machine learning in apache spark. *The Journal of Machine Learning Research*, 17(1):1235–1241, 2016.

Multivariate Projection Techniques to Reduce Dimensionality in Large Datasets

I. Barranco-Chamorro

Department of Statistics and Operations Research, University of Sevilla, Sevilla (Spain)

S. Muñoz-Armayones

Datrik Intelligence, Sevilla (Spain)

A. Romero-Losada and F. Romero-Campero

Department of Computer Science and Artificial Intelligence, University of Sevilla, Sevilla (Spain)

Plant Development Unit Institute for Plant Biochemistry and Photosynthesis, Sevilla (Spain)

CONTENTS

1 INTRODUCTION

Constant development of technology in our era results in an increasing generation of a considerable amount of data. As a consequence, the development of mathematical tools to analyse large datasets is required. In this context, one of the main challenges is to find techniques able to reduce complexity and to extract relevant and quality information from these big datasets.

In general, large and high-dimensional datasets comprise variables measured on categorical, discrete, or continuous scales, and possibly a mixture of these. This point is crucial and must be taken into account in order to apply an appropriate projection method. Keeping this in mind, in this paper, we focus on multivariate projection methods, such as Principal Component Analysis (PCA), Correspondence Analysis (CA), and Canonical Correlation Analysis (CCA). All of them can be used as descriptive and exploratory tools to deal with high-dimensional datasets. Applications to real omic datasets are carried out by using R packages from Bioconductor. The outline of this chapter is, after an explanation of omics data in Section 2, the basis of PCA, CA, and CCA are given in Sections 3–6, respectively. Each technique is described and practical applications are carried out. Methods and results are explained in detail.

Moreover, in order to illustrate the use of methodologies presented in this chapter, an interactive web page based on the R package shinyR is included as supplementary material. In this page, an application of PCA is given. Researchers and students interested in the application of this multivariate projection technique to reduce dimensionality in large omics datasets will be able to change key parameters and observe the effect over the results.

2 OMICS DATA

Recently, several methodologies have been developed to enable molecular biologists to detect and quantify the molecules from a sample with a high sensibility and specificity. This has led to the development of the so-called omics. These techniques can provide scientists with a snapshot of the current molecular state of a sample. Specifically, transcriptomics provides an accurate estimation of the number of transcripts produced by a gene in a sample, how genes are expressed is measured in this way. Nevertheless, huge amounts of data are generated that need to be analysed in order to extract relevant information, making omics data an ideal field for the application of multivariate projection techniques to reduce dimensionality in large datasets.

The boom of this kind of biological data is due to the outstanding technological development in our era. High-throughput technologies are generating increasingly massive and complex omics datasets in laboratories all around the world. Data from large-scale studies have been deposited in public repositories. So, there exists an increasing need of tools to store and analyse these datasets. Fortunately, the parallel development of powerful algorithmic techniques led to computational advances that allow us to deal with this kind of data. Therefore, the development of this type of techniques mainly serves two areas: one is the the analysis of omics data helps scientists to answer important biomedical and biological issues, and the other is that it is useful for data analysts. From the statistical point of view, the main challenge is to develop techniques to deal with a very large number of variables and a really small sample size.

3 PRINCIPAL COMPONENT ANALYSIS

PCA is a multivariate analysis technique that was introduced by Pearson in 1901, and developed by Hotelling in 1933. PCA is useful to visualize clusters and outliers in multivariate data. Nowdays, it is one of the main techniques used to reduce the dimensionality of a large multivariate dataset. In this paper, the theoretical foundations of this technique will be briefly described along with applications of practical interest (mainly in the field of Biomedicine). First, the problem we face will be introduced, that is, given a set of observations of continuous and possibly correlated variables, we aim to reduce the dimensionality of the given dataset through linear combinations of the original variables. Explicitly, given a p-dimensional random vector of continuous random variables $\underline{X} = (X_1, \ldots, X_p)'$, it is assumed that there exist $\underline{\mu}$ (the mean vector) and Σ (the covariance matrix). The method aims to express the variability of the original variables $\underline{X} = (X_1, \ldots, X_p)$ in decreasing order of importance by using $\underline{Y} = (Y_1, \ldots, Y_p)$, where Y_j's are *linear combinations* of $X_1, \ldots, X_p$, and called the *j*th principal component (PC) of $\underline{X}$.

3.1 Method

Applying PCA is a multivariate analysis method that allows us to obtain a set of new variables, called PCs which are linear combinations of the original variables and are uncorrelated. The PCs are defined in such a way that, the so-called first PC explains as much as possible of the variability in our original data, and each succeeding PC has the highest variance possible under the constraint that it must be orthogonal to all the preceding components. In this way, the resulting PCs form an uncorrelated orthogonal basis. The main uses of PCA are as follows:

1. *To reduce the dimensionality* when dealing with a large number of continuous variables. This application makes sense when a few of the first PCs explain a large proportion of the variability in our data. Criteria to choose the number of components to keep in our analysis will be given (percentage criterion and Kaiser's criterion, among others).

2. *As a tool in exploratory data analysis*. This application is based on the fact that PCA provides an orthogonal transformation of the original variables. Therefore, the distance between original and transformed data are preserved, that is

$$d^2(\underline{x}_h, \underline{x}_j) = d^2(\underline{y}_h, \underline{y}_j),$$

where $\underline{x}_j$ denotes the original values observed for the $j - th$ individual and $\underline{y}_j$ denotes the *scores* (i.e., the sample values of the PCs) for the $j - th$ individual. By exploiting this property, PCA technique is really useful to recognize clusters and identify outliers in high-dimensional data.

3. To *deal with the problem of collinearity in linear regression*. This application is based on the fact that PCs are orthogonal. So, they can be used as predictors in linear regression if such a problem exists.

Next, notation and the theoretical foundations of this technique are introduced.

Notation. Given a continuous random vector $\underline{X} = (X_1, \ldots, X_p)'$. Let us assume that there exist μ and Σ. Recall that the mean vector of $\underline{X}$ is given by $\underline{\mu} = E(\underline{X}) = (\mu_1, \ldots, \mu_p)'$ and the covariance matrix of $\underline{X}$ is given by

$$\sum = Cov(\underline{X}) = \begin{pmatrix} \sigma_{11} & \cdots & \sigma_{1p} \\ \vdots & \ddots & \vdots \\ \sigma_{p1} & \cdots & \sigma_{pp} \end{pmatrix}$$

where $\sigma_{ij} = Cov(X_i, X_j) = E((X_i - \mu_i)(X_j - \mu_j))$, $i \neq j$, and $\sigma_{ii} = Cov(X_i, X_i) = Var(X_i)$. This situation will be denoted as $\underline{X} \sim (\underline{\mu}, \Sigma)$.

Principal Components. The jth PC, Y_j, is an *appropriate linear combination* of the original variables, $(X_1, \ldots, X_p)$, that is

$$Y_j = t_{j1}X_1 + \ldots + t_{jp}X_p, \qquad t_{ji} \in \mathbb{R}$$

or equivalently, by using vectorial notation $Y_j = \underline{t}_j'\underline{X}$ where $\underline{t}_j' = (t_{j1}, \ldots t_{jp})'$ and $\underline{X} = (X_1, \ldots, X_p)'$.

Properties of linear transformations of variables are the basis to study PCs. They are listed below.

Properties. Let $\underline{X} \sim (\underline{\mu}, \Sigma)$ and $Y_j = \underline{t}_j'\underline{X}$. Then,

1. $E(Y_j) = \underline{t}_j'\underline{\mu}$ since $E(Y_j) = E(\underline{t}_j'\underline{X}) = \underline{t}_j'\underline{\mu}$.

2. $Var(Y_j) = \underline{t}_j'\Sigma\underline{t}_j$ since $Var(Y_j) = Var(\underline{t}_j'\underline{X}) = \underline{t}_j'\Sigma\underline{t}_j$.

3. Covariance between Y_i and Y_j is $Cov(Y_i, Y_j) = \underline{t}_i'\Sigma\underline{t}_j$ since $Cov(Y_i, Y_j) = Cov(\underline{t}_i'\underline{X}, \underline{t}_j'\underline{X}) = \underline{t}_i'Cov(\underline{X}, \underline{X})\underline{t}_j = \underline{t}_i'Var(\underline{X})\underline{t}_j = \underline{t}_i'\Sigma\underline{t}_j$.

Properties of the covariance matrix. We highlight that Σ is a $p \times p$ symmetric and semidefinite positive matrix. Since Σ is a *symmetric matrix*, the Jordan decomposition theorem (or spectral theorem) can be applied. This theorem provides us a representation of a symmetric matrix in terms of its eigenvalues and eigenvectors. The *eigenvectors belonging to the largest eigenvalues* indicate the *main directions* of the data. Since Σ is symmetrical and positive semi-definite, their eigenvalues are real and positive

$$\lambda_1 \geq \lambda_2 \ldots \geq \lambda_p \geq 0.$$

Let $\underline{e}_i$ the unit eigenvector, $\| \underline{e}_i \|^2 = 1$, associated to λ_i. The eigenvectors are orthogonal, i.e.,

$$\underline{e}'_i \underline{e}_j = 0, \quad for \quad i \neq j .$$

Let $\mathbf{E}$ be the matrix whose columns are $\underline{e}_i$, $\mathbf{E}_{p \times p} = [\underline{e}_1, \underline{e}_2, \dots, \underline{e}_p]$. The matrix $\mathbf{E}$ is orthogonal

$$\mathbf{E}'\mathbf{E} = \mathbf{E}\mathbf{E}' = I_p$$

By applying Jordan decomposition theorem to Σ we have the next results.

Theorem (Spectral decomposition theorem). Under previous conditions,

$$\Sigma = \mathbf{E}\Lambda\mathbf{E}' = \sum_{i=1}^{p} \lambda_i \underline{e}_i \underline{e}'_i$$

where $\Lambda = diag\{\lambda_1, \lambda_2, \dots, \lambda_p\}$ with λ_i the eigenvalues of Σ and $\mathbf{E}_{p \times p} = [\underline{e}_1, \underline{e}_2, \dots, \underline{e}_p]$ is an orthogonal matrix consisting of the eigenvectors of Σ. Moreover,

1. $\mathbf{E}'\Sigma\mathbf{E} = \Lambda = diag\{\lambda_1, \lambda_2, \dots, \lambda_p\}$.
2. $Trace(\Sigma) = Trace(\Lambda) = \sum_{j=1}^{p} \lambda_j$.

Calculus of PCs. The first PC is $Y_1 = t_{11}X_1 + \dots + t_{1p}X_p$, with $t_{1i} \in \mathbb{R}$ such as $Var[Y_1] = \underline{t}'_1 \Sigma \underline{t}_1$ is maximum. Since $Var[Y_1]$ increases with $\underline{t}'_1$, we impose the restriction $\underline{t}'_1 \underline{t}_1 = 1$. Therefore, the problem is to obtain $\underline{t}_1 = (t_{11}, \dots, t_{1p})'$ such that

$$max(\underline{t}'_1 \Sigma \underline{t}_1)$$
$$s.a. : \underline{t}'_1 \underline{t}_1 = 1$$

By applying Lagrange multipliers method, $\underline{t}_1$ is the eigenvector (of norm unit) corresponding to the largest eigenvalue λ_1 of the covariance matrix Σ. Note that $Var[Y_1] = \lambda_1$.

As for the second PC, $Y_2 = t_{21}X_1 + \dots + t_{2p}X_p$, $t_{2i} \in \mathbb{R}$ is such that Y_2 must capture the majority of variance in our data not captured by Y_1. Then, Y_2 must be *uncorrelated* to Y_1, i.e., $Cov(Y_2, Y_1) = Cov(\underline{t}'_2 \underline{X}, \underline{t}'_1 \underline{X}) = \underline{t}'_2 \Sigma \underline{t}_1 = 0$. So, the problem is to obtain $\underline{t}_2 = (t_{21}, \dots, t_{2p})'$ such that

$$max(\underline{t}'_2 \Sigma \underline{t}_2)$$
$$s.a. : \underline{t}'_2 \underline{t}_2 = 1$$
$$\underline{t}'_2 \Sigma \underline{t}_1 = 0$$

$\underline{t}_2$ is the eigenvector (of norm unit) corresponding to the largest second eigenvalue λ_2 of the covariance matrix Σ. Similarly, the ith-CP, Y_i, is the (normalized) linear combination of maximum variance uncorrelated to $Y_1, \ldots, Y_{i-1}$, i.e.,

$$\sigma^2_{y_i} = \sup_{\{\underline{t} \in \mathbb{R}^i \,:\, \underline{t}'\underline{t}=1, \underline{t}'\Sigma\underline{e}_s=0 \; s=1,\ldots,i-1\}} \sigma^2_{\underline{t}'\underline{x}} \qquad i = 1, \ldots, p \tag{1}$$

Properties of CPs.

1. $Var[Y_j] = \lambda_j$.

2. The PCs are uncorrelated.

3. From $\lambda_1 \geq \ldots \geq \lambda_p$ it follows that $Var[Y_1] \geq \ldots \geq Var[Y_p]$.

4. We have that

$$\sum_{j=1}^{p} Var[Y_j] = Trace(\Sigma) = \sum_{j=1}^{p} \lambda_j$$

So, the *proportion of the variability* in our data *explained by* the PC, Y_i, is

$$\frac{\lambda_i}{\sum_{s=1}^{p} \lambda_s}$$

5. The proportion of the variability in our data not explained by the k first PCs is

$$\frac{\sum_{i=k+1}^{p} \lambda_i}{\sum_{s=1}^{p} \lambda_s}$$

Sample features. Given a p-dimensional random vector of continuous random variables $\underline{X} = (X_1, \ldots, X_p)'$ whose μ and Σ exist, and a simple random sample of size n from $\underline{X}$. Let us denote this sample as follows:

$$\mathbf{X} = \begin{pmatrix} x_{11} & \cdots & x_{1p} \\ \vdots & \ddots & \vdots \\ x_{n1} & \cdots & x_{np} \end{pmatrix} = \begin{pmatrix} \underline{x}_1 \\ \vdots \\ \underline{x}_n \end{pmatrix} = \left(\underline{x}_{(1)}, \cdots, \underline{x}_{(p)} \right).$$

X is a $n \times p$ matrix where the jth column $\underline{x}_{(j)}$ is a $n \times 1$ vector which contains the sample of size n from the random variable $X_j, j = 1, \ldots, p$. The ith row contains the observations of $(X_1, \ldots, X_p)$ for the ith sample unit. So, the rows $\underline{x}_1, \ldots, \underline{x}_n$ are a simple random sample of size n from the vector $\underline{X} = (X_1, \ldots, X_p)'$.

In practice, the PC technique should be applied by replacing the population features by their respective estimators. That is, $\underline{\mu}$ should be replaced by the vector with the sample means, $\mathbf{\Sigma}$ by its $\widehat{\mathbf{\Sigma}}$, and so on.

Standarization. The PC technique is sensitive to scale changes. If we multiply one variable by a scalar, we obtain different eigenvalues and eigenvectors. This is due to the fact that an eigenvalue decomposition is performed on the covariance matrix and not on the correlation matrix. The PC technique should be applied to data that have approximately the same scale in each variable. Then, it is better to work with the *standardized data*, which is equivalent to work with the correlation matrix. So, in practice, we should consider the matrix containing the standardized data

$$X_{(s)} = \begin{pmatrix} \frac{x_{11}-\bar{x}_1}{\hat{\sigma}_1} & \cdots & \frac{x_{1p}-\bar{x}_p}{\hat{\sigma}_p} \\ \vdots & & \vdots \\ \frac{x_{n1}-\bar{x}_1}{\hat{\sigma}_1} & \cdots & \frac{x_{np}-\bar{x}_p}{\hat{\sigma}_p} \end{pmatrix}.$$

Choosing the number of PCs. Usual criteria are based on scree plots (plots for the eigenvalues). We can cite the following ones: cumulative percentage greater than a threshold; to choose those eigenvectors whose eigenvalues are greater than the mean (if PC is based on the correlation matrix, then they would be those greater than 1); to look at plot of eigenvalues (we see from eigenvalues in which we have similar values on this plot); by applying hypotheses tests to take a decision (multivariate normality should be assumed in this case), etc. In practice, they can differ a little.

Relations between the original variables and PCs. We highlight that

$$Cov(\underline{X}, \underline{Y}) = \mathbf{\Sigma E} = \mathbf{E \Lambda E' E} = \mathbf{E \Lambda}.$$

Therefore, the linear correlation coefficient between X_i and Y_j, ρ_{X_i, Y_j}, is

$$\rho_{X_i, Y_j} = \frac{\sqrt{\lambda_j} e_{ji}}{\sigma_i}.$$

It is verified that

$$\sum_{j=1}^{p} \rho_{X_i,Y_j}^2 = \frac{\sum_{j=1}^{p} \lambda_j e_{ij}^2}{\sigma_i^2} = \frac{\sigma_i^2}{\sigma_i^2} = 1.$$

Correlation circle. This plot is based on previous properties and it is useful to visualize relationships betweeen the original variables and the PCs., if PCs are based on the matrix correlation, then the sample linear correlation coefficient between the original variables, X_i and the jth PC, Y_j, r_{X_i,Y_j}, is

$$r_{X_i,Y_j} = \hat{e}_{ij}\sqrt{\hat{\lambda}_j}$$

This is the basis of the correlation circle, useful to identify the original variables more correlated to the first and second PCs. The correlation circle is a plot of r_{X_i,Y_1} versus r_{X_i,Y_2}. This plot shows which of the original variables are most strongly correlated with the PCs, namely those that are close to the periphery of the circle of radius 1. (It can be applied to any pair of PCs, not necessarily Y_1, Y_2).

Next, practical illustrations of PCA are given by using R packages from Bioconductor. Two real datasets are considered.

3.2 Application: PCA as a Tool to Detect Batch Effect

Batch effect is one of the most serious problems when dealing with omic data. PCA can be used as a exploratory tool to visualize data and carry out tests to detect this problem. In this section, breastCancer dataset is considered.

Dataset description. breastCancer dataset consists of 16 samples and 12,630 gene expression levels. It is available at GEO (Gene Expression Omnibus) database. Three factors are also included: Treatment, Time, and Batch (A or B).

FactoMine R package. FactoMine is an R package devoted to multivariate Exploratory Data Analysis. It is developed and maintained by Francois Husson, Julie Josse, Sébastien Le, d' Agrocampus Rennes, and J. Mazet. It performs PCA, CA, Multiple Correspondence Analysis (MCA), and other advanced methods. The latest news about this package can be found on http://factominer.free.fr/install.html.

Other packages of interest that can be installed jointly with FactoMineR are: Factoshiny to have a graphical interface that draws graph interactively, missMDA to handle missing values, and FactoInvestigate to obtain automatic description of your analyses.

Analysis and visualization of results.
First, the data file must be read.

```
>   bcData<-   read.table("Breast_Cancer.txt",   header=T,sep="\t",
dec=".", row.names=1)
> class(bcData)
[1] "data.frame"
> dim(bcData)
[1]    18 12630
```

Rownames are shortened in order to facilitate the reading of results.

```
> rownames(bcData)<- substr(rownames(bcData),4,8)
```

The two first rows are eliminated because they are control data. Therefore, the data frame dimensions we analyse are 16 ×12,630. We see the variables and define as factors Treatment, Time, and Batch. Their basic summaries are also obtained.

```
> bcData<- bcData[-(1:2),]
> head(names(bcData))
[1] "Treatment"                "Time"        "Batch"
[4] "Treatment.Combination" "X100_g_at"   "X101_at"
> for(i in 1:3) bcData[,i]<- as.factor(bcData[,i])

> summary(bcData$Treatment)
Control   E2   E2+ICI   E2+Ral   E2+TOT
      0    4        4        4        4
> summary(bcData$Time)
8    48
8     8
> summary(bcData$Batch)
A    B
8    8
```

PCA is applied. Only the most relevant results are shown for cases and variables.

```
> res.pca = PCA(bcData[,-4], quali.sup=1:3, graph=F)
> summary(res.pca)


Call:
PCA(X = bcData[, -4], quali.sup = 1:3, graph = F)


Eigenvalues
                     Dim.1       Dim.2       Dim.3 ............     Dim.15
Variance          2145.250    1426.411    1249.825 ............    452.176
% of var.           17.026      11.321       9.919 ............      3.589
Cumulative % of var 17.026      28.347      38.266 ............    100.000


Individuals (the 3 first)
                Dist    Dim.1   ctr    cos2    Dim.2    ctr    cos2
13099       | 124.565 | 60.994 10.839 0.240 | 10.537  0.486  0.007 |
13138       | 116.159 |-41.266  4.961 0.126 |-59.426 15.473  0.262 |
13139       | 133.028 | 89.899 23.545 0.457 |-57.436 14.454  0.186 |
```

	Dim.3	ctr	cos2
13099	-20.336	2.068	0.027 |
13138	-32.974	5.437	0.081 |
13139	-21.334	2.276	0.026 |

Variables (the 3 first)

	Dim.1	ctr	cos2	Dim.2	ctr	cos2	Dim.3	ctr
X100_g_at	| 0.364	0.006	0.132 |	-0.018	0.000	0.000 |	-0.343	0.009
X101_at	| -0.199	0.002	0.040 |	-0.459	0.015	0.210 |	0.286	0.007
X102_at	| 0.768	0.027	0.589 |	0.004	0.000	0.000 |	-0.182	0.003

	cos2
X100_g_at	0.118 |
X101_at	0.082 |
X102_at	0.033 |

Supplementary categories

	Dist	Dim.1	cos2	v.test	Dim.2	cos2	v.test
E2	| 63.713 |	24.946	0.153	1.204 |	-47.038	0.545	-2.785 |
E2+ICI	| 54.156 |	-28.200	0.271	-1.361 |	21.910	0.164	1.297 |
E2+Ral	| 51.475 |	-7.199	0.020	-0.348 |	15.105	0.086	0.894 |
E2+TOT	| 49.558 |	10.452	0.044	0.505 |	10.023	0.041	0.593 |
Time 8	| 33.218 |	-17.948	0.292	-1.501 |	10.387	0.098	1.065 |
Time 48	| 33.218 |	17.948	0.292	1.501 |	-10.387	0.098	-1.065 |
A	| 41.098 |	31.590	0.591	2.642 |	19.788	0.232	2.029 |
B	| 41.098 |	-31.590	0.591	-2.642 |	-19.788	0.232	-2.029 |

	Dim.3	cos2	v.test
E2	-25.005	0.154	-1.582 |
E2+ICI	-12.736	0.055	-0.806 |
E2+Ral	15.188	0.087	0.961 |
E2+TOT	22.553	0.207	1.426 |
Time 8	-12.985	0.153	-1.423 |
Time 48	12.985	0.153	1.423 |
A	-16.493	0.161	-1.807 |
B	16.493	0.161	1.807 |

1.0 -0.343 0.009

We see that the three first PCs explain 38.266% of variability in our data. Results for individuals and variables are given. Analysis of the supplementaries categories for the first PCs, their correlation, and a normality test ("v.test") are included. In v.test, *batch* is the grouping factor. The confidence ellipses, given in Figure 7.1, are based on this summary and can be obtained as follows.

```
> aa=cbind.data.frame(bcData[,3],res.pca$ind$coord)
> bb=coord.ellipse(aa, bary=TRUE)
> plot.PCA(res.pca, habillage=3, ellipse=bb)
```

In Figure 7.1, we distinguish between samples processed in batch A (black color) or B (red color). Ellipses in this plot do not overlap. This suggests the existence of batch effect in this dataset.

3.3 Application in Algae

In this example, PCA is applied to explore previously published microarray data generated from the microalgae *Ostreococcus tauri* over a complete cycle comprising 24 hours; details can be seen in Monnier et al. [1]. The microalgae were cultivated during 24 hours cycles comprising 12 hours of light simulating the day and 12 hours of dark simulating the night. Samples were collected every three hours starting at the time point known as ZT0 when lights are switch on simulating dawn. The time point ZT12 represents dusk when the lights are switch off. Day time points consist of ZT3, ZT6, and ZT9 and night time points correspond to ZT15, ZT18, and ZT21. For each time point, three independent biological replicates were taken. After pre-processing of microarray data and differential expression analysis, each time point replicate consists

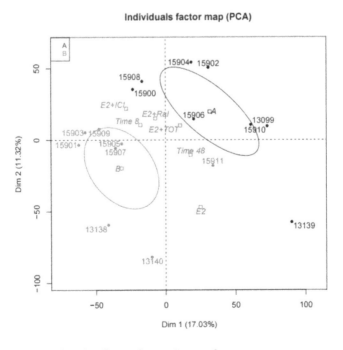

FIGURE 7.1   PCA to detect batch effect in breastCancer dataset

of 4458 gene expression values. Therefore, our input data matrix has 24 rows (8 time points times 3 biological replicates) and 4458 columns (differentially expressed genes).

In Figure 7.2, the hierarchical clustering, scree plot, PCA map, and PCA plot with confidence ellipses are given. From them, we observe that, after data rotation, the first two components are explained over 80% of the total variance, whereas the rest of the components only contribute marginally. Therefore, we only kept these two first components in the projection. Representing the data after rotation and projection revealed that the different time point replicates cluster together and that different time points assemble themselves in a circle like structure resembling a clock. This provides evidence of good data quality and

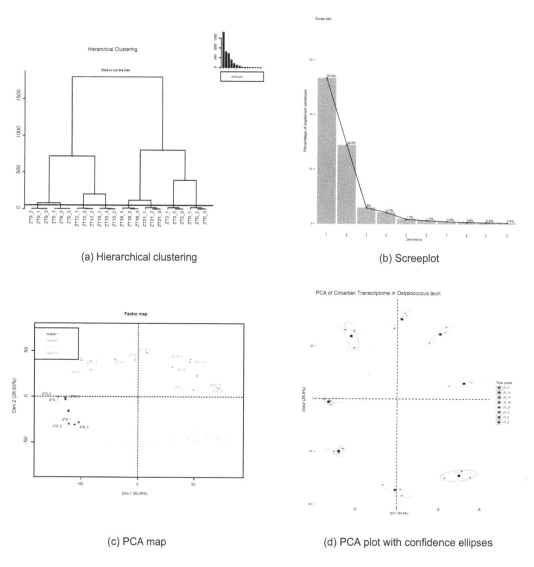

(a) Hierarchical clustering

(b) Screeplot

(c) PCA map

(d) PCA plot with confidence ellipses

FIGURE 7.2   PCA for microalgae *Ostreococcus tauri* (Monnier et al. dataset [1]). (a) Hierarchical clustering, (b) Scree plot, (c) PCA map, (d) PCA plot with confidence ellipses.

that the data truly captured the cyclic daily behavior. Clustering analysis over the rotated and projected data unveiled that the morning transcriptome (ZT0 and ZT3) is more similar to the night transcriptome (ZT18 and ZT21) forming a cluster than to the afternoon transcriptome (ZT6 and ZT9) that forms a separate cluster with the evening transcriptome (ZT12 and ZT15).

4 SINGULAR VALUE DECOMPOSITION

Singular Value Decomposition (SVD) is a tool used to decompose a rectangular matrix as product of other matrices. It is the basis of projection methods studied in next sections. We highlight the properties of this technique that will be used in next sections.

PCA, described in Section 3, is based on the spectral decomposition of the covariance matrix, Σ, of a p-dimensional continuous random vector. Σ is a $p \times p$ symmetric matrix. However, when dealing with other high-dimensional multivariate techniques, such as CA or CCA, we will have a $n \times p$ rectangular matrix, X, whose dimensions we aimed to reduce. In this context, SVD is of interest because SVD is an algebraic tool that allows us to decompose the rectangular matrix as the product of three matrices. In this way, it provides a matrix approximation of lower dimensions than those of the original matrix. The method is described next.

Theorem. Let X be a $n \times p$ matrix, $p \leq n$, and such that its rank is p, $rank(X) = p$. Then, the SVD of X is given by

$$X = \Gamma D_\lambda \Delta' \tag{2}$$

where the matrix Γ contains the eigenvectors of XX', the matrix Δ the eigenvectors of $X'X$, and the diagonal matrix $D_\lambda = diag(\lambda_1^{1/2}, \ldots, \lambda_p^{1/2})$ contains $\lambda_1 \geq \lambda_2 \geq \ldots \geq \lambda_p$, the so-called singular values of X.

We highlight that $\lambda_1 \geq \lambda_2 \geq \ldots \geq \lambda_p$ are the eigenvalues of XX' (they agree with the eigenvalues of $X'X$).

The decomposition given in (2) allows us to obtain a matrix approximation to X of lower dimensions.

Matrix approximation. Let $\widehat{X}$ be a matrix approximation to X in the sense that

$$\min\left\{trace\left[(X - \tilde{X})(X - \tilde{X})'\right]\right\} = trace\left[(X - \widehat{X})(X - \widehat{X})'\right]$$

with $rank(\widehat{X}) = r < rank(X) = p$. Then, $\widehat{X} = \Gamma D_r \Delta'$, where D_r is the diagonal matrix containing the r first singular values of X.

These results will be applied in Section 5 to the rectangular matrix C obtained from the contingency table associated to two categorical variables, and in Section 6 to the rectangular matrix K obtained from the covariance matrix associated to two continuous random vectors. In this way, an efficient reduction of dimensionality will be achieved.

5 CORRESPONDENCE ANALYSIS

CA is a multivariate technique designed to deal with categorical variables. CA aims to discover the relationships between features and samples by using certain indexes, called principal and standard coordinates. They are obtained from the decomposition of a χ^2 statistic. An application to an omic dataset is included by using Bioconductor package made4.

5.1 Method

The basis of CA method is to calculate indexes revealing the underlying relationships between the rows and columns in a contingency table. The indexes are listed in decreasing order of importance.

CA can be applied to test the homogeneity of n independent populations and the independence of two characters. Both problems are briefly described next.

1. *Homogeneity of n independent populations.* In this setting, a categorical feature, denoted by B, with p modalities is studied in n independent populations. The null hypothesis is that the n populations are homogeneous.

$$H_0 : P_1(B_j) = P_2(B_j) = \ldots = P_n(B_j), \quad j = 1, \ldots, p. \tag{3}$$

2. *Independence of two characters.* In this setting, two categorical features, denoted by A and B, with n and p modalities, respectively, are considered. The null hypothesis of independence is

$$H_0 : P(A_i \cap B_j) = P(A_i)\, P(B_j), \quad \forall i, j. \tag{4}$$

In both cases, an $n \times p$ contingency table can be defined, which contains the observed frequency distribution of the variables, $(N_{ij})_{i=1,\ldots,n; j=1,\ldots,p}$ with N_{ij} the observed frequency of cell (i, j). Let N be the total number of elements in our table, $N_{i.}$ the marginal frequencies by rows, and $N_{.j}$ the marginal frequencies by columns. From all of them, the indexes we are looking for will be calculated.

χ^2 *decomposition algorithm.* Recall that the χ^2 statistic is given by

$$\chi^2 = \sum \frac{(N_{ij} - E_{ij})^2}{E_{ij}}, \quad where\ E_{ij} = \widehat{E}_{H_0}(N_{ij}) = \frac{N_{i.}N_{.j}}{N}. \tag{5}$$

Let us consider the matrix C whose elements are

$$c_{ij} = \frac{(N_{ij} - E_{ij})}{E_{ij}^{1/2}}. \tag{6}$$

The elements c_{ij} measure the (weighted) departure between the observed frequencies, N_{ij}, and the expected values, E_{ij}, under the null hypothesis of homogeneity or independence. Let us denote by $R = rank(C) \leq \min\{(n-1), (p-1)\}$. Consider the SVD of C

$$C = \Gamma D_\lambda \Delta' \tag{7}$$

where Γ contains the eigenvectors of CC', Δ the eigenvectors of $C'C$, and $D_\lambda = diag(\lambda_1^{1/2}, \dots, \lambda_R^{1/2})$ with $\lambda_1 \geq \lambda_2 \geq \dots \geq \lambda_R$ the eigenvalues of CC' (they agree with the eigenvalues of $C'C$).

The key fact in CA is the following relationship:

χ^2 *decomposition statistic*

$$\chi^2 = \sum_{i=1}^{n} \sum_{j=1}^{p} c_{ij}^2 = \sum_{k=1}^{R} \lambda_k \tag{8}$$

That is, the total χ^2 value can be decomposed as the sum of R indexes, $\lambda_k's$, which explain the variability of this statistic in decreasing order of importance. $\lambda_k's$ are the eigenvalues of CC'.

In many applications, a few of first eigenvalues explain a high percentage of the total χ^2. In this case, the associated eigenvectors will be used to obtain approximations to the distance between the corresponding rows and columns from the contingency table.

Common ad hoc suggestions upon the number of eigenvalues to retain are as follows:

- To retain just enough eigenvalues to explain certain specified large percentage of the total variability in our data. Usually, values between 70% and 90% are recommended. However, when dealing with n and p large, it is only possible to keep quite smaller percentages of variability with a reduced number of eigenvalues. We must be conscious of this fact.

- A number of authors suggest to examine the so called scree plot; this is a plot of the eigenvalues λ_k against k. The number of eigenvalues selected is the value k corresponding to an *elbow* in the plot, that is, a change of slope from steep to shallow. The first point on the straight line is then taken to be the last eigenvalue to be retained.

Principal Coordinates. Let $A = diag(N_{1.}, \dots, N_{n.})$ and $B = diag(N_{.1}, \dots, N_{.p})$ be the diagonal matrices with the marginal frequencies. For $k = 1, \dots, R$, the principal coordinates for the rows and columns, $\underline{r}_k$ and $\underline{s}_k$, are given by

$$\underline{r}_k = A^{-1/2} C \underline{\delta}_k = \sqrt{\lambda_k} A^{-1/2} \underline{\gamma}_k \tag{9}$$

$$\underline{s}_k = \boldsymbol{B}^{-1/2}\boldsymbol{C}'\underline{\gamma}_k = \sqrt{\lambda_k}\boldsymbol{B}^{-1/2}\underline{\delta}_k \tag{10}$$

$\underline{r}_k$ and $\underline{s}_k$ are the principal coordinates for the rows and columns.

Remark. In (9) and (10), $\underline{\gamma}_k$ and $\underline{\delta}_k$ are the eigenvectors of $\boldsymbol{CC}'$ and $\boldsymbol{C}'\boldsymbol{C}$ contained in Γ and Δ, respectively. $\underline{\gamma}_k$ and $\underline{\delta}_k$ are referred to as row factor and column factor.

Properties of principal coordinates. The means of the principal coordinates are zero, $E(\underline{r}_k) = E(\underline{s}_k) = 0$, and the variances are

$$Var(\underline{r}_k) = \frac{\lambda_k}{N}, \quad Var(\underline{s}_k) = \frac{\lambda_k}{N}. \tag{11}$$

From (11), it follows that $\dfrac{\lambda_k}{\sum_{j=1}^{R}\lambda_j}$ is the proportion of the variablility of the χ^2 statistic explained by the factor k.

CA in practice. Plots can be carried out on the axes $k = 1, 2, \ldots, R$. In these plots, the rows and columns of the contingency table are represented by points, whose coordinates are given by the corresponding elements of $\underline{r}_k$ and $\underline{s}_k$. Typically, two-dimensional plots are carried out. They are appropriate if the cumulated percentage of variance explained by the two factors is large enough. Once the plot is obtained, the following points must be taken into account.

- The origin is the average of $\underline{r}_k$ and $\underline{s}_k$. Hence, a point (row or column) whose projection is closed to the origin indicates an average profile.

- There exists association between the points when they are far away from 0. In this case, the proximity of two rows (or two columns) indicates similar conditional distributions in these rows. The opposite occurs when the two rows are far apart.

- The proximity of a row to a column indicates that this row has an important weight in this column. On the other hand, a row quite distant from a column indicates that there are almost no observations in this column for this row (and vice versa).

Obviously, previous interpretations depend on the quality of the plot which is evaluated by using the cumulative percentage of variance.

5.2 Application

In this subsection, we consider a microarry gene expression dataset from Khan et al. [2]. This dataset is available at Bioconductor package made4. MADE4 provides graphical and visualization tools useful to carry out multivariate analysis of microarray data.

Dataset description. The dataset Khan provides us gene expression profiles of four types of small round blue cell tumors of childhood (SRBCT): NB (neuroblastoma), RMS (rhabdomyosarcoma), BL (Burkitt's lymphoma), EWS (Erwing's sarcoma). This dataset contains gene expression levels for 306 genes (variables) for 64 patient samples (cases).

R package made4. made 4 is an R package for multivariate analysis of gene expression data. It has a widespread use in biomedicine and life sciences, with a large number of papers in these areas citing it, as it can be seen for instance in the digital repository PubMed Central. made 4 provides tools useful to visualize microarray data and carry out CA. made4 contains functions that require the R packages ade4 and scatterplot3d. To install this package, follow the instructions appearing on http://bioconductor.org/packages/release/bioc/html/made4.html

The following functions allow us to carry out CA.

- **overview**. It plots a dendrogram (or hierarchical tree) of our dataset by classes, boxplot, and histogram. The basic use is

```
overview(dataset, classvec=NULL)
```

In classvec, a factor or vector describing the classes in our dataset can be indicated. In this case, the dendrogram will be colored by classes.
- **ord**. The function ord runs (symmetric) CA, PCA, or non-symmetric CA on gene expression data. The basic use is

```
ord(dataset, type=c("coa", "pca", "nsc") )
```

The input is gene expression data given in a matrix or data frame. The rows and columns must contain the variables (genes) and cases (array samples), respectively. As for *type*, the options are "coa" (symmetric correspondence analysis), "pca" (PC analysis), "nsc" (non-symmetric correspondence analysis). The default type is "coa".

Aditional details and other functions can be seen on www.rdocumentation.org/packages/made4

Analysis of Khan dataset. The R packages ade4, made4, and scatterplot 3d must be loaded into the session. First, we look at the Khan dataset and an exploratory data analysis is carried out.

```
> data(khan)

> class(khan) [1] "list"

> names(khan)
 [1] "train"              "test"         "train.classes"    "test.classes"
 [5] "annotation"  "gene.labels.imagesID" "cellType"

> summary(khan)
                Length Class        Mode
train           64     data.frame   list
test            25     data.frame   list
train.classes   64     factor       numeric
test.classes    25     factor       numeric
annotation       8     data.frame   list
```

```
gene.labels.imagesID  306        -none-      character
cellType                64        -none-      character
```

Khan dataset is a list with 7 elements whose names are given above. The data were divided into a training set (khan$train) of 64 cases, and a test set (khan$test). Other elements have information about the classes of tumor in our data (factors train.classes and test.classes), kind of annotation, and other information about genes. khan$cellType indicates if gene expression profile samples were obtained from tumor biopsy ("T") or cell line ("C").

```
> khan$cellType
 [1] "T" "T" "T" "T" "T" "T" "T" "T" "T" "T" "T" "T" "T" "C" "C" "C" ...
(truncated)
```

The training set is used as illustration. Its overview is given in Figure 7.3. The dendrogram and boxplot have been colored by tumor class.

```
> k.data<-khan$train
> dim(k.data)
 [1] 306 64
> k.class <- khan$train.classes
> overview(k.data, classvec=k.class, labels=k.class)
```

The dendrogram or hierarchical tree is a cluster analysis tool which allows us to detect groups or classes in multivariate analysis. It can be applied to the rows or columns in a contingency table. In this case, it has been applied to columns containing the 64 cases. They are represented on the horizontal axis. The vertical axis represents the dissimilarity between clusters. As result, this plot suggests two big groups, one of them containing mostly individuals with the type of tumor "RMS," and the other one with the three remaining types.

A boxplot for each individual has been carried out with the values of the 306 variables.

The histogram represents on the horizontal axis the range of the variables, and on the vertical axis the frequencies of each value for the 64 samples.

Next, the ord function is used to run (symmetric) CA of this dataset.

```
> k.coa<-ord(k.data, type="coa")
```

As output from ord, a list of two elements is obtained: the results ($ord) and a factor ($fac) if input.

Next we focus on the results (k.coa$ord).

```
> k.coa$ord
 Duality diagramm
 class: coa dudi
 $call: dudi.coa(df = data.tr, scannf = FALSE, nf = ord.nf)
```

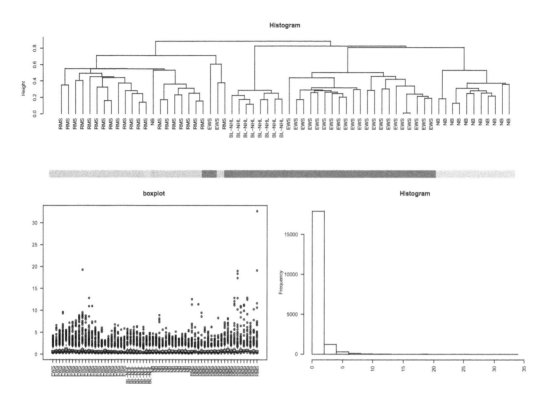

FIGURE 7.3   Overview Khan dataset.

```
$nf: 63 axis-components saved
$rank: 63
eigen values: 0.1713 0.1383 0.1032 0.05995 0.04965 ...
  vector length mode       content
1 $cw      64    numeric   column weights
2 $lw      306   numeric   row weights
3 $eig     63    numeric   eigen values

  data.frame  nrow  ncol  content
1 $tab        306   64    modified array
2 $li         306   63    row coordinates
3 $l1         306   63    row normed scores
4 $co         64    63    column coordinates
5 $c1         64    63    column normed scores
other elements: N
```

k.coa$ord is a list of results. This list includes 63 eigenvalues ($eig), column weight vector of length 64 ($cw), and the row weight vector of length 306 ($lw). Moreover, the row principal coordinates (the projected coordinates of the genes, 306 genes) r_j ($li) and column principal coordinates s_j ($co, 64 microarray samples) and their standardized versions ($l1) and ($c1).

Take a look at the 3 first principal coordinates row and columns for the two first genes ($li) and individuals ($co).

```
> k.coa$ord$li[1:2, 1:3]
            Axis1        Axis2        Axis3
 25725   0.7001400  -0.08693461  -0.1278178
193913  -0.2486831   0.64857220  -0.2381108
> k.coa$ord$co[1:2, 1:3]
            Comp1        Comp2         Comp3
EWS.T1  -0.3923287  -0.3255404  -0.02589332
EWS.T2  -0.3461686  -0.2956390   0.05687684
```

The sum of the 63 indexes is the total χ^2 statistic. From (11), the percentage of variability of χ^2 statistic explained by each factor is given by

```
>k.coa$ord$eig*100/sum(k.coa$ord$eig)
[1] 16.947461298 13.683297888 10.207338717 5.931017086 4.911896717 3.810337299
[7] 3.027912076 3.004793647 2.419837082  2.319143755  2.042227963  1.886343953
:
:
[58] 0.151730905 0.142298857 0.129021644 0.115421971 0.106023909 0.008629433
```

The cumulative percentage of variability explained by the *k*th first factors can be calculated by applying the function cumsum() to previous results (only 6 dimensions (out of 63) are shown)

```
> head(cumsum(k.coa$ord$eig*100/sum(k.coa$ord$eig)))
 [1] 16.94746 30.63076 40.83810 46.76911 51.68101 55.49135
```

Note that, in this case, the first two eigenvalues explain 30.63% of the variability of our data.

Visualization of results

CA plots of the data can be obtained plotting usually the first two coordinates for column categories and for row categories. Assuming that a two-dimensional solution provides an adequate description for the data, row points that are close together represent row categories that have similar profiles (conditional distributions) across columns. Column points that are close together indicate columns with similar profiles down the rows. As for the joint plot, row points that lie close to column points represent a row/column combination that happens more frequently than would be expected if the row and column variables were independent. Conversely, row and column points that are distant from one another indicate a cell in the table where the count is lower than would be expected under independence.

There are many functions in ade4 and made4 for visualizing results obtained in CA. The simplest way is to use plot. plot(k.ord) will draw a plot of the eigenvalues, along with plots of the variables (genes) and a plot of the cases (microarray samples). Microarray samples are color-coded by the kind of tumor (k.class); see Figure 7.4.

- On the top-left corner, a plot for the eigenvalues is given. This plot is useful to choose the number of eigenvalues that properly explain the variability in our data. Looking at the point where the slope of plot is leveling off, in this case, it seems that two might be adequate.

- Plot for the cases (microarray samples). Patients are plotted on $\underline{s}_1$ and $\underline{s}_2$ axis, since they are the columns in the original contingency table. Those individuals that are close together in this plot have similar profiles. Examining the plot obtained in Figure 7.4, part b), it could be said that $\underline{s}_1$ axis distinguishes between RMS tumor and the other kinds. On the other hand, it seems that $\underline{s}_2$ axis separates those samples corresponding to NB and BL from the rest of the cases.

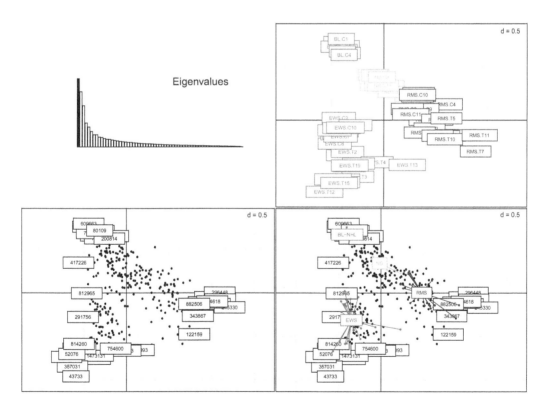

FIGURE 7.4 Plot of CA for Khan dataset. a) Eigenvalues. b) Projections of microarrays for the patients with different kinds of tumors. c) Projections for the genes. d) Biplot for genes and samples.

- Plot for the variables (genes). Genes (rows in the original contingency table) are plotted on $\underline{r}_1$ and $\underline{r}_2$ axes. Those genes that are close together exhibit a similar behavior. It is observed that the axes separate certain groups of genes from others. This groups must be studied in detail for expertise.

- Plot for rows and columns on the same diagram. Genes and samples have been plotted together, along with the kinds of tumors and proper labels to clearly differentiate between them. Those genes that lie close to sample points represent gene/sample combination that exhibits strong association. So, the existing association between genes and the type of tumor is also displayed.

6 CANONICAL CORRELATION ANALYSIS

CCA was introduced by Hotelling (1935) as a projection technique to explore dependence structure between complex multivariate datasets. The aim is to analyse the existing correlation between two given continuous random vectors. Next, a method to find the two first canonical correlation vectors is studied in detail. Canonical correlation variables are given, and significance tests are proposed to choose the most relevant ones. CCA is applied to omic data obtained from a nutritional study in mice.

6.1 Method

Let us consider two continuous random vectors of dimensions p and q with $p > q$ denoted as $\underline{X} = (X_1, \ldots, X_p)$ and $\underline{Y} = (Y_1, \ldots, Y_q)$. A simple random sample of $\underline{X}$ and $\underline{Y}$ will be given in the matrices $X_{n \times p}$ and $Y_{n \times q}$, where columns correspond to variables and rows to cases.

The aim of CCA is to measure the existing correlation between $\underline{X}$ and $\underline{Y}$ by using indexes based on the covariance analysis of projections of the variables. These projections will be called *canonical correlation variables* and it can be calculated exactly, $m = \min(p, q)$.

It will be supposed that for $\underline{X}$ and $\underline{Y}$, next features exist $E[\underline{X}] = \underline{\mu}$, $E[\underline{Y}] = \underline{\nu}$, $Var[\underline{X}] = \Sigma_{XX}$ of dimensions $p \times p$, $Var[\underline{Y}] = \Sigma_{YY}$ of dimensions $q \times q$, and $Cov[\underline{X}, \underline{Y}] = E\left[(\underline{X} - \underline{\mu})(\underline{Y} - \underline{\nu})'\right] = \Sigma_{XY} = \Sigma_{YX}'$ of dimensions $p \times q$.

Let us consider the matrix K defined as

$$K = \Sigma_{XX}^{-1/2}\Sigma_{XY}\Sigma_{YY}^{-1/2}. \tag{12}$$

CCA is based on the SVD of the matrix K

$$K = \Gamma D \Delta'$$

with $\Gamma = (\underline{\gamma}_1, \underline{\gamma}_2, \ldots, \underline{\gamma}_m)$ eigenvectors of KK', $\Delta = (\underline{\delta}_1, \underline{\delta}_2, \ldots, \underline{\delta}_m)$ eigenvectors of $K'K$, λ_i $(i = 1, \ldots, m)$ the m nonzero eigenvalues of KK', and D the diagonal matrix with diagonal elements $\sqrt{\lambda_i}$, $i = 1, \ldots, m$.

Main result. For $i = 1, \ldots, m$, the pairs of canonical correlation variables are given by

$$\eta_i = \underline{a}'_i \underline{X} = \Sigma_{XX}^{-1/2} \underline{\gamma}_i \underline{X} \tag{13}$$

$$\psi_i = \underline{b}'_i \underline{Y} = \Sigma_{YY}^{-1/2} \underline{\delta}_i \underline{Y} \tag{14}$$

where $\underline{\gamma}_i$ is the ith eigenvector in Γ and $\underline{\delta}_i$ is the ith eigenvector in Δ associated to the eigenvalue λ_i.

For the ith canonical correlation coefficient $\rho_i = \rho_i(\eta_i, \psi_i)$ (linear correlation coefficient between η_i and ψ_i), we have that $\rho_i = \lambda_i^{1/2}$.

Properties. Let ρ_i be the ith canonical correlation coefficient. If it is assumed that $\rho_1 < \rho_2 < \ldots < \rho_m$, then

1. $\eta_1, \eta_2, \ldots, \eta_m$ and $\psi_1, \psi_2, \ldots, \psi_m$ are uncorrelated.

2. $Cov(\eta_i, \psi_j) = 0$ for $i \neq j$.

Once the m pairs of canonical variables are obtained, if multivariate normality can be assumed, hypothesis tests, such as Barlett–Lawley or independence tests, may be carried out. These tests allow us to choose the number of pairs of canonical variables which are significantly different to zero. In this way, a significant reduction of the dimension of our problem will be reached.

6.2 Application

CCA can be used as an exploratory tool in multivariate analysis which allows us to show the existing correlation between two datasets measured on the same sample units. The fact that when dealing with omic datasets the number of variables is much bigger than the number of cases must be taken into account. An application is given in which the first two pairs of canonical correlation variables provide a good description of the relationship between the two datasets under consideration.

Dataset description. In *nutrimouse* dataset, 40 mice are cross-classified according to their genotype and diet. There are 141 variables, 120 gene expression levels, and 21 hepatic fatty acids. This dataset is available at CCA package.

R package CCA. The CCA package is available at http://cran.r-project.org/web/packages/CCA/index.html.

This package is specially recommended to analyse omic data, since it provides techniques to carry out CCA when the number of variables is greater than the number of cases. It also includes tools to deal with missing values.

Analysis of nutrimouse dataset

First, we take a look at nutrimouse dataset and obtain somme summaries of variables on it.

```
> class(nutrimouse)
[1] "list"
> str(nutrimouse)
List of 4
 $ gene   :'data.frame': 40 obs. of 120 variables:
  ..$ X36b4   : num [1:40] -0.42 -0.44 -0.48 -0.45 -0.42 -0.43 -0.53 -0.49
    -0.36 -0.5 ...
  ..$ ACAT1   : num [1:40] -0.65 -0.68 -0.74 -0.69 -0.71 -0.69 -0.62 -0.69
    -0.66 -0.62 ...
         :
 :
 .. [list output truncated]
 $ lipid   :'data.frame': 40 obs. of 21 variables:
  ..$ C14.0   : num [1:40] 0.34 0.38 0.36 0.22 0.37 1.7 0.35 0.34 0.22 1.38 ...
  ..$ C16.0   : num [1:40] 26.4 24 23.7 25.5 24.8 ...
  ..$ C18.0   : num [1:40] 10.22 9.93 8.96 8.14 9.63 ...
 :
 :
  ..$ C22.6n.3: num [1:40] 10.39 2.61 2.51 14.99 6.69 ...
 $ diet    : Factor w/ 5 levels "coc","fish","lin",..: 3 5 5 2 4 1 3 3 2 1 ...
 $ genotype: Factor w/ 2 levels "wt","ppar": 1 1 1 1 1 1 1 1 1 1 ...
```

nutrimouse is a list of 4 elements: "nutrimouse$gene" is a dataframe (40 × 120) containing the expression levels of 120 genes in 40 mice; "nutrimouse$lipid" is a dataframe (40 × 21) containing the values of 21 hepatic fatty acids in 40 mice; "nutrimouse$diet" and "nutrimouse$genoType" are factors whose levels are given below.

```
> summary(nutrimouse$genotype)
 wt ppar
 20  20

> summary(nutrimouse$diet)
 coc fish lin ref sun
  8   8   8   8   8
```

Those data related to gene expression levels are stored in matrix X, and those related to lipids in matrix Y. CCA will be applied to these matrices.

```
> X<- as.matrix(nutrimouse$gene)
```

```
> Y <- as.matrix(nutrimouse$lipid)
> View(X)
> dim(X)
 [1] 40 120
> dim(Y)
 [1] 40 21
```

Next the correlation matrices, Σ_{XX}, Σ_{YY}, and Σ_{XY}, are calculated

```
>correl<-matcor(X,Y)
>str(correl)
 List of 3
 $Xcor :num [1:120, 1:120] 1 0.328 0.107 0.262 0.491 ...
 ..- attr(*, "dimnames")=List of 2
 .. ..$ :chr [1:120] "X36b4" "ACAT1" "ACAT2" "ACBP" ...
 .. ..$ :chr [1:120] "X36b4" "ACAT1" "ACAT2" "ACBP" ...
 $Ycor :num [1:21, 1:21] 1 0.00935 -0.59087 0.65744 0.97197 ...
 ..- attr(*, "dimnames")=List of 2
 .. ..$ :chr [1:21] "C14.0" "C16.0" "C18.0" "C16.1n.9" ...
 .. ..$ :chr [1:21] "C14.0" "C16.0" "C18.0" "C16.1n.9" ...
 $XYcor: num [1:141, 1:141] 1 0.328 0.107 0.262 0.491 ...
 ..- attr(*, "dimnames")=List of 2
 .. ..$ :chr [1:141] "X36b4" "ACAT1" "ACAT2" "ACBP" ...
 .. ..$ :chr [1:141] "X36b4" "ACAT1" "ACAT2" "ACBP" ...
```

The correlations are visualized by using img.matcor function, whose result is given in Figure 7.5.

```
> img.matcor(correl, type=2)
```

To illustrate the use of this technique, 10 variables are randomly selected. A seed is set so that our results can be checked.

```
> ## set a seed
> set.seed(24)
> Xr <- X[, sample(1:120, size=10)]
```

In order to apply CCA, the matrices must be scaled

```
> Xscale<-scale(Xr)
> Yscale<-scale(Y)
```

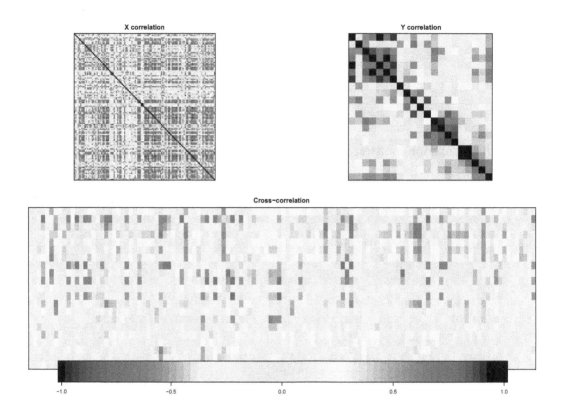

FIGURE 7.5   Plot of CCA

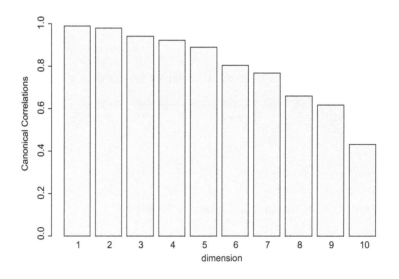

FIGURE 7.6   Plot of CCA.

We see the CCA results. A barplot is also included; see Figure 7.6.

```
> res.cc <- cc(Xscale, Yscale)
> names(res.cc)
[1] "cor"  "names"  "xcoef"  "ycoef" "scores"
> barplot(res.cc$cor, xlab="dimension", ylab="Canonical Correlations",
names.arg=1:10,
          ylim=c(0,1), col="lightblue")
```

Final plots are given in Figure 7.7.

```
> ## Final Plots
> plt.cc(res.cc, var.label = TRUE, ind.names =paste(nutrimouse$geno-
type,nutrimouse$diet, sep = "-"))
```

In Figure 7.7, the first two canonical correlation variables are plotted. We see that the first CC variable η_1 (Dimension 1) distinguishes the cases by their genotype. $PPAR_\alpha$-defficient mice (ppar_xx) are on the left-hand side, whereas wild (wt_xx) type are on the right one. On the other hand, the second CC variable η_2 (Dimension 2) distinguishes the cases by the kind of diet. This distinction is less precise for $PPAR_\alpha$ mice.

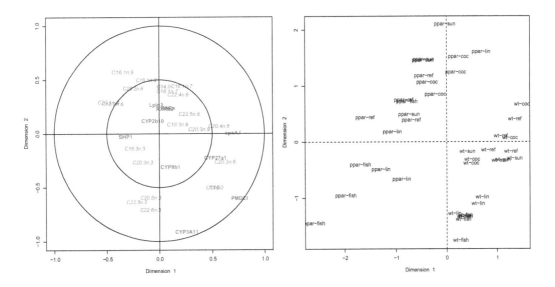

FIGURE 7.7   Plot of CCA for nutrimouse dataset.

7 SUPPLEMENTARY MATERIAL

Throughout the text, links to datasets, and R and Bioconductor packages have been included.

The shiny R application is available at link

https://frannetworks.shinyapps.io/web_app/

Additional details about the statistical techniques we have dealt with in this paper and more applications can be seen in references [2–13] and [14].

REFERENCES

1. Monnier A., Liverani S., Bouvet R., Jesson B., Smith J.Q., et al. Orchestrated transcription of biological processes in the marine picoeukaryote Ostreococcus exposed to light/dark cycles. *BMC Genomics* 22(11):192, 2010.
2. Khan J., Wei J.S., Ringner M., Saal L.H., Ladanyi M., et al. Classification and diagnostic prediction of cancers using gene expression profiling and artificial neural networks. *Nature Medicine* 7:673–679, 2001.
3. Culhane A. Introduction to multivariate analysis of microarray gene expression data using MADE4. 2014.
4. Culhane A., Thioulouse J., Perriere G., and Higgins D.G. MADE4: AnR package for multi-variate analysis of gene expression data. *Bioinformatics* 21(11):2789–2790, 2005.
5. Everitt B., and Hothorn T. *An Introduction to Applied Multivariate Analysis with R.* New York, NY: Springer, 2015.
6. González I., and Déjean S. CCA: Canonical correlation analysis. R package version 1.2. 2012. http://CRAN.R-project.org/package=CCA.
7. Greenacre M. *Correspondence Analysis in Practice.* 2nd Edition. Boca Raton, FL: Chapman & Hall/CTC, 2007.
8. Hardle W.K., and Simar L. *Applied Multivariate Statistical Analysis.* Berlin, Heidelberg: Springer-Verlag, 2015.
9. Husson F., Josse J., Le S., and Mazet J. (2015). FactoMineR: Multivariate exploratory data analysis and data mining. R package version 1.31.4. http://CRAN.Rproject.org/package=FactoMineR.
10. Muñoz Armayones S. Técnicas Multivariantes para el Análisis de Datos Ómicos. 2016. https://idus.us.es/xmlui/bitstream/handle/11441/43809/Mu.
11. R Core Team. *R: A Language and Environment for Statistical Computing.* Vienna, Austria: R Foundation for Statistical Computing, 2018. www.R-project.org/.
12. R Studio. www.rstudio.org/.
13. Meng C., Kuster B., Culhane A.C., Gholami A.M. A multivariate approach to the integration of multi-omics datasets. *BMC Bioinformatics* 15:162, 2014 May 29.
14. Sánchez A. Multivariate methods for the integration and visualization of omics data. http://eib.stat.ub.edu/Integrative+Analysis+of+Omics+Data.

CHAPTER 8

Geo-Distributed Big Data Analytics Systems

An Online Learning Approach for Dynamic Deployment

Yixin Bao and Chuan Wu

Department of Computer Science, The University of Hong Kong, Hong Kong, China

CONTENTS

G eo-distributed big data analytics systems have appeared in recent years, which extend a single cluster-based MapReduce, Spark, or parameter server-based system to the Wide Area Network (WAN), to process data generated in different geographic locations. A fundamental issue in a geo-distributed data analytics system is to effectively place tasks in different processing stages of a job according to locations of the data and the network conditions among the processing sites (e.g., data centers or the edge clouds), in order to minimize job completion time or the resource costs. The problem is challenging given its combinatorial nature, as well as uncertainties in task execution time and data transmission time across data centers. To deal with job deployment in terms of such runtime uncertainties, existing studies mostly use a regression or supervised learning approach, inferring a function to predict running or transmission time using large training datasets of prior job logs. In this chapter, we design an online learning-based algorithm which does not rely on offline training, but can learn the near-optimal decisions for placing each type of jobs over time. Our algorithm is based on the multi-armed bandit online learning framework, and aims at joint minimization of job completion time and resource costs, by balancing exploitation of available information and exploration of uncertainty. Fully utilizing characteristics of representative big data analytics systems and outcomes of previous decisions, the algorithm provides a sequence of online decisions, including the data center and the resource type for running each task, under the current job progress. We rigorously prove an $O(\ln T)$ regret bound for the online learning algorithm. Practical effectiveness of the algorithm is evaluated using both trace-driven simulation and testbed experiments, which demonstrate that our algorithm consistently outperforms commonly adopted heuristic and statistical approaches.

1 INTRODUCTION

Big data analytics frameworks have been designed, deployed, and thriving in recent years, for analyzing large volumes of data in various realms such as social networks, online advertising, web hosting, bioinformation, and e-health. While most frameworks (e.g., MapReduce/Hadoop [1], Spark [2], Tensorflow [3]) were designed to run in a single cluster, there have been recent proposals to extend them to the WAN (Wide Area Network) or to the edge, for processing data produced in dispersed geographic locations (see more discussions in Section 2). Geo-distributed datasets are common in various networked systems: a social networking or content distribution system deploys servers in different regions to serve users locally, and collects user logs from users in respective regions; a banking system owns user data in different branches/regions; an IoT (Internet of Things) platform collects data in different homes.

To analyze geo-distributed datasets, a common approach is to aggregate all data to a central location, where a MapReduce, Spark, or Tensorflow-like framework will run. The centralized processing approach is time-consuming (leading to slow query responses) due to transmitting large volumes of data over bandwidth-constrained WAN links, and is costly for resource consumption (e.g., WAN bandwidth). In addition, due to regulatory constraints and privacy/security concerns, raw datasets may not be allowed to be sent out of their origins [4,5]. All these lead to the arising of geo-distributed data analytics systems, which deploy computing tasks close to input datasets and dispatch intermediate data only (often at much reduced volumes with much less sensitive content) across different locations, for multi-stage processing in a fully decentralized fashion [6–8].

A fundamental issue in a geo-distributed data analytics system is to effectively place tasks in a job according to locations of data and network conditions among data processing sites (e.g., data centers, edge clouds), in order to minimize job completion time or resource costs. The job processing logic is commonly described by a staged, directed graph, where tasks belonging to a stage can only be started once all tasks in the prior stage have been completed and intermediate data are received from them, e.g., as in Spark [2] and synchronous training mode of a Tensor Flow-like distributed machine learning system [3,9]. When the big data analytics system is deployed over geo-distributed data centers or edge clouds, we further need to decide the type of virtual machine (VM) or container to use for running each task in a selected location, which may lead to different task execution durations. The problem is challenging given its combinatorial nature, even when we assume all task execution time and inter-datacenter network bandwidths are known. In practice, how long a task takes to complete on a specified type of VM or container may vary, due to interference from concurrent jobs running on the same physical server [10]; the available bandwidth between tasks deployed on different data centers may fluctuate as well, because of various cross-traffic between data centers [11]. Efficient job deployment is further challenging given such runtime uncertainties.

To deal with uncertainties, existing work-scheduling big data analytics jobs assume that the bandwidth can be measured in real time [6,8], and the task execution time can be predicted based on historical runtime logs of jobs of the same type [12]. However, inter-datacenter bandwidth varies significantly according to real-world measurements [11]. It is also inaccurate to measure the bandwidth each time before actually running a task/job, as interferences due to cross-traffic appear in real time. Further, in pay-as-you-go cloud platforms such as Amazon EC2, users are allowed to test bandwidth only after they have launched a VM instance and made the payment. Running time skewness of big data analytics tasks of the same type has been observed by many studies [13], due to the many factors that influence task completion time, including the size and content of data to be processed and the interference from concurrent jobs on the same machine, competing for CPU and I/O. Although linear regression and SVM regression models have been proposed for predicting task/job completion time [14,15], they can hardly make an accurate prediction in the absence of substantial prior knowledge, and provide no proven accuracy.

In this chapter, we design an online learning-based algorithm which does not rely on offline training, but can learn the near-optimal decisions for placing big data analytics jobs over time. Our algorithm is based on the multi-armed bandit online learning framework [16], and aims at joint minimization of job completion time and resource costs, by balancing exploitation of available information and exploration of uncertainty. Fully utilizing characteristics of representative big data analytics systems and outcomes of previous decisions, the algorithm provides a sequence of online decisions, including the data center and the resource type for running each task, under the current job progress. We rigorously prove an $O(\ln T)$ regret bound for the online learning algorithm, where T is the total time that the system spans. Practical effectiveness of the algorithm is evaluated using both trace-driven simulation and testbed experiments, which demonstrate that our algorithm consistently outperforms commonly adopted heuristic and statistical approaches.

The rest of the chapter is organized as follows: we present related work in Section 2, problem model in Section 3, detailed online algorithm and its analysis in Section 4, simulation and experiment results in Section 5, and conclusion in Section 6.

2 BACKGROUND AND RELATED WORK

2.1 Scheduling of Geo-Distributed Big Data Analytics Jobs

A number of big data analytics systems have been proposed and implemented to run over the WAN, together with efforts on optimal task placement in geo-distributed analytics jobs. Iridium [6] is a geo-distributed analytics query system, achieving low query response time using an online heuristic for joint placement of data and tasks of the queries. Geode [7] is a Hive-based wide-area SQL analytics system, which orchestrates query execution and data replication plans across data centers to minimize bandwidth cost while respecting regulatory constraints. WANalytics [17] applies a greedy heuristic to decide workflow execution plans and replicates data. Pixida [18] is a task placement scheduler that minimizes data movement across resource-constrained links, by formulating and solving a graph-partitioning problem. Flutter [8] is a task-scheduling algorithm to improve completion time of geo-distributed big data processing jobs, by solving an optimal task placement problem for each stage of a job, based on the assumption that the execution time of the tasks in a stage is uniform. Gaia [19] is a geo-distributed machine learning system which minimizes communication over WANs, by eliminating insignificant communication across different data centers. These studies design either approximation or heuristic algorithms to optimize one-shot placement of tasks, ignoring uncertainties in task execution, or propose online heuristics to adjust task placement by reacting to system dynamics, without proving the long-term efficiency of the algorithms.

2.2 Estimating Task Running Time

A number of efforts have been made on predicting completion time of data analytics tasks/jobs, for optimizing resource utilization. Some are based on analysis of previous logs. Kavulya et al. [20] study 10-month worth of MapReduce logs, and conclude that the job completion time follows a long-tailed distribution. Song et al. [21] propose a weighted linear regression model for job completion time prediction. These approaches rely heavily on prior knowledge which is not always available.

Other studies apply simple heuristic or statistic methods. Bardhan et al. [22] model the execution time as a function of the number of parallel sub tasks. Zhang et al. [14] characterize it as a function of the processed data. They assume a linear function and use linear regression to identify the parameters. Wang et al. [12] predict the running time of a Spark job based on the historical average. These studies do not provide theoretical guarantees of the prediction efficiency, nor make sufficient adjustment of their prediction models after a training phase, making it hard to adapt to dynamic environments.

2.3 Multi-Armed Bandit Optimization

Multi-armed bandit optimization is an effective online learning and optimization framework [16]. In a multi-armed bandit problem [16], an agent faces a set of arms (actions) and needs to select one arm repeatedly in a sequence of rounds. After pulling an arm, the agent incurs a loss (or receives a reward) on the pulled arm, which is a realization of the unknown, underlying loss (or reward) distribution associated with that arm. The goal is to incur the minimal cumulative loss (or obtain the maximal cumulative reward) over the whole time horizon. The focus of bandit algorithm design is to achieve a good tradeoff between *exploration* and *exploitation*, i.e., to try some less attempted arms that might provide a better return (*exploration*), or stick to the arm that has brought low loss (or high reward) so far (*exploitation*). The performance of a bandit algorithm is evaluated by regret, which is the gap between the overall loss incurred (or reward obtained) by the offline optimal strategy and the expected loss (or reward) of the bandit algorithm.

Multi-armed bandit optimization has been applied for online recommendation [23], influence maximization [24], lax communication [25], etc., to model uncertain human behavior or unknown channel characteristics. To our knowledge, we are the first in applying bandit optimization to make optimal task placement decisions in big data analytics systems, in the face of various runtime uncertainties. Different from most bandit optimization approaches which maximize a summation of expected outcomes of the base arms, our bandit optimization model maximizes an expected extreme value, where only few studies exist. In [26], the agent chooses a subset of all arms in each round and the reward is the largest reward by an arm among the selected arm set. An $O(\log T)$ regret is proven under the assumption of Bernoulli distribution associated with each arm. Gopalan et al. [27] propose a bandit algorithm based on Thompson sampling to minimize the maximum running time of a set of jobs whose running time follows an unknown distribution. Distribution belonging to a canonical exponential family [28] is assumed. Lin et al. [29] require initialization of exponentially many arms to ensure a regret bound, which is impractical. We do not assume any concrete forms of the distributions leading to runtime uncertainties in our model, nor rely on exploring/initializing all arms in our algorithm.

3 PROBLEM MODEL

3.1 Geo-Distributed Big Data Analytics Job

We consider a system spanning T rounds, and a set of data analytics jobs which can be described by the same directed acyclic graph (DAG),[1,2] arrive at different rounds. In real-world systems, it is common to run the same type of analytical jobs (e.g., those that can be described by the same DAG) repeatedly: in a recommendation system, the service provider recommends a set of items to each user regularly; a website provider analyzes user data such as the click history on a daily basis; and a system operator analyzes the system log every day. The input data sizes to be processed by the jobs are similar, and the contents and locations of the input data sets may differ from one round to another. For example, Jalaparti et al. point out that the input data sizes of the repeated jobs change within an interval and may follow a sinusoidal wave [30]. The DAG describing tasks and their precedence in a job can be divided into consecutive *stages* $1, 2, \ldots, K$

---

[1] Jobs of different DAGs can be treated separately using our online algorithm.

[2] We understand that workflow in a TensorFlow-like distributed machine learning system cannot be modeled as a DAG; nonetheless, our proposed algorithm can be applied to handle resource allocation for parameter server architecture-based machine learning jobs, by placing workers together with respective input datasets and then deciding good locations for the parameter servers [3,9].

(e.g., as in Spark [2]): each stage k contains a set of A_k tasks, which are of the same type, i.e., carrying out the same data processing function/logic; the tasks in stage $k+1$ can only start execution after all tasks in stage k have been completed and their intermediate data produced have been fetched. Figure 8.1 illustrates such a big data analytics job.

There are D data centers, each providing M types of VMs. We assume input data to each job are stored in a subset of the data centers. We choose the data center to place each task in a job, as well as decide the type of VM to use for running the task. Different tasks of the same job can be potentially deployed in different data centers. Due mainly to interference from concurrent workload on the same physical server and the different data content to process, the running time of the same task on the same type of VM may vary from one run to another. Let τ_{ki}^m denote the running time of task i in stage k of a job on a type-m VM. Each VM hosts at most one task. Without loss of generality, suppose the running time of each type of tasks on a specific type of VM follows an unknown and i.i.d. distribution. Let p_m be the cost for using one type-m VM per unit of time. The cost for completing task i on a type-m VM is hence $\tau_{ki}^m p_m$. Let b_{de} be the available bandwidth per connection between data center d and data center e, which fluctuates over time following an unknown distribution, due to cross-traffic on the links between the data centers [31]. q_{de} denotes the cost for transmitting a unit amount of data from datacentre d to data center e. We have $q_{de} = 0$ if d and e are the same data center.

3.2 The Bandit Optimization Problem

Upon each job arrival, we aim to choose the best task deployment strategy that jointly minimizes the job completion time and the resource costs, including the costs for VMs and data transmission. We decide task deployment in a job in a stage-by-stage manner: for each task in a stage, a data center and a VM in the data center are selected for running the task; after all tasks in the previous stage are completed and intermediate data volumes are known, we deploy tasks in the next stage in selected VMs and data centers. After tasks in the next stage are deployed, they fetch intermediate data from tasks in the previous stage.

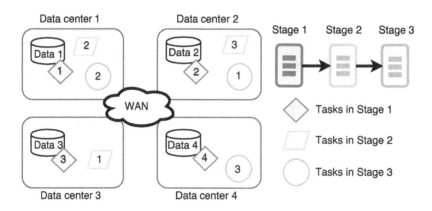

FIGURE 8.1 Big data analytics job.

When all intermediate data a task depends on are received, the task starts running. In this way, all tasks in stage $k + 1$ start fetching data at the same time, but their execution start time may differ. Such stage-by-stage scheduling of tasks in a job is well supported in today's big data analytics frameworks, e.g., Spark splits a job into stages by shuffle dependency and launches tasks in one stage altogether when its parent stages are completed.

In round t, let $x_{ki}^d(t)$ indicate whether task i in stage k of the job in the round is deployed on data center d ($x_{ki}^d(t) = 1$) or not ($x_{ki}^d(t) = 0$). Let $y_{ki}^m(t)$ denote whether to run task i in stage k of the job on a type-m VM ($y_{ki}^m(t) = 1$) or not ($y_{ki}^m(t) = 0$). $s_{ki}^j(t)$ is the size of input data block for task i in stage k, to be fetched from task j in the previous stage. When k is the first stage in the job, the input data is to be fetched from the origin locations of the data. Input data sizes (i.e., output intermediate data sizes from the previous stage if the current stage is not the first one) $s_{ki}^j(t)$'s are known when we decide task deployment in stage k (e.g., in Spark, we can get them from *MapOutputTracker* after each stage has ended). $g_{ki}^d(t)$ is the time taken for task i in stage k to receive all needed output data from tasks in stage $k - 1$, if the task is deployed in data center d. If k is the first stage of the job, $g_{ki}^d(t)$ is the time taken to fetch input data for processing from the origin(s). All notations are summarized in Table 8.1.

Note that for the input stage, the optimal solution of (5) is to place the task at the location of its input dataset. The solution corresponds to the regulatory constraints, as we do not move the input datasets to other data centers than their origins.

In Equation (1) below, we formulate the completion time of stage k of the job in round t. The completion time of a task i in stage k includes the time for fetching intermediate data from tasks in stage $k - 1$ and the task execution time; the completion time of the stage is the time when all tasks are completed, i.e., the maximum task running time in that stage. Since intermediate data transmission time and task execution time are random, we use expected completion time to capture the average performance of the deployment decisions. Equation (2) represents the expected overall VM cost for running tasks in stage k of the job in round t. Equation (3) formulates the expected overall cost for data transmission from tasks in stage $k - 1$ to tasks in stage k of the job in round t. The cost is due to inter-datacenter data transfer. Here, d_j denotes the data center that task j is deployed in, which is known when we deploy tasks in stage k if task j is in the previous stage. We use $[S]$ to denote the set $1, \ldots, S$ in this chapter.

$$l_k^1(\vec{x}_k(t), \vec{y}_k(t)) = \mathbb{E}[\max_{i \in [A_k]}(\sum_{d \in [D]} x_{ki}^d(t) g_{ki}^d(t) + \sum_{m \in [M]} y_{ki}^m(t) \tau_{ki}^m)] \tag{1}$$

$$l_k^2(\vec{x}_k(t), \vec{y}_k(t)) = \sum_{i \in [A_k]} \sum_{m \in [M]} y_{ki}^m(t) \mathbb{E}[\tau_{ki}^m] p_m \tag{2}$$

$$l_k^3(\vec{x}_k(t), \vec{y}_k(t)) = \sum_{i \in [A_k]} \sum_{d \in [D]} (x_{ki}^d(t) \sum_{j \in [A_{k-1}]} s_{ki}^j(t) q_{d_j d}) \tag{3}$$

The objective function to minimize by our deployment decisions is defined as

$$l_k(\vec{x}_k(t), \vec{y}_k(t)) = \lambda_1 l_k^1(\vec{x}_k(t), \vec{y}_k(t)) + \lambda_2 l_k^2(\vec{x}_k(t), \vec{y}_k(t)) + \lambda_3 l_k^3(\vec{x}_k(t), \vec{y}_k(t)) \quad (4)$$

where λ_1, λ_2 and λ_3 are non-negative weights, gauging the priorities in minimizing task completion time, VM cost, and data transport cost. We formulate the optimal task deployment problem for stage k of the job in round t in (5).

$$\min l_k(\vec{x}_k(t), \vec{y}_k(t)) \quad (5)$$

subject to:

$$\sum_{d \in [D]} x_{ki}^d(t) = 1, \ \forall i \in [A_k] \quad (5a)$$

$$\sum_{m \in [M]} y_{ki}^m(t) = 1, \ \forall i \in [A_k] \quad (5b)$$

$$g_{ki}^d(t) = \max_{j \in [A_{k-1}]} \frac{s_{ki}^j(t)}{b_{d_j d}}, \ \forall i \in [A_k], d \in [D] \quad (5c)$$

$$x_{ki}^d(t) \in \{0, 1\}, \ \forall i \in [A_k], d \in [D] \quad (5d)$$

$$y_{ki}^m(t) \in \{0, 1\}, \ \forall i \in [A_k], m \in [M] \quad (5e)$$

Constraints (5a) and (5b) indicate that each task should be scheduled on only one data center and one VM, respectively. Constraint (5c) gives the time for task i in stage k to receive all required output data from tasks in stage $k - 1$. Note that $b_{d_j d}$ is very large if d_j and d are the same data center. We do not consider limitations of resources (VM and bandwidth) in each data center, since resources in cloud data centers are typically much more than required for serving one data analytics job.

In the context of bandit optimization, there are two types of arms in our problem: (i) A pair (i, m) which denotes task i is deployed on a type-m VM, $\forall i \in [A_k]$, $m \in [M], \forall k \in [K]$. The loss of selecting such an arm is the combination of task running time and the VM cost incurred, i.e., $\lambda_1 \tau_{ki}^m + \lambda_2 \tau_{ki}^m p_m$. The task execution time is only revealed after task i has been deployed and completed on a type-m VM. (ii) A connection (d, e) from data center d to data center e, $\forall d, e \in [D]$. Choosing such a connection for intermediate data transport leads to a bandwidth b_{de} achieved and a cost q_{de} incurred for intermediate data transport. The bandwidth is only revealed after a task j in stage $k - 1$ has been placed in data center d, a task i in stage k has been placed in data center e, and intermediate data has been transmitted from task j to task i. The effect of choosing such an arm is reflected by the combination of intermedia data transport time and bandwidth cost incurred, i.e., $\lambda_1 \frac{s_{ki}^j(t)}{b_{de}} + \lambda_3 s_{ki}^j(t) q_{de}$.

TABLE 8.1 Notation

M	# of VM types
D	# of data centers
K	# of stages
k	the $k - th$ stage of the job
A_k	# of tasks in stage k
τ_{ki}^m	Running time of task i in stage k of a job on a type-m VM
b_{de}	The available bandwidth per connection from data center d to data center e
$s_{ki}^j(t)$	Size of data block fetched by task i in stage k from task j in stage $k - 1$
$g_{ki}^d(t)$	Time taken for task i in stage k deployed in DC d to obtain all required data from tasks in stage $k - 1$
d_j	The data center that task j is deployed in
q_{de}	Cost for transmitting a unit amount of data from data center d to data center e
p_m	Cost for using one type-m VM per unit of time
$x_{ki}^d(t)$	Decision variable of whether task i in stage k in round t is deployed on data center d
$y_{ki}^m(t)$	Decision variable of whether to run task i in stage k of the job in round t on a type-m VM
$\hat{B}_{de}$	Historical mean value of bandwidth b_{de}
$\hat{C}_{ki}^m$	Historical mean value of the execution time τ_{ki}^m
$N^B(d, e)$	# of times the arm (d, e) is played till current stage in current round
$N_k^C(i, m)$	# of times the arm (i, m) of stage k is played till current round

Considering all tasks in a stage, the value of $l_k(\vec{x}_k(t), \vec{y}_k(t))$ in (4) is hence the *loss* incurred by per-stage task deployment decisions in each round, in the context of multi-armed bandit optimization. Considering all stages, $\sum_{k \in [K]} l_k(\vec{x}_k(t), \vec{y}_k(t))$ represents the overall loss incurred by deploying the job in round t. We seek to design an online bandit algorithm for task scheduling of all jobs over $[T]$, targeting overall loss minimization as follows:

$$\min \sum_{t=1}^{T} \sum_{k=1}^{K} l_k(\vec{x}_k(t), \vec{y}_k(t)) \tag{6}$$

subject to constraints (5a)–(5e), $\forall k \in [K]$, $t \in [T]$.

The regret of the online bandit algorithm is the gap between the expected overall loss incurred by our bandit strategy and the expected total loss of the (approximate) optimal solution, to be formally defined in Section 4.3.

4 ONLINE BANDIT ALGORITHM

The first challenge of designing an efficient bandit algorithm to minimize (6) is that the overall loss not only depends on the means of the random variables but also on the entire range of the variable values, due to the *max* operators included in computing

$l_k^1(\vec{x}_k(t), \vec{y}_k(t))$ in (1) and (5c). Almost all existing bandit optimization techniques rely on the estimation of mean values of the unknown distributions [32–34]. In our objective function, the expectation of the extreme value of a combination of random variables cannot be represented by the mean values of the distributions. We may need to evaluate the value achieved by each combination of random variables, leading to exponential algorithm complexity.

Instead of taking this native approach, we reduce our loss function to one that relies only on the expectations of the random variables, and prove that the revised loss function provides a non-trivial upper bound to the original one (Section 4.1). Then, we design an efficient online bandit algorithm to minimize the revised loss function (Section 4.2). We prove the regret bound achieved by the online algorithm on the original problem in Section 4.3.

4.1 Reformatting the Objective Function

Given a set of random variables $X_1, X_2, \ldots, X_n$, we present the upper bound of $E[\max_{i \in [n]} X_i]$ in the following theorem.

Theorem 1.1 *Given a set of random variables $X_1, X_2, \ldots, X_n$ with support $[a, b]$, we can find a convex function $\varphi(\cdot)$ such that $\ln \mathbb{E}[\exp\{\lambda X_i\}] \varphi(\lambda)$ for all $i \in [n]$ and $\lambda \geq 0$. Then, we have $\mathbb{E}[\max_{i \in [n]} X_i](b - a)\sqrt{\frac{\ln n}{2}} + \max_{i \in [n]} \mathbb{E}[X_i]$.*

The proof can be found in Section 7.

Based on Theorem 1.1, regarding $\sum_{d \in [D]} x_{ki}^d(t) g_{ki}^d(t) + \sum_{m \in [M]} y_{ki}^m(t) \tau_{ki}^m, \forall i \in [A_k]$ in (1) as a set of random variables, we have an upper bound of $l_k^1(\vec{x}_k(t), \vec{y}_k(t))$ as follows:

$$l_k^1(\vec{x}_k(t), \vec{y}_k(t)) \leq (R_{1k} - L_{1k})\sqrt{\frac{\ln A_k}{2}} + \max_{i \in [A_k]} \mathbb{E}\left[\sum_{d \in [D]} x_{ki}^d(t) g_{ki}^d(t) + \sum_{m \in [M]} y_{ki}^m(t) \tau_{ki}^m\right]$$

$$\leq (R_{1k} - L_{1k})\sqrt{\frac{\ln A_k}{2}} + (R_{2k} - L_{2k})\sqrt{\frac{\ln A_{k-1}}{2}}$$

$$+ \max_{i \in [A_k]}\left(\sum_{d \in [D]} x_{ki}^d(t)\left(\max_{j \in [A_{k-1}]} \frac{s_{ki}^j(t)}{\mathbb{E}[b_{d_jd}]}\right) + \sum_{m \in [M]} y_{ki}^m(t) \mathbb{E}[\tau_{ki}^m]\right)$$

where R_{1k} and L_{1k} are the upper bound and the lower bound of the support of $\sum_{d \in [D]} x_{ki}^d(t) g_{ki}^d(t) + \sum_{m \in [M]} y_{ki}^m(t) \tau_{ki}^m, \forall i \in [A_k]$, under constraint (5d)–(5e), and R_{2k} and L_{2k} are the upper bound and lower bound of the support of $\frac{s_{ki}^j(t)}{E[b_{d_jd}]}, \forall d \in [D], i \in [A_k]$, $j \in [A_{k-1}]$. The second inequality is obtained by applying Theorem 1.1 to $E[g_{ki}^d(t)]$, as $g_{ki}^d(t)$ is also an extreme value of random variables.

Denote

$$\tilde{l}_k^1(\vec{x}_k(t), \vec{y}_k(t)) = a(k) + \max_{i \in [A_k]}(\sum_{d \in [D]} x_{ki}^d(t)(\max_{j \in [A_{k-1}]} \frac{s_{ki}^j(t)}{E[b_{d_j d}]}) + \sum_{m \in [M]} y_{ki}^m(t)E[\tau_{ki}^m])$$

where

$$a(k) = (R_{1k} - L_{1k})\sqrt{\frac{\ln A_k}{2}} + (R_{2k} - L_{2k})\sqrt{\frac{\ln A_{k-1}}{2}}, \tag{7}$$

and let

$$\tilde{l}_k(\vec{x}_k(t), \vec{y}_k(t)) = \lambda_1 \tilde{l}_k^1(\vec{x}_k(t), \vec{y}_k(t)) + \lambda_2 l_k^2(\vec{x}_k(t), \vec{y}_k(t)) + \lambda_3 l_k^3(\vec{x}_k(t), \vec{y}_k(t)). \tag{8}$$

The revised optimization problem for each stage k in each round t is:

$$\min \tilde{l}_k(\vec{x}_k(t), \vec{y}_k(t)) \tag{9}$$

subject to constraints (5a), (5b), (5d), (5e)

The reduced problem is a submodular minimization problem, since the term $\max(\cdot)$ in (8) is submodular in terms of the random variables. The overall loss minimization problem becomes:

$$\min \sum_{t=1}^{T} \sum_{k=1}^{K} \tilde{l}_k(\vec{x}_k(t), \vec{y}_k(t)) \tag{10}$$

s.t. constraints (5a), (5b), (5d), (5e), $\forall k \in [K], t \in [T]$

The following theorem shows that by using $\tilde{l}_k^1(\vec{x}_k(t), \vec{y}_k(t))$ to approximate $l_k^1(\vec{x}_k(t), \vec{y}_k(t))$ in (5), the decisions made will not incur much loss in optimality.

Theorem 1.2 *At any round t, for any stage k, let $(\vec{x}_k^B(t), \vec{y}_k^B(t))$ denote the decisions derived by the bandit algorithm, $(\vec{x}_k^A(t), \vec{y}_k^A(t))$ be the optimal decisions that solve problem (9), and $\vec{x}_k^*(t), \vec{y}_k^*(t)$ be the optimal solutions of the original problem (5). We have $\tilde{l}_k(\vec{x}_k^B(t), \vec{y}_k^B(t)) - \tilde{l}_k(\vec{x}_k^A(t), \vec{y}_k^A(t)) \geq l_k(\vec{x}_k^B(t), \vec{y}_k^B(t)) - l_k(\vec{x}_k^*(t), \vec{y}_k^*(t)) - \lambda_1 a(k)$, where a(k) is defined in (7).*

The proof is given in Section 7.

The theorem shows that if we design a bandit algorithm to minimize (9) in each stage of each round and use the decisions to evaluate the original loss function in (5), the regret of the bandit algorithm evaluated using the revised loss function and that evaluated with the original loss function differ by at most a constant term. Note that the gap $\lambda_1 a(k)$ increases with the number of tasks in each stage and the variances of the unknown distributions. In this way, we use expectations of task running time and inter-DC bandwidth to replace the combinatorial extremes in the loss function, so as to avoid exponential algorithm complexity, and are able to come up with an efficient bandit algorithm. In Section 4.3, we will show that we can bound the regret of our bandit algorithm in terms of the original loss functions based on Theorem 1.2.

4.2 Bandit Algorithm

Algorithm 1: Online Bandit Algorithm for Task Placement (*BAT*)

Input: $T, K, A_k, \forall k \in [K]$
Output: data centers and VMs for task placement, i.e., $\vec{x}_k(t), \vec{y}_k(t), \forall k \in [K], t \in [T]$
1: initialize $\hat{C}^m_{ki} = L^k_C$, $\hat{B}_{de} = R_B$, $N^C_k(i,m) = 0$, $N^B(d,e) = 0$, $\forall i \in [A_k], d, e \in [D]$, $k \in [K], m \in [M]$
2: **for** $t = 1$ to T **do**
3:   **for** $k = 1$ to K **do**
4:     **if** $k = 1$ **then**
5:       obtain sizes $s^j_{ki}(t)$ and locations d_j of input data sets of the new job in t, $\forall i \in [A_1]$, where j denotes different input data blocks
6:     **else**
7:       obtain size of intermediate data produced $s^j_{ki}(t)$ and location d_j of task j in stage $k - 1$, $\forall j \in [A_{k-1}], i \in [A_k]$
8:     **end if**
9:     replace b_{de} by $\min\{\hat{B}_{de} + rad^B_{tk}(d,e), R_B\}$ and τ^m_{ki} by $\max\{\hat{C}^m_{ki} - rad^C_{tk}(i,m), L^k_C\}$ in problem (9)
10:    solve problem (9) by Alg. 2 to obtain $\vec{x}_k(t)$ and $\vec{y}_k(t)$; deploy and run tasks in this stage to the selected VMs and data centers
11:    observe bandwidth $b_{de}(t,k)$ and task execution time $\tau^m_{ki}(t)$ experienced for all $i \in [A_k], j \in [A_{k-1}], m \in [M], d, e \in [D]$, such that $x^d_{ki}(t) = 1$, $x^e_{(k-1)j}(t) = 1$, and $y^m_{ki}(t) = 1$
12:    **for** all data center pairs $(d,e), d, e \in [D]$ **do**
13:      Update the historical mean value $\hat{B}_{de} = P(\hat{B}_{de}, b_{de}(t,k), N^B(d,e), x^d_{ki}(t))$
14:      Update the sampling time $N^B(d,e) = Q(N^B(d,e), x^d_{ki}(t))$
15:    **end for**
16:    **for** all (task, VM type) assignments $(i,m), i \in [A_k], m \in [M]$
17:      Update the historical mean value $\hat{C}^m_{ki} = P(\hat{C}^m_{ki}, \tau^m_{ki}(t), N^C_k(i,m), y^m_{ki}(t))$
18:      Update the sampling time $N^C_k(i,m) = Q(N^C_k(i,m), y^m_{ki}(t))$
19:    **end for**
20:   **end for**
21: **end for**

Algorithm 2 Greedy Oracle for Solving Problem (1.9)

Input: $k, t, s^j_{ki}(t), \tau^m_{ki}$ and $b_{de}, \forall i \in [A_k], j \in [A_{k-1}], m \in [M], d, e \in [D]$
Output: data centers and VMs for task placement in stage k of round t, i.e. $\vec{x}_k(t), \vec{y}_k(t)$

1: **for** $i = 1$ to A_k **do**

2:     Select $(d, m) \in \arg\min_{d \in [D], m \in [M]} \{\tilde{l}_k(\vec{x}_{i-1,k}(t) \cup x_{ki}^d(t), \vec{y}_{i-1,k}(t) \cup y_{ki}^m(t))$

      $- \tilde{l}_k(\vec{x}_{i-1,k}(t), \vec{y}_{i-1,k}(t))\}$

3:     $\vec{x}_{i,k}(t) = \vec{x}_{i-1,k}(t) \cup x_{ki}^d(t)$

4:     $\vec{y}_{i,k}(t) = \vec{y}_{i-1,k}(t) \cup y_{ki}^m(t)$

5: **end for**

6: $\vec{x}_k(t) = \vec{x}_{A_k,k}(t), \vec{y}_k(t) = \vec{y}_{A_k,k}(t)$

We next design an online multi-armed bandit algorithm to minimize the overall loss in (10). The main idea of the algorithm is as follows. Over the rounds, we maintain estimates of the task running durations (corresponding to each arm of a task–VM-type pair (i, m)), and of the inter-DC bandwidths (corresponding to each arm of a DC-to-DC connection (d, e)), respectively. Each estimation is the sum of two parts: (i) the historical mean value, computed as the average of the past observations, which is the *exploitation* component in bandit optimization; (ii) the adjustment, which is inverse proportional to the sampling times, designed to weaken error in the estimation made based on the historical mean value, and serves as the *exploration* component in the bandit algorithm. The adjustment enables larger possibilities to pull arms with less sampling times. At the beginning of each stage k in each round, the estimated task running durations and inter-DC bandwidths are used together with locations of tasks in stage $k - 1$ and sizes of intermediate data produced by each task in stage $k - 1$, to solve problem (9) for deployment decisions of tasks in stage k.

The bandit algorithm is given in Alg. 1. In the algorithm, $\hat{B}_{de}$ and $\hat{C}_{ki}^m$ are the historical mean values of per-connection bandwidth from data center d to data center e, and task running time when task i is assigned to a type-m VM, respectively, which are the average of previous observations. L_B and R_B (L_C^k and R_C^k) are lower and upper bounds of the support of the random variable associated with arm (d, e) (arm (i, m)). $N^B(d, e)$ and $N_k^C(i, m)$ are the sampling times of arm (d, e) and arm (i, m), respectively, after completing stage k in round t, i.e., the number of times the inter-datacenter bandwidth or the task running time is observed. $rad_{tk}^B(d, e) = R_B \sqrt{\frac{3 \ln\left(\left(\sum_{s=2}^{K} A_{s-1} A_s\right) t\right)}{2N^B(d,e)}}$ and $rad_{tk}^C(i, m) = R_C^k \sqrt{\frac{3 \ln(A_k t)}{2N_k^C(i,m)}}$, which are the confidence radius, i.e., the radius of the confidence interval of the estimated bandwidth for arm (d, e) and the estimated task running time for arm (i, m) to be pulled in stage k in round t, respectively, with realizations $b_{de} \in [L_B, R_B]$ and $\tau_{ki}^m \in [L_C^k, R_C^k]$. $I\{\cdot\} \in \{0, 1\}$ is the indicator function.

In the algorithm, we obtain sizes and locations of intermediate data produced by a previous stage (lines 4–8), and use the estimated inter-DC bandwidths and task running times to solve problem (9) (line 9). Then, we update the historical mean values of inter-DC bandwidths and the number of times each inter-DC connection has been explored (lines 12–15), by calculating the mean value of the feedbacks and counting the pulling times of each arm from previous observations. The functions used to calculate the historical mean values and the sampling times from beginning to the current round are as follows:

$$\mathcal{P}(\hat{B}_{de}, b_{de}(t,k), N^B(d,e), x^d_{ki}(t))$$

$$= \frac{\hat{B}_{de} \cdot N^B(d,e) + \sum\limits_{i \in [A_k]} \sum\limits_{j \in [A_{k-1}]} \mathrm{I}\{d_j = e, x^d_{ki}(t)\} \cdot b_{de}(t,k)}{N^B(d,e) + \sum\limits_{i \in [A_k]} \sum\limits_{j \in [A_{k-1}]} \mathrm{I}\{d_j = e, x^d_{ki}(t)\}}$$

$$Q(N^B(d,e), x^d_{ki}(t)) = N^B(d,e) + \sum\limits_{i \in [A_k]} \sum\limits_{j \in [A_{k-1}]} \mathrm{I}\{d_j = e, x^d_{ki}(t)\}$$

We also update the historical mean values of task running times on different VMs and the number of times each task–VM-type assignment (i,m) has been made (lines 16–19), following the functions:

$$\mathcal{P}(\hat{C}^m_{ki}, \tau^m_{ki}(t), N^C_k(i,m), y^m_{ki}(t)) = \frac{\hat{C}^m_{ki} \cdot N^C_k(i,m) + \sum\limits_{j \in [A_k]} y^m_{kj}(t) \cdot \tau^m_{kj}(t)}{N^C_k(i,m) + \sum\limits_{j \in [A_k]} y^m_{kj}(t)}$$

$$\mathcal{Q}(N^C_k(i,m), y^m_{ki}(t)) = N^C_k(i,m) + \sum\limits_{j \in [A_k]} y^m_{kj}(t)$$

Note that in line 1, we can use a small value as the estimated L^k_C and a large value as the estimated R_B. In line 9, the estimation of b_{de}, $\min\{\hat{B}_{de} + rad^B_{tk}(d,e), R_B\}$, is the upper bound of the confidence interval that we estimated for bandwidth of arm (d,e), to be pulled in stage k in round t. We adopt such an optimistic estimation, as we wish the bandwidth to be as large as possible. The estimation of $\tau^m_{ki}(t)$ is $\max\{\hat{C}^m_{ki} - rad^C_{tk}(i,m), R^k_C\}$, where $\hat{C}^m_{ki} - rad^C_{tk}(i,m)$ is the lower bound of confidence interval that we estimated for task running time of arm (i,m). We adopt this pessimistic estimation since we wish the execution time to be as smaller as possible.

In Alg. 2, which solves problem (9), we select a pair of data center and VM for deploying each task i in stage k of round t, that leads to the smallest increment in the loss, beyond the aggregate loss incurred by tasks 1 to $i-1$. We randomly choose one if there are more than one such pair. Here, $\vec{x}_i$ and $\vec{y}_i$ denote the vectors of deployment decisions for the first i tasks; $\vec{x}_{i-1} \cup x^d_i$ and $\vec{y}_{i-1} \cup y^m_i$ means adding the deployment decisions of task i into the decision vectors; and $\tilde{l}_k(\vec{x}_{i,k}(t), \vec{y}_{i,k}(t))$ denotes the cumulative loss after deploying task 1to task i.

Alg. 2 is a fast greedy algorithm to solve the integer program (9), which utilizes submodularity of the objective function. The marginal increment in loss by deploying a new task is smaller if the number of deployed tasks is larger. The following theorem gives the approximation ratio achieved by Alg. 2, as compared to the optimal solution of problem (9).

Theorem 1.3 *Alg. 2 achieves an* $O(\frac{A_k}{l_k(\vec{x}_k^A(t), \vec{y}_k^A(t))})$ *approximation ratio for solving integer program (9), for any stage* $k \in [K]$ *in any round* $t \in [T]$. *The exact approximation ratio is*

$$\beta = 1 + \frac{\lambda_1 A_k \max_{i \in [A_k]} (\max_{d \in [D], m \in [M]} (\bar{g}_{ki}^d + \bar{\tau}_{ki}^m))}{l_k(\vec{x}_k^A(t), \vec{y}_k^A(t))}, \text{ where } \bar{g}_{ki}^d = \max_{j \in [A_{k-1}]} \frac{s_{ki}^j(t)}{E[b_{d_j d}]} \text{ and } \bar{\tau}_{ki}^m = E[\tau_{ki}^m].$$

The proof can be found in Section 7.

Note that in our bandit algorithm (Alg. 1), in each stage of a round, an arm may be repeatedly pulled, i.e., when task deployment leads to multiple tasks deployed on the same type of VMs and connections between the same DC pairs are exploited for transmitting intermediate data. This is different from the existing work (e.g., [29,33]), in which each arm can be pulled for at most once in one round. Such a characteristic of our bandit algorithm leads to fast convergence since we may have more than one feedback for an arm in each round. But the loss may increase if we try a suboptimal arm for multiple times in one round. There is hence a tradeoff in the impact of task numbers per stage on the performance of our algorithm.

4.3 Regret Analysis

We now analyze the performance of *BAT* by an α-approximation regret. The α-approximation regret [33] has been widely adopted for analysis of online learning algorithms when their underlying offline problems are NP-hard. In view of the approximation incurred to solve the offline optimal problem, the regret is to compare the loss of the online learning algorithm with α fraction of the offline optimal loss. The α-approximation regret in our problem model is defined as follows.

Definition 1.1 (α-approximation regret) *The* α-*approximation regret of Alg. 1 after* T *rounds using Alg. 2 as an oracle is*

$$Reg^\alpha(T) = \sum_{t=1}^{T} \sum_{k \in [K]} l_k(\vec{x}_k(t), \vec{y}_k(t)) - \alpha \sum_{t=1}^{T} \sum_{k \in [K]} l_k(\vec{x}_k^*(t), \vec{y}_k^*(t))$$

where $\alpha = \frac{1}{1 - \frac{\lambda_1 a(k)}{\tilde{l}(\vec{x}_k^A(t), \vec{y}_k^A(t))}} \beta$.

The approximation ratio α in our problem is caused by two approximation steps: (i) The approximation due to using the reduced loss function in (9) to approximate the original loss function (5). Based on the inequality in Theorem 1.2 connecting $\tilde{l}_k(\vec{x}_k^A(t), \vec{y}_k^A(t))$ and $l_k(\vec{x}_k^*(t), \vec{y}_k^*(t))$, we can obtain the approximation ratio of using (9) to approximate (5), $\frac{1}{1 - \frac{\lambda_1 a(k)}{\tilde{l}(\vec{x}_k^A(t), \vec{y}_k^A(t))}}$, computed by dividing the original loss function value evaluated at the solution obtained by solving (9) ($l_k(\vec{x}_k^A(t), \vec{y}_k^A(t))$) by the optimal loss ($l_k(\vec{x}_k^*(t), \vec{y}_k^*(t))$). The proof can be found in Section 7. (ii) The approximation due to using the greedy algorithm in Alg. 2 to find an approximated optimal solution of (9), with an approximation ratio β is proven in Theorem 1.3. The approximation ratio of Alg. 1 in solving (5) is hence derived by multiplying the ratios in the above two steps.

We next identify the relationship between the α-approximation regret and a β-approximation regret defined below, such that we can bound the α-approximation regret by bounding the β-approximation regret instead.

Definition 1.2 (β-approximation regret) *The β-approximation regret of Alg. 1 after T rounds using Alg. 2 as an oracle is*

$$Reg(T) = \sum_{t=1}^{T} \sum_{k \in [K]} \tilde{l}_k(\vec{x}_k(t), \vec{y}_k(t)) - \beta \sum_{t=1}^{T} \sum_{k \in [K]} \tilde{l}_k(\vec{x}_k^A(t), \vec{y}_k^A(t))$$

Theorem 1.4 *The β-approximation regret is larger than the α-approximation regret, i.e.,*

$$Reg^{\alpha}(T) \leq Reg(T)$$

The proof can be found in Section 7.

The β-approximation regret is equal to the sum of the gaps in losses incurred by suboptimal arms selected, i.e., a set of arms whose corresponding losses are larger than the upper bound of approximate optimal loss. Therefore, our regret bound analysis mainly relies on bounding the sampling times of suboptimal arms under Alg. 1. We divide the arms into two disjoint sets based on a threshold: one set includes all arms whose number of times selected is less than the threshold; the other set includes the other arms. We prove that the probability of the under-sampled event, i.e., that the sampling time of an arm does not exceed the threshold, can be bounded by the sampling threshold, and the probability of the sufficiently sampled event, i.e., that the sampling time of an arm exceeds the threshold, can be bounded using the historical mean value plus an adjustment term. Then, by multiplying the maximum possible difference between losses achieved by suboptimal decision and optimal decision by the sampling times of suboptimal arms, we can bound the regret. Detailed analysis steps can be found in Section 7.

Theorem 1.5 *The β-approximation regret of Alg. 1 after T rounds using the greedy oracle Alg. 2 is at most*

$$\sum_{k=1}^{K} \left(\frac{1}{\left(\sum_{k=2}^{K} A_{k-1} A_k \right)^2} + \frac{1}{A_k^2} \right) \frac{\pi^2}{3} \cdot \Delta_{\max}$$

$$+ \sum_{(d,e) \in B} \max_{t \in [T], k \in [K]} \frac{6 R_B^2 \ln \left(\left(\sum_{k=2}^{K} A_{k-1} A_k \right) T \right)}{f_{tk}^{-1} (\Delta_{t,k,\min}^{B,d,e})^2} \cdot \Delta_{\max}$$

$$+ \sum_{(i,m)\in C} \sum_{k=1}^{K} \max_{t\in[T]} \frac{6(R_C^k)^2 \ln(A_k T)}{f_{tk}^{-1}(\Delta_{t,k,\min}^{C,i,m})^2} \cdot \Delta_{\max} + 2 \cdot \Delta_{\max}$$

Here, $B = \{(d,e), \ \forall d,e \in [D]\}$ is the set of arms corresponding to DC pairs. $C = \{(i,m), \forall i \in [A_k], m \in [M], k \in [K]\}$ is the set of arms corresponding to task–VM-type assignments. $\Delta_{t,k,\min}^{B,d,e}$ is the minimum gap between losses incurred by deployment decisions related to an arm $(d,e), \forall d,e \in [D]$, and by the optimal solution in stage k of round t. $\Delta_{t,k,\min}^{C,i,m}$ is the minimum gap between losses incurred by deployment decisions related to an arm $(i,m), \forall i \in [A_k], m \in [M], k \in [K]$ and by the optimal solution in stage k of round t. $f_{tk}(\cdot)$ is a smoothness function associated with the objective function in stage k and round t, mapping the variances of variables to the variance of objective function. $\Delta_{\max}$ is the maximum difference in losses incurred by suboptimal decisions and optimal decisions over all stages in the entire time span T.

According to Theorem 1.4, the α-approximation regret of Alg. 1 is also bounded by the bound in Theorem 1.5. The bound in Theorem 1.5 is $O(\ln T)$ and polynomial with the numbers of arms. Especially, the bound is the sum of product of the expected sampling times of suboptimal arms and $\Delta_{\max}$, while the sampling threshold depends on the minimum gaps $\Delta_{t,k,\min}^{B,d,e}$ and $\Delta_{t,k,\min}^{C,i,m}$. The number of tasks in each stage also influences the regret. In each stage of decision-making in Alg. 1, one arm may be pulled for multiple times but its mean value estimation is only updated after the stage ends. Therefore, we can obtain more feedback of one arm in each stage, but the loss caused by sticking to a suboptimal arm may be larger as the feedback is not that timely used to update the estimation, as compared to traditional bandit models. This explains why A_k appears both in the denominator and in the numerator in the bound. When T is large enough, the average regret in each round is close to zero.

5 PERFORMANCE EVALUATION

We evaluate the performance of *BAT* using both trace-driven simulation and testbed experiments. The focus of trace-driven simulation is to show the performance with production workload in large scale, while testbed experiments are designed to demonstrate the effectiveness in real-world data analytics applications, as well as to verify simulation results.

5.1 Trace-Driven Simulation

Setup. We use the job logs of BDBench from [35]. BDBench is a big data benchmark [36], consisting of jobs for exploratory SQL queries, join queries, and page-rank-like queries. Especially, we simulate a page-rank-like query job. The job consists of 8 stages and the number of tasks in each stage is among 100, 200 and 248. To obtain the amount of data to be transmitted from one task in stage $k-1$ to one task in stage k, we divide the output data volume from the previous stage among tasks in the next stage following a normal distribution. Since the BDBench traces were collected when all jobs are running on the same type of VMs, we combine the traces with the Google cluster data [37] to produce more task running durations on different types of VMs. The Google cluster data record information of data analytics jobs running on the Google cluster, including resource consumption (CPU cores, memory, and disk) of tasks, and timestamps for start and end of each task. We treat tasks using different numbers of cores in the Google cluster data as different types of VMs. There are 9 different types of VMs simulated in this way. We then map the VM used in the BDBench job logs to the most powerful VM in the Google cluster data, and create more task execution durations on different types of VMs by scaling the task running durations in the BDBench job logs proportionally, according to the ratio of the number of cores used in each type of VMs over that used by the most powerful VM. We simulate 8 data centers as shown in Figure 8.2. We randomly deploy input data sets for each job among the data centers. We use bandwidth measurements collected among the 8 data centers every 5 minutes for 35 hours from [11], and randomly choose one bandwidth value from the set of measurements between two data centers, each time when a connection between the two data centers is used for data transfer. We set the unit bandwidth prices according to [38] and the unit VM cost is set according to the number of cores each VM uses, i.e., the more powerful a VM is, the more expensive it is. We set $\lambda_1 = 0.1, \lambda_2 = 0.1, \lambda_3 = 0.1$ by default in our simulations.

Schemes for Comparison. We compare *BAT* with the following methods, which are representative of existing work discussed in Section 2. Note that other existing methods require substantially more prior knowledge, and hence would not render a fair comparison.

(1) *Historical Average (Ave).* This algorithm uses the historical mean values as the estimated bandwidths and task running durations, to be used in task placement decision-making [12,39,40].

(2) *Random Algorithm (Rand).* With this approach, we select a data center and a VM to deploy each task uniformly randomly among all data centers and VM types.

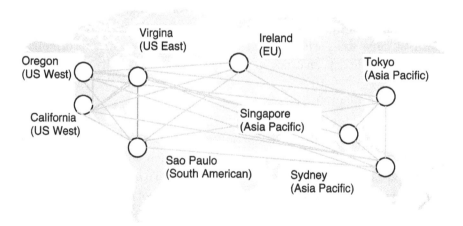

FIGURE 8.2   Data center topology.

(3) *Dynamic Linear Regression (DLR).* In this approach, a linear relationship is assumed between the data size and the time taken for data processing or transfer, and linear regression is used to predict the task execution time and data transfer time [14], to be used in task placement decision-making. In each round, all historical information and input in the current round are used for computing the coefficients in the regression model. In this case, the complexity of DLR is in the order of T, which is much higher than that of *BAT*, which does not depend on T and can be regarded as a constant.

(4) *Static Algorithm (Stat).* We collect some measurements on task execution time and bandwidth as prior information before carrying out our simulation. Then, we use this prior information as the estimation in each round without considering any uncertainties. This method is similar to that of Hu et al. [8], where they collect some bandwidth measurements before running a job.

(5) *Optimal Solution (Opt).* We also compare with the approximate optimal overall loss computed for each stage in each round using Alg. 2 in Section 4.2, assuming full knowledge of inter-DC bandwidths and task running durations.

Results. We plot the expected loss in each round incurred by different algorithms in Figures 8.3 to Figures 8.5. Figure 8.3 shows that BAT performs close to the approximate optimum, and its performance improves after more rounds of learning. The algorithm based on historical average relies heavily on exploitation and cannot make adjustment timely if the previous observations are inaccurate. Performance of the random algorithm is stable but cannot get improved over rounds. With the dynamic linear regression approach, more time is needed to train the linear prediction model, and the performance is not as good as *BAT*, due to the lack of exploration. The performance of the static method does not improve over time either. Figure 8.4 and Figure 8.5 show the results when the loss to minimize includes only job completion time (i.e., $\lambda_2 = 0$ and $\lambda_3 = 0$), and resource costs (i.e., $\lambda_1 = 0$). Note that in these two cases, the

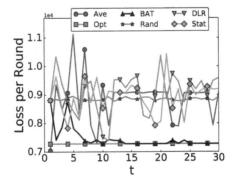

FIGURE 8.3 Loss per round: $\lambda_1 = 0.1, \lambda_2 = 0.1, \lambda_3 = 0.1$.

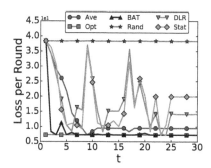

FIGURE 8.4   Loss per round: $\lambda_1 = 0.1, \lambda_2 = 0, \lambda_3 = 0$.

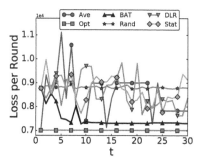

FIGURE 8.5   Loss per round: $\lambda_1 = 0, \lambda_2 = 0.1, \lambda_3 = 0.1$.

approximation ratio of Alg. 2 is 1. We observe that *BAT* always performs the best, with a per-round loss close to the optimum.

In Figure 8.6, we evaluate the influence of the number of tasks per stage on the overall loss (over a total of $T = 30$ rounds), since it represents a tradeoff of the regret achieved by *BAT*. The number of tasks in Figure 8.6 is the average number of tasks per stage, over the 8 stages of the job. We scale down the job size proportionally from the trace data, in order to produce jobs of different average numbers of tasks per stage. We observe that the difference in loss is smaller if the number of tasks is larger. This is because the loss incurred by the optimal solution and that of *BAT* do not increase much with a larger number of tasks, such that the impact of more feedbacks on the loss is larger than that of a suboptimal arm. Therefore, a smaller regret can be achieved with more sampling times.

Figure 8.7 shows the overall regret over all rounds achieved when the total number of rounds T varies. The regret is computed as the difference between the loss incurred by an algorithm and the optimal loss. Note that this regret is stronger than the α-approximation regret in our theoretical analysis. We observe that the regret of *BAT* is logarithmic with T, which is consistent with our theoretical analysis. However, other algorithms lead to near-linear regret with T.

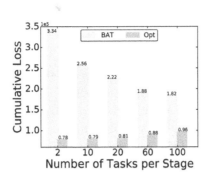

FIGURE 8.6   Overall loss with different # of tasks per stage.

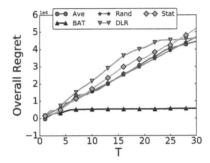

FIGURE 8.7   Overall regret.

5.2 Testbed Experiments

Testbed Implementation. We implement our task scheduling algorithm in Spark [2], by overriding the default Spark scheduler modules. After each stage of tasks is done, we obtain the output data sizes and locations from MapOutputTracker, a module in Spark designed to keep track of the output of a stage. We then make task deployment decisions for the next stage: the DAG scheduler creates a TaskSet and feeds it to a TaskScheduler; the TaskScheduler waits for resources from Scheduler-Backened and also decides which task should be launched on which type of VM. After resources are offered, i.e., an idle VM, *BAT* verifies the VM location and type: if there is no task for this type of VM according to the deployment decisions made, *BAT* just ignores this resource offer; otherwise, it picks a corresponding task from the pending queue, creates the task description, and sends it to CoarseGrainedSchedulerBackend for launching the task. For intermediate data transport, each task sends request by evoking ShuffleBlockFetcherIterator and fetches data blocks using the BlockTransferService.

The Spark system is deployed on a cluster of 6 IBM blade servers, each with 32 cores, 80GB memory, 600GB disk, and two 10GbE NICs connected to a 10GbE switch. We treat each server as one data center. Each server runs KVM-QEMU [41] to launch 32 VM instances, each with 1 core and 2 GB memory. To emulate different types of VMs within a data center, we vary the CPU frequency of each VM instance between 1.2GHz and 2.0GHz. We use one VM instance as the Spark master node and all other instances are worker nodes. We deploy Hadoop Distributed File System (HDFS) [42] among servers to store the input and output of Spark jobs. The block size of HDFS is 128MB and the replication number is 2. To emulate inter-DC bandwidth, we use linuxtc [43] to enforce specified bandwidth between servers following the varying bandwidths measured in [11]. An illustration of the testbed architecture is given in Figure 8.8.

Experiment Setup. We implement two applications on Spark.

(1) *WordCount.* There are two stages of processing and 24 tasks in each stage. We use 5GB of Wikipedia dump data as the input [44].

(2) *PageRank.* There are 7 stages of processing and 8, 24, or 12 tasks in each stage. We use a directed graph with 875,713 nodes and 5,105,039 edges released by Google [45] as the input.

The input file is divided into several blocks with the size of 128MB each and deployed on servers randomly picked. To emulate the interference among workload in real-world data centers, we run additional workload on the physical servers. Following Google cluster data [37], we allow each server to be half loaded on average by adding colocated workload.

Experimental Results. We observe that *BAT* still performs the best among all online algorithms both in the case of WordCount jobs (Figure 8.9) and PageRank jobs (Figure 8.10). Due to the interference of background workload, individual observations of inter-DC bandwidths and task running durations can be far from the expectation. Without sufficient adjustment over the rounds, future decisions may stick to bad ones due to inaccurate previous observations. The algorithm using historical average cannot recover well in this case. *BAT* takes the uncertainties into consideration, by assigning the arms

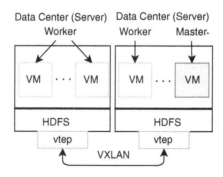

FIGURE 8.8   Testbed.

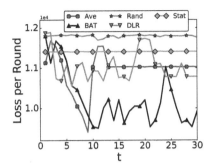

FIGURE 8.9 Loss in WordCount.

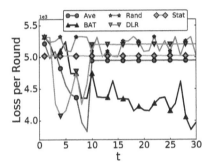

FIGURE 8.10 Loss in PageRank.

with fewer sampling times with a larger exploration probability, and is able to adapt well in highly dynamic environments. The random algorithm does not work well as it does not utilize feedback to make improvement. The dynamic linear regression approach does not track the change in the relationship between data and processing/transmission time well enough too. The static method is stable and does not achieve much improvement over time either.

In addition, we observe that our algorithm runs efficiently in the experiments. The algorithm to compute task deployment in each stage of each job finishes within 1600ms for 500 tasks, 10 data centers, and 9 VM types. Except that the random algorithm is apparently a few times faster, running times of the other algorithms are similar. The time consumption of the dynamic linear regression approach is not much higher than that of *BAT*, as the number of rounds is not large enough in our experiments. We omit detailed figures due to space limit.

6 CONCLUSION

This chapter investigates online optimal deployment of big data analytics jobs across geo-distributed regions, with unknown and uncertain information of inter-datacenter bandwidths and task execution durations on different VMs. We design an online learning algorithm, *BAT*, based on multi-armed bandit optimization to guide data center and VM type selection for task deployment over multiple rounds, aiming to minimize the overall loss, a mixture of job completion time and resource costs, over the entire time horizon. The algorithm is designed to balance the tradeoff between exploiting real-world feedback from previous decisions and the exploration of new choices, with continuous updates on preference between exploration and exploitation. *BAT* does not require any prior information but is able to achieve a bounded regret, compared with the approximate optimal solution derived with full knowledge. We also implement the algorithm in a real-world Apache Spark system. Trace-driven simulation and experiments with real-world workload validate that our algorithm is more adaptive than previous heuristic and statistical methods, and approaches the optimum after a small number of rounds of online learning. In future work, we seek to investigate the multiple job scheduling problem with resource constraints in similar cases of runtime uncertainties.

7 APPENDIX

Proof of Theorem 1.1

We use Hoeffding's lemma [46] to bound the moment-generating function of any bounded random variable.

Lemma 1.1 (Hoeffding's Lemma) *Let X be any real-valued random variable such that $a \leq X \leq b$ for some $a, b \in \mathbb{R}$. Denote $\mu = \mathbb{E}[X]$. Then, $\mathbb{E}[\exp\{\lambda(X - \mu)\}] \leq \exp\left\{\frac{\lambda^2(b-a)^2}{8}\right\}$ for all $\lambda \in \mathbb{R}$.*

Lemma 1.2 (Jensen's Inequality [47]) *If $\varphi(\cdot)$ is a convex function and X is a random variable, we have $\varphi(\mathbb{E}[X]) \, \mathbb{E}[\varphi(X)]$, provided that the expectations exist and are finite.*

Proof 1.1 *We construct $\lambda(\cdot)$ for all X_i, $i \in [n]$ first. Let $\mu_{\max} = \max_{i \in [n]} \mathbb{E}[X_i]$ and $\mu_i = \mathbb{E}[X_i]$. Note that*

$$\mathbb{E}[\exp\{\lambda(X_i - \mu_i)\}] = \exp\{-\lambda\mu_i\} \cdot \mathbb{E}[\exp\{\lambda X_i\}]$$

Based on Lemma 1.1, for all $\lambda \in \mathbb{R}$ and for all $i \in [n]$, we have

$$\ln(\mathbb{E}[\exp\{\lambda X_i\}]) \leq \frac{\lambda^2(b-a)^2}{8} + \lambda\mu_i$$

Then, we set $\varphi(\lambda) = \frac{\lambda^2(b-a)^2}{8} + \lambda\mu_{\max}$, which can satisfy the requirement.

Since $\ln(\cdot)$ is strictly concave and $-\ln(\cdot)$ is strictly convex. By Lemma 1.2, we have $\ln(\mathbb{E}[X_i]) \geq \mathbb{E}[\ln(X_i)]$ for all $i \in [n]$. Then, for any $\lambda \geq 0$, we have

$$\mathbb{E}[\max_{i \in [n]} X_i] = \frac{1}{\lambda} \mathbb{E}[\ln \exp\{\lambda \max_{i \in [n]} X_i\}]$$

$$\leq \frac{1}{\lambda}\ln(\sum_{i\in[n]}\mathbb{E}[\exp\{\lambda X_i\}]) \leq \frac{1}{\lambda}(\ln n + \varphi(\lambda))$$

Thus, we have

$$\mathbb{E}[\max_{i\in[n]} X_i] \leq \frac{\ln n}{\lambda} + \frac{\lambda(b-a)^2}{8} + \mu_{\max} \qquad (11)$$

By taking deviation on λ in (11), we can minimize the upper bound of $\mathbb{E}[\max_{i\in[n]} X_i]$, which is $(b-a)\sqrt{\frac{\ln n}{2}} + \mu_{\max}$.

Proof of Theorem 1.2

Proof 1.2 *Since $\max_{i\in[n]}\mathbb{E}[X_i] \leq \mathbb{E}[\max_{i\in[n]} X_i]$, we have $\tilde{l}_k^1(\vec{x}_k(t),\vec{y}_k(t)) - a(k) \leq l_k^1(\vec{x}_k(t), \vec{y}_k(t)) \leq \tilde{l}_k^1(\vec{x}_k(t),\vec{y}_k(t))$, for all $(\vec{x}_k(t),\vec{y}_k(t))$ in the set of feasible solutions $\mathcal{F}$ of the problem in (5). Note that $(\vec{x}_k^*(t),\vec{y}_k^*(t)) = \arg\min_{\vec{x},\vec{y}\in\mathcal{F}} l_k(\vec{x},\vec{y})$ and $(\vec{x}_k^A(t),\vec{y}_k^A(t)) = \arg\min_{\vec{x},\vec{y}\in\mathcal{F}} \tilde{l}_k(\vec{x},\vec{y})$. Then, we have the following inequalities:*

$$\tilde{l}_k(\vec{x}_k(t),\vec{y}_k(t)) - \lambda_1 a(k) \leq l_k(\vec{x}_k(t),\vec{y}_k(t)) \leq \tilde{l}_k(\vec{x}_k(t),\vec{y}_k(t))$$

$$\tilde{l}_k(\vec{x}_k^A(t),\vec{y}_k^A(t)) \leq \tilde{l}_k(\vec{x}_k^*(t),\vec{y}_k^*(t))$$

The relationship between the optimal value of $\tilde{l}_k(\vec{x}_k(t),\vec{y}_k(t))$ and $l_k(\vec{x}_k(t),\vec{y}_k(t))$ is

$$\tilde{l}_k(\vec{x}_k^A(t),\vec{y}_k^A(t)) - \lambda_1 a(k) \leq \tilde{l}_k(\vec{x}_k^*(t),\vec{y}_k^*(t)) - \lambda_1 a(k) \leq l_k(\vec{x}_k^*(t),\vec{y}_k^*(t))$$

$$\tilde{l}_k(\vec{x}_k^A(t),\vec{y}_k^A(t)) \leq l_k(\vec{x}_k^*(t),\vec{y}_k^*(t)) + \lambda_1 a(k)$$

Then, we can use the optimal solution of $\tilde{l}_k(\vec{x}_k(t),\vec{y}_k(t))$ as the approximated optimal solution of $l_k(\vec{x}_k(t),\vec{y}_k(t))$.

Proof of Theorem 1.3

Proof 1.3 *From the greedy step in Alg. 2, we have*

$$\tilde{l}_k(\vec{x}_{i,k}(t),\vec{y}_{i,k}(t)) - \tilde{l}_k(\vec{x}_{i-1,k}(t),\vec{y}_{i-1,k}(t))$$

$$\leq \tilde{l}_k(\vec{x}_{i,k}^A(t),\vec{y}_{i,k}^A(t)) - \tilde{l}_k(\vec{x}_{i-1,k}(t),\vec{y}_{i-1,k}(t)), \; \forall i \in [A_k]$$

where the first $i-1$ components in $\vec{x}_{i,k}^A(t)$ and $\vec{y}_{i,k}^A(t)$ are the same as the first $i-1$ components in $\vec{x}_{i,k}(t)$ and $\vec{y}_{i,k}(t)$, while the ith component is the optimal decision of $\tilde{l}_k(\vec{x}_k(t),\vec{y}_k(t))$. Let $x_{ki}^{d,A}(t)$ and $y_{ki}^{m,A}(t)$ be the corresponding optimal decision variables, respectively.

Summing over i, we have

$$\tilde{l}_k(\vec{x}_k(t), \vec{y}_k(t)) \leq \lambda_1 \sum_{z \in [A_k]} \left(\sum_{d \in [D]} g_{kz}^d x_{kz}^{d,A}(t) + \sum_{m \in [M]} \tau_{kz}^m(t) y_{kz}^{m,A}(t) \right)$$

$$+ \lambda_2 l_k^2(\vec{x}_k^A(t), \vec{y}_k^A(t)) + \lambda_3 l_k^3(\vec{x}_k^A(t), \vec{y}_k^A(t))$$

$$\leq \tilde{l}_k(\vec{x}_k^A(t), \vec{y}_k^A(t)) + \lambda_1 A_k \max_{i \in [A_k]} (\max_{d \in [D], m \in [M]} (\bar{g}_{ki}^d + \bar{\tau}_{ki}^m))$$

where $\bar{g}_{ki}^d = \max_{j \in [A_{k-1}]} \frac{s_{ki}^j(t)}{\mathbb{E}[b_{d_j d}]}$ *and* $\bar{\tau}_{ki}^m = \mathbb{E}[\tau_{ki}^m]$.

We can get the approximation ratio β of the greedy algorithm, which is

$$1 + \frac{\lambda_1 A_k \max_{i \in [A_k]} (\max_{d \in [D], m \in [M]} (\bar{g}_{ki}^d + \bar{\tau}_{ki}^m))}{\tilde{l}_k(\vec{x}_k^A(t), \vec{y}_k^A(t))}$$

Proof of Theorem 1.4

Proof 1.4 *Note that from Theorem 1.2, we can also convert the gap to a ratio of* $\frac{1}{1 - \frac{\lambda_1 a(k)}{\tilde{l}(\vec{x}_k^A(t), \vec{y}_k^A(t))}}$. *Then we have* $l_k(\vec{x}_k^A(t), \vec{y}_k^A(t)) \leq \tilde{l}_k(\vec{x}_k^A(t), \vec{y}_k^A(t)) \leq \frac{1}{1 - \frac{\lambda_1 a(k)}{\tilde{l}(\vec{x}_k^A(t), \vec{y}_k^A(t))}} \cdot l_k(\vec{x}^*(t), \vec{y}^*(t))$.
Then, we have

$$\beta \tilde{l}_k(\vec{x}_k^A(t), \vec{y}_k^A(t)) \leq \frac{1}{1 - \frac{\lambda_1 a(k)}{\tilde{l}(\vec{x}_k^A(t), \vec{y}_k^A(t))}} \beta l_k(\vec{x}_k^*(t), \vec{y}_k^*(t)) = \alpha l_k(\vec{x}_k^*(t), \vec{y}_k^*(t))$$

$$\tilde{l}_k(\vec{x}_{t,k}^B, \vec{y}_{t,k}^B) - \beta \tilde{l}_k(\vec{x}_k^A(t), \vec{y}_k^A(t)) \geq l_k(\vec{x}_{t,k}^B, \vec{y}_{t,k}^B) - \alpha l_k(\vec{x}_k^*(t), \vec{y}_k^*(t))$$

Proof of Theorem 1.5

With the reformation in Section 4.1, the original problem (5) is reduced to (10). The reformulated problem (10) is a combinatorial multi-armed-bandit problem [33,34] which is composed of the expectation of each random variable. Therefore, we analyze the sampling time of each arm set which does not belong to optimal decision, and prove the upper bound based on Chernoff bound [48]. The analysis shows that the estimation of each arm is accurate enough if the arm is sampled for enough times.

We refer to each decision $(\vec{x}_k(t), \vec{y}_k(t))$, corresponding to a set of arms, as a super arm S. Note that one arm in one super arm can be repeatedly selected. We introduce the definition of the loss of a super arm as $\tilde{l}_t^k(S) = \tilde{l}_t^k(\vec{x}_k(t), \vec{y}_k(t))$. Denote the super arm corresponding to DC pairs as $\mathcal{B}$ and the super arm corresponding to task–VM-type assignment in stage k as $\mathcal{C}_k$.

We prove that expected loss function $\tilde{l}_k(\vec{x}_k(t), \vec{y}_k(t))$ satisfies the required properties in the standard combinatorial multi-armed-bandit problem [33].

Lemma 1.3 (Monotonicity) *At any round t and any stage k, the expected loss of playing any super arm S is monotonically nondecreasing with respect to the expectation of each arm. That is, for any super arm S, if $\forall (d, e) \in S \cap \mathcal{B}$, $E[b_{de}] \leq E[b'_{de}]$, and $\forall (i, m) \in S \cap \mathcal{C}_k$, $E[\tau_{ki}^m] \geq E[\tau_{ki}'^m]$, we have $\tilde{l}_{k, \vec{b}, \vec{\tau}}(S) \geq \tilde{l}_{k, \vec{b}', \vec{\tau}}(S)$. $\tilde{l}_{k, \vec{b}, \vec{\tau}}(S)$ means we use $\vec{b}$ and $\vec{\tau}$ as the parameter vector, representing $b_{de}, \tau_{ki}^m, \forall i \in [A_k], m \in [M], d, e \in [D]$.*

Proof 1.5 *From (9), we can find that $\tilde{l}_k(\vec{x}_k(t), \vec{y}_k(t))$ is monotonically non-increasing with b_{de} and monotonically nondecreasing with τ_{ki}^m.*

Lemma 1.4 (Bounded smoothness) *At any round t and any stage k, there exists a bounded smoothness function $f_{tk}(\cdot)$ with $f_{tk}(0) = 0$, which is continuous, strictly increasing and invertible, such that for any two expectation vectors $(\vec{b}, \vec{c})$ and $(\vec{b}', \vec{c}')$, given any super arm S, if $b'_{de} \geq b_{de}$ and $\tau_{ki}'^m \leq \tau_{ki}^m$, $\max_{(d,e) \in S \cap \mathcal{B}} b'_{de} - b_{de} \leq z_1$, $\max_{(i,m) \in S \cap \mathcal{C}_k} \tau_{ki}^m - \tau_{ki}'^m \leq z_2$, then $\tilde{l}_{k, \vec{b}, \vec{\tau}}(\vec{x}_k(t), \vec{y}_k(t)) - \tilde{l}_{k, \vec{b}', \vec{\tau}}(\vec{x}_k(t), \vec{y}_k(t)) \leq f_{tk}(\max\{z_1, z_2\})$.*

Proof 1.6 *Note that with these two expectation vectors, the super arm S and the decision $\vec{x}_k(t), \vec{y}_k(t)$ are fixed. Let the task and the task in its parent stage, i.e., $(i_1, j_1) = \arg\max_{ij} \tilde{l}_{k, \vec{b}, \vec{\tau}}^1(\vec{x}_k(t), \vec{y}_k(t))$ and $(i_2, j_2) = \arg\max_{ij} \tilde{l}_{k, \vec{b}', \vec{\tau}}^1(\vec{x}_k(t), \vec{y}_k(t))$. d_1 and d_2 are the data centers associated with i_1 and i_2, respectively. Since $\frac{s_{ki_2}^{j_2}(t)}{b'_{d_2 d_{j_2}}} + \tau_{ki_2}'^{m_2} > \frac{s_{ki_1}^{j_1}(t)}{b'_{d_1 d_{j_1}}} + \tau_{ki_1}'^{m_1}$, we have*

$$\tilde{l}_{k, \vec{b}, \vec{\tau}}(\vec{x}_k(t), \vec{y}_k(t)) - \tilde{l}_{k, \vec{b}', \vec{\tau}}(\vec{x}_k(t), \vec{y}_k(t)) \leq \lambda_1 \left(s_{ki_1}^{j_1}(t) \left(\frac{1}{b_{d_1 d_{j_1}}} - \frac{1}{b'_{d_1 d_{j_1}}} \right) \right.$$

$$+ \tau_{ki_1}^{m_1} - \tau_{ki_1}'^{m_1} \right) + \lambda_2 \sum_{i \in [A_k]} (\tau_{ki}^m - \tau_{ki}'^m) p_m y_{ki}^m(t)$$

$$\leq \lambda_1 \left(\frac{\max\limits_{j \in [A_{k-1}], i \in [A_k]} s_{ki}^j(t)}{L_B^2} z_1 + z_2 \right) + \lambda_2 A_k \max_{m \in [M]} p_m z_2$$

where L_B is the lower bound of the support of distributions among all bandwidth distributions $b_{de}, \forall d, e \in [D]$. We set $f_{tk}(z) = \lambda_1 \left(\frac{\max_{j \in [A_{k-1}], i \in [A_k]} s_{ki}^j(t)}{L_B^2} + 1 \right) z + \lambda_2 A_k \max_{m \in [M]} p_m z$, which is a strictly increasing linear function.

Following the standard proofs in combinatorial multi-armed bandit [33,34], we can bound the regret in Theorem 1.5 by bounding the sampling time of each suboptimal super arm. See [33,34] for more details.

BIBLIOGRAPHY

1. Jeffrey Dean and Sanjay Ghemawat. MapReduce: Simplified data processing on large clusters. In *Proc. of USENIX OSDI*, 2004.
2. Matei Zaharia, Mosharaf Chowdhury, Michael J. Franklin, Scott Shenker, and Ion Stoica. Spark: Cluster computing with working sets. In *Proceedings of USENIX HotCloud*, 2010.
3. Martjn Abadi, Paul Barham, Jianmin Chen, Zhifeng Chen, Andy Davis, et al. TensorFlow: A system for large-scale machine learning. In *Proceedings of USENIX OSDI*, 2016.
4. Prashanth Mohan, Abhradeep Thakurta, Elaine Shi, Dawn Song, and David Culler. GUPT: Privacy preserving data analysis made easy. In *Proceedings of ACM SIGMOD*, 2012.
5. Martin Rost and Kirsten Bock. Privacy by design and the new protection goals. In *Datenschutz und Datensicherheit 35*, 2011.
6. Qifan Pu, Ganesh Ananthanarayanan, Peter Bodik, Srikanth Kandula, Aditya Akella, et al. Low latency geo-distributed data analytics. In *Proceedings of ACM SIGCOMM*, 2015.
7. Ashish Vulimiri, Carlo Curino, P. Brighten Godfrey, Thomas Jungblut, Jitu Padhye, and George Varghese. Global analytics in the face of bandwidth and regulatory constraints. In *Proceedings of USENIX NSDI*, 2015.
8. Zhiming Hu, Baochun Li, and Jun Luo. Flutter: Scheduling tasks closer to data across geo-distributed datacenters. In *Proceedings of IEEE INFOCOM*, 2016.
9. Mu Li, David G Andersen, Jun Woo Park, Alexander J. Smola, Amr Ahmed, et al. Scaling distributed machine learning with the parameter server. In *Proceedings of USENIX OSDI*, 2014.
10. Ripal Nathuji, Aman Kansal, et al. Q-Clouds: Managing performance interference effects for Qos-aware clouds. In *Proceedings of EuroSys*, 2010.
11. Hong Zhang, Kai Chen, Wei Bai, Dongsu Han, Chen Tian, et al. Guaranteeing deadlines for inter-datacenter transfers. In *Proceedings of EuroSys*, 2015.
12. Kewen Wang and Mohammad Maifi Hasan Khan. Performance prediction for Apache spark platform. In *Proceedings of IEEE HPCC, CSS, ICESS*, 2015.
13. YongChul Kwon, Magdalena Balazinska, Bill Howe, et al. Skewtune: Mitigating skew in Mapreduce applications. In *Proceedings of ACM SIGMOD*, 2012.
14. Zhuoyao Zhang, Ludmila Cherkasova, and Boon Thau Loo. Benchmarking approach for designing a MapReduce performance model. In *Proceedings of ACM/SPEC ICPE*, 2013.
15. Hailong Yang, Zhongzhi Luan, Wenjun Li, and Depei Qian. MapReduce workload modeling with statistical approach. *Journal of Grid Computing*, 10(2):279–310, 2012.
16. Sebastien Bubeck. Regret analysis of stochastic and nonstochastic multi-armed bandit problems. *Foundations and Trends in Machine Learning*, 5(1):1–122, 2012.
17. Ashish Vulimiri, Carlo Curino, Brighten Godfrey, Konstantinos Karanasos, and George Varghese. WANalytics: Analytics for a geo-distributed data-intensive world. In *Proceedings of CIDR*, 2015.
18. Konstantinos Kloudas, Margarida Mamede, Nuno Preguiça, and Rodrigo Rodrigues. Pixida: Optimizing data parallel jobs in wide-area data analytics. In *Proceedings of VLDB*, 2015.
19. Kevin Hsieh, Aaron Harlap, Nandita Vijaykumar, Dimitris Konomis, Gregory R. Ganger, et al. Gaia: Geo-distributed machine learning approaching LAN speeds. In *Proceedings of USENIX NSDI*, 2017.
20. Soila Kavulya, Jason Tan, Rajeev Gandhi, and Priya Narasimhan. An analysis of traces from a production MapReduce cluster. In *Proceedings of IEEE CCGrid*, 2010.
21. Ge Song, Zide Meng, Fabrice Huet, Frederic Magoules, Lei Yu, and Xuelian Lin. A Hadoop MapReduce performance prediction method. In *Proceedings of IEEE HPCC. EUC*, 2013.
22. Shouvik Bardhan and Daniel A Menasce. Queuing network models to predict the completion time of the map phase of MapReduce jobs. In *Proceedings of the CMG*, 2012.

23. Lijing Qin, Shouyuan Chen, and Xiaoyan Zhu. Contextual combinatorial bandit and its application on diversfied online recommendation. In *Proceedings of SIAM ICDM*, 2014.

24. Yixin Bao, Xiaoke Wang, Zhi Wang, Chuan Wu, and Francis CM Lau. Online influence maximization in non-stationary social networks. In *Proceedings of IEEE IWQoS*, 2016.

25. Orly Avner and Shie Mannor. Multi-user Lax communications: A multi-armed bandit approach. In *Proceedings of IEEE INFOCOM*, pages 1–9, 2016.

26. Max Simchowitz, Kevin Jamieson, and Benjamin Recht. Best-of-K-bandits. In *Proceedings of COLT*, 2016.

27. Aditya Gopalan, Shie Mannor, and Yishay Mansour. Thompson sampling for complex online problems. In *Proceedings of ICML*, 2014.

28. Tze Leung Lai and Herbert Robbins. Asymptotically efficient adaptive allocation rules. *Advances in Applied Mathematics*, 6(1):4–22, 1985.

29. Tian Lin, Jian Li, and Wei Chen. Stochastic online greedy learning with semi-bandit feedbacks. In *Proceedings of NIPS*, 2015.

30. Virajith Jalaparti, Peter Bodik, Ishai Menache, Sriram Rao, Konstantin Makarychev, and Matthew Caesar. Network-aware scheduling for data-parallel jobs: Plan when you can. In *Proceedings of ACM SIGCOMM*, 2015.

31. Yingying Chen, Sourabh Jain, Vijay Kumar Adhikari, Zhi-Li Zhang, and Kuai Xu. A first look at inter-data center traffic characteristics via Yahoo! Datasets. In *Proceedings of IEEE INFOCOM*, 2011.

32. Yi Gai, Bhaskar Krishnamachari, and Rahul Jain. Combinatorial network optimization with unknown variables: Multi-armed bandits with linear rewards and individual observations. In *IEEE/ACM Transactions on Networking*, 20(5):1466–1478, 2012.

33. Wei Chen, Yajun Wang, and Yang Yuan. Combinatorial multi-armed bandit: General framework and applications. In *Proceedings of ICML*, 2013.

34. Wei Chen, Yajun Wang, Yang Yuan, and Qinshi Wang. Combinatorial multi-armed bandit and its extension to probabilistically triggered arms. *Journal of Machine Learning Research*, 17(1):1746–1778, 2016.

35. Kay Ousterhout, Ryan Rasti, Sylvia Ratnasamy, Scott Shenker, and Byung-Gon Chun. Making sense of performance in data analytics frameworks. In *Proceedings of USENIX NSDI*, 2015.

36. Andrew Pavlo, Erik Paulson, Alexander Rasin, Daniel J Abadi, David J DeWitt, et al. A comparison of approaches to large-scale data analysis. In *Proceedings of ACM SIGMOD*, 2009.

37. Charles Reiss, Alexey Tumanov, Gregory R Ganger, Randy H Katz, and Michael A Kozuch. Heterogeneity and dynamicity of clouds at scale: Google trace analysis. In *Proceedings of ACM SoCC*, 2012.

38. Yuan Feng, Baochun Li, and Bo Li. Jetway: Minimizing costs on inter-datacenter video traffic. In *Proceedings of ACM MM*, 2012.

39. Jorda Polo, David Carrera, Yolanda Becerra, Malgorzata Steinder, and Ian Whalley. Performance-driven task co-scheduling for MapReduce environments. In *Proceedings of IEEE NOMS*, 2010.

40. Xicheng Dong, Ying Wang, and Huaming Liao. Scheduling mixed real-time and non-real-time applications in MapReduce environment. In *Proceedings of IEEE ICPADS*, 2011.

41. KVM-QEMU. www.linux-kvm.org/.

42. Apache Hadoop. http://hadoop.apache.org/, 2018.

43. Linux Advanced Routing & Traffic Control. http://lartc.org/.

44. Wikimedia Downloads. https://dumps.wikimedia.org/.

45. Jure Leskovec, Kevin J Lang, Anirban Dasgupta, and Michael W Mahoney. Community structure in large networks: Natural cluster sizes and the absence of large well-defined clusters. *Internet Mathematics*, 6(1):29–123, 2009.

46. Ramon van Handel. Probability in high dimension. Technical Report, DTIC Document, 2014.
47. Stephen Boyd and Lieven Vandenberghe. *Convex Optimization*. Cambridge University Press, 2004.
48. Anne Auger and Benjamin Doerr. *Theory of Randomized Search Heuristics: Foundations and Recent Developments*. World Scientific, 2011.

CHAPTER 9

The Role of Smart Data in Inference of Human Behavior and Interaction

Rute C. Sofia, Liliana Carvalho, and Francisco M. Pereira

COPELABS, Universidade Lusófona, Lisboa, Portugal

CONTENTS

S mart data captured via pervasive, mobile sensing technology is relied upon to model different aspects of human activities and human behavior. The data capture, data processing, and inference via pervasive mobile sensing platforms bring in several challenges both from a software and networking architecture perspective.

1 INTRODUCTION

A first challenge concerns the development of light methods for inference of behavior. Such methods have to frequently handle small amounts of extracted data, and often to support fast data transmission rates. They have also to be devised in a way that does not endanger the privacy of the involved citizens. Ideally, data should be stored locally or as close to the user as possible, which also implies that smart data processing methods can benefit from distributed inference [1,2].

A second challenge to overcome is to ensure that the technology used to capture smart data is the least intrusive. Even though the participation of citizens is required in environments such as Smart Cities, data needs to be captured seamlessly. Such capture must not endanger the citizen's privacy or anonymity. And the data must be kept as close to the end-user as possible, so that only the user has access to it.

A third challenge concerns taking advantage of opportunities in time and space to perform sensing. *Opportunistic sensing* [3,4] methods are best suited to large-scale environments, as the user is not actively participating in the whole data capture process.

A fourth and major challenge to address in the context of relying on smart data to infer aspects of human interaction behavior is to devise methods that support in close-to-real-time the correlation of contextual conditions and individual characteristics (e.g., age and lifestyle) encountered in large-scale mobile sensing systems, and the integration of multiple data representing the same real-world activity into a consistent, accurate, and useful representation.

To assist in addressing the aforementioned challenges, this chapter explores features and concepts, and provides guidelines on the role and applicability of smart data captured in a non-intrusive way, in the inference and contextualization of human behavior and interaction.

For this purpose, the chapter starts (Section 2) with a brief introduction to concepts concerning modeling of human interaction; for instance, how to define and how to best model physical and psychological proximity; models for social awareness and social contextualization. Such introduction is relevant to assist the reader in understanding the basics of human interaction modeling in the context of computer science. It is also relevant to guide the reader in understanding the need for an interdisciplinary view on proximity and human interaction aspects.

Section 3 deals with interaction inference and interaction contextualization: classification models that best suit the inference of behavior via smart data; challenges regarding small data capture and behavior inference derived from small data, in particular when considering decentralized, mobile cyber-physical systems; guidelines to model interaction based on pervasive wireless sensing systems, including available middleware and systems (tools). In Section 4, we go over a specific case of application of smart data, namely, *Points of Interest (PoI)* detection. The chapter concludes with a set of recommendations in Section 5.

2 HUMAN INTERACTION ASPECTS

In regular daily routines, several factors affect interaction between people. One of the most relevant factors is the way that people define and perceive the surrounding space. Aspects such as distance, orientation towards others, density of people around us, and noise levels are features that can be captured today via any personal mobile device and that can assist in better understanding the physical proximity between people, the social proximity between people, and the relation of people towards the use of spaces. This means that personal technology can be relied upon to capture indicators that can measure both *physical* and *social* proximity. By measuring the different dimensions of proximity, one can better define personal spaces; develop tools that can stimulate social cohesion, and stimulate a better relation towards spaces around us.

2.1 Physical and Psychological Proximity

Indicators of proximity, such as distance or geolocation, and individual motion are preferential indicators to characterize physical proximity today via pervasive mobile technology. Technology today assists also the measurement of interaction of devices over time and space, surrounding sound level, and similarities in motion or in mobility. Nevertheless, to better model proximity, it is necessary to work upon an interdisciplinary approach which considers physical proximity indicators and notions of psychological proximity. In particular, notions on how people perceive personal spaces.

More recently, there has been a surge of interest in supporting device-to-device communication due to exploiting direct communication between nearby devices. Taking advantage of the temporal–spatial device proximity, it is feasible to improve spectrum utilization, overall throughput, and energy consumption. This optimization is relevant in the context of exploring new peer-to-peer and location-based applications, and services. Proximity modeling is relevant as well to devise new communication models, complementary to current infrastructures, e.g., people-to-people communication in emergency scenarios.

For instance, in the context of *device-to-device (D2D)* communications, proximity-based services are provided, derived from notions of device proximity in time and space. Without recurring to pervasive sensing, the discovery of surrounding services would be a high-energy consuming process.

The notion of *proximity services* has first been debated and introduced by M. S. Corson et al. [5], by allowing a direct device discovery mechanism referred to as *Aura-Sense*. Aura-Sense enables D2D communication via a licensed *Time Division Duplex (TDD)*-based air-interface (FlashLinQ), in combination with a namespace system, which allows application-driven discovery among nearby devices. Li and Sinha introduced a low power consumption direct device discovery based on recursive binary time partitioning [6]. Such a proposal is more generic, and thus not fully aligned with the 3GPP perspective, since it is not relying on network discovery, but requires sophisticated scanning and additional security procedures. LTE-Direct [7] is another proposal for proximity services where devices rely on session/application layer semantics for service discovery, while the network assists in device authentication and in coordinating radio resources used for discovery.

Quantification of social interaction via pervasive wireless sensing systems is a recent line of research, for which some aspects have already been addressed in related literature. Most work has been focused on distance estimation via sensing technology (*Wi-Fi* (*Wireless Fidelity*) or *Bluetooth* (*BT*)) and via the relation of distance and capacity to grasp real-world social interaction patterns [8–10].

Smart data captured via overhearing can further assist in better modeling and contextualizing proximity, thus becoming closer to human interaction. For this purpose, pervasive sensing can rely on different properties such as motion, physical proximity, social strength, and surrounding sound level to assist in a seamless characterization of people' s proximity, and hence contribute to a better modeling of social interaction.

However, as explained before, proximity is a time and space notion, and related with each individual belief and perception of interpersonal spaces. It is therefore relevant to revisit notions of psychological proximity, and analyse how it can be modeled with pervasive technology.

Psychological proximity relates with interaction (interconnections) between people. The study of borders of a 'social network', i.e., the distinction between acquaintances and friends, is not a trivial subject—social connections cannot be defined per se as a complete closed system. Hence, what is usually done in social sciences is to define borders of a network via additional information, e.g., an institutional definition (e.g., an organization), or via the linking to a specific individual (*betweenness*). The latter approach can be identified in an influential classical theory in social psychology, as happens with Lewin's field theory [11], which defines an individual's 'life space' in terms of 'push' and 'pull' motivational forces related with the individual's interconnections.

While the interconnectedness of a social network can be seen as a basic feature to define boundaries in *groups*, it is not enough to define interconnection borders. Typically, groups are considered smaller than social networks. Moreland and Levine have analyzed how groups develop and how socialization is performed in perceived groups [12], by considering that interactions that bring people together can be categorized in specific activities. The authors explain that small groups of interconnected individuals emerge from larger social networks, and this is facilitated by *propinquity* (i.e., the degree of proximity that enhances the probability of direct contact).

Nevertheless, differentiating a network of individuals from a group of individuals does not yet have a clear methodology to be applied. Campbell proposed the concept of *entitativity*, i.e., the perception of a group as a pure (mental abstraction) entity [13]. Operationally, entitativity can be defined by different metrics, e.g., spatial proximity; 'similarity' between members; interdependence; common routine aspects (e.g., synchrony in movement). Roulston and Young relied on GPS tracking to examine spatial mobility of communities of citizens in common geographic areas [14]. Here, spatial proximity and routine similarity are used to assist in identifying groups.

In the next section, we shall go over how these notions can be integrated into computer science modeling, to improve the inference of human interaction with the aid of smart data.

2.2 Modeling Proximity with an Interdisciplinary Perspective

The aspects mentioned are relevant in the context of defining algorithms that rely on interaction between devices, as such interaction derives from the interaction levels of their human carriers. Hence, hypotheses involving the role of social psychological mechanisms in the facilitation of the formation of group-based structures are helpful and should, in our opinion, be integrated in current computer science models. Such hypotheses should start from the assumption that propinquity is an indicator that can facilitate the development and growth of group-based networks. Hence, we propose the following hypotheses:

- **Affiliation and closeness based on face-to-face interaction are expected to facilitate group emergence and cohesion**. The rationale is that affiliation and closeness assist in increasing trust (reciprocity) and assist in sharing/exchange of resources.

- **Group cohesion (communal sharing needs) is usually satisfied via face-to-face interaction**. An indicator for such interaction is, for instance, frequency of close encounters.

- **Equality matching in interaction is relevant to assist in strengthening groups**. Reciprocity is therefore an indicator of equality matching. However, the need to maintain balance could limit the speed of interactions or contributions to the system, aspects which have to be taken into consideration when modeling reciprocity.

- **Social similarity and propinquity contribute to stronger network connections** [15]. Propinquity refers to the physical and/or psychological proximity between people. It has been studied mostly to understand how interpersonal relations develop within the same space. For instance, people living in the same floor of a building attain a higher propinquity than those living on different floors. Two people sharing similar beliefs also attain a higher propinquity than those that do not share beliefs. Hence, propinquity is a property that is highly relevant to consider when defining, in networked systems, social interaction contextualization.

- **Market pricing approaches can assist in modeling cohesion.** Influence modeling can be relevant in terms of modeling costs for interest in a specific group, but not as the basis for the construction of group-based networks.

These are aspects that can assist in a better modeling of human interaction and contribute to a better development of proximity-based services.

As shall be seen in the next section, smart data brings in the possibility to better contextualize different levels of interaction, of proximity, and of personal spaces. In other words, smart data is relevant not only in terms of accurately inferring real-time interaction, but also of inferring strong and weak social ties between people, i.e., a level of *nearness* contextualized via mediating technology. Nearness inference, however, needs to consider both psychological (social) proximity and physical proximity aspects.

2.3 Social Awareness, the NSense Example

NSense [4][1] is an open-source tool licensed under LGPLv3.0, which has been designed to capture data via multiple sensors (Wi-Fi, BT, accelerometer, microphone) in a seamless and modular way, as illustrated in Figure 9.1. NSense has the purpose of analysing features of social interaction. Smart data captured with NSense is expected to be used in interaction studies, assisted by data reports generated in csv format. Locally, the data captured is worked via different *pipelines*. A pipeline corresponds to a set of operations performed by a classification model over a set of sensors that classify activity in terms of social proximity, relative distance, location, motion, and surrounding sound level.

To analyse interaction (nearness), NSense relies on two developed utility functions: *propinquity* (p) and *social interaction* (si). *Propinquity* (p) [15] is a probabilistic utility

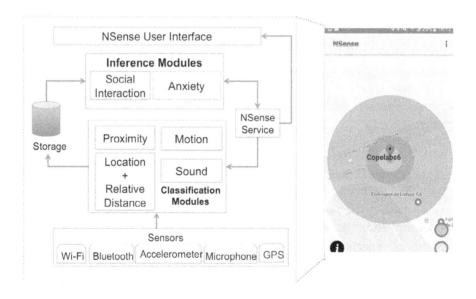

FIGURE 9.1   The NSense architecture.

[1] NSense is available via https://play.google.com/store/apps/details?id=cs.usense and via GitHub: https://github.com/COPELABS-SITI/NSense.

function which provides the likelihood of devices to enrol in future social interaction. Owners of devices that are in close range to each other, or that meet often, are expected to have a higher propinquity than owners of devices that do not meet as often. Other aspects, such as environmental sound, or distance between devices, can assist in inferring propinquity.

The *social interaction si* function provides an indication on how much owners of devices have been interacting over time and space, derived from aspects such as node degree and motion; the relative distance between devices; the sound level activity around the devices; the type of movement of the devices; and the cost, *social strength*, between pairs of devices.

The *social strength* of node i towards node j in a specific hourly sample h, for day d, $s(i,j)_{d,h}$ [16] is derived from contact duration between nodes i and j during a specific time window h in a passive way. The relative distance between devices i and j, $d(i,j)_t$, corresponds to an exponential moving average of the euclidean distance between the two nodes, following a propagation loss model. Finally, the surrounding sound level is measured by the device based on a sound activity detection algorithm which classifies the environmental sound context based on noise level.

Figure 9.2(a) provides an example of the type of feedback that NSense provides to the user, over time, where the X-axis corresponds to days of the month, and the Y-axis provides the value for the social interaction and propinquity functions. For instance, on 13th March, the result shows that the interaction of this device towards others was lower while propinquity was higher. This means that while this device was surrounded by 'familiar' devices (devices it has encountered often before), the interaction (Wi-Fi and BT sightings and encounters) was actually lower.

With this type of modeling, it is feasible to further articulate more complex aspects based on initial calibration, or a baseline, for instance, whether or not a user is not interacting on purpose.

2.4 Social Contextualization

Context is "*any information that can be used to characterize the situation of an entity. An entity is a person, place, or object that is considered relevant to the interaction between a user and an application, including the user and applications themselves*".

In the realm of applications, context-awareness has been dealt with in an *active manner*, by immediately presenting context to the user, or in a *passive manner*, by storing context that later can be retrieved.

With the technology evolution and with new computing and networking paradigms such as IoT, research has been extensively dealing with context-aware computing solutions derived from a (limited) number of sensors. For smart data–based applications and services, context-awareness becomes more critical as it can assist in better selecting data to be relied upon and where as well as when to process data.

Contextual awareness can assist several aspects of networking. Its relevancy in the context of challenged networking scenarios, such as in *Internet of Things (IoT)*, is well covered by several surveys [17]. The most recent evolution of contextualization in IoT concerns Fog Computing [18]; social interaction in IoT [19]; and the use of

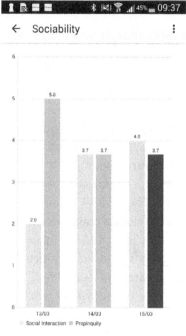

(a) Average levels

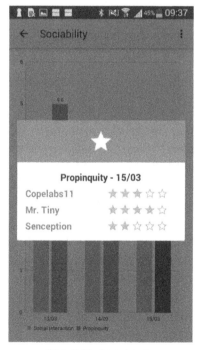

(b) Individual propinquity

FIGURE 9.2 NSense sociability modeling based on propinquity and social interaction functions.

contextualization to improve aspects of network operation such as routing [20]. *Network contextualization* is derived from network data mining and measurement, e.g., smart data concerning individual and collective roaming habits; network and device usage. Being able to characterize roaming habits and to capture/measure internal device usage in a way that does not endanger anonymity and data privacy is therefore essential. Such characterization goes beyond the integration of movement prediction and/or anticipation mechanisms in the network operation, e.g., in routing or mobility management.

Personalized behavior inference poses some challenges in terms of training personalized classification models, since these have to be adjusted to the unique features of each user. Then, they also require a large amount of labeled data from each user. The burden of manually collecting and annotating sensor data falls upon the user, making personalization ill-suited for general use in large-scale mobile sensing systems.

2.4.1 The UMOBILE Contextual Agent Example

In the H2020 UMOBILE project [20], context-awareness follows the line of interdisciplinary work being described in this chapter with the main goal of improving the social routine of Internet users via technology-mediated approaches. One example is, for instance, to assist people-to-people communication in emergency scenarios, where access to the Internet may be intermittent due to infrastructure damage.

For that purpose, the UMOBILE architecture integrates a Contextual agent, the CMContextual Manager *Contextual Manager (CM)*. The CM is an application for end-user devices that capture both external (roaming) and internal (usage) data to improve the operation of other network services. For instance, routing can be improved via the weights for node availability, centrality, or node similarity that the CM computes based on spatial and temporal context for each node [21]. The CM can also assist in resource management, by feeding priorities. Data sharing can be improved by relying on interest matching.

The CM architecture integrates three main modules: capture, storage, and inference, as illustrated in Figure 9.3.

The data captured by the CM remains solely on the device, and on the internal memory database, thus just being accessible via the developed binary. Data captured is based on overhearing and on an interface specifically created to operate via Wi-Fi Direct and Bluetooth, so that neighboring CMs exchange data concerning peers. It has three sub-modules: *peers; visited networks; resource usage*. The visited networks capture concerns Wi-Fi overheard data from regular Wi-Fi scans, thus integrating information concerning *Access Points (APs)* that are in the range of the device. The peer usage concerns information about neighbors and is captured via Wi-Fi Direct and via Bluetooth. The resource usage concerns information about internal resources such as battery level, CPU, storage, and memory status. Such data is captured to provide, via the inference module, a measure of node availability.

The data inference module takes care of using the different indicators stored, and combining them via different utility functions to characterize a node's affinity network

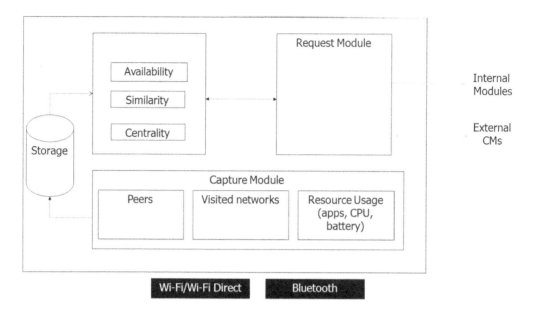

FIGURE 9.3   The UMOBILE Contextual Manager.

(neighborhood and its variation over time and space) and to characterize a node' s usage and to give a measure of similarity between adjacent nodes. Such weights can assist aspects such as whether or not the device is in good shape (e.g., to transmit data); if the device (and hence its carrier) is isolated (betweenness); and if it holds some form of similarity towards other devices around.

The next section further debates on behavior inference and contextualization aspects.

3 INTERACTION INFERENCE AND CONTEXTUALIZATION ASPECTS

Contextual aspects such as distance, orientation towards others; density of people around us, and noise levels are features that can assist in better understanding the physical proximity between people, the social proximity between people, and the relation of people towards the use of spaces. As discussed and exemplified, such context can today easily be collected by regular sensorial devices, carried or controlled by people. Hence, personal mobile technology can be relied upon to capture indicators that can measure both physical and social proximity. By measuring proximity, one can better define personal spaces; develop tools that can stimulate social cohesion, and stimulate a better relation towards spaces around us.

A relevant aspect in what concerns the adequate use of smart data derived from pervasive wireless and cellular systems [22] is data mining techniques that can be performed locally, on each device, before being sent to the cloud. Eager classification models such as neural networks have been the preferential choice for pattern detection for wireless sensor data [23, 24]. Inference of behavior can be simplified and some activities should be performed locally, in mobile devices. First, because it allows to consider extraction of data in a more secure way, keeping user anonymity. Second, this approach reduces the cost associated with data transmission to a cloud. Therefore, the allocation of local computational tasks for the classification of sensed data is of key importance for mobile sensing systems. To perform smart data classification as close to the user as possible, it is necessary to reduce the computational weight of current classification models.

3.1 Classification Models

Local classification, e.g., on mobile devices, can be feasible by using lazy classification models based on the phenomenon of reasoning from memories of specific episodes [25,26]. This theory contrasts with much of the current work in similarity-based learning, which tacitly assumes that learning is equivalent to the automatic generation of rules.

Eager learner algorithms such as *Decision Trees* or *Neural Networks* construct general and explicit description of the target function based on the provided training examples. Generalization beyond the training data set is tried before receiving queries.

Lazy learning algorithms, often applied in the context of wireless sensor networks, of which the *k-nearest neighbor (k-NN)* algorithm is an example, store training data and wait until a query (test tuple) is performed [27]. Hence, this category of algorithms achieves a low computational cost during the training phase, but may have high computational cost during the query. In the context of smart data analysis, it may be necessary to constantly re-train an eager learner algorithm. Running a lazy learning algorithm with storage in the cloud may prove to be beneficial and improve computational performance.

Case-Based Reasoning (CBR) [28] is an artificial intelligence methodology that aims at mimicking human logic and reasoning. It stores 'cases,' namely, prior experience sets and the solution for those prior experiences. CBR assumes that problems recur and that similar problems have similar solutions, hence it provides a simplistic way to solve its (prior) dataset of problems. CBR is often used for recommendation systems [29,30] and is a lazy learning method that uses a k-NN approach.

Memory-Based Reasoning (MBR) [26] is a lazy learning method that relies as well on k-NN to operate. The process here is to store all the training data and retrieve instances from memory similar to the query instance, which are then used to classify the given instance by assigning the value of the target function estimated for the current instance. The method requires no models to be fitted or function to be estimated. MBR relies completely on similar examples from memory found in the training data and avoids the knowledge engineering phase employed by other artificial intelligence approaches. This property makes it a powerful tool for classification in the context of analysis of fused data from pervasive sensing devices which generally do not suffer from the curse of dimensionality, which is a major drawback for MBR systems.

In Table 9.1, a comparison of the different classification models being applied on different pervasive wireless tools is shown. As can be seen, the usage of eager classification models based on data collected from a single sensor is commonplace.

For instance, BeWell [32] relies on the Jigsaw continuous sensing engine classification models [33] for the classification of physical activity. Jigsaw considers a DT model for

TABLE 9.1 Examples of classification models in pervasive sensing tools.

Tool	Classification Model	Sensors	Indicator	Activity detected
NSense	MTracker [31]	Wi-Fi; Wi-Fi direct	Wi-Fi visited networks; fusion location; RSSI of all neighbors	Location
	Time-evolving contact duration algorithm	Bluetooth	Duration of contacts with neighbors	Proximity
	Decision tree	Accelerometer	Walking, standing, running	Physical activity
	Deterministic approach	Microphone	Quiet, normal, alert, noisy	Surrounding sound
EmotionSense	Gaussian mixture model	Microphone	Comparing audio samples with preloaded models	Speaker identities
	Gaussian mixture model	Microphone	Comparing audio samples with preloaded models	Emotions
	Discriminant function classifier	Accelerometer	Movement/Non-movement	Physical activity
BeWell	Gaussian model	Accelerometer, microphone, battery	Phone recharging; phone stationary, or in silence environment	Sleep pattern
	Decision tree; Naive Bayes; Gaussian mixture models	Microphone	Voicing, non-voicing	Social interaction
	Decision tree	Accelerometer	Driving, stationary, running, walking	Physical activity
CenceMe	Discriminant function classifier	Microphone	Deviation of the DFT power	Human voice/ Surrounding sound
	Decision tree	Accelerometer	Sitting, standing, walking, running	Physical activity
	Rolling window filters	Microphone	Rolling window of N phone audio primitives	Conversation
SocioMeter	Hidden Markov model	Microphone	Detect the pair-wise conversation	Group interactions
		IR	Pattern of IR signal	

the accelerometer data; DT and Naive Bayes for the classification of social interaction; and Gaussian mixture models for microphone data.

In fact, there is not consensus about the best classification model for specific types of sensor data. For instance, BeWell and NSense classify physical activity based on decision tree models, while EmotionSense [34] relies on a discriminant function classifier.

Furthermore, the efficiency of eager classification models highly depends on the type of data being classified. For instance, the classification evaluation provided in Jigsaw for physical performance activity data, which considers DT, multivariate Gaussian model, support vector machine, and Naive Bayes based only on accelerometer data [33], shows that the average classification performance increases if a split-and-merge process is used, particularly for the Naive Bayes classifier, although the best performance is achieved with a support vector machine classifier.

While the classification of simple activities (e.g., motion, surrounding sound, conversation, proximity, location) is normally performed based on data collected from a single sensor, the classification of more complex activities, such as social interaction and sleep patterns, requires data from more than one sensor. For instance, SocioMeter makes use of a Hidden Markov model to classify group interactions based on microphone and infrared data, while NSense classifies social interaction and propinquity based on Wi-Fi Direct, BT, accelerometer, and microphone data. In what concerns sleep patterns, BeWell uses Gaussian models to derive patterns related to phone movement, and surrounding sound, based on data collected from the accelerometer, microphone, and information about the battery usage.

Independently of the need to classify simple or complex activities, current smart data sensing solutions are normally based on eager classification models. However, eager classification models present significant limitations to operate locally in mobile devices due to the amount of required resources (e.g., CPU, energy). They also suffer with the need for continuous sensing strategies able to supply significant amount of data.

To mitigate such limitations, researchers have been investigating methods to allow the deployment of people-centric sensing systems based on eager classification models by reducing resources used in continuous sensing activities, and relying on classification learning processes that run in cloud systems. As an example of methods aiming to reduce resources used in sensing activities, we can enumerate hierarchical sensor management strategies [35], balancing the performance of applications and sensing activities [33], or monitoring topology changes and adapting the rate of sensing queries [36].

3.2 Challenges for Smart Data Classification in Mobile Crowd Sensing Scenarios

Smart Data is highly relevant to assist in adequately modeling and estimating aspects related with social interaction. Future solutions are expected to be based on frameworks that reside in end-user personal devices and on the edges of the network. These frameworks are expected to perform distributed functions, and individual smart data is expected to be collected non-intrusively during the daily routines of people. We envision such frameworks to have at least modules concerning data capture, learning, inference, and feedback (individual and collective). For that purpose, there are a few challenges that need to be addressed, as explained next.

3.2.1 Sensing

Current solutions rely in their majority on opportunistic sensing due to the availability of a large variety of sensors in personal devices. Nevertheless, there is no consensus about the best paradigm for pervasive sensing systems, namely, in what concerns the role assumed by people within such systems: to what extent should people be conscious active participants in meeting sensing application requirements.

Both opportunistic and participatory sensing have performance implications. With participatory sensing, people consciously opt to meet a sensing application request out of personal or financial interest. A participatory approach incorporates people into significant decision stages of the sensing system, such as deciding what data is shared and to what extent privacy mechanisms should be allowed to impact data fidelity. With opportunistic sensing, sensing entities may not be aware of active applications. Instead a sensing device (e.g., cell phone) is utilized whenever its state (e.g., geographic location, body location) matches the requirements of an application.

While participatory and opportunistic sensing approaches may be complementary, previous experimental results show that the opportunistic sensing design approach yields a system better suited for large-scale distributed deployments.

Independently of the data-sensing approach selected, the amount of data, information, and knowledge being generated in the most varied applicability scenarios tends to increase. Moreover, the use of multiple sensors and data fusion needs in the context of services or for activity recognition is expected to increase as well. Therefore, behavior analysis and inference based on smart data, the extraction of relevant data, the composition of information, and the resulting inference representation needs to be carefully addressed. If poorly selected, composed, and generated, the results not only put in cause the functioning of the full solution, but also the privacy and the well-being of users.

3.2.2 Adequate Contextualization

Currently, in related literature, social interaction is often modeled in a simplistic way, usually associated to encounter duration. Proximity is, however, tied both to a time and spatial dimensions and directly linked to the social and physical contexts in which they arise, which are also dynamic themselves. Context to be identified and modeled are physical (space, co-presence), social (embedded in groups), and relational (identification of basic relational types based on dynamics and physical aspects of recent interactions and interest affinity).

As discussed in this chapter, context can be extracted from the natural overheard footprint derived from the use of cellular/wireless technologies and this is not an aspect that should be overlooked.

Adequate contextualization requires local storage and computational support, and hence is tightly related with classification mechanisms that can be applied in a distributed way, and/or in the edges of the network.

Furthermore, context does not necessarily require capture and storage of personal information. Aspects such as waypoints traversed in a wireless or cellular network, and the correlation of such roaming context, can be applied in multiple applicability scenarios, as shall be explained in Section 4.

3.2.3 Privacy and Anonymity

Any sensing framework focused on quality of living and/or well-being needs to take into consideration the need to ensure privacy and anonymity at all times, even for the cases when observations shall take into consideration social interaction. Data can be tracked only at an individual level, and kept in the user device, obfuscating fields that may hold sensitive information. For instance, assuming a large-scale event (such as a music festival), data to be exchanged would track an increase in, e.g., device movement, or surrounding noise in a specific cluster of devices, not the devices nor their users, nor conversations being held.

Aspects such as location and location privacy shall be taken into consideration, by providing always the aggregate data perspective, instead of the individual data profile. All data, including identifiers of the devices, are to be made anonymous. Furthermore and above all, independently of data being locally stored, or sent to the cloud, the user must provide his/her prior consent.

3.2.4 Classification

Routine modeling and an adequate identification of a digital behavior footprint across time and space require pervasive solutions to passively learn and adjust to the individual user routine. The challenge resides in the creation of mechanisms to track smart data without endangering the privacy of users and of peers of such user. Prediction of behavior patterns is useful for assessment and detection of abnormal behavior, which works as a control trigger in the system, leading to potential adjustments, namely in what concerns the patterns of data collection. Such adjustment should take into consideration not only the prior digital footprint, but also external commodities (the context in time and space) that may or may not contribute to a deviation from the usual pattern modeled.

It is relevant to bring smart data classification and caching as close as possible to the end-user devices. Classification should also be based on hierarchical methodologies. For instance, the use of discriminate features on a first instance, followed by the classification of specific datasets. This can assist in providing different levels of classification, and in further reducing misclassification.

4 APPLICABILITY ASPECTS

In this section, we shall go over a specific applicability example for smart data use for the detection of PoIs in Smart Cities. PoIs are usually considered to be existing landmarks that exhibit some form of affluence (e.g., public spaces, monuments). The definition of PoIs is usually static and provided by municipalities. However, the majority of citizens may not even become aware of them. Smart data brings in the possibility to perform PoI detection over time, and to understand metrics related with PoI evolution, relevancy, and affluence. Such metrics are highly relevant for smart cities, as they can assist in better dimensioning multiple aspects related with human routine and behavior.

For that, it is possible to rely on individual and collective behavior inference via smart data obtained, upon consent, from regular personal devices and from embedded devices and considering the following assumptions:

- Citizens provide, upon consent and based on pervasive, non-intrusive middleware, non-personal data (e.g., roaming patterns based on visited networks, location not associated with the person; time spent in specific areas).

- The city infrastructure may include devices that in addition collect, upon consent, non-personal data, such as number of people (devices) in specific locations and affluence.

- The data is available for the framework to use. In other words, it is not up for this framework to generate data.

- Data is transmitted in close-to-real time.

- Connectivity may be intermittent.

4.1 Can Smart Data Derived from Wireless and Cellular Networks be Relevant to Detect Human Interaction?

In the context of smart cities, smart data that characterizes aspects of human interaction can be obtained in a non-intrusive way while citizens develop their social daily routines from wireless and cellular networks, based on mobile personal devices such as smartphones.

With the different types of smart data collected in cities, it is feasible to gather an understanding of the roaming habits of daily users. While geolocation is a way to gather such data, an interesting alternative is to consider contextual data such as the one described in Section 3. This has the advantage of working indoors, incurring in less battery spending, and being less intrusive from an end-user and network perspective.

For instance, context awareness derived from preferred network visits is relevant to understand individual PoIs. Such PoIs can be mapped in space and in time—hour, day of the week, month. An example for this illustrated in Figure 9.4.

The data represented in the Figure reflects data of 50 users captured during May 2017, with the free middleware *PerSense Mobile Light* (PML)[2] [37], and presented over different days of the week, where day 6 corresponds to Friday, while day 1 corresponds to Sunday. The data shows that there is a higher affluence of users during day 6 and a stronger incidence on a specific geographic area for this particular set of users. This simple example illustrates how smart network data can be used to infer in close-to-real-time affluence and preference areas in smart cities. Such smart data is derived from *wireless overhearing*, i.e., the natural digital footprint left in wireless and cellular networks, and therefore does not add a cost to the network operation nor to the end-user.

4.1.1 How to Define a PoI with Smart Data?

Defining PoIs based on wireless and cellular smart data requires developing heuristics based on human interaction indicators, such as proximity and social interaction. Such heuristics can be locally computed without endangering user and data privacy. For some people, a PoI is only a location for which information is available, such as a simple set of

---

[2] PML is developed by Senception Lda and freely available for Android, https://play.google.com/store/apps/details?id=com.senception.persensemobilelight

FIGURE 9.4 Wireless waypoints of 50 users aggregated per day of the week. 1 corresponds to Sunday while 7 corresponds to Saturday.

coordinates, a name, or a place. Others go further and consider PoIs a most fundamental requirement of any spatial data infrastructure, and see their importance in the commercial sector for navigation applications and social networks.

Heuristics to define a PoI in real time need to consider that a PoI is a product of space and time, and some measure of influence/attraction. For instance, Lim et al. define a framework for personalized tour recommendations based on user interests and PoI visits' duration [38]. Their work assumes that there are already pre-established PoIs (municipality data) and the focus is on the recommendation for specific, existing PoIs.

What we advocate in this chapter is to detect existing and future PoIs, derived from the learning of similarities in roaming habits of citizens. In this context, there is a slight difference between *waypoint* and PoI. Both identify a location PoI, but the first one is commonly used to mark locations that can serve any interest, while the second is connected with special preferences of some collective or individual interest. For instance, a person can, in its daily routine, stop on a specific location due to its interest in interacting with others (not necessarily due to an event, activity, or location) [39]. Hence, a PoI, from an individual perspective, is also the results of individual interest in social interaction and in particular of similarity patterns in such interaction.

For PoI detection and inference via smart data, it is relevant to consider seamless ways to correlate the data from different users in a seamless way. Such data may be then correlated with existing PoIs (geolocation) as well. To detect personal PoIs, derived from the intersection of individual paths, it is feasible to consider the following approaches:

- **Based on edge betweenness**. The relevancy of a PoI is its centrality. A PoI is based upon the number of individual paths that cross such a PoI within a specific time window.

- **Based on spatial correlation**. A PoI can be defined by measures concerning cluster density over time and space. For both cases, it is relevant to consider other individual parameters:

  - **Speed**. Average speed that an individual user experiences during his/her periodic routine is relevant to further characterize PoIs. For instance, when possible, the time cycle used in certain PoIs of the course, by considering aspects such as speed and acceleration, and by considering speed of displacement between PoIs and crossing them with the other users.

  - **Stationary time**. The time each user spends on a potential PoI is relevant to define the relevancy of such PoI for a cluster of users.

  - **Time granularity**. In addition to the daily route, there has to be a weekly, monthly, or even annual, not just one, but multiple users.

4.1.2 How to Extract Similarities in Individual Behavior?

Analysing similarities of behavior derived from wireless and cellular smart data is feasible by performing both a spatial and a time characterization of roaming routines, and of affinity networks.

In terms of roaming routine, examples of smart data relevant for a spatial characterization are: distance traversed between crossed wireless networks; encountered and connected wireless hotspots; spatial relation of connected and crossed wireless hotspots [?].

In what concerns spatial characterization, it is feasible to consider aspects such as daily/monthly/yearly connectivity patterns; duration of visits and encounters.

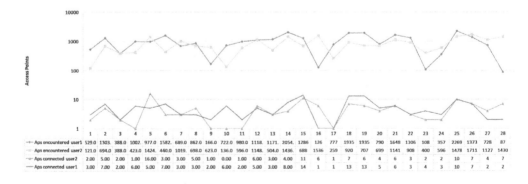

	1	2	3	4	5	6	7	8	9	10	11	12	13	14	15	16	17	18	19	20	21	22	23	24	25	26	27	28
Aps encountered user1	529.0	1303.	388.0	1002.	977.0	1582.	689.0	862.0	166.0	722.0	980.0	1118.	1171.	2054.	1286	126	777	1935	1935	790	1648	1306	108	357	2269	1373	728	87
Aps encountered user2	121.0	694.0	388.0	423.0	1424.	440.0	1019.	698.0	623.0	136.0	596.0	1148.	504.0	1436.	688	1536	259	920	707	699	1141	908	400	596	1478	1711	1127	1430
Aps connected user2	2.00	5.00	2.00	1.00	16.00	3.00	3.00	5.00	1.00	0.00	1.00	6.00	3.00	4.00	11	6	1	7	6	4	6	3	2	2	10	7	4	7
Aps connected user1	3.00	7.00	2.00	6.00	5.00	7.00	3.00	3.00	2.00	6.00	2.00	5.00	3.00	8.00	14	1	1	13	13	5	6	3	4	3	10	7	2	2

FIGURE 9.5 Similarity patterns from smart wireless data, 2 users with strong similarity, encountered and visited APs [37].

An example is provided in Figure 9.5, derived from a study carried out for one month with 7 devices, where strong similarity in routine can be extracted, derived from wireless mining [37]. In the Figure, the x-axis corresponds to days, and the y-axis corresponds to the total number of APs (connected or crossed) by 2 users, user1 and user2.

Cluster-based analysis is another methodology that can be applied to understand similarities in behavior, derived from smart data. An example on how such analysis can be performed is provided based on data collected in 2017 by three different users, in the city of Portimão, Portugal, for one day, with the PML tool, as illustrated in Figure 9.6.

Cluster similarity based on different parameters is shown in Figure 9.7.

We have then considered similarity detection via cluster similarity analysis based on geolocation (cf. Figure 9.7(a)), speed (cf. Figure 9.7(b)), or visited networks (cf. Figure 9.7(c)).

5 CONCLUSIONS

This chapter explores features and concepts, and provides guidelines concerning the role and applicability of smart data captured in a non-intrusive way, in the inference and contextualization of human behavior and interaction. The chapter addresses concepts such as the need to redefine aspects of human interaction detection, such as proximity modeling, in a way that stems from an interdisciplinary perspective, providing examples on how such proposal can be achieved.

Challenges concerning the applicability of smart data in mobile crowd sensing systems are then debated, and the chapter concludes with a section on smart data applicability aspects.

FIGURE 9.6   User traces obtained with the tool PML in the City of Portimão, Portugal.

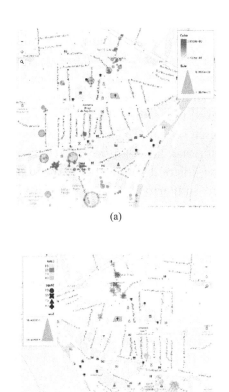

(a)

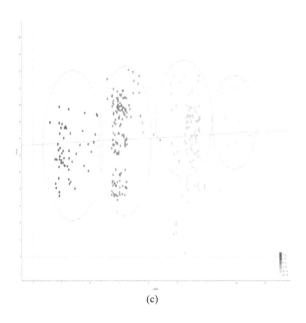

(b)

(c)

FIGURE 9.7 Cluster similarity analysis of the same data set, different approaches. (a) Geolocation, (b) Speed, (c) Visited wireless networks.

Smart data has a relevant role in the context of social routine improvements via mediating technology. Today, such role is already being acknowledged in the form of the most varied tools that provide levels of awareness about oneself. Furthermore and as exemplified in this chapter, the natural networking footprint that is available in mobile personal devices, derived from the natural operation of both cellular and wireless networks as well as by the fact that personal mobile devices are carried around by humans, is relevant to assist in exploring new computational systems and services that can best serve the society.

Acknowledgements

The work carried out and described in this chapter has received funding from the Fundaçãopara a Ciência e Tecnologia (FCT), project 'Proxemics Data lab', COPELABS, references UID/MULTI/04111/2013, UID/MULTI/04111/2016, UID/MULTI/04111/2019, and the H2020 UMOBILE project, grant number 645124.

BIBLIOGRAPHY

1. N. Lane, Y. Xu, H. Lu, S. Eisenman, T. Choudhury, and A. Campbell. Cooperative Communities (CoCo): Exploiting social networks for large-scale modeling of human behavior. In *IEEE Pervasive Computing, Special Issue on Large-Scale Opportunistic Sensing*, vol. 10, Oct 2011.
2. R. Reichle, M. Wagner, M. U. Khan, K. Geihs, J. Lorenzo, M. Valla, C. Fra, N. Paspallis, and G. A. Papadopoulos. A comprehensive context modeling framework for pervasive computing systems. In *IFIP International Conference on Distributed Applications and Interoperable Systems*. Oslo, Norway, 2008.
3. N. D. Lane, S. B. Eisenman, M. Musolesi, E. Miluzzo, and A. T. Campbell. Urban sensing systems: Opportunistic or participatory? Feb 2008.
4. R. Sofia, S. Firdose, L. A. Lopes, W. Moreira, and P. Mendes. NSense: A people-centric, non-intrusive opportunistic sensing tool for contextualizing nearness. In *2016 IEEE 18th International Conference on e-Health Networking, Applications and Services (Healthcom)*, pp. 1–6. IEEE, 2016.
5. M. S. Corson, R. Laroia, J. Li, V. Park, T. Richardson, and G. Tsirtsis. Toward proximity-aware internet working. *Wireless Communications, IEEE*, 17:26–33, Dec 2010.
6. D. Li and P. Sinha. RBTP: Low-power mobile discovery protocol through recursive binary time partitioning. *IEEE Transactions on Mobile Computing*, 13:263–273, Feb 2014.
7. S. Balraj. LTE Direct overview. Tech. Rep., Qualcomm Research, Jul 2012.
8. V. Osmani, I. Carreras, A. Matic, and P. Saar. An analysis of distance estimation to detect proximity in social interactions. *Journal of Ambient Intelligence and Humanized Computing*, 5:297–306, Jun 2014.
9. N. Palaghias, S. A. Hoseinitabatabaei, M. Nati, A. Gluhak, and K. Moessner. Accurate Detection of Real-world social interactions with smartphones. In *2015 IEEE International Conference on Communications (ICC)*, pp. 579–585. IEEE, Jun 2015.
10. M. Porcheron, A. Lucero, A. Quigley, N. Marquardt, J. Clawson, and K. O'Hara. Proxemic mobile collocated interactions. In *Proceedings of the 2016 CHI Conference Extended Abstracts on Human Factors in Computing Systems - CHI EA '16*, New York, NY, pp. 3309–3316. ACM Press, 2016.
11. K. Lewin. *Field theory in social science*. Harper, 1951.
12. R. L. Moreland and J. M. Levine. Group dynamics over time: Development and socialization, 1998.

13. D. T. Campbell. Common fate, similarity, and other indices of the status of aggregates of persons as social entities. *Behavioral Science*, 3:14–25, Feb 2007.

14. S. Roulston and O. Young. GPS tracking of some Northern Ireland students' patterns of shared and separated space: Divided we stand? *International Research in Geographical and Environmental Education*, 22:241–258, Aug 2013.

15. R. Reagans. Close encounters: Analyzing how social similarity and propinquity contribute to strong network connections. *Organization Science*, 22:835–849, Aug 2011.

16. R. C. Sofia, S. Firdose, L. A. Lopes, W. Moreira, and P. Mendes. NSense: A people-centric, non-intrusive opportunistic sensing tool for contextualizing social interaction - Technical Report, COPE-SITI-TR-16-02. Tech. Rep., COPELABS, ULHT, 2016.

17. G. D. Abowd, A. K. Dey, P. J. Brown, N. Davies, M. Smith, and P. Steggles. Towards a better understanding of context and context-awareness, pp. 304–307. Springer, Berlin, Heidelberg, 1999.

18. F. Bonomi, R. Milito, J. Zhu, and S. Addepalli. Fog computing and its role in the Internet of Things. In *Proceedings of the First Edition of the MCC Workshop on Mobile Cloud Computing - MCC '12*, New York, NY, p. 13. ACM Press, 2012.

19. B. Guo, D. Zhang, Z. Wang, Z. Yu, and X. Zhou. Opportunistic IoT: Exploring the harmonious interaction between human and the Internet of Things. *Journal of Network and Computer Applications*, 36:1531–1539, Nov 2013.

20. C.-A. Sarros, S. Diamantopoulos, S. Rene, I. Psaras, A. Lertsinsrubtavee, C. Molina-Jimenez, P. Mendes, R. Sofia, A. Sathiaseelan, G. Pavlou, J. Crowcroft, and V. Tsaoussidis. Connecting the edges: A universal, mobile-centric, and opportunistic communications architecture. pp. 136–143, February 2018.

21. P. Mendes, R. Sofia, V. Tsaoussidis, S. Diamantopoulos, and C.-A. Sarros. Information-centric routing for opportunistic wireless networks. Tech. Rep., 2018.

22. R. Sofia and P. Mendes. User-provided networks: Consumer as provider. *IEEE Communications Magazine*, 46:12, 2008.

23. T. Bilgin and S. Erdogan. A data mining approach for fall detection by using k-nearest neighbour algorithm on wireless sensor network data. *IET Communications*, 6:3281–3287, Dec 2012.

24. R. V. Kulkarni, A. Forster, and G. K. Venayagamoorthy. Computational intelligence in wireless sensor networks: A survey. *IEEE Communications Surveys & Tutorials*, 13 (1):68–96, 2011.

25. C. Stanfill and D. Waltz. Toward memory-based reasoning. *Communications of the ACM*, 29:1213–1228, Dec1986.

26. M. J. A. Berry and G. Linoff. *Data mining techniques: For marketing, sales, and customer support*. Wiley, 1997.

27. M. A. Alsheikh, S. Lin, D. Niyato, and H.-P. Tan. Machine learning in wireless sensor networks: Algorithms, strategies, and applications, 2015.

28. R. C. Schank. *Dynamic memory: A theory of reminding and learning in computers and people*. Cambridge University Press, 1982.

29. A. Kofod-Petersen and A. Aamodt. Contextualised ambient intelligence through case-based reasoning, pp. 211–225. Springer, Berlin, Heidelberg, 2006.

30. J. Kolodner, *Case-based reasoning*. Elsevier Science, 2014.

31. R. Sofia. A tool to estimate roaming behavior in wireless architectures, 2015.

32. N. Lane, M. Lin, M. Rabi, X. Yang, A. Doryab, H. Lu, S. Ali, T. Choudhury, A. Campbell, and E. Berke. Bewell: A smartphone application to monitor, model and promote wellbeing. In *5th ICST/IEEE Conference on Pervasive Computing Technologies for Healthcare*. IEEE Press, 2011.

33. H. Lu, J. Yang, Z. Liu, N. D. Lane, T. Choudhury, and A. T. Campbell. The Jigsaw continuous sensing engine for mobile phone applications. In *Proceedings of the 8th ACM Conference on Embedded Networked Sensor Systems, SenSys '10*, New York, NY, pp. 71–84, ACM, 2010.

34. K. K. Rachuri, M. Musolesi, C. Mascolo, P. J. Rentfrow, C. Longworth, and A. Aucinas. EmotionSense: A mobile phones based adaptive platform for experimental social psychology research. In *Proceedings of the 12th ACM International Conference on Ubiquitous Computing, UbiComp '10*, New York, NY, USA, pp. 281–290. ACM, 2010.

35. A. Liu, V. K. N. Lau, L. Ruan, J. Chen, and D. Xiao. Hierarchical radio resource optimization for heterogeneous networks with enhanced inter-cell interference coordination (eICIC), *CoRR*, vol. abs/1305.5, 2013.

36. N. Banerjee, S. Agarwal, P. Bahl, R. Chandra, A. Wolman, and M. Corner. Virtual compass: Relative positioning to sense mobile social interactions. In *Proceedings of the 8th International Conference on Pervasive Computing, Pervasive'10*, Berlin, Heidelberg, pp. 1–21. Springer-Verlag, 2010.

37. R. C. Sofia, I. Dos Santos, J. Soares, S. Diamantopoulos, C.-A. Sarros, D. Vardalis, and V. Tsaoussidis. UMOBILE Deliverable: D4.5, Report on data collection and inference. Tech. Rep., UMOBILE, 2017.

38. K. H. Lim, J. Chan, and C. Leckie. Personalized tour recommendation based on user Interests and points of interest visit durations. *IJCAI*, 15, 2015.

39. A. Ribeiro and R. C. Sofia. A survey on mobility models for wireless networks. Tech. Rep. SITI-TR-11-01, COPELABS (SITI), University Lusofona, Feb 2011.

CHAPTER 10

Compression of Wearable Body Sensor Network Data

Robinson Raju, Melody Moh, and Teng-Sheng Moh

Department of Computer Science, San Jose State University, San Jose, CA, USA

CONTENTS

1 INTRODUCTION

As the population of the world rises and healthcare costs increase worldwide, human health monitoring has become a critical research area, since it helps tremendously in containing the expenses related to healthcare and enhancing the customer experience [1]. Though there have been devices to measure vital statistics from a person's body, they have mostly been wired, large, and conspicuous. Recent trends towards improvements in micro-electro-mechanical systems (MEMS) technology [2], wireless communications, and digital electronics have allowed the development of miniature, low-cost, low-power, multi-functional sensor that can sense and transmit data wirelessly.

One family of these devices is wearable Body Sensor Networks (BSNs), which are IoT (Internet of Things) devices that can transmit health-related data from a person wirelessly to a node. The data can be used to monitor vital signs and provide real-time feedback. The data can also be used for machine learning and predictive analytics, to foresee medical infrastructure needs and lead the world towards a future of ubiquitous healthcare monitoring. Since real-time data analysis is critical in many cases, transmitting the data from sensors to sink nodes with speed and ease is vital.

The sensors in the BSN have limited battery and memory available, and this makes data compression crucial in a BSN. Also, since the data in question is related to health information, it should be accurate, and the compression algorithms have to be lossless. As the technology improves, the number of sensors and the amount of data that a sensor can capture and transmit also increases. This is another reason to focus on data compression at the sensor nodes.

The primary objective of the chapter is to evaluate the performance of classical data compression algorithms and Two Thresholds Two Divisors (TTTD) data chunking algorithm on BSN data. The chapter starts by giving a background on BSN, the general architecture, and types of sensors, followed by data processing steps common in most BSNs. It then reviews existing research on compression of BSN data. After this, it gives a short overview of lossless compression algorithms like Huffman, LZW, and RLE and data chunking technique called TTTD. It then reviews the results of experimental evaluation of the aforementioned algorithms on BSN data. It establishes that TTTD can be used to compress BSN data with different sets of parameters and has performance that is comparable to or superior than other algorithms. After the experimental evaluations, the chapter proposes an approach to combine TTTD and Huffman (TTTD-H) algorithms to compress data more efficiently. This algorithm, TTTD-H, is then evaluated on BSN data from multiple sources. The chapter includes an analysis on energy consumption of the compression algorithms, and concluded that the proposed TTTD-H algorithm, compared with existing algorithms, not only improves the compression factor, but also reduces its power consumption. Early results of this work have been reported [3].

2 BACKGROUND

2.1 General Architecture of a BSN

A BSN is a wireless network of wearable computing devices. BSNs may be embedded inside the body as implants, placed on the body in a fixed position, or in accompanied devices which people carry around, like in pockets, by hand, in a bag, and so forth.

Figure 10.1 describes the general architecture of a BSN. The sensor nodes at different parts of the body collect physical data and transmit to the sink node which then transmits it to the base station. Some sensors directly transmit to the base station or send data via Bluetooth to smartphones.

2.2 Sensors in a BSN

Sensors are IoT devices that connect the physical world with the measuring system and, eventually, the Internet. They collect information about the surrounding and are responsible for processing information and transmitting them. A sensor node ordinarily consists of the following modules: sensor module, processor module, wireless communication module, and power supply module [4].

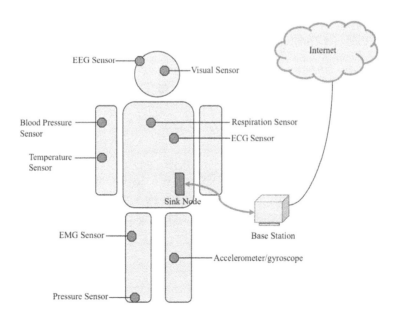

FIGURE 10.1   Architecture of a body sensor network.

While the sensor module collects and converts physical data into electrical signals, the wireless communication module transports the signal to various devices. The processor module controls the sensor nodes, and the power supply module provides energy to the nodes.

2.2.1 Classification of Sensors

Sensors could be classified by BSN attributes like types of signals, transmission media, deployment position, and so forth [4].

Classification by Types of Measured Signals

a) *Sensors that collect continuous time-varying signals:* This type of sensor collects data continuously, and the main requirement here would be real-time transfer of information. The continuous signal sensors can also generate a lot of data. Accelerometers or gyroscopes used in Smart watches, ECG, EEG, and EMG sensors are examples of these types of sensors.

b) *Sensors that collect discrete time-varying physiology signals:* This type of sensor collects signals in discrete intervals. For example, temperature and humidity sensors capture measurements every "x" minutes or hours, and monitor and measure blood pressure every hour or day.

Classification by data transmission media

c) *Wireless sensors:* These sensors employ wireless communication technologies like Bluetooth, Zigbee, RFID, and so forth to communicate with other devices.

d) *Wired sensors:* These sensors are physically connected to other devices and transmit the data through wires.

e) *Human body communication (HBC) sensors:* These sensors use the human body as the transmission medium and they adopt sub-GHz frequencies for transmission.

Other Classifications

a) The sensors can also be classified based on deployment position as Wearable, Implantable, or Surrounding. They can also be classified based on the automatic adjustment ability whether they are self-adapting or not.

2.2.3 Commonly Used Sensors in BSNs

TABLE 10.1 Commonly used sensors in BSNs.

Sensors	Signal Type	Frequency	Position
Accelerometer	Continuous	High	Wearable
Artificial cochlea	Continuous	High	Implantable
Artificial retina	Continuous	High	Implantable
Blood-pressure sensor	Discrete	Low	Wearable
Camera pill	Continuous	High	Implantable
Carbon dioxide sensor	Discrete	Low/Very low	Wearable
ECG/EEG/EMG sensor	Continuous	High	Wearable
Gyroscope	Continuous	High	Wearable
Humidity sensor	Discrete	Very low	Wearable
Blood oxygen saturation sensor	Discrete	Low	Wearable
Pressure sensor	Continuous	High	Wearable/Surrounding
Respiration sensor	Continuous	High	Wearable
Temperature sensor	Discrete	Very low	Wearable
Visual sensor	Continuous/Discrete	High/Low	Wearable/Surrounding

2.3 Data Processing in BSNs

Data Processing, also referred to as Data fusion, is a process for handling the data from the sensors in an efficient manner. BSNs produce a considerable amount of data, and data processing techniques are needed to filter noise efficiently, combine data from multiple sensors, extract necessary information, and transmit to devices that need the information for analysis. The following is a summarization of different steps in data fusion [4].

a) *Preprocessing*: Since the wireless and implantable sensors are constantly in a dynamic environment, the data that comes out of these sensors can many times have lot more information than what is pertinent to being measured. "Preprocessing" is a step to remove the noise from the data without losing the vital information. Some of the techniques used for preprocessing are Fourier Transform, Wavelet Transform [5], Mathematical morphology filters [6], Kalman filter [7], Low-pass median value filter, Laplacian Transform, Gaussian filter, and so forth.

b) *Feature Extraction*: The principal objective of this step is to extract features that represent the characteristics of the original data accurately. The classifiers use the features as inputs. Techniques regularly used in feature extraction include Support Vector Machine (SVM), K-Means Clustering, Principal Component Analysis (PCA), Independent Component Analysis (ICA), and so forth. Commonly used features are *time-Domain Features* like Variance and Root Mean Square (RMS),

Frequency-Domain Features like Spectral Energy and Spectral Entropy, *Time-Frequency Domain Features* like Wavelet Coefficients, *Heuristic Features* like Signal Magnitude Area (SMA), Signal Vector Magnitude, and Inter-Axis Correlation and *Domain-Specific Features* like Time-Domain Gait Detection [8].

c) *Data Processing (Computing)*: The chief objective of the data computing step is to use algorithms to analyze the data. Machine Learning Algorithms could be used to do Classification or Clustering. As per Lai et al. [4], the commonly used algorithms include threshold-based classification, hierarchical methods, decision trees, and K-Nearest Neighbor (KNN), Support Vector Machines (SVM), Artificial Neural Net-works (ANN), Hidden Markov Models (HMM), and so forth. Peng et al. [9] recognized fourteen physical activities using a binary decision-tree with a Naïve Bayes classifier. Krishnan et al. [10] conducted research on how AdaBoost, HMM, and KNN are used to analyze data from accelerometers to identify human hand activity.

d) *Data Compression*: After noise reduction, feature extraction, and optionally data fusion, the sensor nodes do compression of the data before sending it to the sink node or the base station. Data compression reduces the amount of data transmission and also lowers power consumption. This is important since power consumption is one of main areas of concern in a WSN or a BSN [11]. Data Compression is the main topic of exploration in this chapter.

3 RELATED STUDIES

3.1 The Need for Compression of BSN Data

As mentioned in the previous section, it is essential to compress the data from WIBSNs since the devices are small and data generated can be very frequent. The reasons for compression can be summarized as follows:

- *Battery power*: The sensors are small and battery has limited power.

- *Network bandwidth*: Compressed data needs less bandwidth. Lot of data from multiple sensors might be sharing the same channel to send information to the base station.

- *Data staleness*: Data loses effectiveness if not sent within a short period of time, especially in cases where it is life-critical.

- *Data security*: Data sent in raw format could be snooped by other devices, thereby compromising the privacy and security of the individual whose data is collected.

3.2 Review of Research on BSN Data Compression

In their survey of BSNs, Lai et al. [4] mention that data compression in BSNs can be done using classical compression algorithms such as source encoding, differential encoding, and Huffman encoding. Sadler et al. [12] did a study on data compression algorithms for energy-constrained devices and proposed a variant of Lempel Zev Welch (LZW) algorithm named s-LZW to reduce the amount of data sent across the network. Yoon et al. [13] used the s-LZW scheme as the compression method to improve energy utilization in solar-powered WSNs. It is also noted in the chapter that s-LZW is a lossless compression algorithm widely used in WSNs. Wu and Tseng [14] did a case study on Pilates motion recognition using BSNs, and they proposed a compression algorithm based on interception and differential encoding techniques. Hu et al. [15] analyzed biomedical signals from low-power BSNs and utilized an algorithm named Joint Orthogonal Matching Pursuit (JOMP) which could control interval times, thereby reducing the amount of data processing and transmission. Charbiwala et al. [16] evaluated the effectiveness of a wireless Neural Recording System (NRS) and proposed using on-chip detection of action potentials, combined with compressive sensing techniques. Manikandan and Dandapat [17] presented an ECG data compression algorithm based on Discrete Sinc Interpolation (DSI) technique which used an efficient Discrete Fourier Transform (DFT) to achieve compression and decompression. Tiwari and Kumar [18] did a survey and experimentation on classical lossless compression techniques like LZW, Huffman, and so forth and proposed a new algorithm named Aggregated Deflate-RLE (ADR) compression technique which combined Deflate and RLE compression techniques and achieved better performance.

4 EXISTING LOSS COMPRESSION TECHNIQUES: ALGORITHMS AND EXPERIMENTAL EVALUATIONS

4.1 Review of Existing Lossless Compression Techniques

A brief description about lossless compression algorithms, such as Run Length Encoding, Huffman Encoding, and Lempel Zev Welch, is given below.

4.1.1 Run Length Encoding Algorithm

Run Length Encoding is an algorithm where characters/symbols that are repeating in sequence are coded just once. For example, the input WWWWWWWBBBWWWB gives the output as 6W3B3W1B when it is passed through the RLE algorithm. The algorithm is efficient if there are a lot of repeating symbols like an image with a line graph where pixels in the background color are the same [19].

4.1.2 Huffman Encoding Algorithm

Huffman encoding is an algorithm where symbols are encoded with bits in such a way that more frequently occurring symbols are assigned smaller bit strings. As an input, Huffman would need an array or lookup table of frequencies for each symbol that may be in the dataset. The frequency can be pre-computed using a test dataset [20].

4.1.3 Lempel Zev Welch (LZW) Algorithm

LZW compression is an algorithm where a sequence of symbols is mapped to a code from a lookup table. The lookup table initially has codes 0–255 to represent single bytes and the algorithm adds more symbol-sequences and codes as it reads the text [21].

4.1.4 Data Chunking and TTTD Algorithm

Data chunking is a technique primarily used in data deduplication systems for deduping data in files to reduce storage costs. During data chunking, the algorithm breaks data into smaller data elements called "chunks." Chunks are then fingerprinted and used later for duplicate detection. The simplest approach of data chunking, called "Fixed size chunking," is to break the input into equal, fixed-size chunks. But this approach has some key issues like "boundary shift problem" and large chunk size variances.

The concerns around boundary-shift problem were addressed by content-defined chunking (CDC) algorithm which was proposed in Low Bandwidth File System (LBFS) [22]. As shown in Figure 10.2, CDC uses a basic sliding window (BSW) technique where the sliding *window W* shifts one byte at a time from the beginning to the end of the file. During every shift, it computes a *hashvalue h* for the data in the window. The hashvalue is computed using Rabin Fingerprinting which makes it faster. The satisfying pre-condition in this instance is *(h mod D) = R*. The divisor *D* is a divisor that is chosen at the beginning depending on the average chunk size desired. *R* could be *0* or some number that is less than *D*. If the pre-condition is met, the algorithm sets that point *P* as the breakpoint for the chunk boundary. Then, a hash of the chunk is done and stored in memory with the key as the hash and value as either the data or compressed data. Before the hash is stored, a lookup is done to see if the hash already exists. If yes, just a pointer to the position is stored thereby reducing the space needed.

The TTTD algorithm, developed by HP laboratory [23], to solve the problem of large chunk sizes, uses the same concept as above with some modifications. As the name suggests, there are two thresholds, maximum threshold (*maxT*) and minimum threshold (*minT*), to limit the chunk sizes between two boundaries. In addition to this, there is a second divisor (second), which is used to determine backup breakpoint. The TTTD-S algorithm, developed at San Jose State University, is an improvement over TTTD where a parameter switch is used to improve the probability of using the main divisor thereby bringing the average chunk size closer to the middle of the two boundaries.

Though the TTTD algorithm is primarily used to optimize file storage in local or cloud storage systems, one of the objectives of this research is to evaluate if this algorithm could also be used for small data sizes with different parameters.

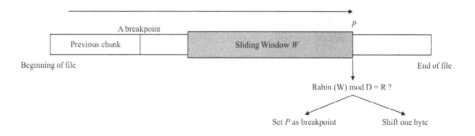

FIGURE 10.2 Sliding window algorithm.

Pseudocode [24]:

```
1  intcurrP = 0, lastP = 0, backupBreak = 0 ;
2
3  for ( ; ! endOfFile ( input ) ; currP++ ) {
4      unsigned char c = getNextByte ( input ) ;
5      unsigned int hash = updateHash ( c ) ;
6
7      if ( currP – lastP < minT ) {
8          continue ;
9      }
10     if (( hash % secondD ) = = secondD – 1 ) {
11         backupBreak = currP ;
12     }
13     if (( hash % mainD ) = = mainD – 1 ) {
14         addBreakpoint (currP ) ;
15         backupBreak = 0 ;
16         lastP = currP ;
17         continue ;
18     }
19     if ( currP – lastP < maxT ) {
20         continue ;
21     }
22     if ( backupBreak != 0 ) {
23         addBreakpoint (backupBreak ) ;
24         lastP = backupBreak ;
25         backupBreak = 0 ;
26     }
27     else {
28         addBreakpoint (currP ) ;
29         lastP = currP ;
30         backupBreak = 0
31     }
32 }
```

4.2 Experimental Evaluations

The metrics used for the analysis of the runtime results of the compression algorithms above are outlined below.

4.2.1 Metrics for Analysis

TABLE 10.2 Metrics for compression analysis.

Metric	Description	Formula
File size (FS)	File size in *bytes*	–
Compressed file size (CS)	File size of the compressed file in *bytes*	–
Compression time (CT)	Time taken to compress the file in *milliseconds*	–
Compression ratio (CR)	*Ratio* of compressed file size to original file size	*CS/FS*
Savings percentage (SP)	*Percentage* of reduction in file size after compression	*100 × ((FS – CS)/FS)*
Compression factor (CF)	*Ratio* of original file size to compressed file size	*FS/CS*

4.2.2 Experimental Objectives

The main objective of the experiments was to run the various algorithms to compute FS, CS, CT, CR, SP, and CF for files with varying sizes. The data characteristics are similar among files. All files were data from Fitbit [25], a wearable device that has sensors like accelerometers and gyroscopes to measure steps and activity intensities during the course of a day. Files of smaller sizes were chosen since sensors typically do not have large RAMs available.

4.2.3 Experimental Configurations

The experiments were conducted on a machine with the following hardware:

- 2.8 GHz Intel Core i7 2.8 GHz processor.

- 16 GB 1600 MHz DDR3 Memory.

- 500GB Flash hard disk drive.

The configuration for the algorithms is as follows:

- *RLE*: Regex to find letters "[0–9] + |[a-zA-Z]."

- *Huffman*: Size of frequency count table, R = 256.

- *LZW*: Number of input chars, R = 256; Codeword width, W = 12; Number of codewords, L = 2^W = 4096.

- *TTTD*: Prior to running this experiment, TTTD algorithm was run on the dataset with different sets of parameters. The initial trial was with the defaults from the original chapter's optimal values by Eshghi et al. [23], which were window size of 48 bytes, main divisor as 540, secondary divisor as 270, and *maxT* and *minT* as 2800 and 460, respectively. These values resulted in the compressed file size being the same as the original file. After different trials, the following parameters were arrived at. These gave an optimal (>50%) reduction in the file sizes.

TABLE 10.3 TTTD parameters.

Parameter Name	Value
Window size (bytes)	4
Main divisor (mainD)	540
Second divisor (secondD)	270
Maximum threshold (maxT)	15
Minimum threshold (minT)	5

TABLE 10.4 Datasets used for the experiments (FitbitData).

Dataset no.	Data name	Data type	File size (Bytes)
#1	Steps per day	*.csv	25,175
#2	Intensities per day	*.csv	70,581
#3	Intensities per hour	*.csv	482,671
#4	Steps per hour	*.csv	796,562
#5	Steps per minute	*.csv	3,481,174

4.3 Experimental Results

The dataset was compressed using the algorithms mentioned above and the results were recorded to have a side-by-side comparison.

TABLE 10.5 Comparison of various compression algorithms.

	FS	CS	CT	CR	SP
Huffman	25,175	11,971	130	0.476	52.45
	70,581	32,634	138	0.462	53.76
	482,671	242,107	155	0.502	49.84
	796,562	399,955	181	0.502	49.79
	3,481,174	1,137,343	311	0.327	67.33
LZW	25,175	9,200	203	0.365	63.46
	70,581	26,825	423	0.380	61.99
	482,671	161,429	7398	0.334	66.56
	796,562	268,850	18865	0.338	66.25
	3,481,174	621,182	199799	0.178	82.16
RLE	25,175	47,021	135	1.868	-86.78
	70,581	117,753	140	1.668	-66.83
	482,671	851,493	182	1.764	-76.41
	796,562	1,432,065	208	1.798	-79.78
	3,481,174	6,769,007	455	1.944	-94.45
TTTD	25,175	24,262	199	0.964	3.63
	70,581	65,543	249	0.929	7.14
	482,671	174,672	402	0.362	63.81
	796,562	363,847	459	0.457	54.32
	3,481,174	989,000	1090	0.284	71.59

4.4 Experimental Observations

- *Compressed File Size (CS):* The compressed file for RLE was larger than the original file and hence RLE would not be a good fit for this type of data.

Table 10.5 shows that compressed file size grows linearly with input size. LZW performs better than Huffman and TTTD algorithms in terms of compressed file size.

- *Compression Ratio (CR):* Compression Ratio is consistent for Huffman Algorithm for files of 25KB, 71KB, 483KB, and 796KB files. For 3.5MB file, the ratio is better than smaller files. Of all the algorithms, LZW had the best CR for all sizes of files, followed by TTTD and then Huffman. LZW and TTTD algorithms perform much better for larger files than smaller ones in terms of CR.

- *Compression Factor (CF):* Since Compression Factor is reciprocal of Compression Ratio, the observations there apply to this also. Huffman is quite stable and LZW has the best compression factor.

- *Savings Percentage (SP):* Huffman is stable in terms of savings percentage. LZW has higher SP in comparison to Huffman but not by a great margin. TTTD has lower SP in comparison to Huffman for smaller files but better SP in comparison to Huffman for larger files.

- *Compression Time (CT):* Compression time is very high for LZW in comparison to other algorithms. LZW took 199 seconds in comparison to 0.3 seconds for Huffman and 1.1 seconds for TTTD. Huffman is best in terms of compression time, followed by RLE and then TTTD.

5 PROPOSED METHOD

5.1 Experiment with Combination of Algorithms

Comparisons of algorithms in the last section gave the following insights:

- TTTD and LZW outranked other algorithms in terms of compressed file size, compression ratio, compression factor, and savings percentage.

- TTTD and Huffman outranked other algorithms in terms of compression time.

- RLE was not suitable for this type of data since the compression ratio was greater than 1.

The above insights brought forth the idea that perhaps multiple algorithms could be used to compress the compressed data and give an overall efficiency to the system. Hence, in the next stage of experiments, the algorithms Huffman, LZW, and TTTD were run in a sequence in different orders with output from the first algorithm being the input for the second. Table 10.6 has the results of performance of different combinations. The sequence *TTTD -> LZW -> Huffman (TLH)* performed better than others in terms of compression ratio. The sequence *TTTD -> Huffman -> LZW (THL)* performed better in terms of compression time. Since LZW takes time, when experiment was run by removing LZW from the chain, the

TABLE 10.6 Performance of algorithms in different combinations.

Algorithm	FS	CS	CT	CR	SP
HLT (Huffman-LZW-TTTD)	3481174	760956	76087	0.219	78.14
HTL (Huffman-TTTD-LZW)	3481174	700017	52449	0.201	79.89
LHT (LZW-Huffman-TTTD)	3481174	613565	194295	0.176	82.37
LTH (LZW-TTTD-Huffman)	3481174	611280	194090	0.176	82.44
THL (TTTD-Huffman-LZW)	3481174	455984	18517	0.131	86.90
TLH (TTTD-LZW-Huffman)	3481174	353831	31703	0.102	89.84
TH (TTTD-Huffman)	**3481174**	**408642**	**1249**	**0.117**	**88.26**
TL (TTTD-LZW)	3481174	355863	31840	0.102	89.78

TTDD ->Huffman (TH) algorithm performed much better in terms of time and was only fractionally different in terms of compression ratio and savings percentage.

Based on the results, the proposal is to run TTTD and Huffman in sequence on the data, with the output of TTTD being the input of Huffman.

5.2 Outline of the Proposed Algorithm

6 PERFORMANCE EVALUATION

The proposed method was run on the data used in the baseline experiments (Fitbit data) and also on additional data to support the research. The second set of data was obtained from UCI (University of California, Irvine)'s "Heterogeneity Activity Recognition Data Set." Fitbit dataset had data about steps and intensities recorded by Fitbit wearable

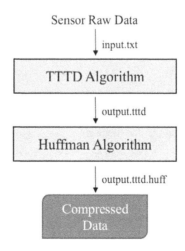

FIGURE 10.3   Outline of the proposed algorithm.

device. The Smartphone dataset has data from readings that were recorded while users executed activities carrying smartwatches and smartphones.

6.1 Fitbit Dataset

The metrics used for the analysis of the runtime results of the proposed compression algorithm are as outlined in Section 4. Below, the results are compared with the existing techniques.

1) *Compressed File Size:* As shown in Figure 10.4, compressed size for TTTD-H is much lower than Huffman, LZW, and TTTD. It is almost half of what Huffman or TTTD has individually. For small file sizes, LZW is better than other algorithms. For 25KB file, LZW compresses it to 9KB while TTTD is only 24KB. The proposed algorithm, TTTD-H, is closer to LZW in terms of compressed file size, compressing the input to 11.5KB. As the file size becomes larger, especially after 100KB, TTTD and TTTD-H easily trump other algorithms. For a 3.5MB file, the output from LZW is 621KB while the output from TTTD-H is only 408KB, 50% better than LZW.

TABLE 10.7 Performance of proposed algorithm in comparison to other compression algorithms

Sl. No	Algorithm	FS (bytes)	CS (bytes)	CT (ms)	CR	SP	CF
1	Huffman	25,175	11,971	130	0.476	52.45	2.10
2	Huffman	70,581	32,634	138	0.462	53.76	2.16
3	Huffman	482,671	242,107	155	0.502	49.84	1.99
4	Huffman	796,562	399,955	181	0.502	49.79	1.99
5	Huffman	3,481,174	1,137,343	311	0.327	67.33	3.06
6	LZW	25,175	9,200	203	0.365	63.46	2.74
7	LZW	70,581	26,825	423	0.380	61.99	2.63
8	LZW	482,671	161,429	7398	0.334	66.56	2.99
9	LZW	796,562	268,850	18865	0.338	66.25	2.96
10	LZW	3,481,174	621,182	199799	0.178	82.16	5.60
11	TTTD	25,175	24,262	199	0.964	3.63	1.04
12	TTTD	70,581	65,543	249	0.929	7.14	1.08
13	TTTD	482,671	174,672	402	0.362	63.81	2.76
14	TTTD	796,562	363,847	459	0.457	54.32	2.19
15	TTTD	3,481,174	989,000	1090	0.284	71.59	3.52
16	TTTD-H	25,175	11,520	398	0.458	54.24	2.19
17	TTTD-H	70,581	30,336	404	0.430	57.02	2.33
18	TTTD-H	482,671	87,531	566	0.181	81.87	5.51
19	TTTD-H	796,562	185,465	616	0.233	76.72	4.29
20	TTTD-H	3,481,174	408,642	1263	0.117	88.26	8.52

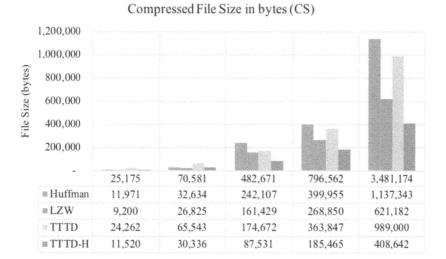

Compressed File Size in bytes (CS)

	25,175	70,581	482,671	796,562	3,481,174
▪ Huffman	11,971	32,634	242,107	399,955	1,137,343
▪ LZW	9,200	26,825	161,429	268,850	621,182
▪ TTTD	24,262	65,543	174,672	363,847	989,000
▪ TTTD-H	11,520	30,336	87,531	185,465	408,642

FIGURE 10.4   Comparison of compressed file sizes with TTTD-H.

2) *Compression Ratio*: As shown in Figure 10.5, the compression ratio for TTTD-H is lower than Huffman, LZW, and TTTD. For smaller files, the compression ratio of TTTD-H is comparable to that of Huffman and LZW, but for larger files, TTTD-H is much better. The ratio is 11.7% for a 3.5MB file in comparison to 17.8% for LZW and 32.7% for Huffman.

3) *Compression Factor*: Compression factor is the reciprocal of compression ratio and the values mirror the results in compression ratio chart in the other direction. As illustrated in Figure 10.6, the compression factor for TTTD-H is higher than Huffman, LZW, and TTTD. Compression factor for TTTD-H is 8.52 for a 3.5MB file in comparison to that of 5.6 for LZW and 3.06 for Huffman.

4) *Savings Percentage*: From Figure 10.7, it is clear that the savings percentage for TTTD-H is higher than Huffman, LZW, and TTTD. The savings percentage is 54% for TTTD-H for 25KB file in comparison to 63% for LZW and 52% for Huffman. For larger files, however, TTTD-H has much better savings which is in line with compression ratio. For a 3.5MB file, the savings percentage is 88% for TTTD-H, which is much higher than other algorithms.

5) *Compression Time*: Illustrated in Figure 10.8, the compression time for TTTD-H is higher than that of TTTD or Huffman but lower than LZW. LZW took close to 200,000 milliseconds to compress a file of size 3.5MB. TTTD-H in comparison took only 1,200 milliseconds.As mentioned earlier, the value for TTTD-H is higher than other but the compression ratio and savings percentages are much higher. Since the value is only 0.2 seconds higher than TTTD for 3.5MB file, this is the small increase to pay for the extra compression ratio. The benefit from making network bandwidth better by reducing the amount of data sent during I/O calls outweighs the compression time concerns.

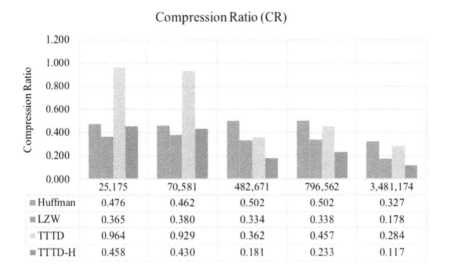

FIGURE 10.5   Comparison of compression ratio with TTTD-H.

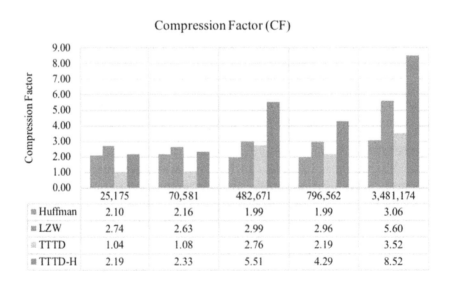

FIGURE 10.6   Comparison of compression factor with TTTD-H.

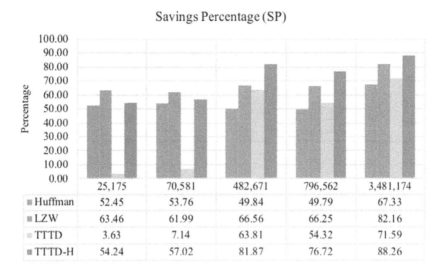

FIGURE 10.7   Comparison of savings percentage with TTTD-H.

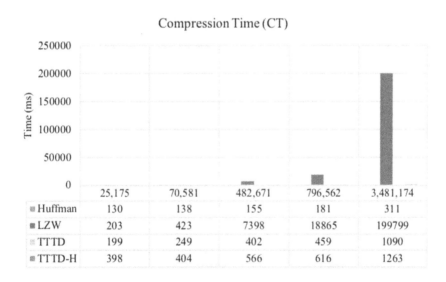

FIGURE 10.8   Comparison of compression time with TTTD-H.

6.2 Heterogeneity Activity Recognition Dataset

Further experiments were conducted with different sets of wearable sensor data to determine if the results were consistent. UCI dataset on *Heterogeneity Activity Recognition* [26] was used for this experiment. This dataset contains the readings of motion sensors from smartphones to track activities like 'Biking,' 'Walking,' 'Walking up the stairs', and so forth. The data was from devices like Samsung Galaxy S3, LG Nexus, Galaxy Gear, and so forth.

TABLE 10.8 Dataset used for the experiments (smartphone data).

Dataset no.	Data name	Data type	File size (Bytes)
#1	Phones accelerometer	*.csv	498,034
#2	Phones gyroscope	*.csv	1,100,585
#3	Samsung Galaxy Gear	*.csv	2,038,622
#4	Watch accelerometer	*.csv	4,322,183
#5	Watch gyroscope	*.csv	6,512,577

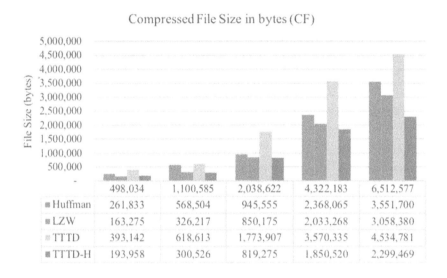

Compressed File Size in bytes (CF)

	498,034	1,100,585	2,038,622	4,322,183	6,512,577
■ Huffman	261,833	568,504	945,555	2,368,065	3,551,700
■ LZW	163,275	326,217	850,175	2,033,268	3,058,380
■ TTTD	393,142	618,613	1,773,907	3,570,335	4,534,781
■ TTTD-H	193,958	300,526	819,275	1,850,520	2,299,469

FIGURE 10.9 Comparison of compressed file sizes with TTTD-H.

1) *Compressed File Size:* As shown in Figure 10.9, compressed size for TTTD-H is much lower than Huffman, LZW, and TTTD. It is almost half of what Huffman or TTTD has individually.

2) *Compression Ratio:* As shown in Figure 10.10, the compression ratio for TTTD-H is lower than Huffman, LZW, and TTTD.

3) *Compression Factor:* As illustrated in Figure 10.11, the compression factor for TTTD-H is higher than Huffman, LZW, and TTTD.

4) *Savings Percentage:* From Figure 10.12, it is clear that the saving percentage for TTTD-H is higher than Huffman, LZW, and TTTD.

5) *Compression Time:* Illustrated in Figure 10.13, the compression time for TTTD-H is higher than that of TTTD or Huffman but much lower than LZW. The savings percentage and compression ratio are much higher for TTTD-H.

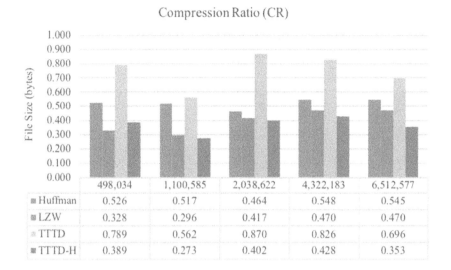

FIGURE 10.10   Comparison of compression ratio with TTTD-H.

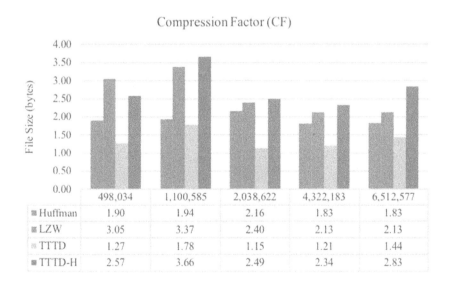

FIGURE 10.11   Comparison of compression factor with TTTD-H.

FIGURE 10.12   Comparison of savings percentage with TTTD-H.

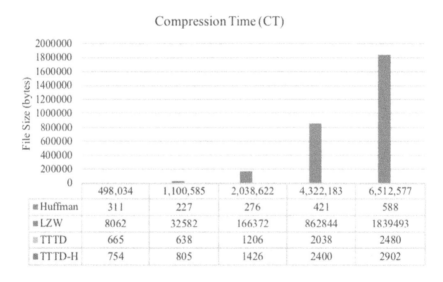

FIGURE 10.13   Comparison of compression time with TTTD-H.

6.3 Analysis of Energy Consumption

6.3.1 Formula for Energy Consumption

Another important criterion to decide on the compression algorithm for BSN data is the rate of energy consumption at the sensor. As mentioned in Section 3.1, the need for compression of BSN data, reducing the battery power, is one of the main goals of compression. Thus, the amount of extra energy needed for compression should be less than the amount of energy that is saved due to the reduced number of bits that are transmitted. Shin et al. [27], in their chapter on *"Analysis of Low Power Sensor Node Using Data Compression,"* formulated this as follows:

$$P_{no\_compression} = P_{memory} + P_{sensing} + P_{processing} + P_{transmission}$$

$$P_{with\_compression} = P_{no\_compression} + \Delta P_{memory} + \Delta P_{processing} - \Delta P_{transmission}$$

where

- $\Delta P_{memory} + \Delta P_{processing}$ are the power consumption increases for extra memory and processing that occurs due to compression.

- $\Delta P_{transmission}$ is the power saving due to lesser amount of data that is being sent.

For compression to be useful, the following condition should be satisfied:

$$\Delta P_{memory} + \Delta P_{processing} < \Delta P_{transmission}$$

The amount of energy needed for computation is more than that needed for storing data in memory. Since $\Delta P_{processing}$ is the upperbound, we could simplify the above formula as

$$2\Delta P_{processing} < \Delta P_{transmission}$$

In their chapter on "Energy-aware lossless data compression," Barr and Asanović [28] performed experiments and summarized the energy consumptions for computations and transmissions of sensor data. As per the analysis, the energy used by the processor for a single ADD is 0.86 nJ (0.86×10^{-9} J) and the energy used for sending a single bit is between 417 nJ (417×10^{-9} J) and 1090 nJ (1090×10^{-9} J). The chapter mentions that sending a single bit is equivalent to performing 485 to 1267 ADD operations. For our computations, we take the average as 700 nJ for sending a single bit. Also, cache miss consumes 78.34 nJ of energy per bit for writing data into memory and cache hit needs 2.41×10^{-9} J of energy. To summarize,

- The energy used for computation = 0.86×10^{-9} J

- The energy used for writing data into memory = 78.34×10^{-9} J

- The energy used for reading data from memory = 2.41×10^{-9} J

- The energy used for transmission of 1 bit = 700×10^{-9} J

If we take the first experiment with Huffman as an example,

$$\Delta P_{processing} = \Delta P_{cache\_hit} + \Delta P_{cache\_miss}$$

$$\Delta P_{processing} = (FS - CS)*8*2.41*10^{-9} + CS*8*78.34*10^{-9} = \textbf{7.76 x 10}^{-3}\textbf{J}$$

where FS = File Size and CS = Compressed File Size, both in bytes.

$$\Delta P_{transmission} = (FS - CS)*8*700*10^{-9} = \textbf{73.94 x 10}^{-3}\textbf{J}$$

We see that $2\Delta P_{processing} < \Delta P_{transmission}$ holds true and energy saved can be calculated as $\Delta P_{transmission} - 2\Delta P_{processing} = 58.43$ mJ.

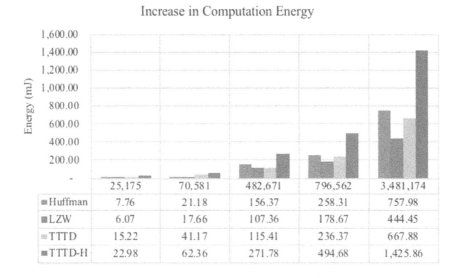

Increase in Computation Energy				
	25,175	70,581	482,671	796,562	3,481,174
▪Huffman	7.76	21.18	156.37	258.31	757.98
▪LZW	6.07	17.66	107.36	178.67	444.45
▪TTTD	15.22	41.17	115.41	236.37	667.88
▪TTTD-H	22.98	62.36	271.78	494.68	1,425.86

FIGURE 10.14   Dataset 1—Comparison of increase in energy during computation.

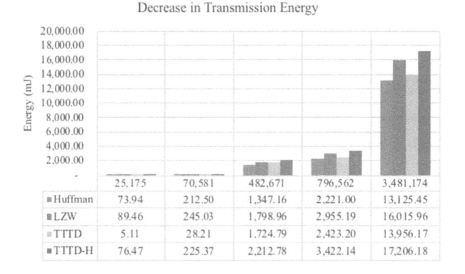

Decrease in Transmission Energy				
	25,175	70,581	482,671	796,562	3,481,174
▪Huffman	73.94	212.50	1,347.16	2,221.00	13,125.45
▪LZW	89.46	245.03	1,798.96	2,955.19	16,015.96
▪TTTD	5.11	28.21	1,724.79	2,423.20	13,956.17
▪TTTD-H	76.47	225.37	2,212.78	3,422.14	17,206.18

FIGURE 10.15   Dataset 1—Comparison of decrease in energy during transmission.

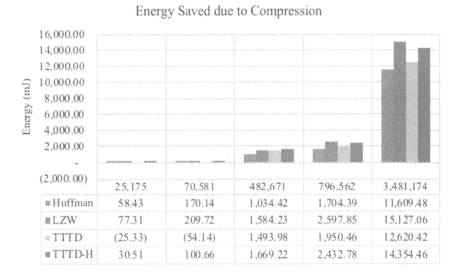

FIGURE 10.16   Dataset 1—Comparison of energy saving due to compression.

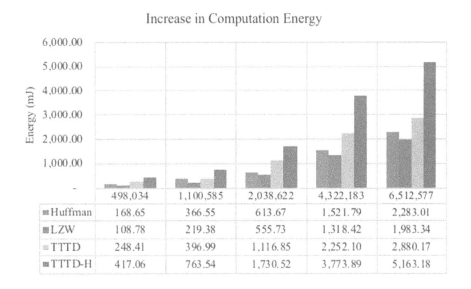

FIGURE 10.17   Dataset 2—Comparison of increase in energy during computation.

6.3.2 Computation of Energy Savings Due to Compression

Figures 10.14–10.19 show the increase in processing time, decrease in transmission time, and the energy saved due to compression for datasets #1 and #2. The actual energy saved due to compression might be larger than the values in the table since we made

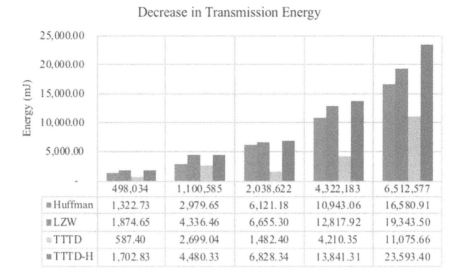

FIGURE 10.18   Dataset 2—Comparison of decrease in energy during transmission.

	498,034	1,100,585	2,038,622	4,322,183	6,512,577
Huffman	1,322.73	2,979.65	6,121.18	10,943.06	16,580.91
LZW	1,874.65	4,336.46	6,655.30	12,817.92	19,343.50
TTTD	587.40	2,699.04	1,482.40	4,210.35	11,075.66
TTTD-H	1,702.83	4,480.33	6,828.34	13,841.31	23,593.40

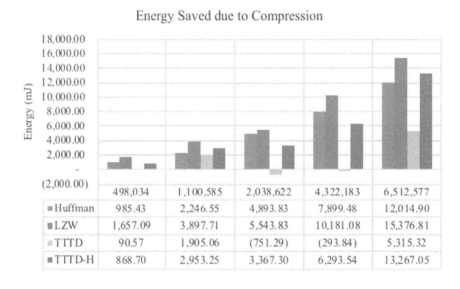

FIGURE 10.19   Dataset 2—Comparison of energy saving due to compression.

	498,034	1,100,585	2,038,622	4,322,183	6,512,577
Huffman	985.43	2,246.55	4,893.83	7,899.48	12,014.90
LZW	1,657.09	3,897.71	5,543.83	10,181.08	15,376.81
TTTD	90.57	1,905.06	(751.29)	(293.84)	5,315.32
TTTD-H	868.70	2,953.25	3,367.30	6,293.54	13,267.05

assumptions on upper bounds for energy consumption due to increased storage in memory.

TTTD-H consumes more energy during compression as expected, and since it compresses more data, the energy saving is higher because the transmission cost is much higher than the power used during computation.

7 CONCLUSION

7.1 Summary

In this chapter, we reviewed the concept of wearable and implantable BSN and their lossless compression techniques, including RLE, LZW, and Huffman. We also reviewed a data chunking algorithm used in many deduplication systems named TTTD. Experiments showed that Huffman is a stable algorithm, and LZW had better compression ratio but takes much longer time. TTTD had less compression ratio than LZW but was much faster. After this, we ran experiments by combining algorithms to determine a combined algorithm that would produce a lower compression ratio using short compression time. Based on these experimental results, we proposed *TTTD -> Huffman (TTTD-H)* algorithm which performed significantly better than all the individual algorithms, with a very slight increase in compression time. We also analyze the energy consumption of these compression algorithms. We found that the result on the significantly improved compression factor of the proposed TTTD-H also yields a much lower power consumption, since a sizable reduction on sensor data to be transmitted implies a substantial saving on transmission energy.

7.2 Future Work

From LifeShirt (intelligent medical garment), STARPATCH (wireless cardiac monitoring), and IntelliDrug (implantable drug dispensing) reviewed by Konstantas [29] in 2007, to implantable chips with the size of a grain of rice in 2017, the last decade has seen an explosion of new sensors entering the market. Processes to analyze and store data for analysis need to adapt to the growing demand and this area needs more research. Since wireless data transmission uses most of the power in the sensor, there is a need to have new methods to reduce the power consumption. This could be achieved by reducing the amount of data sent across by compression, as discussed in the chapter, and by reducing the amount of data sent across by sampling or by doing local processing. These efforts, especially "local processing," would need sensors to have bigger memories. Sensors with more computing capability is another hot topic of research. Along with research on sensors with increased computing power, a key area of focus could be to understand energy consumption in comparison to increased computation.

Also, the algorithm proposed in the chapter can be further enhanced in multiple ways. Data from TTTD algorithm can be stored in a compressed form after a chunk is found. The chunk key lookup can be done using BloomFilter to make the lookup faster.

Another area of future research and development could be to store the data from sensors in the cloud after running through a data deduplication algorithm like TTTD. TTTD-S [24] which is an improvement over TTTD would be better suited to dedupe large amount of sensor data before storing them in the cloud. Storage in the cloud would help in getting more insights from historical data. Processing data using TTTD can also be parallelized. That means a large amount of data from multiple sensors can be deduped and stored by using MapReduce frameworks like Hadoop.

REFERENCES

1. Dimitrov, D. V. Medical internet of things and big data in healthcare. *Healthcare Informatics Research*, 22(3):156–163, 2016.
2. Darwish, A. and Hassanien, A. E. Wearable and implantable wireless sensor network solutions for healthcare monitoring. *Sensors*, 11(6):5561–5595, 2011.
3. Robinson, R., Moh, M., and Moh, T.-S. Compression of wearable body sensor network data using improved two-threshold-two-divisor data chunking algorithms. In *Proceedings of IEEE International Conference on High Performance Computing and Simulation*, Orleans, France, July 2018.
4. Lai, X., Liu, Q., Wei, X., Wang, W., Zhou, G., and Han, G. A survey of body sensor networks. *Sensors*, 13(5):5406–5447, 2013.
5. Song, K. T.and Wang, Y. Q. Remote activity monitoring of the elderly using a two-axis accelerometer. In *Proceedings of the CACS Automatic Control Conference*, pp. 18–19, November 2005.
6. Chen, Y. and Duan, H. A QRS complex detection algorithm based on mathematical morphology and envelope. In *IEEE-EMBS 2005. 27th Annual International Conference of the Engineering in Medicine and Biology Society, 2005*, pp. 4654–4657, January 2006. IEEE.
7. Dong, L., Wu, J., Bao, X., and Xiao, W. Extraction of gait features using a wireless body sensor network (BSN). In *2006 6th International Conference on ITS Telecommunications Proceedings*, pp. 987–991, June 2006. IEEE.
8. Avci, A., Bosch, S., Marin-Perianu, M., Marin-Perianu, R., and Havinga, P. Activity recognition using inertial sensing for healthcare, wellbeing and sports applications: A survey. In *2010 23rd International Conference on Architecture of Computing Systems (ARCS)*, pp. 1–10, February 2010. VDE.
9. Peng, H., Long, F., and Ding, C. Feature selection based on mutual information criteria of max-dependency, max-relevance, and min-redundancy. *IEEE Transactions on Pattern Analysis and Machine Intelligence*, 27(8):1226–1238, 2005.
10. Krishnan, N. C., Juillard, C., Colbry, D., and Panchanathan, S. Recognition of hand movements using wearable accelerometers. *Journal of Ambient Intelligence and Smart Environments*, 1(2):143–155, 2009.
11. Akyildiz, I. F., Su, W., Sankarasubramaniam, Y., and Cayirci, E. Wireless sensor networks: A survey. *Computer Networks*, 38(4):393–422, 2002.
12. Sadler, C. M., and Martonosi, M. Data compression algorithms for energy-constrained devices in delay tolerant networks. In *Proceedings of the 4th International Conference on Embedded Networked Sensor Systems*, pp. 265–278, October 2006. ACM.
13. Yoon, I., Kim, H., and Noh, D. K. Adaptive data aggregation and compression to improve energy utilization in solar-powered wireless sensor networks. *Sensors*, 17(6):1226, 2017.
14. Wu, C. H. and Tseng, Y. C. Data compression by temporal and spatial correlations in a body-area sensor network: A case study in Pilates motion recognition. *IEEE Transactions on Mobile Computing*, 10(10):1459–1472, 2011.
15. Hu, F., Li, S., Xue, T., and Li, G. Design and analysis of low-power body area networks based on biomedical signals. *International Journal of Electronics*, 99(6):811–822, 2012.
16. Charbiwala, Z., Karkare, V., Gibson, S., Markovic, D., and Srivastava, M. B. Compressive sensing of neural action potentials using a learned union of supports. In *2011 International Conference on Body Sensor Networks (BSN)*, pp. 53–58, May 2011. IEEE.
17. Manikandan, M. S. and Dandapat, S. ECG signal compression using discrete sinc interpolation. In *Third International Conference on Intelligent Sensing and Information Processing, 2005. ICISIP 2005*, pp. 14–19, December 2005. IEEE.

18. Tiwari, B. and Kumar, A. Aggregated Deflate-RLE compression technique for body sensor network. In *2012 CSI Sixth International Conference on Software Engineering (CONSEG)*, pp. 1–6, September 2012. IEEE.

19. Kriegl, A. 3.3.1 Run-length encoding. July 2003. Retrieved March 08, 2018, from www.mat. univie.ac.at/%#x007E;kriegl/Skripten/CG/node44.html.

20. Rosettacode.org. Huffman coding. March 2018. Retrieved March 10, 2018, from https:// rosettacode.org/wiki/Huffman_coding.

21. Saikia, A. R. LZW (Lempel–Ziv–Welch) compression technique. n.d. Retrieved March 10, 2018, from www.geeksforgeeks.org/lzw-lempel-ziv-welch-compression-technique.

22. Muthitacharoen, A., Chen, B., and Mazieres, D. A low-bandwidth network file system. In *ACM SIGOPS Operating Systems Review*, Vol. 35, No. 5, pp. 174–187, October 2001. ACM.

23. Eshghi, K. and Tang, H. K. A framework for analyzing and improving content-based chunking algorithms. Hewlett-Packard Labs Technical Report TR, 30, 2005.

24. Moh, T. and Chang, B. A running time improvement for the two thresholds two divisors algorithm. In *Proceedings of the 48th Annual Southeast Regional Conference on – ACM SE '10*, 2010. doi:10.1145/1900008.1900101.

25. Ismail, S. Health datasets from Fitbit. 2018. Retrieved February 2018 from https://github.com/ health-hacks/datasets/tree/master/fitbit.

26. UCI machine learning repository: Heterogeneity activity recognition data set. October 2015. Retrieved February 2018 from https://archive.ics.uci.edu/ml/datasets/Heterogeneity Activity Recognition.

27. Shin, H. D., Ahn, S. W., Song, T. H., and Baeg, S. H. Analysis of low power sensor node using data compression. *IFAC Proceedings Volumes*, 42(3):34–39, 2009.

28. Barr, K. C. and Asanović, K. Energy-aware lossless data compression. *ACM Transactions on Computer Systems (TOCS)*, 24(3):250–291, 2006.

29. Konstantas, D. An overview of wearable and implantable medical sensors. *Yearbook of Medical Informatics*, 7(1), 66–69, 2007.

30. Bo, C., Li, Z. F., and Can, W. Research on chunking algorithms of data de-duplication. In *Proceedings of the 2012 International Conference on Communication, Electronics and Automation Engineering Advances in Intelligent Systems and Computing*, pp. 1019–1025, 2013. doi:10.1007/978-3-642-31698-2_144.

31. Rabin, M. O. *Fingerprinting by Random Polynomials*. Cambridge, MA: Center for Research in Computing Techn., Aiken Computation Laboratory, Univ.

CHAPTER 11

Population-Specific and Personalized (PSP) Models of Human Behavior for Leveraging Smart and Connected Data

Theodora Chaspari

Texas A&M University, College Station, TX, USA

Adela C. Timmons

Florida International University, Miami, FL, USA

Gayla Margolin

University of Southern California, Los Angeles, CA, USA

CONTENTS

1 INTRODUCTION

Recent computational and algorithmic advances can fully leverage the vast amount of information obtained on a 24/7 basis from smart-sensing devices for conventional applications, such as computer vision and speech processing. This is not always the case in affective computing, behavioral analytics, and human-related applications, where the high diversity of people and behaviors renders such data hard to manage and process [1, 2]. The ideal view of a system that can be generalized to fully capture the behavioral and clinical characteristics of a large group of people requires longitudinal multimodal information from extensive and systematic data collection procedures that are usually hard to implement for a large number of participants. Furthermore, even if the acquisition of such data was feasible, the long processing times and computational power required from the corresponding machine learning algorithms render such applications almost prohibitive for the average user. These challenges have created the need to develop computationally efficient models that can address the inherent data sparsity issues and high variability present in human-related applications.

Emerging advances in machine learning can leverage person-specific information to design individualized models of human behavior that can yield accurate predictors of the human state. The main premise behind such models is that the same phenomenon can be expressed differently for various types of people; therefore, population-specific and personalized (PSP) models that are built using a subset of individuals who are similar to each other might be more effective at detecting and predicting facets of human behavior, compared with a general model constructed based on the entire data sample. For example, anger, a common human emotion, is experienced and expressed in distinct ways for different types of people: passive individuals tend to internalize their feelings of anger, whereas aggressive people tend to directly express anger to the other person in order to hurt them emotionally, physically, or psychologically [3]. These distinct expressions of anger manifest differently in terms of bio-behavioral signals, e.g., change in speech intonation might be a more informative measure of anger for an aggressive individual compared to a passive one.

The current chapter discusses novel signal processing and machine learning approaches that can be used to develop PSP models for human-related applications. Using examples from the lifesciences, we explain why general models are not sufficient for capturing multiple facets of human behavior (Section 2). We then describe fundamental concepts regarding the design and implementation of PSP models (Section 3) and review state-of-the-art work at the crossroads of computer science, physical well-being, mental health, and human behavior (Section 4). Finally, we summarize findings, identify current gaps in the literature, and discuss promising research directions for future work (Section 5).

2 DIVERSITY OF HUMAN BEHAVIOR: EVIDENCE FROM LIFE SCIENCES

Psychological science and related fields have long recognized that human behavior and health are affected by a variety of person- and context-specific factors. These include global factors, such as childhood exposure to family violence, and fluctuating factors, such as concurrent stress levels. Each of these variables may separately predict outcomes of interest or may interact to produce outcomes when they coincide, e.g., history of childhood exposure to family violence interacts with stress on a given day to increase the likelihood of marital conflict on the same day [4]. A variety of statistical methods have been developed and employed to model how different variables occurring at various levels of analysis interact in complex ways to predict human behavior. These include more standard techniques, such as regression, as well as specialized methods, such as structural equation modeling, multilevel modeling, and dynamical systems modeling [5, 6, 7]. Such models are most typically theory-driven, with researchers positing an expected relationship between predictor and outcome variables a priori and then fitting a model to either confirm or disconfirm the hypothesized association. In contrast to this traditional framework, predictive machine learning techniques use the outcome of interest as the criterion by which the factors are selected, which are in turn confirmed via cross-validation. Machine learning techniques also allow for the identification of complex associations between the input space and outcome of interest, which are hard to model using statistical analysis. While statistical and machine learning methods differ, they are complementarily informative approaches. For example, information gleaned from psychological theory and research can be used to identify a range of potential predictor variables, which are then fed into the model and selected via machine learning techniques. In turn, variables identified via machine learning can inform the development of psychological theories, which can subsequently be tested via confirmatory statistical methods.

3 BASIC CONCEPTS ON POPULATION-SPECIFIC AND PERSONALIZED (PSP) MODELS OF HUMAN BEHAVIOR

3.1 Defining a Population

In the context of this chapter, population refers to a group of subjects from the original pool of participants that share one or more common characteristics with each other.

A fundamental challenge is the criterion being used to cluster a group of individuals into a population [8]. The three main clustering criteria include: (a) personal traits (e.g., demographics, personality traits, family history); (b) contextual information (e.g., time of day, alcohol/caffeine/drug consumption, work load, frequency of interventions); and (c) decision boundaries defined from data-driven approaches (e.g., clustering of the input features or input trajectories or the likelihoods of a machine learning system). As we will see in Sections 4 and 5, various benefits and drawbacks are associated with each criterion in terms of their implementation and performance.

3.2 Defining Personalized and Population-Specific Models

Personalized models of human behavior make decisions separately by using a different learner for each participant. Such models are based on previously seen data from the subject of interest, while samples from the rest of the dataset can be included to enhance the generalizability of these models. In contrast, population-specific models do not rely on data from the test subject. Rather, they use different learners for different subsets of participants (or "populations," as explained in Section 3.1) and include participants similar to the test subject in order to make the final decision.

Personalized models tend to be more accurate, since they incorporate person-dependent information. However, they are difficult to implement in practice and may fail to adequately generalize: it is not always possible to obtain prior information for each person, and there may not be enough training samples for each outcome of interest—especially those related to extreme conditions, which are highly relevant to health applications. While population-specific models tend to generalize better for unseen data, the clustering criterion is an important factor affecting their performance.

3.3 Establishing Baselines with respect to Conventional Machine Learning Approaches

Evaluation of PSP systems can be done by comparing the predictive power of PSP to that of baseline models. Typically, three main baselines are used, which include general models trained on the entire dataset (general), models learned using a random subset of the original dataset (random), and models with a subset of people different compared with the one of interest (alternate). Other ways of evaluating PSP models include effectiveness measures of feedback and interventions performed based on the output of PSP systems (e.g., personalized recommender systems), although these are out of the scope of the current book chapter.

4 EMERGING WORK ON PSP MODELS OF HUMAN BEHAVIOR

This section provides an overview of previous work on PSP models. Such approaches are summarized into two main categories: (a) signal-based approaches measuring participants' divergence from a baseline; and (b) machine learning models that are learned separately or jointly for each person or population. Table 11.1 provides an overview of previous work summarizing the methods that have been proposed for each of the two categories, including the signal processing and machine learning algorithms

TABLE 11.1 Overview of population-specific and personalized models of human behavior.

PSP model	Reference	Proposed algorithm	Population clustering criteria	Application of interest	Evaluation metric and performance	Baseline description and performance
Signal-based	Aigrain et al. [9]	Person-specific normalization of features	N/A	Stress detection (N=14)	Binary classification accuracy, 65–80%	Unnormalized features, 63–68%
Signal-based	Giakoumis et al. [10]	Signal-based physiological indices measuring ratio between task of interest and rest	Fully personalized	Stress detection (N=24)	5-class classification accuracy, 95%	Common electrodermal activity and electrocardiogram features, 86%
Signal-based	Reimer et al. [11]	Person-dependent decision thresholds of physiological features	Fully personalized	Stress detection (N=34)	Deployment of proposed algorithm in mobile application. Results not available yet	N/A
Signal-based	De Santos et al. [12]	Template matching, trajectory of physiological indices across different conditions	N/A	Stress detection (N=80)	Binary classification precision and recall, 92–99% and 86–97%	N/A
Signal-based	Zeevi et al. [13]	Enhancing the feature space with person-specific features	Microbiome, blood tests, questionnaires on lifestyle indices, anthropometrics	Prediction of post-prandial glycemic response (PPGR) for diabetes (N=900)	Correlation between predicted and actual PPGR, 0.68 ($p<0.01$)	Correlation between PPGR and unimodal independent variables without person-specific features, 0.33–0.38 ($p<.01$)
Machine learning-based (Separate)	Bertsimas et al. [14]	K-Nearest Neighbor regression	Similarity metrics on individual characteristics and medical history	Diabetes management (N=10,806)	R^2 difference between actual and predicted outcomes, 0.2–0.54	General models, 0.24–0.53
Machine learning-based (Separate)	Che et al. [15]	Separate models per person using the N most similar participants	Similarity score of time-sequences using dynamic temporal matching	Prediction of Parkinson's disease (N=683)	Binary classification F1-score, 71–76%	General models, 38–75%

(Continued)

TABLE 11.1 (Cont.)

PSP model	Reference	Proposed algorithm	Population clustering criteria	Application of interest	Evaluation metric and performance	Baseline description and performance
Machine learning-based (Separate)	Kallus [16]	Classification and regression tree with recursive partitioning to find globally optimal partition	Fully personalized	Medication intake (N=5410)	Average risk of predicted dosage, 0.35–0.50	General models, 0.38–0.60
Machine learning-based (Separate)	Koldijk et al. [17]	K separate support vector regression models	K-means clustering on signal-based metrics from computer activity, facial expression, and body posture	Stress detection (N=25)	Correlation between actual and predicted self-assessment scores, 0.16–0.87	General models, 0.15–0.80
Machine learning-based (Separate)	Xu et al. [18]	K separate neural network regression models	K-means clustering on signal-based metrics of baseline data	Stress detection (N=22)	Normalized difference between actual and predicted self-assessment scores, 0.15	Alternate models, 0.27
Machine learning-based (Hierarchical)	Gujral et al. [19]	Multi-task learning with neural networks	K-means clustering on person- and couple-dependent characteristics, and signal-based indices	Detection of interpersonal conflict between couples (N=87)	Binary classification F1-score, 75%	Separate models, 69%; General models, 64%
Machine learning-based (Hierarchical)	Jaques et al. [20]; Taylor et al. [21]	Multi-task Learning; Hierarchical Bayesian logistic regression where the weights of each cluster follow a different prior distribution	K-means clustering on personality and demographics; Soft clustering based on the similarity of relationship between input features and outcome of interest	Prediction of stress and well-being (N=250)	Binary classification accuracy, 72–82%	General models, 60–67%

Machine learning-based (Hierarchical)	Lopez-Martinez and Picard [22]	Multi-task learning with neural networks	Fully personalized	Pain detection (N=87)	Binary classification accuracy, 62–82%	General models, 59–78%
Machine learning-based (Adaptive)	Clifton et al. [23]	Personalized Gaussian process with learned parameters for each subject	Fully personalized	Abnormality detections for readmission to ICU (N=200)	Mean square error between actual and predicted data, 0.72	Personalized model, 0.64
Machine learning-based (Adaptive)	Hernandez et al. [18]	SVMs with modified loss function incorporating class prior of test subject and assigning more weight to train samples closest to test	K-means clustering (K=2) on signal-based metrics (i.e., frequency and amplitude of skin conductance responses)	Stress recognition from physiological signals (i.e., electrodermal activity) for call center employees (N=9)	Binary classification accuracy, 73%	Fully personalized models, 78%
Machine learning-based (Adaptive)	Liu et al. [24]	Personalized Gaussian process superimposed on neural network outcomes	Fully personalized	Automatic pain estimation (N=25)	Mean absolute error, 2.18–2.41	General models, 2.48–3.67
Machine learning-based (Adaptive)	Peterson et al. [25]; Utsumi et al. [26]	Gaussian process trained on general population and adapted on each individual	Fully personalized	Prediction of Alzheimer's disease progression (N=1737)	3-class classification accuracy, 89–92%	General models, 65–87%
Machine learning-based (Ensemble)	Kächele et al. [8]	Ensemble models providing final decision based on similarity criteria	Similarity measures based on individual characteristics, signal indices, and model outcomes (i.e., confidence on which samples are classified)	Pain intensity assessment (N=87)	5-class classification accuracy, 35–40.4%	General and random models, 35–39.5%
Machine learning-based (Ensemble)	Lane et al. [27]	Ensemble learning with weights specified based on similarity metrics	Similarity network between users based on physical, lifestyle, and signal-based indices	Classification of physical and social activities (3 datasets, N=41, 51, 120)	3,4,6-Class classification accuracy, 55–69%	General, separate, and random models, 29–57%

and population clustering criteria. The table also denotes the applications for which each PSP model was evaluated (e.g., stress detection, mood prediction), the number of participants, and the experimental setup, including evaluation metrics (e.g., classification or regression metrics), baseline methods, and corresponding results.

4.1 Signal-Based Approaches for PSP Models

A large body of work on signal-based PSP approaches has proposed using measures of signal divergence that compare a baseline state (e.g., rest) to a condition of interest. These approaches are based on the idea that individuals exhibit short-term physiological fluctuations during rest that are due to inner thoughts or overall emotional arousal [28]; therefore, personalized features can be computed as deviation measures from baseline. Such deviation measures have been computed with respect to the considered feature space [9] or its nonlinear transformations (e.g., defined on the basis of Legendre polynomials) [10]. Other studies have proposed the use of signal trajectories across varying tasks to quantify person-dependent deviations between conditions of interest [29]. In addition, it is possible to identify individualized data-driven thresholds for different behavioral states using extreme signal values across different tasks [11]. A final set of approaches involves augmenting the feature space with person-dependent characteristics, such as genetic information or blood samples, which, along with momentary indices, can be used as input for the machine learning classifier [13].

While signal-based PSP approaches are intuitive and computationally inexpensive, they are hard to implement and scaleup in practice, especially because it is not always possible to capture baseline data for each subject. Furthermore, the implementation of baseline procedures can be subjective, with different designs potentially biasing results towards detecting positive or negative change [30]. Finally, such signal-based measures only rely on the input space without taking into account the corresponding outcomes of interest (or labels). As outlined below, machine learning PSP approaches can integrate outcomes of interest, which could lead to increased system performance.

4.2 Machine Learning Approaches for PSP Models

Four types of machine learning approaches have been proposed for designing PSP models: (a) separate models independently learned for different groups of participants or for each participant alone (separate); (b) hierarchical models whose initial components correspond to corpus-wide information, while the later ones contain the PSP information (hierarchical); (c) adaptation techniques involving a two-stage process, where initial estimates of the model parameters are obtained via corpus-wide information and are refined using the PSP information (adaptive); and (d) ensemble methods providing outcome estimates based on the subset of data that are most relevant to the sample of interest (ensemble).

4.2.1 Separate Models

An extensive amount of research has proposed separate learners for PSP models trained independently for groups of participants or for each participant alone. The majority of these studies have used pre-determined population clustering criteria, such as demographics and medical history, to split the original participants into independent groups, and have trained separate models for each population. For example, in an effort to detect worker stress in an office environment, previous research clustered users into two populations with respect to level of computer activity, facial expressions, and body movement [17]. Similarly, other studies have trained learners for each test subject separately based on the N most similar participants [14, 15]. While the training of each learner was performed independently in the aforementioned studies, other approaches have used separate learners trained on joint optimization criteria for the entire dataset. For example, separate nonlinear regression models per population were jointly trained through an additive criterion that included the sum of prediction errors from all learners [31]. Other studies have integrated the population clustering procedure into the optimization process, rather than using predetermined populations. For instance, a single learning task that jointly learns the parameters of different regression models for each population and recursively partitions the data has also been proposed [16].

Research to date generally shows that machine learning models trained on separate populations tend to outperform general models learned on the entire dataset [14, 15, 16, 17], as well as random subsets of the data [31]. Detecting and predicting the behavior of an individual using a portion of the original data, selected based on some pre-defined criterion, may be particularly useful, given that the same phenomenon might be manifested in different ways across different people. It is important to note that some of the population clusters might clearly outperform the baseline, while others might perform similarly or worse to the baseline [17], suggesting a potential bias in the clustering procedure. Such findings might also indicate various levels of association between the input features and outcomes for the various populations, contributing to an exploratory analysis of the data of interest. Moreover, data-driven clustering—where data partitioning into separate populations is jointly performed with the learning of the models—may outperform models trained on pre-determined populations [16].

Separate models per person or population are computationally efficient, simple to implement, and intuitive to the final user. However, such models might not be generalizable enough, since they do not incorporate general knowledge from the entire dataset. Furthermore, some populations might have fewer data samples compared with others or might not have enough data related to all outcomes of interest, therefore increasing the risk of overfitting the corresponding models. Previous work has compared separate machine learning models with more advanced approaches (Sections 4.2.2–4.2.4), indicating that the latter tend to perform best because they integrate general and population-specific information to predict the outcome of interest [27, 19].

4.2.2 Hierarchical Models

Hierarchical models typically rely on multi-level regressors or classifiers, whose first levels leverage information common across all individuals and whose last levels are built using data from the population of interest. Such models have been operationalized through hierarchical and multi-task learning using deterministic (e.g., multi-task neural networks) and probabilistic (e.g., hierarchical Bayesian learning) classifiers [20, 22, 21, 19]. Various implementations of hierarchical approaches seem to be comparable, with multi-task neural networks slightly outperforming the other approaches [20, 21]. Current research generally supports the superiority of such techniques compared to general and separate machine learning models [20, 21, 19].

One advantage of using hierarchical models is that such models make decisions based on clusters of people with common characteristics, therefore reducing the amount of data needed for training and increasing system accuracy: smaller models can still incorporate flexibility in terms of data representation, while they avoid drawbacks related to overfitting. Even so, such models tend to be complicated and lack interpretability. For example, multi-task neural networks learn different feature combinations for different populations; yet, the complexity of the considered networks decreases the interpretability of the resulting models, therefore limiting data exploration opportunities.

4.2.3 Adaptive Models

In the adaptive model approach, a model developed for the entire dataset is reused as a starting point and adapted for the data specific to a participant or a population. Implementation of such transfer learning techniques has been performed with Gaussian processes, in order to take time-dependencies of the input data into account [23, 24, 25, 26]. Alternate approaches have used modified optimization criteria that assign increased weight to samples close to the sample of interest, therefore promoting similarity between like data during learning [18].

Although no direct comparison has been attempted between hierarchical and adaptation approaches for PSP models, these are conceptually similar to each other with similar benefits and drawbacks.

4.2.4 Ensemble Models

Ensemble methods take into account a set of decisions from multiple participants, resulting in highly discriminative power [27, 8]. The set of participants on which decisions are made is determined through pre-determined population clustering criteria, as well as the likelihood and confidence measures of the corresponding classifiers [8]. Other studies have proposed a combination of decisions made through models trained on different populations, each defined through different clustering criteria. For example, "Similarity Networks" were used to find a set of similar people according to a certain criterion (e.g., physical characteristics, lifestyle). Different models were then trained based on populations determined via each Similarity Network, with the final decision made by combining all partial decisions through boosting [27].

Ensemble methods have been compared with various baselines—including models trained on the entire dataset and separate models for each population—and have been shown to depict a clear advantage due to the high generalization ability of the multiple used learners [27]. However, such approaches are computationally expensive compared with separate models for each population. Furthermore, ensemble PSP methods tend to assign the same test subject in multiple populations. Because different population clustering criteria are used for every model, interpretability is sometimes compromised.

5 DISCUSSION

This section summarizes findings from previous work on PSP models, identifies gaps in the literature, and provides recommendations for future work in the context of smart data and human-related applications.

5.1 Comparison between the Different PSP Models

As summarized in Table 11.2, each type of PSP model has various benefits and drawbacks. Signal-based PSP approaches tend to adopt an unsupervised approach by comparing facets of the same person over multiple environments and situations. Although no systematic comparison between signal-based and machine learning-based PSP approaches has been performed so far, the unsupervised nature of the latter could potentially compromise its overall performance. Simpler approaches, such as separate models for each population, usually need less data to train, have a smaller computational cost, and tend to be quite interpretable. These models also tend to be more robust to overfitting and have better generalizability to unseen data. The component-wise structure of hierarchical and adaptive models renders them more interpretable compared with ensemble methods, while the large number of variable components embedded in the latter makes them hard for humans to understand. In terms of performance, more complex machine learning-based PSP models tend to outperform general, random, and alternate models [31, 20, 14, 15, 16, 24, 22, 21, 19, 17, 26]. A small number of studies further suggest that complex methods tend to depict higher discriminatory power compared with the separate models [27, 19]. However, no research to date has compared performance across the hierarchical, adaptation, and ensemble methods. Systematic studies determining which of these approaches provide more reliable PSP descriptors conducted over multiple datasets would be highly informative.

5.2 Comparison between the Different Population Clustering Criteria

The studies reviewed here have used a variety of criteria to perform population clustering. Meta-information criteria included person-specific information mostly obtained through

TABLE 11.2 Empirical properties of the different population-specific and personalized machine learning approaches

Property	Separate models	Hierarchical/adaptation models	Ensemble models
Ability to generalize	Low	Medium/High	Medium/High
Amount of data required	Low	Medium/High	High
Computational cost	Low	Medium/High	Medium/High
Interpretability	High	Medium	Low/Medium

one-time assessments, such as demographics, microbiome information, blood tests, medical history, lifestyle indices, personality traits, and anthropometrics (e.g., height, body mass indices). On the contrary, signal-based criteria are extracted from the input signals captured through physiological, audiovisual, and computer-based activity sensors. Such information is not only used for population clustering, but also comprises the input of machine learning systems on which the output is being predicted. The limited number of existing studies on this topic are thus far inconclusive as to which type of clustering criteria performs best [27, 19]. Combining both types of criteria into a single system is a promising direction for boosting performance [27].

For clustering methods, K-Means was the most common approach [18, 31, 20, 21, 19, 17], while alternative techniques have been proposed to assess the similarity of each user in a graph-based structure [27]. To implement these algorithms, different types of deterministic and statistical-based similarity metrics have been used, including the Euclidean and Mahalanobis distances. Previous methods have employed both static [18, 31, 19, 17] and time-dependent [15] approaches to model signal-based similarity.

For clustering assignment, the majority of methods have involved assigning each individual into one population group. However, a person might belong to more than one population cluster, given that multiple contextual factors, such as events that occurred that day, could apply to the same person. To address this issue, other studies have explored soft clustering approaches [21]. Although such approaches have not shown significant benefits in terms of performance, they did indicate that a small number of individuals do belong to more than one cluster.

5.3 Relation between System Performance, Number, and Size of Populations

As expected, extant research shows that system performance increases with population size. At the same time, the benefits of population size eventually plateau, as arbitrarily large populations do not improve system performance [8, 16]. In fact, some studies show that very large population sizes might actually harm performance, since decisions may be based on individuals who are not necessarily relevant to the test subject [31, 15].

Current research further indicates that arbitrarily splitting datasets into a very large number of populations is not beneficial [27]. The optimal number of populations is dependent upon the nature of the dataset and the clustering criteria being used. Theoretical analysis could potentially reveal more systematic relations between the nature of the data, the number and size of populations, and the resulting system performance.

5.4 Research Findings Using PSP Models

A number of studies have attempted to shed light into several groups of people identified via population clustering. For example, in a study predicting mood indices, clusters of participants that intuitively matched with the "happy" population were recovered [20]. In fact, the hierarchical machine learning models proposed by these authors were able to find a significant part of the "happy" population by identifying their unique relation between the input and output features, without looking at any type of meta-information. In another example, different types of workers based on momentary signal indices were identified, including "writers and copy-pasters" during a computer activity, "highly expressive and less expressive" individuals, and "active and less active" groups of people [17]. Similarly, research has recovered various clusters of people based on self-reported lifestyle habits, such as 9am–5pm workers and individuals with erratic sleeping and activity patterns [27].

Attention has also been given to the types of features that are most predictive of the outcome of interest for each population. For mood recognition, previous work observed that measures of social interaction (e.g., daily positive social interaction, interpersonal interaction before sleep) were most predictive of "agreeable" people's mood, while indices of phone-based communication were most important for individuals with high sleep quality, and physical activity features worked best for predicting mood in judgmental and sensitive people [21]. Similarly, features related to the motions of the lips were most informative for detecting mental effort of "non-expressive" individuals, while features associated with the eyes, brows, and chin performed best for the rest of people [17].

5.5 Recommendations for Future Research
5.5.1 Interpretability of PSP Models
Interpretable computational models can help users understand the inner mechanisms of the algorithms and find explanations regarding the predicted outcomes, therefore increasing their trust and confidence in the decisions of the automated systems. However, the interpretability of a model is highly dependent on its complexity, i.e., the more complex a system, the less interpretable it is. While there has been a significant amount of research assessing the interpretability of PSP systems for understanding diversity in human behavior [27, 20, 21, 17], more work is needed to maximize its usefulness for the life sciences. Such findings could shed light into unexplored facets of human behavior and could eventually be used to develop novel behavioral and therapeutic interventions for improving mental and physical health outcomes in at-risk and vulnerable populations.

5.5.2 Availability of Meta-Information in Publicly Available Human-Related Datasets
PSP methods rely heavily on person-specific meta-information to perform population clustering and to develop the corresponding learners. Although such data are increasingly available for public use [32], more data are needed to support its implementation on a large scale. Human behavior is a multi-faceted phenomenon affected by multiple person-dependent and contextual factors. Signal-based indices, which capture human behavior in-the-moment, might not always be adequate; researchers are advised to record and take into account multiple sources of person-specific and contextual meta-information, such as demographics, physical traits, environmental indices, family history, and medical exams, to provide enriched and unified descriptors of human behavior that increase the predictive power and performance of machine learning systems. Depending on the application, such information can be highly sensitive and subject to a variety of ethical constraints. Therefore, researchers should adopt safe data practices to anonymize information and store data in secure physical and digital locations.

5.5.3 Development of PSP Signal Representations

While a large body of work has used machine learning methods to identify and understand human behavior, less research has focused on signal-based representations [33, 34]. Such methods model direct representations of raw signals and therefore are able to more reliably capture fine-grain signal fluctuations, which might include important PSP information. These models are based on the assumption that various parts or trends of the corresponding signals (e.g., rate of increase or decrease) can be relevant in a different way to different population groups [35]. Computational models of human behavior could greatly benefit from such approaches, making it possible to preserve relevant PSP information by directly capturing signal trends, which are not always maintained through conventional feature extraction approaches.

5.5.4 Personalized Recommender Systems for Human-Related Applications

Though out of the scope of the current chapter, a promising line of work lies in the use of PSP recommender systems that provide personalized recommendations to modify human behavior. Such systems can improve the delivery and understanding of medical content, suggest personalized recommendations related to health and well-being, as well as contribute to individualized learning curves for optimizing learning outcomes [36, 37]. Despite their promise, due to practical constraints and ethical reasons, PSP systems might be difficult to implement in real life, although a growing body of literature has initiated such efforts [13]. Such systems will likely see increased use and development in coming years.

REFERENCES

1. Weiss, J. C., Natarajan, S., Peissig, P. L., McCarty, C. A., & Page, D. (2012). Machine learning for personalized medicine: Predicting primary myocardial infarction from electronic health records. *AI Magazine, 33*, 33.
2. Schork, N. J. (2015). Personalized medicine: Time for one-person trials. *Nature, 520*, 609–611.
3. DiGiuseppe, R., & Tafrate, R. C. (2007). *Understanding anger disorders.* Oxford University Press, Oxford, UK.
4. Timmons, A. C., Arbel, R., & Margolin, G. (2017). Daily patterns of stress and conflict in couples: Associations with marital aggression and family-of-origin aggression. *Journal of Family Psychology, 31*, 93–104.
5. Peugh, J. L. (2010). A practical guide to multilevel modeling. *Journal of School Psychology, 48*, 85–112. doi: 10.1016/j.jsp.2009.09.002.
6. Kline, R. B. (2011). *Principles and practices of structural equation modeling.* New York, NY: Guildford Press.
7. Ferrer, E., & Helm, J. M. (2013). Dynamical systems modeling of physiological coregulation in dyadic interactions. *International Journal of Psychophysiology, 88*, 296–308. doi: 10.1016/j.ijpsycho.2012.10.013.
8. Kächele, M., Thiam, P., Amirian, M., Schwenker, F., & Palm, G. (2016). Methods for person-centered continuous pain intensity assessment from bio-physiological channels. *IEEE Journal of Selected Topics in Signal Processing, 10*(5), 854–864.
9. Aigrain, J., Dubuisson, S., Detyniecki, M., & Chetouani, M. (2015, May). Person-specific behavioral features for automatic stress detection. In *2015 11th IEEE International Conference and Workshops onAutomatic Face and Gesture Recognition (FG)* (Vol. 3, pp. 1–6). IEEE.

10. Giakoumis, D., Tzovaras, D., & Hassapis, G. (2013). Subject-dependent biosignal features for increased accuracy in psychological stress detection. *International Journal of Human-Computer Studies, 71*, 425–439.

11. Reimer, U., Laurenzi, E., Maier, E., & Ulmer, T. (2017, January). Mobile stress recognition and relaxation support with smartCoping: User-adaptive interpretation of physiological stress parameters. In *Proceedings of the 50th Hawaii International Conference on System Sciences.*

12. De Santos, A., Sánchez-Avila, C., Guerra-Casanova, J., & Bailador-Del Pozo, G. (2011). Real-time stress detection by means of physiological signals. In *Recent Application in Biometrics.* InTech.

13. Zeevi, D., Korem, T., Zmora, N., Israeli, D., Rothschild, D., Weinberger, A., Ben-Yacov, O., Lador, D., Avnit-Sagi, T., Lotan-Pompan, M., Suez, J., Mahdi, J.A., Matot, E., Malka, G., Kosower, N., Rein, M., Zilberman-Schapira, G., Dohnalová, L., Pevsner-Fischer, M., Bikovsky, R., Halpern, Z., Elinav, E., & Segal, E. (2015). Personalized nutrition by prediction of glycemic responses. *Cell, 163*(5), 1079–1094.

14. Bertsimas, D., Kallus, N., Weinstein, A. M., & Zhuo, Y. D. (2017). Personalized diabetes management using electronic medical records. *Diabetes Care, 40*, 210–217.

15. Che, C., Xiao, C., Liang, J., Jin, B., Zho, J., & Wang, F. (2017, June). An RNN architecture with dynamic temporal matching for personalized predictions of Parkinson's disease. In *Proceedings of the 2017 SIAM International Conference on Data Mining* (pp. 198–206). Society for Industrial and Applied Mathematics.

16. Kallus, N. (2017, July). Recursive partitioning for personalization using observational data. In *International Conference on Machine Learning* (pp. 1789–1798).

17. Koldijk, S., Neerincx, M. A., & Kraaij, W. (2018). Detecting work stress in offices by combining unobtrusive sensors. *IEEE Transactions on Affective Computing, 9*(2), 227–239.

18. Hernandez, J., Morris, R. R., & Picard, R. W. (2011, October). Call center stress recognition with person-specific models. In *Proceedings of the International Conference on Affective Computing and Intelligent Interaction* (pp. 125–134). Springer, Berlin, Heidelberg.

19. Gujral, A., Chaspari, T., Timmons, A.C., Kim, Y., Barrett, S., & Margolin, G. (2018, October). Population-specific detection of couples' interpersonal conflict using multitask learning. In *Proceedings of the 2018 ACM International Conference on Multimodal Interaction (ICMI '18).* ACM, New York, NY, USA, 5 pages.https://doi.org/10.1145/3242969. 3243007

20. Jaques, N., Taylor, S., Nosakhare, E., Sano, A., & Picard, R. (2016). Multi-task learning for predicting health, stress, and happiness. In *Proceedings of the NIPS Workshop on Machine Learning for Healthcare.*

21. Taylor, S. A., Jaques, N., Nosakhare, E., Sano, A., & Picard, R. (2017). Personalized multitask learning for predicting tomorrow's mood, stress, and health. *IEEE Transactions on Affective Computing, 1*, 1.

22. Lopez-Martinez, D., & Picard, R. (2017). Multi-task neural networks for personalized pain recognition from physiological signals. In *Proceedings of the), 2017 ACM Affective Computing and Intelligent Interaction (ACII) International Conference.* ACM.

23. Clifton, L., Clifton, D. A., Pimentel, M. A., Watkinson, P. J., & Tarassenko, L. (2013). Gaussian processes for personalized e-health monitoring with wearable sensors. *IEEE Transactions on Biomedical Engineering, 60*, 193–197.

24. Liu, D., Peng, F., Shea, A., & Picard, R. (2017, August). DeepFaceLIFT: Interpretable personalized models for automatic estimation of self-reported pain. In *First International Workshop on Affective Computing (AC), Proceedings of Machine Learning Research.*

25. Peterson, K., Guerrero, R., & Picard, R. W. (2017, December). Personalized Gaussian processes for future prediction of Alzheimer's disease progression. In *Proceedings of the ML4H:Machine Learning for Health, 31st Conference on Neural Information Processing Systems.*

26. Utsumi, Y., Peterson, K., Guerrero, R., & Picard, R. W. (2018). Personalized Gaussian processes for forecasting of Alzheimer's disease assessment scale-cognition sub-scale (ADAS-Cog13). *arXiv preprintarXiv:1802.08561.*

27. Lane, N. D., Xu, Y., Lu, H., Hu, S., Choudhury, T., Campbell, A. T., & Zhao, F. (2014). Community similarity networks. *Personal and Ubiquitous Computing, 18*(2), 355–368.

28. Healey, J. A., & Picard, R. W. (2005). Detecting stress during real-world driving tasks using physiological sensors. *IEEE Transactions on Intelligent Transportation Systems, 6,* 156–166.

29. De Santos, A., Sánchez-Avila, C., Guerra-Casanova, J., & Bailador-Del Pozo, G. (2011). Real-time stress detection by means of physiological signals. In *Recent Application in Biometrics.* InTech.

30. Fishel, S. R., Muth, E. R., & Hoover, A. W. (2007). Establishing appropriate physiological baseline procedures for real-time physiological measurement. *Journal of Cognitive Engineering and Decision Making, 1,* 286–308.

31. Xu, Q., Nwe, T. L., & Guan, C. (2015). Cluster-based analysis for personalized stress evaluation using physiological signals. *IEEE Journal of Biomedical and Health Informatics, 19*(1), 275–281.

32. Koldijk, S., Sappelli, M., Verberne, S., Neerincx, M., & Kraaij, W. (2014). The SWELL knowledge work dataset for stress and user modeling research. In *Proceedings of the 16th ACM International Conference on Multimodal Interaction (ICMI2014)* (Istanbul, Turkey, 12–16 November 2014).

33. Chaspari, T., Tsiartas, A., Duker, L. I. S., Cermak, S. A., & Narayanan, S. S. (2016, August). EDA-gram: Designing electrodermal activity fingerprints for visualization and feature extraction. In *2016 IEEE 38th Annual International Conference of the Engineering in Medicine and Biology Society (EMBC)* (pp. 403–406). IEEE.

34. Chaspari, T., Tsiartas, A., Stein, L. I., Cermak, S. A., & Narayanan, S. S. (2015). Sparse representation of electrodermal activity with knowledge-driven dictionaries. *IEEE Transactions on Biomedical Engineering, 62,* 960–971.

35. Shu, X., Tang, J., Li, Z., Lai, H., Zhang, L., & Yan, S. (2018). Personalized age progression with bi-level aging dictionary learning. *IEEE Transactions on Pattern Analysis and Machine Intelligence, 40,* 905–917.

36. Buder, J., & Schwind, C. (2012). Learning with personalized recommender systems: A psychological view. *Computers in Human Behavior, 28,* 207–216.

37. Wiesner, M., & Pfeifer, D. (2014). Health recommender systems: Concepts, requirements, technical basics and challenges. *International Journal of Environmental Research and Public Health, 11,* 2580–2607.

CHAPTER 12

Detecting Singular Data for Better Analysis of Emotional Tweets

Kiichi Tago

Graduate School of Human Sciences, Waseda University, Japan

Kenichi Ito

School of Human Sciences, Waseda University, Japan

Qun Jin

Faculty of Human Sciences, Waseda University, Japan

CONTENTS

There are many studies that examine users' emotional expressions and relationships on Twitter. However, datasets of users and tweets may include considerable noise. Data analysis may become inaccurate if the datasets are used without removing the noise. Therefore, we need to remove the noisy data that are outliers. In this chapter, we introduce analyses that consider outlier users on Twitter. We examined the influence of emotional tweets on user relationships using two emotion dictionaries. In our experiment, we verified how the analysis result changes with the extraction criterion for outlier users.

The analysis results showed almost the same between the two dictionaries if the extraction criterion of outlier users was strict. Furthermore, we adopted a strict criterion in another experiment that changed the emotion evaluation method. The results obtained by this change were almost the same as those for the first experiment. From these results, it is seen that we must exclude outlier users carefully for high-quality analysis.

1 INTRODUCTION

In recent years, social networking services (SNS) such as Twitter have been used as a platform by people across the world for easily posting messages. Users post several tweets in a day and these tweets are used as text data for studies on natural language processing, community detection, and emotion analysis, among others [1–3].

When analyzing the data for various purposes, it is necessary to clean the dataset [4]. On Twitter, various accounts such as bots, users who rarely post, and malicious users, exist. Such users are judged as outliers as they may degrade the quality of analysis. According to Xu et al. [5], outliers who have a little influence on network are existent in data from SNS. Generally, it is necessary to preprocess the dataset for excluding these outliers. However, there has been less focus on the removal of singular data for natural language processing. To exclude such users, it is necessary to study in detail according to the purpose of research.

In our previous studies [6,7], we proposed an approach for analyzing the influence of emotional expression on user relations on Twitter. In these studies, we set several conditions for excluding singular data and compared the results by a statistical test. The results greatly varied according to the conditions. Moreover, by applying the effective condition obtained in the first experiment, better results could be obtained in the second experiment.

In this chapter, we introduce our studies and discuss how to better analyze and use data smartly.

2 OVERVIEW OF BIBLIOGRAPHY

Data preparation and preprocess are important, and they are generally performed before starting a purposeful analysis. Camargo et al. [8] divided their big data analytics system into two layers: data processing layer and data analytics layer. In the data processing layers, the system extracted information such as username, tweet text, place, and latitude/longitude from a raw tweet. Horng [9] analyzed the relationship between the user behavior in SNS and the indicator of Google Analytics. They regarded the increased number of homepage visitors as outliers when special events have occurred and removed outliers using statistic values such as average and standard deviation. Iglesias et al. [10] presented an approach for automatically investigating the user profiles of a specific community on Twitter. In their study, they stated that inadequate profiles for the analysis data should be removed during preprocessing.

Exclusion of outlier data based on graph theory has also been conducted in network analysis. Xu et al. [5] proposed an algorithm for detecting clusters, hubs, and outliers in the networks. Consequently, they found that hub users are connected to multiple communities and have much influence on every community they belong to. On the other hand, outlier users connected to a single community rarely have an influence on others. Jeon et al. [11] showed a method to graph and analyze the text of an e-mail and removed outlier data in the process. When building a network centered on user relations, they removed nodes that do not have any connection with other nodes, or nodes whose meanings overlap with other similar words. Kaur [12] proposed the outlier detection method using k-means and a neural network. Liu et al. [13] proposed a system for text summarization on comment streams. They detected meaningless words as outliers, and revealed that over 90% of comments are meaningless texts.

Additionally, there are studies for detecting malicious attackers as outliers. Anahita and Mainak [14] defined users performing profile injection attacks in social networks as outlier users. In order to detect these attackers, they proposed a method that evaluates users using three indicators: user-item rating matrix, user-connection matrix, and similarity between users. Chan-Tin et al. [15] proposed a new attack method called frog-boiling against a network coordinate system. They showed that the attack method was effective against outlier detection method based on Mahalanobis distance or Kalman filter.

3 DETECTING SINGULAR DATA FOR BETTER ANALYSIS

While processing big data, it is very important to enhance the quality of a dataset. If the analysis processing is performed using noise data, the obtained findings may not be universal, and they may be a feature peculiar to the dataset. For example, if a dataset includes bots or commercial accounts, then the result of the research is greatly altered.

In order to have a better analysis and obtain a more accurate result, it is necessary to detect singular data and exclude them. Additionally, it is important to assess how the result changes depending on the condition. The quality of a dataset may be further improved by excluding singular data carefully.

The characteristic which is not easily influenced by outliers is called "robust," and there are many studies related to it in the field of statistics. Robustness for excluding outliers should also be considered in big data analysis, and needs to be investigated in detail.

In the next section, we discuss two experiments, in which we apply a statistical test while setting several different conditions for outlier data.

4 EXPERIMENTS AND DISCUSSIONS

4.1 Influence Analysis of Emotional Tweets on User Relationships

Twitter users post their feelings and get other's reactions easily through their tweets. We assume that if a user tends to post positive expression, then his/her relationships will increase, whereas if he/she posts negative expressions, then his/her relationships will decrease. In other words, we consider that emotional expression influences user relationships. We investigate whether a user's relationship is constructed differently for positive and negative users. Moreover, in the analysis, we verify how the statistical result changes when several outlier conditions are set.

The flow of our approach is shown in Figure 12.1. First, we set conditions for identifying users, and further, select sample users randomly. We construct a Twitter corpus using the tweets of these selected users.

Next, an emotion score is attached to each tweet. In order to attach an emotion score, we apply two emotional word dictionaries in the first experiment and leverage the Naive Bayes in the second experiment. Both of the emotional word dictionaries have an emotion score or label for each word. Naive Bayes is a type of machine learning algorithm. Using this algorithm, all words of a tweet can be used for emotion evaluation.

We then calculate the average emotion score for each user. This score is calculated by averaging the emotion scores of randomly selected tweets or all emotional tweets per user and represents the emotional trend of the user.

After calculating the average emotion score, we define two groups, namely the positive (P-Group) and negative (N-Group) groups. While creating P/N-Goups, we set up several conditions for excluding outliers and verify the difference of statistical test result.

Finally, we analyze the difference of user relationships between P-Group and N-Group, and investigate the influence of emotional behaviors on the user relationships on Twitter.

In order to create a tweet corpus, we set conditions and got 5,000 users using Twitter API. However, because of the strict limitation of Twitter API, we could not gather all their tweets and detailed user attributes such as their followee and follower list. For this reason, we randomly sampled 600 users from the 5,000 users and collected their tweets. However, since a number of these 600 users are non-public, we excluded the non-public users and finally obtained 574 users. The acquisition period is from March 13 to April 13, 2017. The total number of tweets is 62,729.

4.2 Experiment 1: Using Emotional Word Dictionaries

In Experiment 1, we measured the emotion score of tweets using the emotional word dictionaries, which had emotional words with a positive/negative score or label attached to them. For evaluating emotions in Japanese text, two emotion dictionaries are

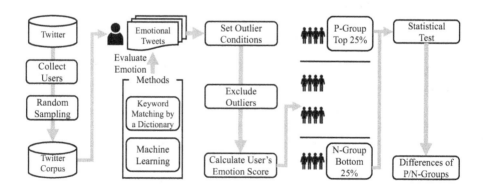

FIGURE 12.1   Overview of our approach.

generally used. The first is the sentiment polarity correspondence table (hereafter, Dict A) [16] and the second is the Japanese sentiment polarity dictionary (hereafter, Dict B) [17,18]. Dict A scores positive words from 0 to +1 and negative words from 0 to −1. Dict B has words labeled as positive, negative, or neutral.

We then attached the emotion score for tweets using Dict A, which contains 55,124 words (49,982 negative words, 20 neutral words, and 5,122 positive words). After morphological analysis, we used Dict A and performed keyword matching between a morpheme and emotional words of Dict A. We adopted a Japanese morphological analysis tool "Mecab" [19] for the morphological analysis.

In case of a word separated by Mecab, the emotion score of the word $ESWA_i$ was attached if it existed in Dict A; otherwise, null was assigned.

$$ESWA_i = \begin{cases} s \Big| \begin{matrix} -1 \leq s \leq +1 \\ \text{if a word } W_i \in \text{Dict A} \end{matrix} \\ null \quad \text{otherwise} \end{cases} \tag{1}$$

The emotion score of a tweet $ESTA$ is the sum of all the emotional words' score in a tweet that exists in Dict A, which is defined as follows:

$$ESTA = \sum_{i=1}^{|ESWA_i|} ESWA_i \tag{2}$$

$$(If\ ESWA_i\ is\ null,\ it\ is\ regarded\ as\ 0)$$

If no emotional word exists, we do not include it in this calculation. We assign the score of null when the tweet does not have any emotional words. Table 12.1 shows the word coverage rate of this dictionary. In this table, the coverage rates of positive and negative words were almost the same. The positive and negative words were extracted in a well-balanced manner, and almost no bias existed. Table 12.2 shows the number of words that matched the dictionary with all the morphemes.

We also used Dict B, which has 18,620 words (5,497 positive words, 8,164 negative words, and 4,959 neutral words). The emotion scores for tweets were attached by the same method with Dict A. We regarded a positive label as +1, negative label as −1, and neutral label as 0.

The emotion score of the word $ESWB_i$ is attached if it exists in Dict B; otherwise, a null is assigned.

$$ESWB_i = \begin{cases} s \Big| \begin{matrix} s \in \{-1, 0, +1\} \\ \text{if a word } W_i \in \text{Dict B} \end{matrix} \\ null \quad \text{otherwise} \end{cases} \tag{3}$$

TABLE 12.1 Coverage rate of Dict A.

	Number of words	Matched	Coverage rate
Positive	5,122	1,407	27.5%
Negative	49,982	13,417	26.8%
Total	55,104	14,824	26.9%

TABLE 12.2 Coverage rate of morphemes using Dict A.

All Kinds of morphemes	1,840,332
Matched	442,316
Coverage rate	24.0%

The emotion score of the tweet *ESTB* is the sum of all the emotional words in the tweet that exists in Dict B.

$$ESTB = \sum_{i=1}^{|ESWB_i|} ESWB_i \tag{4}$$

(*If ESWB$_i$ is null, it is regarded as 0*)

Table 12.3 presents the word coverage rate of this dictionary. The coverage rates of both positive and negative words were between 25 and 30%. We considered that this dictionary could also extract emotional words in a well-balanced manner. Table 12.4 shows the number of words that matched the dictionary with all morphemes, and the rate of matching was very low. We think that the reason for this low rate is that, although the dictionary has many vocabularies, the vocabulary of the Twitter corpus was quite limited.

First, we excluded 51 outlier users who posted ten or fewer tweets during the experiment period because we assumed that they have a negligible influence on others. Therefore, we obtained a dataset of 523 users. We designed three experiments with different conditions as follows.

Case 1: Calculate the average emotion score by randomly sampling 15 emotional tweets for each user. The total number of samples was 523.
Case 2: Calculate the average score of all emotional tweets excluding outlier users whose emotional tweets were equal or fewer than nine, which was a quarter of the average of emotional tweet count. The total number of samples was 425.
Case 3: Calculate the average score of all emotional tweets excluding outlier users whose emotional tweets were equal or fewer than 19, which was half of the average of emotional tweet count. The total number of samples was 311.

We regarded a tweet as an emotional tweet only when there were scores by both dictionaries. We analyzed the differences in the fluctuation of user relationships between the P-Group and N-Group by using Dict A and B, respectively.

TABLE 12.3 Coverage rate of Dict B.

	Number of words	Matched	Coverage rate
Positive	5,497	1,626	29.6%
Negative	8,164	2,029	24.9%
Total	13,661	3,655	27.4%

TABLE 12.4 Coverage rate of morphemes using Dict B.

All kinds of morphemes	1,840,332
Matched	30,103
Coverage rate	1.6%

In order to confirm the differences between the two groups, we applied the Brunner–Munzel test, which is a statistical test. The flow of the Brunner–Munzel test is as follows. We first sampled values that are ranked in each group and the combined group of the two in descending order. Basic statistic values such as W-value and t-value are calculated based on these ranks and sample size. The p-value decreases as the absolute value of t-value increases. This indicates the possibility supporting the null hypothesis that there is no significant difference between the two groups. If the p-value is less than 0.05, a difference is considered to exist, and if it is lower than 0.01, then it is assumed that a difference certainly exists.

Table 12.5 shows the result of Brunner–Munzel test. In Case 3, it was confirmed that there was a significant difference in the number of followee, follower, and mutual follow for both dictionaries. It can be seen that the result significantly changes depending on the outlier condition. The detailed results of Case 3 are shown in Tables 12.6 and 12.7. In both tables, P-Group has a larger value than N-Group. This means that positive users tend to have more relationships than negative users, not in a one-sided manner, but rather bilaterally.

4.3 Experiment 2: Using Naive Bayes

The Naive Bayes classification is one of the machine learning methods. Words that are not in the dictionary can be used for emotion evaluation by training Naive Bayes using training corpus. We used the same Twitter corpus as in Experiment 1 for the experiment and collected tweets for training the Naive Bayes separately.

We collected 48,978 tweets for training and classified them into three emotions, positive (P), negative (N), and neutral (Nt). One evaluator judged tweets for positive and negative emotion, and tweets which were judged neither positive nor negative were labeled as neutral. As a result, we obtained 287 positive tweets and 371 negative tweets. The remaining 48,320 tweets were regarded as neutral. Therefore, we assumed that these tweets were not emotional tweets. Table 12.8 shows the ratio of each emotion classified by the evaluator. If all neutral tweets are used for training,

TABLE 12.5 t-Values when tested with different conditions in Experiment 1.

	t-Value (Dict A)			t-Value (Dict B)		
	Case 1	Case 2	Case 3	Case 1	Case 2	Case 3
Followee fluctuation	$-0.181^{n.s.}$	$-1.000^{n.s.}$	-2.055^{*}	-3.158^{**}	-2.246^{*}	-2.022^{*}
Follower fluctuation	$-0.597^{n.s.}$	$-1.114^{n.s.}$	-2.418^{*}	-3.174^{**}	-3.147^{**}	-2.566^{*}
Mutual follow fluctuation	$-0.809^{n.s.}$	$-0.848^{n.s.}$	-2.749^{**}	-3.047^{**}	-2.225^{*}	-2.930^{**}
Emotional tweet count	$1.542^{n.s.}$	-3.912^{**}	$-1.432^{n.s.}$	$-0.515^{n.s.}$	$0.523^{n.s.}$	$-1.311^{n.s.}$
All tweet count	-3.018^{**}	$0.427^{n.s.}$	$-1.721^{n.s.}$	$1.728^{n.s.}$	$-1.311^{n.s.}$	$0.528^{n.s.}$

$^{*}p<0.05$, $^{**}p<0.01$, n.s.: not significant.

TABLE 12.6 Comparison of P/N groups using Dict A (Case 3).

	Total Sample ($N = 311$)			P-Group ($N = 78$)			N-Group ($N = 78$)			
	Median	Mean	SD	Median	Mean	SD	Median	Mean	SD	t-Value
Followee fluctuation	2.000	5.531	16.5595	2.000	10.64	25.357	1.000	3.090	9.361	-2.055^{*}
Follower fluctuation	1.000	5.029	16.959	1.500	1.19	29.236	1.000	1.577	4.186	-2.418^{*}
Mutual follow fluctuation	0.000	3.768	14.109	1.000	8.462	24.657	0.000	1.128	3.955	-2.749^{**}
Count of emotional tweets	45.000	56.940	43.737	49.500	72.83	64.780	44.500	58.540	40.887	$-1.432^{n.s.}$
Count of all tweets	143.000	169.900	110.297	124.000	169.000	128.856	113.000	133.650	81.876	$-1.721^{n.s.}$

$^{*}p<0.05$, $^{**}p<0.01$, n.s.: not significant.

TABLE 12.7 Comparison of P/N groups using Dict B (Case 3).

	Total Sample ($N = 311$)			P-Group ($N = 78$)			N-Group ($N = 78$)			
	Median	Mean	SD	Median	Mean	SD	Median	Mean	SD	t-Value
Followee fluctuation	2.000	5.531	16.5595	2.000	8.060	20.636	1.000	3.359	6.915	-2.022^{*}
Follower fluctuation	1.000	5.029	16.959	1.000	7.633	23.484	0.000	2.385	7.256	-2.566^{*}
Mutual follow fluctuation	0.000	3.768	14.109	1.000	6.227	19.853	0.000	1.333	3.620	-2.930^{**}
Count of emotional tweets	45.000	56.940	43.737	44.500	62.170	19.853	39.000	50.370	30.506	$-1.311^{n.s.}$
Count of all tweets	143.000	169.900	110.297	126.500	160.200	111.538	137.000	164.000	112.463	$0.528^{n.s.}$

$^{*}p<0.05$, $^{**}p<0.01$, n.s.: not significant.

TABLE 12.8 Ratio of each emotion classified by the evaluator.

Emotion	Classified Number	Ratio
P	287	0.5%
N	371	0.7%
Nt	48,320	98.8%
Total	48,978	100%

then it may give rise to a problematic situation where almost all tweets will be classified as neutral. To avoid this problem, 329 tweets (329 being the average of the number of positive and negative tweets) were extracted at random, and used as neutral training data.

In order to calculate a user's emotion score, we used the score of each category of the Naive Bayes. Further, we calculated the user's average emotion score, which is the average score of emotional tweets. The average emotion score represents a user's emotional tendency. If a user has a high score, it is assumed that he/she tends to post a positive tweet. On the other hand, if the user has a small score, it is assumed that he/she tends to post a negative tweet. The tweets classified as Nt are not included in the calculation of the average emotion score.

We used software called KHCoder [20] for constructing the Naive Bayes. This is natural language processing software, which can construct a Naive Bayes and verify its accuracy. In order to verify the accuracy of the Naive Bayes, we performed a five-fold cross-validation. The results of the cross-validation are shown in Table 12.9, and the overall accuracy rate of 65.8% is close to the result of Yamamoto's study [21].

In addition to the five-fold cross-validation, we prepared 150 tweets for verifying the accuracy of classifying the following new tweets: 50 positive, 50 negative, and 50 neutral tweets. These 150 tweets were selected from another dataset by one evaluator, and this evaluator was the same person who judged P/N/Nt emotions for creating the training dataset. The results of classifying these 150 tweets are shown in Table 12.10. For this test, the overall accuracy rate is 68%, and the classification accuracy of each emotion is around 70%.

Using this Naive Bayes, we attached the emotion labels for tweets in the Twitter corpus. Table 12.11 shows the number of tweets classified into each emotion. About 50% tweets were classified as Nt, about 15% as P, and about 35% as N.

Finally, we created P/N-Groups and applied the Brunner–Munzel test in the same way as in Experiment 1. For the outlier condition, we excluded 201 users whose emotional tweets were less than 30, which is the half the average tweet count, i.e., 60. The total number of samples was 322.

In Experiment 1, the result of Brunner–Munzel test for Case 3 showed similar tendencies for both dictionaries. In Experiment 2, when we adopted the same criterion of Case 3 as in Experiment 1, we obtained a similar result. Tables 12.12 and 12.13 show

TABLE 12.9 Matching result by five cross-validation.

		By Naive Bayes Classification				
		P	N	Nt	Total	Matching Rate
By the evaluator	P	187	54	45	286	65.4%
	N	29	282	60	371	76.0%
	Nt	53	96	180	329	54.7%
	Total	269	432	285	986	65.8%

TABLE 12.10 Matching result for a new dataset.

		By Naive Bayes Classification				
		P	N	Nt	Total	Matching Rate
By the evaluator	P	33	7	10	50	66.0%
	N	4	36	10	50	72.0%
	Nt	6	11	33	50	66.0%
	Total	43	54	53	150	68.0%

TABLE 12.11 Ratio of each emotion classified by Naive Bayes for the Twitter Corpus.

Emotion	Classified Number	Ratio
P	9,747	15.5%
N	21,819	34.8%
Nt	31,163	49.7%
Total	62,729	100%

the results of Experiments 1 and 2. Significant differences were confirmed in the number of followee, follower, and mutual follow fluctuations.

4.4 Discussions

In Cases 1 and 2 of Experiment 1, the results of the statistical test for both dictionaries were inconsistent. In Case 3, we adopted the strict condition for outlier users, and the result was almost the same between Dict A and B. Significant differences were confirmed in the number of followee, follower, and mutual follow fluctuations. By setting the strict outlier condition, we could improve the quality of the dataset and analyze better than the case of not excluding outlier users.

TABLE 12.12 *t*-Values for all users and P/N-Groups.

	Total Sample ($N = 311$)			P-Group ($N = 78$)			N-Group ($N = 78$)			
	Median	Mean	SD	Median	Mean	SD	Median	Mean	SD	*t*–Value
Followee fluctuation	1.500	5.186	17.473	2.000	4.827	16.198	0.000	2.543	8.939	-3.218^{**}
Follower fluctuation	1.000	5.236	16.860	1.000	5.235	9.606	0.000	1.802	6.895	-2.826^{**}
Mutual follow fluctuation	0.000	3.801	13.927	0.000	3.395	7.317	0.000	1.358	5.976	-2.907^{**}
Count of emotional tweets	71.000	86.990	56.016	64.000	75.730	37.948	63.000	78.770	44.872	$-0.157^{n.s.}$
Count of all tweets	143.500	171.800	107.114	132.000	152.800	74.526	127.000	155.100	85.032	$0.020^{n.s.}$

$^{*}p<0.05$, $^{**}p<0.01$, n.s.: not significant.

TABLE 12.13 *t*-Values for Experiment 1 and Experiment 2.

	DictA (Case3)	DictB (Case3)	Naive Bayes
Followee fluctuation	-2.055^{*}	-2.022^{*}	-3.218^{**}
Follower fluctuation	-2.418^{*}	-2.566^{*}	-2.826^{**}
Mutual follow fluctuation	-2.749^{**}	-2.930^{**}	-2.907^{**}
Count of emotional tweets	$-1.432^{n.s.}$	$-1.311^{n.s.}$	$-0.157^{n.s.}$
Count of all tweets	$-1.721^{n.s.}$	$0.528^{n.s.}$	$0.020^{n.s.}$

$^{*}p<0.05$, $^{**}p<0.01$, n.s.: not significant.

Based on the above result, we assumed that users who posted emotional tweets had a greater influence on other users. In order to test the hypothesis, we analyzed the top seven users who had the most emotional tweets when evaluating emotion using the emotional word dictionaries. Figure 12.2 shows the relationship fluctuation of the top seven users. As a result, the average of the followee, follower, and mutual follow fluctuations of these seven users was much larger than negative users and all other users for each average. The result shows that our research results are more reliable owing to the exclusion of outlier users.

In Experiment 2, when we applied the outlier condition obtained in the first experiment to the second experiment, we got almost the same results as in Experiment 1. The result shows that detecting and excluding outlier users is effective even if the way of emotion evaluation is changed.

For using big data in a smart way, the exclusion criterion and the items used for exclusion is important, and should be considered. In our experiments, we excluded outlier users according to the number of followers of the user. Xu et al. [5] also revealed that users who have few followers have little influence on other users' relationships. Actually, our result has been greatly altered with the criterion for outliers. By gradually

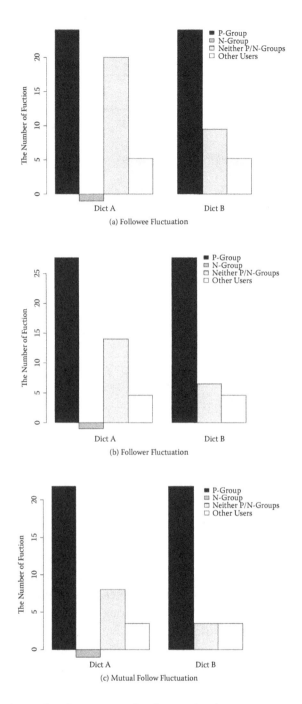

FIGURE 12.2   User relationship fluctuation of each item for the top seven users.

changing the outlier criterion, we can improve the quality of the dataset and obtain more reliable results.

5 SUMMARY

In order to analyze the dataset in a more efficient and effective manner, it is important to raise the quality of data to the highest possible level. In this chapter, we introduced our approach for detecting singular data for improved analysis and discussed two experiments. In order to perform an improved analysis on the influence of emotional tweets on user relationships, we investigated how the results changed based on the conditions of outliers in Experiment 1. Consequently, under the strictest condition, the statistical test results between two dictionaries had a similar tendency. Moreover, while using the Naive Bayes for the emotion evaluation and adopting the outlier condition in Experiment 2, it was seen that the result of Experiment 2 was consistent with that of Experiment 1. The quality of the dataset can be improved by setting outlier condition; therefore, we can obtain more reliable results.

In summary, the preprocessing for both tweets and outlier users significantly affects the result of the study. For better analysis, it is necessary not only to remove noise data, but also to detect and exclude singular data.

BIBLIOGRAPHY

1. H. Kwak, C. Lee, H. Park, and S. Moon. What is twitter, a social network or a news media? Categories and subject descriptors. In *Proceedings of the 19th international conference on World wide web*, pages 591–600, 2010.
2. M. Ozer, N. Kim, and H. Davulcu. Community detection in political twitter networks using nonnegative matrix factorization methods. In *Proceedings of the IEEE/ACM International Conference on Advances in Social Networks Analysis and Mining*, pages 81–88, 2016.
3. A. Pak and P. Paroubek. Twitter as a corpus for sentiment analysis and opinion mining. In *Proceedings of the International Conference on Language Resources and Evaluation*, pages 320–326, 2010.
4. J. Victoria. Hodge and Jim Austin. A survey of outlier detection methodologies. *Artificial Intelligence Review*, 22(2):85–126, Oct 2004.
5. X. Xu, Z. Feng, N. Yuruk, and T. A. J. Schweiger. Scan: A structural clustering algorithm for networks. In *Proceedings of the 13th ACM international Conference on Knowledge Discovery and Data Mining*, pages 824–833, 2007.
6. K. Tago and Q. Jin. Analyzing inuence of emotional tweets on user relationships by naive Bayes classification and statistical tests. In *Proceedings of the Service Oriented Computing and Applications (SOCA)*, pages 217–222, 2017.
7. K. Tago and Q. Jin. Influence analysis of emotional behaviors and user relationships based on twitter data. *Tsinghua Science and Technology*, 23(1):104–113, 2018.
8. J. E. Camargo, C. A. Torres, O. H. Martinez, and F. A. Gpmez. A big data analytics system to analyze citizens' perception of security. In *Proceedings of the Smart Cities Conference (ISC2)*, pages 1–4, 2016.
9. S. M. Horng. Analysis of users' behavior on web 2.0 social network sites: An empirical study. In *Proceedings of the 7th International Conference on Information Technology: New Generations*, pages 454–459, 2010.

10. J. A. Iglesias, A. Garcia-Cuerva, A. Ledezma, and A. Sanchis. Social network analysis: Evolving twitter mining. In *Proceedings of International Conference on Systems, Man, and Cybernetics*, pages 1809–1814, 2016.

11. S. Jeon, Y. Khosiawan, and B. Hong. Making a graph database from unstructured text. In *Proceedings of the 16th IEEE International Conference on Computational Science and Engineering*, pages 981–988, 2013.

12. P. Kaur. Outlier detection using kmeans and fuzzy min max neural network in network data. In *Proceedings of the 8th International Conference on Computational Intelligence and Communication Networks*, pages 693–696, 2016.

13. C. Y. Liu, M. S. Chen, and C. Y. Tseng. Incrests: Towards real-time incremental short text summarization on comment streams from social network services. *IEEE Transactions on Knowledge and Data Engineering*, 27(11):2986–3000, 2015.

14. D. Anahita and C. Mainak. Detection of profile injection attacks in social recommender systems using outlier analysis. In *Proceedings of the IEEE International Conference on Big Data*, pages 2714–2719, 2017.

15. E. Chan-Tin, D. Feldman, N. Hopper, and Y. Kim. *The Frog-Boiling Attack: Limitations of Anomaly Detection for Secure Network Coordinate Systems*, pages 448–458. Springer, Berlin, Heidelberg, 2009.

16. H. Takamura, T. Inui, and M. Okumura. Extracting semantic orientations of words using spin model. In *Proceedings of the 43rd Annual Meeting of the Association for Computational Linguistics (ACL)*, pages 133–140, 2005.

17. M. Higashiyama, K. Inui, and Y. Matsumoto. Learning sentiment of nouns from selectional preferences of verbs and adjectives. In *Proceedings of the 14th Annual Meeting of the Association for Natural Language Processing*, pages 584–587, 2008 (in Japanese).

18. N. Kobayashi, K. Inui, Y. Matsumoto, K. Tateishi, and T. Fukushima. Collecting evaluative expressions for opinion extractionl. *Journal of Natural Language Processing*, 12(3):203–222, 2005 (in Japanese).

19. T. Kudo, K. Yamamoto, and Y. Matsumoto. Applying conditional random fields to Japanese morphological analysis. In *Proceedings of the 2004 Conference on Empirical Methods in Natural Language Processing (EMNLP)*, pages 230–237, 2004.

20. K. Higuchi. Quantitative analysis of textual data: Differentiaiton and coordination of two approches. *Sociological Theory and Methods*, 19(3):101–115, 2004.

21. M. Yamamoto, S. Tsuchiya, S. Kuroiwa, and F. Ren. Emotion classification for emotion corpus construction. In *IEICE technical report, No. 2007-NL-180*, pages 25–30, 2007 (in Japanese).

CHAPTER 13

Smart Data Infrastructure for Respiratory Health Protection of Citizens against PM2.5 in Urban Areas

Daniel Dunea, Stefania Iordache, Alin Pohoata, and Emil Lungu

Valahia University of Targoviste, Targoviste, Romania

CONTENTS

1 INTRODUCTION

In recent decades, city air pollution has become one of the most important environmental issues because of the clear evidences regarding the negative effects on human health in urban environments and on surrounding ecosystems. Epidemiological studies have shown a clear association between air pollution and adverse health effects [1,2]. Particulate matter (PM) contains small airborne particles, ranging in size from less than 1 micron to about 100 microns. The smallest fractions of such particles remain suspended in the air for long periods and absorb, reflect, and scatter solar radiation, thus reducing the visibility. When someone breathes in an environment that presents fine particles, they can penetrate deep into the lungs, up to pulmonary alveolus, resulting in increased morbidity of population [3]. The attention has particularly focused on the fine fraction, i.e., PM2.5 due to the current well-established standards and robust instruments for measurements [4]. In particular, citizens living in cities are exposed to high levels of PM [5]. There is evidence that long-term reduced levels of PM result both in health benefits and in reduced national health costs, e.g., improving life expectancy, diminishing hospitalization time, and associated treatment [6]. Furthermore, quantitative knowledge about emission sources, emission levels, and the trends in emission of primary PM and precursor gases is important for the best control strategy to reduce health risks at spatiotemporal scales [7].

1.1 Smart Data for Protecting the Health of Urban Residents against Air Pollution Episodes

The smart city concept involves 12 smart application areas identified by Lim and Maglio [8] from a textual analysis of 1234 articles, i.e., device, environment, home, energy, building, transportation, logistics, farming, security, health, hospitality, and education. In the context of smart health application, a smart city requires cyberinfrastructures that are adapted to the specific conditions of the city (climatic, topographic, pollution sources, social, economic, greenness, etc.) to support a proper environment for a better life quality of inner citizens by monitoring weather and air pollution parameters in realtime. With the help of a smart urban sensing system, the adverse impact of heat waves and air pollution episodes on human health can be diminished due to a better transfer of the synthesized information towards the citizens, thus raising their awareness. Internet of Things (IoTs) is employed as a component of the newly developed sensing and monitoring systems for air pollution, noise, and meteorological surveillance in a smart city. Monitored raw data are usually processed using machine learning techniques in conjunction with other information such as social media, transport patterns, traffic data, and lately with health information. The digital urban data enabled by the IoT are projected to grow exponentially to optimize energy and environmental efficiency [9]. Major achievements are expected from the IoT in improving air quality, because it provides the potential to use advanced monitoring tools, i.e., end-to-end service delivery development involving new powerful forms of decision-support for pollution prevention as well as management of resources [10]. Because of the recent progress of low-cost instruments and sensors regarding the accuracy and robustness, cyberinfrastructures, communication and Web-based GIS technologies, machine learning and modeling tools, the IoT has important premises in interfacing the physical world in the Internet environment. For smart health, the increasing number of portable monitoring devices (micro-sensors) capable of assessing the air pollution levels as well as a number of functional human physiological probes will provide a great amount of data regarding the environmental sustainability of a city. Another data source could be the integration of Volunteered Geographic Information (VGI) component by encouraging the citizens to contribute quasi-empirical georeferenced data, e.g., GPS tracks, heart and breath rates, sky and street pictures, physical symptoms, respiratory events, and visual observations of emissions. These sources of information can be further processed and extrapolated based on state-of-the-art models and expert information systems to improve the characterization of outdoor microenvironments in a city [11]. In a smart city, such systems must provide intelligent online information to the users with portable devices such as smartphones and tablets enabling their feedback regarding the urban spatiotemporal dynamics of air pollution [12]. Their implementation can enhance the communication between urban spatiotemporal dynamics, stakeholders, and urban policymaking facilitating the understanding of ecological consequence for human health and welfare [13].

1.2 Modeling of PM Concentrations

Models for estimating PM2.5 concentrations have a large number of applications, including those that complement and/or supplement in situ air quality monitoring [14], providing key support in elaborating warnings and mitigation plans. The non-deterministic models involved in forecasting of PM can be divided into three broad categories as follows: *Statistical methods* (regression methods, autoregressive methods, stochastic methods, spectral methods, etc.), *Artificial Intelligence methods* (Artificial Neural Networks, Fuzzy-Logic, Predictive Data Mining, Support Vector Machines, etc.), and *Hybrid Methods* (Adaptive Neuro-Fuzzy Inference System, Wavelet-Neural Networks, etc.). For example, a novel hybrid model that is capable of predicting the daily average concentrations of PM2.5 two days in advance was built by applying the trajectory-based geographic model and wavelet transformation into an adapted neural network [15]. Likewise, the integration of a wavelet preprocessor into a hybrid neural network for air pollution forecasting should help the experts in subsequent assessments increasing the role of the pollution modeling tools to understand how to reduce local or regional emissions towards safer levels for human health [16].

Considering the abovementioned aspects, there is an actual need for further development of the existing state-of-the-art tools to model PM levels for smart health applications in urban environments. Algorithms and models developed for smart analysis of air quality data should provide reliable outputs to characterize the specific impact of air pollution episodes and exposure on sensitive population in various urban microenvironments.

In this context, the chapter describes an Environmental Decision Support System (EDSS) with web-based GIS capabilities that was developed to allow the examination of airborne particulate matter data acquisition near schools, kindergartens, and playgrounds in two Romanian cities. The EDSS components include the spatiotemporal analysis tools that present air quality data according to the corresponding geographic location and spatial topologies of the analysed area. The system was designed to integrate air pollution records from the official monitoring network, PM2.5 measurements from mobile monitoring instruments, and PM2.5 measurements from 8 micro-stations, meteorological data, and dispersion modeling results.

The current chapter focuses on two modeling problems, i.e., enhancement of the interpolation of the continuous measurements performed in 4 points by using the results obtained in 11 points from sequential monitoring campaigns, and assessment of the personal exposure to PM2.5 when the user is selecting routes between various points in cities.

The EDSS with web-based GIS capabilities is a component of the cyberinfrastructure that was designed and developed in the ROKIDAIR research project funded by EEA

Grants (www.rokidair.ro/en) focusing on the PM effects on children's health, in two industrialized cities of Romania, i.e., Targoviste and Ploiesti.

The cyberinfrastructure includes 4 main components: Data Acquisition and Management Structure, Network Monitoring System, Web-based GIS Module, and Decision Support System (Forecasting and Early Warning modules; Fig. 13.1). The cyberinfrastructure was described in [17], the relational database in [18], and the Web-based GIS module in [19]. The EDSS integrates data provided by the monitoring network, forecasts from FANN hybrid model, expert messages and early warnings from DSS module, and

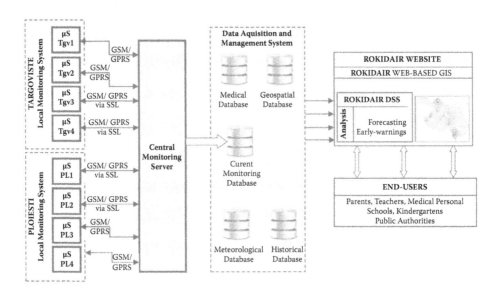

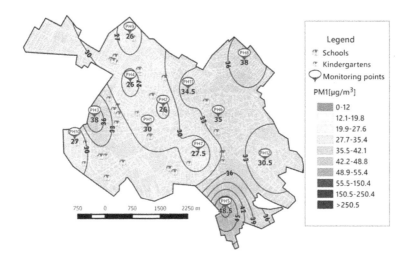

FIGURE 13.1   The architecture of the ROKIDAIR cyberinfrastructure; µS = PM2.5 micro-station; map of Ploiesti city showing the sequential monitoring points and interpolated isolines of concentration.

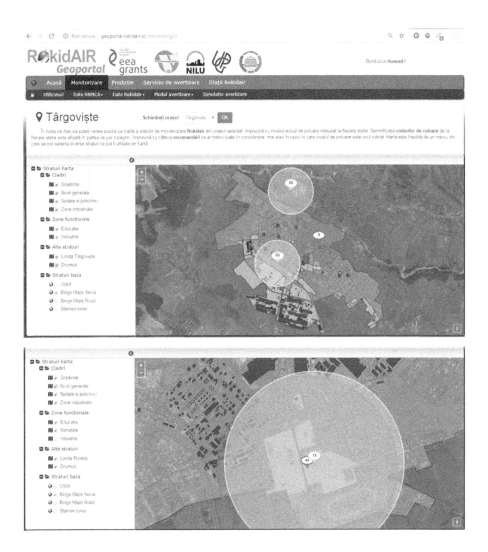

FIGURE 13.2   The main interface of the Environmental Decision Support System (EDSS) showing the positions of real-time measurements provided by the micro-stations and various thematic layers, e.g., green dots—schools and kindergartens; yellow dots—hospitals; purple areas—industry; numbers represent the hourly average concentration of PM2.5.

automates the sending of SMS messages and e-mails to the users in case of PM air pollution episodes to protect the respiratory health of population.

The data processing functions include the graphical representation of time series for each monitoring point (Fig. 13.2), the calculation of the descriptive statistics for the selected parameters (average, median, coefficient of variation, distribution coefficients, etc.), and the histogram (the user can select the number of categories); see Fig. 13.3. The system allows the export of data for the selected interval and performs the associative statistics, testing the statistical significance of bivariate correlations between the selected parameters (pollutant–meteorological parameter;

FIGURE 13.3   Visualization of the recorded PM2.5 time series from 3 micro-stations and the corresponding statistical indicators (count, average, median, min, max, coefficient of variation, skewness, and kurtosis).

pollutant–pollutant; meteorological parameter–meteorological parameter). The meaningful results (warnings, reports, expert messages, etc.) are submitted via SMS to the end-user (Fig. 13.4).

FIGURE 13.4   Historical list of the warning messages transmitted via SMS.

1.3 Structure of the Model

The forecasting and interpolation model was developed using a hybrid wavelet-neural network coupled with an enhanced interpolation mechanism that allows the estimation of the concentrations with increased accuracy in various locations of a city. Figure 13.5 describes the general structure of the model. In the first stage, PM2.5 time series that were acquired hourly by a micro-station were decomposed using a Daubechies Db3 wavelet in four components. Each of these components was used as an input in a feedforward artificial neural network (FANN) together with other inputs that were found to have a significant influence on PM2.5 concentrations (hour of the day, atmospheric stability, and other pollutants). The outputs representing the values of one hour in advance for each Db3 component were recomposed to form the modeled series. The same cycle was applied to all the time series acquired from the 4 micro-stations. Later on, they were used in the enhanced interpolation mechanism to provide the values for each square of the grid in the mapping step.

In the last stage, the resulted forecasted values were used to calculate the potential exposure of a user following the selection of a route in the city.

The following subsections provide the details regarding the calculations performed to achieve the forecasting and exposure assessment using the constructed model.

1.3.1 Hybrid Neural Network Component

Previous tests have shown that the application of Daubechies Db3 wavelet as a decomposing preprocessor of hourly average time series of PM2.5 has significantly improved

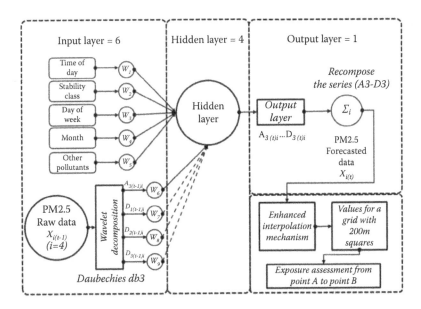

FIGURE 13.5 The structure of forecasting and interpolation model using a hybrid wavelet-neural network coupled with an enhanced interpolation mechanism.

the out-of-sample forecasted values [16,20,21] compared with the sole use of FANN. The components resulted from the decomposition of time series (A3, D1, D2, and D3) were used one by one, as inputs in an optimal FANN architecture established in previous works, i.e., Rprop algorithm (6–4–1). The simulated FANN output of each component was recomposed to form the modeled series of the original pollutant time series and the network performance was analysed using MSE, MAE, RMSE, and r. Early stopping procedure was applied to avoid overfitting. Wavelet integration contributed also to the overfitting reduction. More details about the FANN setup, testing, and optimization can be found in [22].

1.3.2 An Enhanced Mechanism for PM2.5 Interpolation

An adequate interpolation mechanism is required to obtain the necessary values for the estimation of PM2.5 values in each square of the grid covering the inhabited area of a city. The case study was performed in Ploiesti city, Romania. The usual interpolation mechanisms must be enhanced due to the specific geometry of the map and considering the displacement of the measuring points in such way to include the continuous hourly measurements of the 4 micro-stations, but also the influence of the measurements performed in 11 discontinuous sampling points. The usual interpolation algorithms, i.e., Inverse Distance Weighting Method (IDW), Kriging, polynomial interpolation, etc., do not provide satisfactory results in this case. Therefore, an optimization method was required to solve this problem. A combination of two interpolation methods was chosen, i.e., one that takes into account the data from 4 continuous measuring points and the other one that includes the influence of the sequential measurements in 11 sampling points. The IDW interpolant was used for the 4 continuous points. A polynomial function containing two variables of degree higher than or equal to 3 was applied to the data obtained from the 11 sequential measuring points.

Consequently, the interpolant has the following form:

$$\varphi(x,y) = u(x,y) + P(x,y),$$

where

$$u(x,y) = \begin{cases} \dfrac{\sum_{i=1}^{4} w_i(x,y)u_i}{\sum_{i=1}^{4} w_i(x,y)} & \text{if } (x,y) \neq (x_i,y_i) \\ u_i & \text{if } (x,y) = (x_i,y_i) \end{cases} \text{ is IDW interpolant}$$

with:

$$w_i(x,y) = \left(\frac{1}{\sqrt{(x-x_i)^2 + (y-y_i)^2}} \right)^p,$$

$p \in [0,2]$ and u_i are the measured values of the concentration in a continuous measurement point (M_i); the polynomial function P should be 0 in the continuous measuring points and should approximate the average daily value in each of the 11 discontinuous measurement points. $P(x, y) = [(y - y_1)(x_2 - x_1) - (x - x_1)(y_2 - y_1)][(y - y_3)(x_4 - x_3) - (x - x_3)(y_4 - y_3)] \, Q_k \, (x, y)$, where Q_k is a polynomial function of degree $k \geq 1$.

We have denoted by s_i the coefficients of the Q_k polynomial.

For establishing s_i values, the least squares method was used to minimize the sum of the squared differences between the daily measured average for each of the 11 points $N_1, \ldots, N_{11}$ and the interpolated daily average of the sequential measurement day. The expression was minimized as follows:

$$E(s_1, s_2, s_3) = \sum_{k=1}^{11} (c_k - \varphi(x_k, y_k))^2$$

where c_k is the daily measured average value of the sequential measurement day, calculated in the discontinuous measurement points and $\varphi(x_k, y_k)$ is the interpolated values in those points. The interpolant φ is calculated using u_i, the daily measured average value of the sequential measurement day, from the continuous measurement stations.

The s_i parameters were used in the polynomial interpolation after calculation, and all the further interpolations were made using those values. The resulted coefficients were maintained until a new campaign of sequential monitoring was performed and then the interpolation algorithm was recalibrated with the new c_i values and new s_i parameters were obtained. Such combined interpolation algorithm was applied to use both real-time measurements of the continuous hourly monitoring and the discontinuous ones.

1.3.3 Quantification of Exposure to PM2.5

Exposure to $PM_{2.5}$ was found to have a direct impact on the asthma mechanism, especially in infants and pre-schoolers, which increases the number of wheezing episodes and the levels of allergic indicators [23]. The real-time exposure assessment may prevent asthma triggers by avoiding air-polluted areas in the city.

Two possible scenarios for outdoor exposure assessment were considered in our study. In the first case, the user may want to get from point A to point B on the shortest way looking for an estimation of the potential exposure to air pollutants. In the second case, the user may want to receive a suggestion for a route to the destination so that the exposure is minimal. In both cases, the problem is to find an optimal path (relative to the route length or exposure) in a graph in which the edges represent road segments of the road network. Depending on the selected scenario, the graph is assessed by the *cost* function, which gives the length for the first case, and respectively the length multiplied by pollutant concentration for the second case.

The *PostGIS pgRouting* extension has been used based on Dijkstra's algorithm to solve the optimization problem. The vector data representing the road network of the city was preprocessed to be adapted to the requirements of this algorithm. In the first phase, the data were changed using the *postgis_topology* extension to have a valid topological structure (each line intersects other lines only at its extremities). In the second phase, data were adjusted using a grid in which each square has a side of 200 m. Each square of this network is covered by a corresponding pixel from the raster obtained from the interpolation of data representing pollutant concentrations collected in the measurement points. Therefore, within each square, the concentration is considered having a constant value. The graph that finds the optimal routes is obtained starting from the trimmed vector data by applying *pgr_createTopology* procedure. Figure 13.6 shows a segment from the road network with nodes obtained at the intersections of original roads with grid lines. The figure also shows the resulted shortest route between points A and B containing 14 segments each of them belonging to a certain square of the grid.

Discrete data representing the concentrations of pollutants measured in all the sampling points were interpolated using the *gdal_grid* tool to obtain a raster having a resolution that complies with the 200 m grid (*www.gdal.org/gdal_grid.html#gdal_grid_algorithms*). The grid and the rectangular area used for interpolation are overlapping and the number of squares in the two directions corresponds to the number of pixels in raster.

Exposure is proportional to the concentration of pollutants and the time spent on a segment in a specific area [24]. Along a route, the calculation of exposure is made using the following equation:

$$E = \sum_{i=1}^{n} C_i t_i$$

where the route from point A to point B is $[A(x_0, y_0), P_1(x_1, y_1), \ldots, P_{n-1}(x_{n-1}, y_{n-1}), B(x_n, y_n)]$.

For each segment $[P_{i-1}P_i]$ of length d_i with $i = \overline{1, n}$ ($A = P_0, B = P_n$), we have the concentration C_i and the time spent on this segment is t_i.

If the average movement speed (V)is known, the formula becomes the next equation:

$$E = \frac{1}{V} \sum_{i=1}^{n} C_i d_i$$

The middle of the $[P_{i-1}P_i]$ segment will be considered to calculate the concentration (to avoid the situation where the segment has both ends on the border's square), and concentration C_i is extracted querying the corresponding value of this point from the concentrations' raster obtained from the interpolation of measurements. The d_i distance is obtained using the *postgis st_length* function.

The resulted geoportal provides messages containing information regarding early warnings and recommendations to protect the health of population, derived from data analysis and existing thematic layers (buildings, streets, functional areas, etc.). The classification of PM2.5 concentrations was performed using the 2012 US EPA revised breakpoints including the associated health effects (from *green—good conditions*, to *brown—maximum health risk*).

A useful function that was integrated in the EDSS is the assessment of exposure and inhaled doses. First, the route is selected by clicking on the map the start and ending points. Second, the user is asked to provide supplementary information regarding the commuting mode, age, start time, etc. Then, the EDSS estimates the route distance, time spent on the route, exposure levels, and potential inhaled doses (Fig. 13.7).

The integration of mobility patterns of specific individuals and temporal changes in human behaviors in correlation with fluctuations of contaminants' concentrations leads to a reliable assessment of human exposure to PM respirable fractions [25]. The temporal dimension is often underemphasized in exposure assessment studies, partly due to insufficient tools for visualizing and examining temporal datasets [26]. In general, personalized routing relies on traveler's preferences based on various criteria, such as shortest, fastest, least traffic, or less expensive [27,28]. Inclusion of the air pollution criterion in selecting routes, especially in the case of walking as a commuting mode, may provide better personal protection of health by avoiding or reducing the time spent in contaminated microenvironments.

Traffic exposure metrics include distance to heavy-traffic roads, traffic volume on nearby roads and traffic within buffer distances, measured pollutant concentrations, land-use regression estimates of pollution concentrations, and other factors. GIS software is useful to estimate traffic exposure using traffic count data and a kernel density calculation to generate a traffic density surface with a resolution of 50 m [29]. In ROKIDAIR EDSS, the contributions of road traffic emissions, which were considered as line sources, were estimated in a simplified way using the rectangular coordinates for the two points defining each major line source, specific emission factors extracted from the

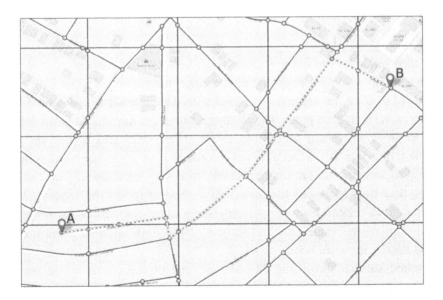

FIGURE 13.6   Example of route selection (from A to B points) for computing potential exposure to fine particulate matter.

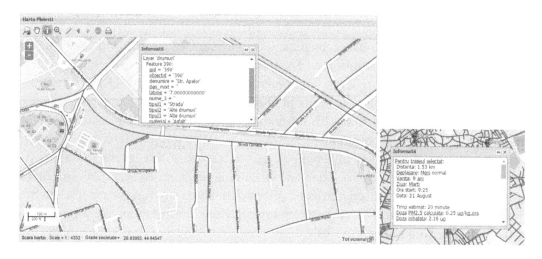

FIGURE 13.7   Road network vectors in Ploiesti city that are used for computing the exposure to air pollution and the result for a route of 1.53 km by walking for a child of 9 years old at a particular day and hour; the system provides the estimated time spent on the route as well as the potential inhaled dose (i.e., 2.16 µg PM2.5 in 20 minutes).

EEA CORINAIR Guidebook, time interval, and statistical indicators regarding the traffic data around the monitoring points. Then, the resulted values were used as weights for the final adjustment of the grid values resulted from the enhanced interpolation. Consequently, the ROKIDAIR EDSS provides spatiotemporal analysis features required for a reliable exposure assessment to PM2.5 in conjunction with other air pollutants monitored in the area of Ploiesti city.

2 MODELING RESULTS

The embedded model in the EDSS provides a spatially improved assessment of the PM2.5 levels in Ploiesti city using the enhanced interpolation mechanism. The time series continuously measured by the 4 micro-stations are used to feed the wavelet-neural network to predict one step-ahead value in each point. The predicted values are introduced in the interpolation algorithm to provide potential concentrations for an extended area beyond the monitored area in Ploiesti based on the historical values recorded in the sequential monitoring.

Figure 13.8 presents an example resulted from the interpolation of the predicted values. The blue dots represent the measured average value of the sequential measurement campaign, calculated from the discontinuous measurement points, while the green dots are the forecasted values in the location of the four micro-stations that perform continuous hourly measurements.

The resulted surface shows the 24-hour average of the combined interpolation of forecasted values in 4 points and the 11 average values of the sequential measurements.

Figures 13.9 and 13.10 present the modeled values of PM2.5 in Ploiesti city. According to these results, it was observed that Ploiesti inner city was characterized by "moderate"

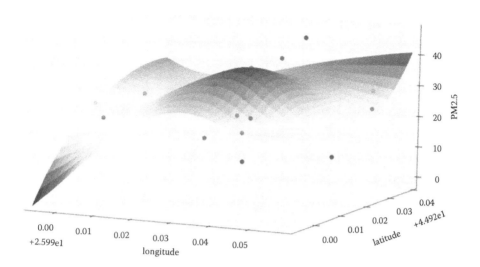

FIGURE 13.8 Modeling of PM2.5 concentrations (μg m^{-3}) for an extended area of Ploiesti city beyond the monitored perimeter obtained using the combined interpolation $\varphi(x,y) = u(x,y) + P(x,y)$ of the forecasted values resulting from the wavelet-neural network (green dots) and the averages of sequential monitoring (blue dots).

FIGURE 13.9 Results of data interpolation showing the isolines of PM2.5 concentrations.

and "unhealthy for sensitive groups" conditions for particulate pollution depending on the area of the city. The spatial distribution of PM2.5 provided by the model shows increased concentrations in the centre of Ploiesti because of traffic jams and adjacent

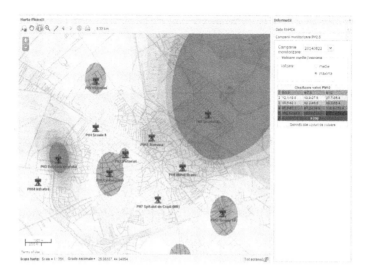

FIGURE 13.10   Raster display of PM2.5 potential levels in Ploiesti and the classification using US EPA 2012 index bands for a specific monitoring campaign.

emissions, in northeast because of the most important oil refinery, and in northwest due to the intense traffic on a national road and industrial sources located in the area. The model performs well for various scenarios involving both low and high concentrations. Resulted outputs were comparable to the real patterns of PM2.5 time series observed in Ploiesti, i.e., recorded maximum values ranged between 60 and 90 μg m^{-3}, and the most frequent values were in the 8 and 16 μg m^{-3} interval.

3 CONCLUSIONS

The systems for air quality monitoring and forecasting are not always able to assess adequately the population outdoor exposure to air pollution at various spatial scales, especially in urban areas with high density of sensitive citizens (children, elders, and ill persons). Therefore, the development and implementation of complementary and/ or supplementary monitoring and data processing solutions (e.g., the use of personal monitors, models, statistical inferences, etc.) to the existing networks could avoid the information hiatus, despite the potential loss of measurement accuracy compared with the environmental standards and technical norms. The Environmental Decision Support System presented in this work facilitates the assessment of exposure to PM2.5 at city scale with sufficient precision. The integrated features include statistical processing of historical air pollution and meteorological data, continuous PM2.5 measurements, sequential monitoring, forecasting of PM2.5 measurements in 4 points, interpolation of data for a better spatial covering of the city, support for route selection, and calculation of potential inhaled doses during the movement on the selected routes.

The current approach requires further calibration to increase the precision of the enhancing interpolation mechanism and to verify the real PM2.5 exposure by employing a mobile monitoring experimental protocol on various routes in the city coupled with an adapted epidemiological study design.

REFERENCES

1. Henschel S., Atkinson R., Zeka A., et al. Air pollution interventions and their impact on public health. *International Journal of Public Health.* 2012; 57(5): 757–768.
2. Liu H.Y., Dunea D., Iordache S., Pohoata A. A review of airborne particulate matter effects on young children's respiratory symptoms and diseases. *Atmosphere.* 2018; 9(4): 150.
3. US EPA. Quantitative health risk assessment for particulate matter. EPA-452/R-10-005; June 2010.
4. Chow J.C., Watson J.G. New directions: Beyond compliance air quality measurements. *Atmospheric Environment.* 2008; 42: 5166–5168.
5. Health effects of particulate matter—Policy implications for countries in Eastern Europe, Caucasus and Central Asia. Available from: www.euro.who.int/__data/assets/pdf_file/0006/189051/Health-effects-of-particulate-matter-final-Eng.pdf
6. Kampa M., Castanas E. Human health effects of air pollution. *Environmental Pollution.* 2007; 151: 362–367.
7. Liu H.-Y., Bartonova A., Pascal M., Smolders R., Skjetne E., Dusinska M. Approaches to integrated monitoring for environment and health impact assessment. *Environmental Health.* 2012; 11: 88.
8. Lim C., Maglio P.P. Data-driven understanding of smart service systems through text mining. *Service Science.* 2018; 10(2): 154–180.
9. Bibri S.E., Krogstie J. On the social shaping dimensions of smart sustainable cities: A study in science, technology, and society. *Sustainable Cities and Society.* 2016; 29: 219–246.
10. Bibri S.E. The IoT for smart sustainable cities of the future: An analytical framework for sensor-based big data applications for environmental sustainability. *Sustainable Cities and Society.* 2018; 38: 230–253.
11. Dunea D., Iordache S., Bohler T., Huber F., Leitner P. Evaluating the air pollution impact using environmental monitoring, dispersion modeling and volunteered geographic information systems. Revista de *Chimie (Bucharest).* 2017; 68(4): 835–840.
12. Govindaraju R.S., Engel B., Ebert D., et al. Vision of Cyberinfrastructure for End-to-End Environmental Explorations (C4E4). http://dx.doi.org/10.1061/(ASCE)1084-0699(2009) 14:1(53).
13. CYRDAS Report, cyberinfrastructure for the atmospheric sciences in the 21st Century. Available from: www.cisl.ucar.edu/cyrdas/cyrdas_report_final.pdf.
14. Dunea D., Iordache S., Radulescu C., Pohoata A., Dulama I.D. A multidimensional approach to the influence of wind on the variations of particulate matter and associated heavy metals in Ploiesti city, Romania. *Romanian Journal of Physics.* 2016; Available from: www.nipne.ro/rjp/accpaps/054-Dunea__53BCA0.pdf.
15. Feng X., Li Q., Zhu Y., Hou J., Jin L., Wang J. Artificial neural networks forecasting of PM2.5 pollution using air mass trajectory based geographic model and wavelet transformation. *Atmospheric Environment.* 2015; 107: 118–128.
16. Dunea D., Pohoata A., Iordache S. Using wavelet – Feedforward neural networks to improve air pollution forecasting in urban environments. *Environmental Monitoring and Assessment.* 2015; 187: 477.

17. Iordache S., Dunea D., Lungu E., et al. A cyberinfrastructure for air quality monitoring and early warnings to protect children with respiratory disorders. In *Proceedings of the 20th International Conference on Control Systems and Computer Science (CSCS20-2015)*. Bucharest, 2015; 789–796. doi: 10.1109/CSCS.2015.39.

18. Dunea D., Iordache S., Oprea M., Savu T., Pohoata A., Lungu E. A relational database structure for linking air pollution levels with children's respiratory illnesses. *Bulletin UASVM CN*. 2014; 71(2): 205–213.

19. Dunea D., Lungu E., Pohoata A. An environmental mapping system for airborne particulate matter monitoring in urban areas. In *Proceedings of the 14th SEPADS '15*, At Dubai, United Arab EmiratesFebruary 22–24, 2015; 85–94. Available from: www.wseas.us/e-library/confer ences/2015/Dubai/SEPADS/SEPADS-10.pdf.

20. Siwek K., Osowski S. Improving the accuracy of prediction of PM10 pollution by the wavelet transformation and an ensemble of neural predictors. *Engineering Applications of Artificial Intelligence*. 2012; 25: 1246–1258.

21. Mihalache S.F., Popescu M., Oprea M. Particulate matter prediction using ANFIS modelling techniques. In *19th International Conference on System Theory Control and Computing (ICSTCC)*, 2015, 895–900.

22. Dunea D., Iordache S. Analyzing the impact of airborne particulate matter on urban contamination with the help of hybrid neural networks – Artificial neural networks-models and applications. *IntechOpen*. 2016. doi: 10.5772/63109.

23. Dunea D., Iordache S., Liu H.-Y., Bøhler T., Pohoata A., Radulescu C. Quantifying the impact of PM2.5 and associated heavy metals on respiratory health of children near metallurgical facilities. *Environmental Science and Pollution Research*. 2016; 23(15): 15395–15406.

24. Liu H.-Y., Skjetne E., Kobernus M. Mobile phone tracking: In support of modelling traffic-related air pollution contribution to individual exposure and its implications for public health impact assessment. *Environmental Health*. 2013; 12: 93. doi: 10.1186/1476-069X-12-93.

25. Dunea D., Iordache S., Pohoata A. Fine particulate matter in urban environments: A trigger of respiratory symptoms in sensitive children. *International Journal of Environmental Research and Public Health*. 2016; 13(12): 1246.

26. Sinha, G., Mark, D.M. Measuring similarity between geospatial lifelines in studies of environmental health. *Journal of Geographical Systems*. 2005; 7(1): 115–136.

27. Peters, J., Theunis, J., Van Poppel, M., Berghmans, P. Monitoring PM10 and ultrafine particles in urban environments using mobile measurements aerosol. *Aerosol and Air Quality Research*. 2013; 13: 509–522.

28. Meliker, J.R., Slotnick, M.J., AvRuskin, G.A., Kaufmann, A., Jacquez, G.M., Nriagu, J.O. Improving exposure assessment in environmental epidemiology: Application of spatio-temporal visualization tools. *Journal of Geographical Systems*. 2005; 7(1): 49–66.

29. Pratt, G.C., Parson, K., Shinoda, N., et al. Quantifying traffic exposure. *Journal of Exposure Science and Environmental Epidemiology*. 2014; 24: 290–296.

CHAPTER **14**

Fog-Assisted Cloud Platforms for Big Data Analytics in Cyber Physical Systems

A Smart Grid Case Study

Md. Muzakkir Hussain, Mohammad Saad Alam, and
M.M. Sufyan Beg

Aligarh Muslim University, Aligarh, India

S. M. Shariff

Department of Electrical Engineering, Taibah University, Al-Madinah Al-Munawwarah, KSA

CONTENTS

1 INTRODUCTION

The introduction of state-of-the-art Information and Communication Technologies (ICT) to next-generation power grid, synonymously Smart Grid (SG), leverages utilities for supporting bidirectional flow of electric power and digital information [1]. The SG is bestowed with advanced synchronization and monitoring facilities with human in the loop, realizing optimized cum automated power delivery network [2]. The SG overhauls the century-old legacy power grid by eradicating the inherent flaws such as unidirectional data flow, energy wastage, upsurge of energy demands, consistency, reliability security, sustainability, and many more [3–5]. The two-way flow support in SG architecture integrates a wide range of stakeholders to actively participate in the decentralized energy trade across the cascaded generation, transmission, distribution, and consumption domain [6,7]. The delineation of energy vendors and consumers is now abridged and are now acting as prosumers (producer plus consumer) [8]. For instance, the SG supports penetration of Electric Vehicles (EVs) to participate in both G2V (grid to vehicle) mode while charging and V2G (vehicle to grid) mode while discharging into energy market. The connected Home Area Networks (HAN) that play role of nano-pico grids are other emerging examples [9]. The SG ensures efficient connection and exploitation of all means of production, provides automatic and real-time management of the electrical networks, allows better measurement of consumption, optimizes the level of reliability, and improves the existing services, thus leading to energy savings and economic energy costs and tariffs [10,11]. Moreover, the SG is adapted to demand peaks as well energy wastage, because such issues are efficiently fixed through efficient implementation of real-time pricing, self-healing, demand response (DR) mechanisms, power consumption scheduling, dynamic energy management (DEM), and efficient demand-side management (DSM) policies [12]. Such policies significantly improve the power quality as well as the efficiency of the grid by maintaining an optimal balance between power generation and its usage [9]. Added to this, the SG aims to achieve steady availability of power, energy sustainability, environmental protection, prevention of large-scale failures, as well as optimized operational expenses (OPEX) of power production and distribution, and reduced future capital expenses (CAPEX) for thermal generators and transmission networks [13].

Recently, the Internet of Things (IoT) had perceived a global endeavor and the SG is considered as one of the largest applications of the IoT [14–16]. Current trend shows that the number of things that use electricity is higher than the number of things connected to the Internet, and essentially everything which uses electricity could be made more efficient by integrating it to the Internet [17]. In coming days, the IoT would be larger than the SG today, and hence it is not possible to assure grid-operational dynamism without the IoT technology [18]. By making the IoT technology a global standard and basis for SG communications, new avenues will be created for maximizing the prospects for future innovations [19–21]. The contemporary SG architectures are being heavily populated with the IoT devices such as sensors, actuators, and smart meters, to support various network functions throughout the generation, transmission, distribution, and consumption land-scapes. The IoT leverages real-time connectivity, automation, and tracking of on premise smart devices, deployed for analysis, monitoring, and control of the power grid. The IoT technology is the key player to the success of SG dynamics as it provides seamless integration and interaction of the power network infrastructure as the physical systems, and information sensing, storage, processing, intelligence, and control as the cyber systems [10,22]. Thus, the SG architecture evolves into an ideal class of cyber-physical systems (CPS) that efficiently conjoins the physical systems and cyber sub-systems [12,23].

The SG is considered to be a system of systems. It comprises a physical-half (power network infrastructure) and a cyber-half that encompasses entities such as IoT devices, sensors, and

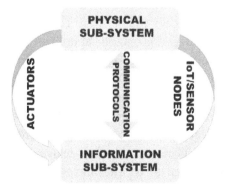

FIGURE 14.1 Smart grid as a cyber-physical system.

actuators. In the context of SG, the IoT services typically include a set of software modules running in multiple locations and meshed through active networks such as 4G, wireless LAN, and the World Wide Web (WWW) [24]. The SG cyber sub-system forms the basis of data-driven analytics, ultimately focused to manage the operation of physical sub-system. The cyber components are seamlessly meshed through a communication backbone that leverages bidirectional information flow across the entities. The integration of physical and cyber subsystem through ad hoc and dedicated communication networks makes SG an ideal example of CPS [25,26]. Figure 14.1 illustrates the role of SG as a CPS. It is an integrated framework of real and virtual worlds where the attributes from the real (physical) as well as virtual (cyber) world are fed as input to the control/data centers (clouds), to generate simulation models for predicting the future mechanisms and transitions. The controlling modules manage the dynamic connections and interactions between components of both worlds, as the system response is essentially defined by their dynamic cooperation. These days, cloud services undertake the SG control and monitoring task [27]. They perform real-time, parallel computation, and distributed information processing of big data streams to deliver optimal and timely decisions to SG application users. The exponential data deluge in SG systems has led to a focus in academia as well as industries to allocate heavy investments on how to effectively extract insights from such data streams, to assist in the SG-CPS design process. The Big Data Analytics (BDA) techniques are employed to guarantee self-adapting, self-organizing, and self-learning nature of SG that can autonomously respond to faults, attacks, and emergencies, ensuring SG resilience, secure, and safe power supply [3,28].

However, the implementation of IoT-aided SG features and services leads to an unprecedented data deluge, to be processed due to the installation of smart meters and various sensors on the network and the development of customer facilities, etc. Consider the case Advanced Metering Infrastructures (AMI); if a smart meter sends customer energy usage logs four times per hour, 96 million reads can be generated by merely one million smart meters and the transactions of merely two million smart metering populations generate more than 20GB of data every day [29]. The IoT forms the backbone of a data-aware SG architecture that intelligently congregates the behaviors and actions of all the stakeholders in the electricity supply chain to deliver energy in smart, sustainable, and secured manner, and ensure economical and environmentally sustainable use. Thus, the avalanche of IoT-aided SG devices embarks and gears up the urgent need of big data management. For SG use-cases, the storage and processing loads will be swarmed up from billions of static as well as mobile IoT nodes spanning over vast geographical domain [30,31]. The IoT–SG marriage comes with the cost of humanitarian as well as monetary expenses incurred during storage, analytics, and management of SG big data [11]. The SG datasets associated to physical and energy sub-system are consumers load demand, energy consumption, network components status, power lines faults, outage management records, forecast conditions, etc. Hence, the utility companies must be equipped with robust hardware, software, and algorithmic support to store, manage, and process such big data deluge in IoT-aided SG infrastructures.

Cloud Computing (CC) emerged to be a technology enabler for data-driven SG infrastructures [32]. The reasons are being its ability to provide convenient and on-demand, anytime, anywhere network access to the shared computing resources, provisioned and released with minimal management effort or service provider interaction. The cloud platforms also free the IoT devices from battery-draining processing tasks by leveraging virtually unlimited pay-per use resources through virtualization. However, the varying modalities of services facilitated by CC paradigms perish to meet the mission-critical requirements of SG [33]. The existing CC paradigm is perishing to welcome its proponents because of its failure in building common and multipurpose platform that can provide feasible solutions to the stringent Quality of Service (QoS) requirements of SG in IoT space [34].

Fog Computing (FC), because of its peculiar property of low latency and highly distributed nature, extends the centralized cloud services to SG network end-points viz. routers, gateways, etc., and overcomes such concerns [10,35]. These days, the notion of FC has perceived a consensus attention among the research community. It has also been realized that the mere of fact of migrating and executing everything to the mega data centres creates major concerns for reliable SG computing and analytics [36]. Thus, eager respondents from academia as well as commercial utilities started to adopt FC platforms for IoT-aware SG architectures where a significant proportion of compute and storage activities are offloaded to geo-distributed nodes termed as Fog Nodes (FNs) [37]. In the context of SG, the FC can be defined as an architectural setup for federated as well as distributed processing where application-specific logic is embedded not only in remote clouds or edge systems, but also across the intermediary infrastructure components such as portable devices, gateways, smart meters, Road Side Units (RSUs), and OBUs at electric vehicular networks, wireless sensors at smart homes, and micro-nano grids and miscellaneous IoT devices. Fog rises as cloud descends to be closer to the end-users. Building on the foundation of past work in related areas and driven by emerging trend of SG mission-critical applications and capabilities, the FC model is now bestowing unique opportunities to R&Ds, SG utilities, academia, and researchers.

Motivated by the mission-critical SG requirements and the downsides of current cloud infrastructures to meet such needs, and having the assumption that the SG community is not in a position to reinvent a remotely owned Internet infrastructure or to develop its own computing platforms and elements from scratch, in this chapter, we present an FC framework whose principle underlies on offloading the time- and resource-critical operations from cOre to edGe, i.e., along the cloud of things continuum. The argument here is not to cannibalize the existing cloud support for SG, but to comprehend the applicability of FC algorithms to interplay with the core-centered CC support. The objective is to develop a viable computational prototype for efficient BDA in SG architectures, in the realm of IoT space. Through proper orchestration and assignment of compute and storage resources to the network endpoint as well as cloud data centers, the CC and FC technologies are tuned to interplay and assist each other in a synergistic way.

The key contributions of this chapter are highlighted as follows:

i. In Section 2, we identify the mission-critical computing needs of IoT-aided SG architectures, through two candidates use-cases namely Smart Homes and electric vehicles charging management.

ii. In Section 3, we examine the current state of cloud platforms towards satisfying the requirements identified in Section 2. Correspondingly, we also analyse the suitability of FC in accomplishing the shortcomings associated with cloud-based big data treatment for SG services.

iii. In Section 4, we present a multi-tier FC framework for BDA in SG and provide a synoptic overview of the varying network and device types in SG deployment scenarios.

iv. In Section 5, we provide a service-oriented software architecture (SOSA) for demonstrating the execution of FC-based analytics on SG data. Conclusions are provided in Section 6.

2 COMPUTING NEEDS OF IOT-AIDED SMART GRID APPLICATIONS

A number of architectures have been proposed for IoT-aided SG systems. Notable architectures are 3-layered architecture [38], 4-layered architecture [9,39], Energy-Efficient Architecture [40], Last-Mile SG architecture [9], and Web-Enabled Smart Grid [41]. A 3-layer architecture for an IoT-integrated SG ecosystem is presented in

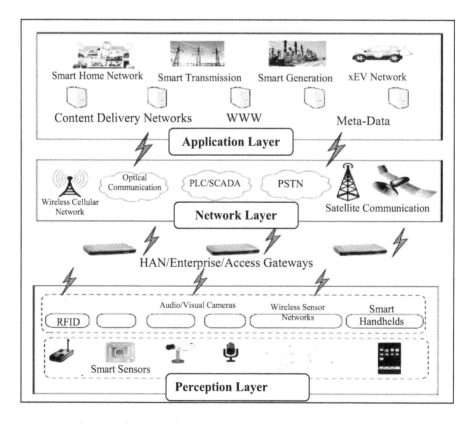

FIGURE 14.2   A 3-layer architecture for an IoT-integrated SG ecosystems [37].

Figure 14.2. In order to efficiently deal with consumed and generated data streams at each layer, i.e. perception layer, network layer, and application layer, such architectures demands multifaceted big data management techniques and tools. The emerging data-driven SG applications also require complex data treatments because of their nature and distribution. The multidimensional attributes of SG data will be mined by BDA utilities to acquire better insights of stakeholder's behavior, consumption, and demand profiles, thus guaranteeing a stable and hassle-free grid dynamics. The prime objective of SG utilities is to get equipped with state-of-the-art BDA tools, platforms, and techniques that can efficiently store, manage, and transform the generated data streams to consecutive information, knowledge, and finally to actionable business decisions. Further, the SG applications demand services in wide degrees of criticality. For instance, the applications for weather forecasting require updates in 12–24 hour time quanta while transmission line monitoring activities demand virtually real-time and context-aware intelligence. To show how large-scale computing must play a key role in the smart power grid, in this section, we analyze two representative SG use-cases and classify requirements of mission-critical BDA in these use-cases.

A Smart Homes

The IoT technologies will result in high penetration of SG-powered home appliances such as smart heating/refrigeration system, smart infotainment services, home security sub-system, and smart emergency response devices like lighting control, fire alarms, temperature monitoring devices, etc. [14,15]. Embedding these appliances into IoT network will enhance transparency in the infrastructure by tracking the activities of the smart city residents. The future SG will be leveraged with a range of AMI and monitoring devices. The IoT sensors and actuators integrated to such systems sense the environment-specific data streams and offload to the controlling module operated by either householders or HAN operators [16]. The operator's prime objective is to dynamically adjust the consumption patterns in order to match the power tariffs and to shape the load surges on the power grid [15]. The smart homes are also meshed-up with sensor networks that assimilate the surveillance data for predicting the occurrence of future events, thus preparing the householders to behave according to the contingencies. For instance, a geyser might be on when power is cheap but the water is allowed to cool when hot water is unlikely to be needed. An air conditioning (AC), washing machine system, or even smart TVs might time themselves to match with usage patterns, power costs, and overall grid state [17]. In fact, there seems to be a one-one mapping between a SCADA system and a Smart Home Network (SHN) and having the realization that the former directly reaches into the smart homes. The smart homes or smart customers may also form communities through Neighbor Area Network (NAN) to have access to shared resources and response intelligently to the community-based cooperative energy consumption schemes [18].

B Electric Vehicle Charging Infrastructures

Electric, plug-in electric, and plug-in hybrid electric vehicles (xEVs) are receiving a global attention from automotive industries, vehicle vendors, R&D organizations, power sectors, and policymakers in the intelligent transportation (ITS) era. Penetration of xEV fleet into the contemporary charging infrastructure(s) in the absence of robust power integration network imbalances the power grid and will potentially jeopardize the execution of power grid horizontals, viz. generation, distribution, transmission, and consumption. However, SG technologies in collaboration with smart charging management strategies can circumvent such operational disparities, thus enabling a reliable, efficient, consistent, and optimal electric energy management in the power system [19,20]. While the integration of xEVs potentially benefits to both power and electrified transportation sectors, it may also threaten the SG reliability by creating energy sinks at random end points. Thus, the statistics of vehicle fleet dynamics needs to be efficiently understood in order to realize a xEV fleet charging management framework that can lead to characteristic economic power tariffs, minimum charging delays, and eliminate the queuing delay at fuel stations. Moreover, the current evolution of V2G market opens a doorway to numerous research and business prospects [19,21]. Thus, the engineering and economic philosophy of V2G market (we term it as Gridonomics) should be critically studied in order to assess the viability of xEV penetration across the SG infrastructures. There is also need for noble business analytics that congregates perspectives of various SG stakeholders such as vehicle vendors, power ISOs, generation bodies, and xEV owners, with a goal to establish a stable and win-win ecosystem [22]. The intelligency provided by a data-driven fleet charging management systems will synergistically integrate the xEV into the SG network. It will also implement vehicle routing algorithms coupled with smart charging schedules that alleviates Electric Vehicle Range Anxiety (EVRA) concerns, a syndrome prevalent in the xEV customer that usually becomes acute during long-drive scenario when the driver is deprived of accurate information of charging station statistics. Now, the default question that arises is about the computational needs implied by such use-cases in SG settings. A brief summary of non-functional computational service needs of multiple SG verticals is given in Table 14.1 [32]. In order to fulfill the requirements shown in this table, the SG requires robust storage and compute framework that can process and serve the service requests accordingly. In this section, we briefly discuss the requirements of BDA activities in IoT-aware smart homes and xEV network (see rows 2 and 7 in Table 14.1).

2.1 Decentralization

The data generation and consumption nodes of SHN and xEV networks are randomly distributed over the whole SG geography. In addition to a centralized control, the sensor and actuator nodes deployed across these networks also demand geo-distributed intelligence. In such circumstances, the information currently captured and consumed in a single regional power system will increasingly need to be visible to neighboring power systems [23]. Similarly, the domain of information transparency may need to be extended from mere SCADA systems to a scale that ensures national-level visibility.

2.2 Scalability

The IoT-aided SG concept brings multitude of new controllable entities into single dais, all demanding infinitely scalable Store Compute and Network (SCN) services for their

TABLE 14.1 Non-functional computational requirements of multiple SG verticals.

	Applications	Decentralization	Consistency	Scalability	Security	Bandwidth	Availability and reliability	Latency
1	Vehicle to Grid (V2G)	Highly decentralized	High	High	High	9.6–56 Kbps, (Target to 100 Kbps)	99–99.99%	2–300 sec
2	EV Charging	Highly decentralized	High	High	High	9.6–56 Kbps, 100 Kbps	99–99.99%	2–300 sec
3	Demand Response	Highly decentralized	High	High	High	14 Kbps–100 Kbps per node/device	99–99.99%	500 ms to several hundred sec
4	Distribution Subsystem	Moderately decentralized	High	High	High	9.6–56 Kbps, 100 Kbps	99–99.99%	15–200 ms
5	Substation Automation	Moderately decentralized	High	High	High	9.6–56 Kbps, 100 Kbps	99–99.99%	15–200 ms
6	Transmission Link Monitoring	Moderately decentralized	High	High	High	9.6–56 Kbps, 100 Kbps	99–99.99%	15–200 ms
7	Home Energy Management	Highly decentralized	High	High	High	9.6–56 Kbps, 100 Kbps	99–99.99%	300–2000 ms
8	Advanced Metering Infrastructures (AMI)	Highly decentralized	High	High	High	10–100 Kbps/node, 500 Kbps for Backhaul	99–99.99%	2000 ms
9	Asset Management	Moderately decentralized	High	High	High	56 Kbps	99%	2000 ms
10	WASA	Yes	High	High	High	600–1500 Kbps	99.999–99.9999%	15–200 ms

execution. It may enable the smart homes to behave as independent candidates for intelligent SCADA control. Similarly, the xEVs may also be coordinated via home energy management systems (HEMS), micro-grid integration, etc. Moreover, the IoT-equipped autonomous vehicles must tap to the dynamic data generated by SG utilities, viz. state of charge (SOC) and load predictions, tariff structures, and miscellaneous attributes that ensure grid stability. Other ideas integrate enormous numbers of small power producing entities into the grid and require non-trivial control adjustments to keep the grid stable. Thus, scalability will be a key requirement—scalability of a kind that dwarfs what the industry has done up to now, and demands a shift to new computational approaches.

2.3 Consistency

The demand for consistency-preserving decision-making analytics is being emerged as the need of the hour to carry up mission-critical requirements of SG utilities. For SG, consistency is a broad term associated with ACID (Atomicity, Consistency, Isolation, and Durability) guarantees, support for state machine replication, virtual synchrony, and deployments having only limited count of node failures. To understand the consistency need of SG use-cases, consider an xEV fleet where multiple vehicles are concurrently communicating to SCADA system over different network paths that lead to different servers that provide the control information. Even if the vehicles are under distributed control, they all should receive the right control instructions. Minute deviation from the communication synchrony may lead to catastrophic deformation in the fleet dynamics. Here, the control data needn't be computed in some sort of radically new, decentralized manner, rather the SCADA computation itself could be localized. Think of contemporary cloud systems where one copy of a video of an important news event is used as a starter. Since replication of data and computation is key to scalability, consistency issues may arise when a client platform requests data from a service replica. In that situation, it is really complex to answer, is this really the most current version of the control policy? Notice that consistency and real-time guarantees are in some ways at odds. For instance, if we want to provide identical data to some set of clients, failures may cause delays, i.e. we lose real-time guarantees of minimal delay. If we want minimal delay, we run the risk that a lost packet or a sudden crash could leave some clients without the most recent data.

2.4 Real-Time Analytics

In order to understand the latency profile of SG applications, we group them into three categories with loosely defined boundaries. The data latency hierarchy of typical SG applications is shown in Figure 14.3. Installation of transmission infrastructures, power delivery road maps, etc. come under Group-A type applications with relaxed timing requirements. For such applications, current computing configurations are able to guarantee service-level agreements (SLA) because of their informal service constraints. Group-B applications are those that need super-paced communication and transport channels, for instance, circulating the smart meter data to regulate SCADA control. Such applications can tolerate delays to only unit to few or tens of microseconds, often caused due to node failures or connectivity disruptions. However, Group-B applications

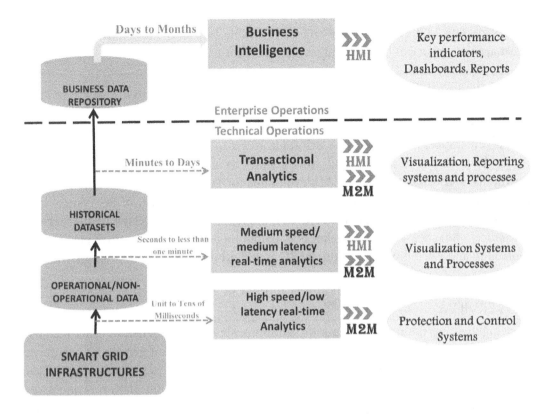

FIGURE 14.3   Service latency hierarchy for typical smart grid applications.

demand real-time response even in the presence of failures. Group-C includes mission-critical SG applications that require high assurance, stringent privacy and security enforcements, robust access control, and consistent behavior across the nodes of action. For such applications acting on real-time data, the BDA framework may produce glitches if exposed stale data. For instance, the SCADA system employed in a modern data-driven SG is so timed that it can malfunction when operated over ubiquitous TCP/IP protocols and cannot sustain the out-of-the-box TCP flow control latencies [24].

2.5 Privacy and Security

The SG applications when embedded with IoT endpoints need robust protective mechanisms that ensure restricted and entrusted access to critical data. The SG confidential data might be of interests to the criminals or manipulating entities seeking edge to energy trade, thus exposing the system to cyber attacks. The denial-of-service (DoS) or distributed denial-of-service (DDoS) attacks on AMI or vehicular data may cause severe vulnerabilities such as bandwidth drainage, excessive CPU utilization, irregular memory surges, and halting the client's or host's operations, etc. [25]. Thus, any computing framework designed for vehicular applications or smart homes should be equipped with robust aggregation algorithms that can guarantee the privacy and data anonymization of respective stakeholders and that motivate consumer's participation [26]. Other security aspects that need to be addressed properly in smart home, xEV use-cases are data outage, threat detection, and cyber-physical attacks [2]. Table 14.2 shows the most important SG threat agents, which can be found in similar form, for example in [42].

2.6 Availability and Reliability

The NIST Guidelines for cyber-security defines availability as the most important security objective for power system reliability [27]. The increasing connectedness due to IoT penetration may expose the SG applications to disrupted Internet traffic caused due to DoS or DDoS attacks and consequently to non-deterministic power failures, brownouts, and blackouts. The SCADA solutions for HEMS, xEV fleet charging utilities still needs high-reliability enforcements because a minor relinquish of SG control layer may put it at grave risk of damage or even complete meltdown. Design of a structured, methodical, holistic, and comprehensive computing model that encompasses both availability and reliability dimensions of SG is still a billion dollar research question.

3 CLOUD AND FOG-ASSISTED CLOUD FOR SMART GRID—A SYNOPTIC OVERVIEW

After highlighting the major computing requirements of future generation SG architectures in Section 2, in this section, we examine the current state of generic CC platforms towards fulfilling these requirements. We also demystify the fact of how fog-assisted cloud or simply FC paradigms will serve as potential ally to cloud platforms and assess how far such a noble mix of both computation models will be successful in satisfying the high assurance and mission-critical computing needs of next-generation SG. It is to be noted that here we present practical realization/status of SG across these aspects, not what proposals/and theoretical solutions provided/found in the literatures.

3.1 Decentralization

The platform as a service (PaaS) resources provided by Cloud Service Providers (CSP) can be hired to install the SCADA systems, a significant portion of which can be shared across power providers, ISOs, distributed generation sources, and decentralized energy markets. For market operations, the PaaS-based analytics will maintain transparency at varying levels of granularity. The web applications running in Software as a Service (SaaS)

TABLE 14.2 Major smart grid threat agents.

	Threat agent	Description
1	Nations, States	Seeking to gain information or cause harm for strategic or political reasons
2	Terrorists	Organizations or individual motivated by ideological or political reasons
3	Malicious attacker	Organizations or individuals seeking to cause harm
4	Activists	Groups or individual motivated socially or politically
5	Economic intruders	Organizations or individual motivated by financial revenue or competitive advantage
6	Recreational criminals	Individuals seeking entertainment or self-promotion, e.g., hackers
7	Hazards	Natural disasters, accidents, human errors

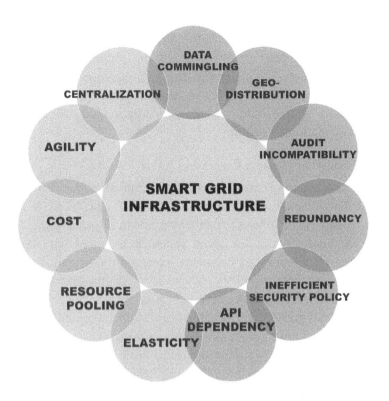

FIGURE 14.4 A summary of opportunities and challenges in a cloud-controlled smart grid.

mode allows authenticated web access to track the status of IoT endpoints. Use of cloud data centers leveraged with high-performance processing elements, for BDA in electrified transportation, will ensure robustness and resiliency in accommodating xEV fleet of any size.

However, the contemporary cloud deployments are still unable to capture the dynamic context of decentralized SG nodes embedded in IoT technology. In cloud-based SG operations, since the visibility delineations are defined by third-party cloud vendors, discrepancies may occur due to biased favors. For illustration, let us consider a decentralized energy market where the xEVs participate in dual mode, i.e., in G2V mode for charging and V2G mode for discharging. In V2G mode, the xEVs will sell the stored electricity into the energy market following an incentive policy. Since the V2G integration and recommendation policy is often done via aggregators, there may be the case that the cloud market policy is more inclined to aggregator's payoff. In that situation, the xEV customers may be deprived of appropriate paybacks. Moreover, in a cloud-based control policy, the degree of transparency enforcements is still in the hand of cloud business giants. Under these circumstances, there may be a slight abuse of decentralization.

The FC platforms, using the intelligence provided in the geo-distributed Fog Computing Nodes (FCN), will provide support for both context and situational awareness. Here, the power-generating bodies may utilize the synchrophasor data from decentralized SCADA components such as Phasor Measurement Units (PMUs) and Phasor Data

Concentrators (PDCs) processed in FCNs, in order to have context-aware operational visibility of SG dynamics. This will enable to prepare themselves respond intelligently to any disturbances that can have catastrophic effects, leading to sudden blackouts or brownouts. As for the same V2G example, the xEV end-user may form communities and rely on local computations performed in associated FCN. In that case, the xEVs will be dependent not only on the "hidden hands of energy market" but also on the outputs of its own recommendation algorithms.

3.2 Scalability, Consistency, and Real-Time Analytics

The cloud-based computational transformation has resulted in the displacement of traditional SCADA-based state estimation models. The traditional SCADA sub-systems are getting derelict because of the inherent scalability problem associated with SG components when deployed on a large scale. The cloud system is bestowed with large numbers of lightweight, inexpensive servers thus becoming irreversibly dominant to support scalable analytical solutions from large numbers of sensors, actuators, customers, and other SG stakeholder's data. A single CC data center might have storage and computing capabilities tens or hundreds of times greater than all of the world's supercomputing facilities combined. This motivates the SG community to migrate high-performance computing (HPC) applications into these data centers. Over time, the cloud PaaS services leave counter-incentive prospects for industry investment in faster HPC systems. Moreover, the horizontal as well as vertical extendibility support provided by cloud platforms enables the SG utilities to expeditiously respond to any market or regulatory changes and to the state-of-the-art products and services. In order to have a detailed, real-time tracking IoT devices' states and transitions, the future SG infrastructures are planned with deployment of a large number of sensors and smart meters (AMI) across various points of the grid. For real-time monitoring of SG applications, the cloud data centers obtain two-way communication and relay data from wireless sensor networks (WSN), and disseminate it for proactive diagnosis and timely response. Fault diagnosis is a mission-critical task, i.e., any erroneous context can lead to transient faults or blackouts in worst case. On the transmission and distribution side, the cloud services can be employed to collect real-time information of wide-area situational awareness (WASA), power grid State of Reserve (SoR), etc, while from the consumer's perspective; real-time estimates of anticipated usage through AMI enables DR controls, thus improving energy utilization efficiency.

To have an uninterrupted SG dynamics, any computing paradigm must be adept to the timing constraints and even if some servers' fiascos occur, the sub-systems should heal themselves with just graceful degradation in QoS and QoE. The contemporary cloud platforms are well matched to Group-A type applications described in Section 2. Though current cloud systems do support Group-B-like services requiring real-time responses, the response time can be disrupted by transient Internet congestion events, or even a single server failure. However, it still lacks the technologies for hosting applications that come under Group-C.

Talking about scalability–consistency preservations, the current cloud vendors seem unilaterally focused to scalability challenge. They are deploying massive but weak storage and processing configurations that often "embrace inconsistency." For high assurance applications, they seem to be annoyed by scalability consistency dilemma. The business behavior is more dedicated to the motto "serve more customers" rather than "serve more critical customers." The cloud-based BDA tools are more exposed to stale data to respond to user's vectored requests, and in such scenarios, the users are made to deal with this. In general, the cloud giants employ the embrace of the Consistency Availability and Partitioning (CAP) [27] to justify their consistency–scalability tradeoffs. The SG applications feed into a service spectrum supporting wide degree of shared access, and thus poor scaling of consistency is not feasible. Though the CAP theorem can also be formalized under weaker assumptions, but the clouds make stronger assumptions in practice and cite such folk logic for offering weak consistency guarantees, although they consider strict consistency assurances for their own needs.

3.3 Privacy and Security

In the context of SG applications security here is to mean the safety and stability of the power grid, rather than protection against malice, which come under the privacy umbrella. The malignancy of casual justification of CAP theorem is manifested in the current position of SG cloud security. In current SG designs, all data finds its way into cloud storages that comprise a huge number of HPC servers and other storage elements having peculiar horizontal and vertical elasticity. Unfortunately, the existing cloud-based security and privacy enforcements are precisely erratic, and many a times the cloud operators became evil if they are intended to do so. In a competitive cum shared cloud SG environments, the worry is that the rivals may spy on property data, leading to cyber-physical war (CPW) in extreme cases. Such platforms though always guarantee that the data center will be on and the applications will keep running, but when analyzed at finer depths, they are still far from ideal for discrete data items and individual computations.

Gartner[1] claimed that the cloud platforms are fraught with security risks and recommends the SG customers to put rigorous questions and specifications before undertaking any service from the cloud service providers [33,34]. They should also consider a guaranteed security assessment from a neutral third party prior to making any commitment. Table 14.3 shows seven key security risks identified by Gartner from perspective of current CSP [33]. The woeful protection services of current cloud deployments often stimulate the cloud vendors to recapitulate their security management folks to "not be evil." Rigorous efforts are on headway across the power system and transportation electrification communities to come up with SG cloud models and platforms, leveraged with robust protective contrivances, where the stakeholders could entrust the storage of sensitive and critical data even under concurrent share and access environments [26].

3.4 Availability Reliability and High Assurance Computing

A subset of SG applications require hardware and software solutions that are "everytime on." Any interruption in computing services may cause increased costs and many

---

[1] www.gartner.com/it-glossary/smart-grid

TABLE 14.3 Key security risks encountered in cloud computing [27].

	Security Risks	Risk description
1	Administrator access	Server provider manager handling sensitive information
2	Audit	Suppliers refused to external audit and certification of security risks
3	Data location	Unknown data location
4	Data isolation	Multi-tenant data shared resource isolation
5	Data recovery	Suppliers of data backup and recovery capabilities
6	Investigative support	Suppliers inappropriate or illegal behavior is difficult to provide evidence to support
7	Long-term survival	Service stability, continuity, migration

a times it may lead to loss of consumer confidence. Because CC by its nature relies primarily on the Internet connectivity, the SG utility vendors interested in starting or expanding their business strategies with current cloud platforms must have rigorous IT consultations for showing them ways to schedule network resources such as bandwidth levels, which will suffice their mobility and availability constraints [7,19]. While conducting technical operations in such remote data centers, the control of SG stakeholders over the infrastructure will be seized. Thus, the manageability is not as robust as when they are used to with SCADA workstations and other controllers.

According to the resource protocols employed in CC, the user's physical control over the outsourced data is relinquished permanently, and hidden data breaches from untrusted cloud vendor(s) may jeopardize SG data confidentiality, data integrity, and data availability. Switching from traditional power grid to SG subsystems, when introduced to an IoT space, may endanger the energy sector with substantial risk factors, an issue that needs to get fixed since its inception. The penetration of autonomous EVs for instance into the modern road transport generates avalanche of multi-dimensional data sets, an asset which if mishandled may befool the execution of whole SG ecosystem. In fact, the data generated due to Cloud-IoT integrated transportation telematics and AMI can prove to be harmful to its stakeholders, specifically for privacy and security [13]. Thus, it's an earnest need for the stakeholders to be assured with stringent protection protocols and be inert from these vulnerabilities. Such scenario necessitates incorporating robust risk analysis procedures that will evaluate and quantify the computational and business risks that persist in such critical infrastructures. Selection followed by implementation of proper risk analysis paradigms is itself a full-fledged realm to dwell on. Risks perceived to be minor in inception phase later elicits tougher public concerns. Though the "pay-for-usage" protocols of CC business models are efficient in satisfying the bulky analytics and computational tasks, the bliss transforms into worries when the applications demand virtually zero-latency services and when the data stream congests the bandwidth-restricted communication buses [13]. Table 14.4 summarizes some yet urgent research topics for a cloud-controlled SG. The aforesaid discussions yet CC, as we've shown, lacks key features that power control and similar SG functionality will need. These include security, consistency, real-time assurances, ways to protect the privacy of sensitive data, and other needs.

TABLE 14.4 Highest priority research thrusts for a cloud-controlled smart grid system.

1	Assessment and quantification of the kinds of service guarantees that cloud computing solutions can offer.
2	Quantify the kinds of service guarantees that are required for a new generation of smart grid control paradigms.
3	Mechanisms of how to reintroduce robust trust properties in data center settings.
4	Efficient standards/protocols to quantify/resolve the possible physical/cyber-attacks against a centrally managed smart grid.
5	Improve attack tolerance and fault diagnosis.
6	Learn to build an Internet with better availability, reliability, and interoperability.

4 FOG COMPUTING FOR BIG DATA ANALYTICS IN SMART GRID

The underlying notion of FC is the distribution of store, communicate, control, and compute resources from the edge to the remote cloud of things continuum. The FC architecture may be either fully distributed, mostly centralized, or somewhere in between. In addition to the virtualization facilities, specialized hardware and software modules can be employed for implementing fog applications. In the context of an IoT-aided SG [37], a customized fog platform will permit domain-specific applications to run anywhere, reducing the need for specialized applications dedicated just for the cloud, just for the endpoints, or just for the edge devices. It will enable applications from decentralized vendors to run on the same physical machine without reciprocated interference. Further, the FC architecture will provide a common lifecycle management framework for all applications, offering capabilities for com posing, configuring, dispatching, activating and deactivating, adding and removing, and updating applications. It will further provide a secure execution environment for SG services and applications. Among the solid list of fog specialties, offered by fog–cloud and fog–fog interfaces, we here define five key advantages of typical FC architecture over generic cloud models, abbreviated as SCALE [43]. Moreover, a summary of performance comparison of Cloud and FC in SG applications is presented in Table 14.5.

4.1 Security

FC enables SG enterprises to standardize on security architectures across the whole range of IoT platforms, vendors, and customers. By design, FC accommodates the unique architectures and vulnerabilities of the IoT. It operates in the cloud-to-things continuum, rather than at the perimeter, to offer distinct privacy advantages. Since fog is built from the ground up for cloud-to-thing IoT security, it offers a new level of defense above and beyond IT perimeter security. The key denominator for how FC resolves security issues for the IoT-SG applications is that it enables service (viz., computing and control, storage, and networking, etc.) continuum that bridges the gap between cloud and things.

4.2 Cognition

The most peculiar property of an FC platform is its cognizance to client-centric objectives, also termed as geo-distributed intelligence. The FC framework is aware of the context of customer requirements and can best determine where to carry out the computing, storage, and control functions along the cloud-to-thing continuum. Thus, the fog applications can be populated at the vicinity of SG endpoints and are ensured to be better aware of and closely reflect customer requirements.

4.3 Efficiency

In FC architectures, the compute, storage, and control functions can be pooled and disseminated anywhere across the cloud and the edge nodes, hence acquiring full advantage of the diverse resources available along the cloud-to-thing continuum. For IoT-aided SG applications, the FC model allows utilities and applications to leverage the otherwise idle computing, storage, and networking resources abundantly available both along the network edge (viz. HAN, NAN, MAN, etc.) and end-user devices such as smart meters, smart home appliances, connected vehicles, and network edge routers. Fog's closer proximity to the IoT end-points will enable it to be more closely integrated with consumer-centric applications.

4.4 Agility

By the virtue of agility, it is usually much faster and affordable to experiment with both client and edge devices in FC. Rather than waiting for vendors of large network and cloud boxes to initiate or adopt an innovation, the FC will make it easier to create an open marketplace for individuals and peer teams to use open application programming interfaces (API), open software development kits (SDKs), and the proliferation of mobile devices to scale, innovate, develop, deploy, and operate innovative services.

4.5 Latency

Since FC enables data analytics at the network edge, it can support latency-sensitive functions for SG like CPS. This is essential for developing not only stable control systems but also for the tactile Internet vision, i.e., to enable embedded AI applications with millisecond response requirements. Such advantages in turn enable new services

TABLE 14.5 Performance comparison of cloud and fog computing in smart grid context.

	Characteristics and Requirements	Pure Cloud Platform	Fog-Assisted Cloud Platform
1	Geo-distribution	Centralized	Distributed
2	Context/Location Awareness	No	Yes
3	Service Node Distribution	Within the Internet	At core as well as edges
4	Latency	High	Low
5	Delay Jitter	High	Low
6	Client-Server Separation	Remote/Multiple hops	Single hop
7	Security	Not defined	Defined degree of security
8	Node Population	Few	Very large
9	Mobility Support	Limited	Rich mobility support
10	Last Mile Connectivity Support	Leased line	Wired/Wireless
11	Real-time Analytics	Supported	Supported
12	En-route Data Attacks/DoS	High probability	Low probability

and business models, and may help broaden revenues and reduce cost, thereby accelerating IoT-aided SG rollouts.

Motivated by the multi-faceted advantages of fog architectures as described above, the pressing economic as well as environmental arguments for the overhaul of the pure cloud architecture, we in this section propose a three-tier fog-assisted cloud analytics framework for IoT-aided SG. Figure 14.3 shows a three-tier fog-assisted CC architecture where a substantial proportion of SG store, control, and computation is non-trivially hybridized to geo-distributed FCNs, alongside the mega-data centers. The hybridization objective is to overcome the disruption caused by the penetration of IoT devices into SG infrastructures, which requires active proliferation of control, storage, networking, and computational resources across the heterogeneous edges or end-points. The Big Data in SG can be defined through seven V's namely volume, variety, velocity, value, variability, veracity, and visualization. In addition, it also exhibits unique location-aware characteristics: geo-distribution, requiring distributed analytics, communication, control, and storage resources closer to the end-users along the cloud-to-things continuum [37]. The proposed framework facilitates the comprehensive enactment of IoT services in fog landscape supporting BDA of SG data and guaranteeing optimal resource provisioning in the fog.

The layer nearest to ground is termed as physical schema or data generator layer, which primarily comprises a wide range of intelligent IoT-enabled devices scattered across the SG network. This is the sensing network consisting of several non-invasive, highly reliable, low-cost wireless sensory nodes and smart mobile devices that are deployed for capturing situational context information from SG verticals. Thus, the physical components of this tier comprise RFIDs, M2M (machine-to-machine) devices, cameras, infrared sensors, laser scanners, global positioning (GPS), and miscellaneous data collection entities. Since the data capturing/generating devices are widely distributed at numerous SG endpoints, the multi-dimensional data streams produced from these geo-spatially distributed sensors have to be processed as a coherent whole. However, this layer may occasionally filter data streams for local consumption (edge computing) and offloads the rest to upper tiers through dedicated gateways. The entities in this layer may be abstracted into application-specific logical clusters, directly or indirectly influenced by the expediency of SG operations. As shown in Figure 14.5, the first cluster (C1) represents vehicular applications where the intelligent Autonomous Vehicles (AV) equipped with sensing units such as on-board sensors (OBS) and the roadside infrastructures such as RSUs and Smart Traffic Sensors (STS) organize themselves to form vehicular fogs, as shown in Figure 14.6.

Often these transportation telematics support such as cellular telephony, OBU, RSU, and smart wearable devices may uncover the computational as well as networking capabilities latent in the underutilized vehicular resources [37]. The underutilized vehicular resources may occasionally be transformed into communicational and analytics use, where a collaborative multitude of end-user clients or near-user edge devices carry out communication and computation, based on better utilization of individual storage, communication, and computational resources of each vehicle [36]. Similarly,

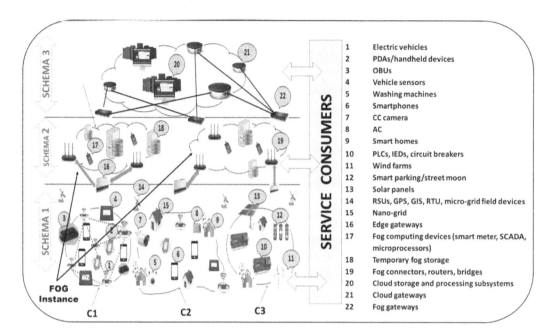

FIGURE 14.5   Multi-tier fog computing architecture for IoT-aided smart grid applications.

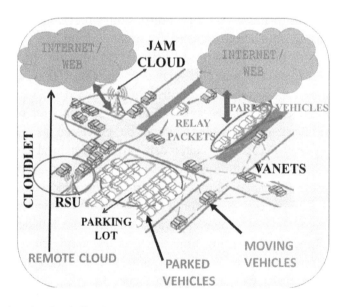

FIGURE 14.6   Vehicular fog (adhoc) computing scenario.

presence of clusters (C2) could also be traced in smart home networks (HAN) that have noteworthy contributions in SG operational dynamics. The intelligent IoT-equipped home gadgets, such as washing machines, AC, freezes, parking lots, and CC camera, are potentially active data generation entities and may also be augmented with actuators to provide storage, analysis, and computational support for satisfying the prompt and local decision-making services (multi-access edge computing) [22].

The third but not the least cluster C3 depicts a similar structure constituted by utilities involved at the power-flow ends of SG, viz. micro-nano grid, PLCs (HAN, MAN, etc.), automated circuit breakers, and other entities associated to whole range of SG generation, transmission, and distribution services. The smart nodes within such clusters sense and cultivate the heterogeneous physical attributes and transmit it to the upper layers through dedicated edge gateways. However, a significant portion of data generated within these physical clusters are accumulated at the interim across access points such as GPS, GIS, RSU, remote terminal units (RTU), intelligent electronic devices (IED), phasor data concentrators (PDC), and other field arrays.

Layer 2 is termed as FC layer, comprising low-power intelligent fog devices such as SCADA, smart meters, routers, switches high-end proxy servers, intelligent agent, and commodity hardware, having peculiar ability of storage, computation, and packet routing. The software-defined networking (SDN) assembles the physical clusters of layer 1, forming virtualized intercluster private networks (ICPN) that route the generated data to the FCNs in layer 2. The fog devices and its associated entities form geographically distributed virtual computing snapshots that are mapped to layer-1 devices, in order to serve the mission-critical computing demands of SG. Each FN is mapped to and responsible for a local cluster of sensors covering a neighborhood or a small community achieving data analytics in virtually real time. However, since the

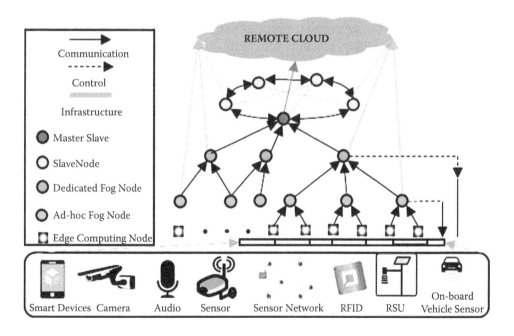

FIGURE 14.7   Data/control flow among FCNs in layer 2.

IoT devices in layer 1 are often dynamic (viz. vehicular sensors), robust mobility management techniques need to be employed that can guarantee flexible association of layer-1 devices with FCNs in layer 2.

Often, the FCNs are paralleled to other nodes lying below in the hierarchy to undertake processing tasks. Also, in some cases, the FCN may form further sub-trees of FCNs, with each node at higher depth in the tree managed by the ones at lower depth, in master slave paradigm. A typical association of such hierarchies is depicted in Figure 14.7. As an illustration, consider the SG power transmission scenario where the FCNs operate on spatial and temporal data to identify potential hazardous events in transmission lines such as power thefts and network intrusion. In such circumstances, these computing nodes will shut down the power supply from the distribution sub-station and the data analysis results will be feed-backed and reported to the upper layer (from village substation to SCADA, to city-wise power distribution center or to generation bodies) for complex, historical, and large-scale behavior analysis and condition monitoring. Hence, the distributed BDA activities from multi-tier FCNs (followed by aggregation analytics in many use-cases) performed at layer 2 will deliver localized "reflex" decisions to avoid potential contingencies. Since a significant fraction of generated IoT-SG applications data don't require to be dispatched to the remote clouds, response latency and bandwidth consumption problems could be easily fixed.

The uppermost layer is the CC layer consisting of network of mega data centres that provide city-wide SG monitoring and global centralization. This is in contrast to localization, geo-distributed intelligence, low latency, and context awareness support provided by layer 2. The HPC processors and storage devices deployed at this layer are focused to produce complex, long-term, and city-wide behavioral analytics such as large-scale event detection, long-term pattern recognition, and relationship modeling, in order to support dynamic decision-making. This will ensure also SG utilities to perform WASA [44], wide-area demand response (WADA), and resource management in case of any natural disaster or large-scale service interruption, blackouts, and brownouts. The processing output of layer 2 can be categorized into two dimensions. The first one comprises analysis and status reports and the corresponding data that demand large-scale and long-term behavior analysis and condition monitoring. Such datasets are offloaded to CC mega data centers situated in layer 3 via high-speed WAN gateways and links. The other portion of output is the inferences, decisions, and quick feedback control to the aligned data consumers.

5 SERVICE-ORIENTED SOFTWARE ARCHITECTURE (SOSA) FOR FOG-BASED BIG DATA ANALYTICS ON SMART GRID DATA

It is clear that the efficiency of multi-tier FC model presented in Section 4 depends on how the resources are cached, scheduled, and provisioned among the computing nodes at different layers, with varying range of store and processing capabilities. For explaining the operations of FC model in the context of SG applications, in this section, we define a SOSA that explains the execution and control flow of BDA in IoT-aided SG environment. Any SG utility coupled with its processing and computational requirements nails down numerous key objectives to be met. The software framework shown in Figure 14.8 consists of four quadrants (**Q1, Q2, Q3,** and **Q4** being **XY′, XY, XY′,** and **X′Y′** coordinate in Cartesian system, respectively); each quadrant schematically depicts what and how to realize such objectives.

5.1 Resource Management (Q1)

Contrast to cloud platforms where the physical resources are mostly homogenous and managed centrally, the FCNs are heterogeneous in nature and deployed in a variety of environments including core, edge, access networks, and other network endpoints. Thus, a typical FC architecture should facilitate seamless resource management (see **Q1** in Figure 14.8) across the diverse set of hardware and software platforms [26]. The hardware platforms have varying levels of RAM, secondary storage, and real states, facilitating peculiar SG functionalities. Moreover, these platforms host numerous breeds of operating systems (OSs) and software applications having dedicated APIs, thus leveraging a strong list of analytics operations. The network infrastructure designed for FC is also heterogeneous in nature, ranging from high-speed links connecting enterprise data centers and the core, to multiple wireless access technologies (e.g. 3G/4G, LTE, WiFi, etc.) towards the edge. For having a full manifestation of such distributed FC architecture and for scalable and efficient virtualization of the

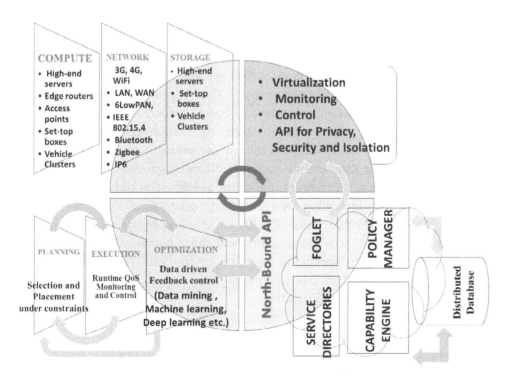

FIGURE 14.8   Service-oriented software architecture for fog computing in smart grid.

key resource classes (shown in second quadrant (**Q2**) of Fig. 14.7), the FCNs rely on the following three key technology enablers:

5.1.1 Compute

In order to virtualize both the computing and I/O resources, proper assignment of compute resources, such as hypervisors, is necessary.

5.1.2 Network

For efficiently managing the network resources listed above, viable and robust Network Virtualization Infrastructures such as Software-Defined Networking (SDN) and Network Functions Virtualization (NFV) techniques should be employed.

5.1.3 Storage

It defines a Virtual File System (VFS) and a Virtual Block and/or Object Store.

5.2 Abstraction Support (Q2)

The sensors and actuators available in the present-day marketplace are not capable of interfacing directly with the FCNs. A software abstraction layer (**Q2**) makes it logically possible to interface such devices with the allocated FCN(s). Abstraction also ensures multi-dimensional generated data to be utilized for BDA activities in upper layers' system and software components. Abstraction is also key to multi-vendor interoperability for both IoT objects and FCNs. It hides the platform heterogeneity and leverages a uniform and programmable interface for seamless resource management and control. It also motivates the developers to design generic APIs for monitoring, provisioning, and controlling the storage, compute, and networking resources. Moreover, the multi-tenant virtualization support provided by the abstraction layer enables vendors and developers to run multiple OSs or service containers on a physical machine, thus improving resource utilization. If properly defined, such abstraction layers can also enable vendors to share meta-data of FC architectural elements they support, thereby fostering multi-vendor data interoperability and service composability. The sharing mechanism also leverages cross-layer optimizations, viz., optimally routing the data streams among FCNs using information-centric networks (ICN) or to create dynamic fog network topologies, as with SDN and NFV. At the "south side" of the architectural application layer, there exist micro-services like Fog Connector Services (FCS) equipped with a range of APIs for enabling higher layer fog services to communicate with devices, sensors, actuators, and other platforms, using the any-edge protocol of choice. The FCSs operate on top of the abstraction layer to translate the data produced and communicated by the IoT "things" into common data structures/formats and then send it into the core infrastructures.

5.3 Utilities for Distributed Service Orchestration (DSO) (Q3)

This quadrant (**Q3**) defines the policies and protocols for dynamic, policy-based life-cycle management of FC services. The orchestration functionality is as distributed as the underlying FC infrastructures, and is realized through the following key components:

5.3.1 Fog Orchestration Control Block (FOCB)

The FOCB is an intelligent software agent running on every FCN having reasonably small footprint but can provide enough support for the orchestration functionality and performance requirements. It could be embedded in numerous FCNs as well as IoT endpoints. It utilizes the abstraction layer APIs to monitor the health and state of the physical machine(s) and also the services installed on that machine. The FOCB serves as the key DSO entity for performing life-cycle management activities such as standing up/down guest OSs, service containers, provisioning and tearing down service instances, etc. Through abstraction layer APIs, the FOCB invokes functions necessary for programmatic management and control. These functionalities can be implemented by the whole set of entities over which the interaction of FOCB is spanned, viz. physical machine, hypervisor, guest OSs, service containers, and service instances.

5.3.2 Policy Manager

The policy manager aids the orchestration framework to facilitate policy-based service routing, i.e., to route an incoming service request to the appropriate service instance that conforms to the relevant business policies. The distributed control provides better resiliency, scalability, and faster orchestration for geographically distributed deployments. Business policies specified via dashboard-style user interface (UI) are pushed to a distributed policy database. When triggered by an incoming service request, the policy manager gathers relevant policies, for instance those pertaining to the service, subscriber, and tenant, from the policy metafile. It also retrieves metadata about currently active service instances from the services directory. The policy manager utilizes these two data attributes in order to find an active service instance that satisfies the policy constraints and forwards the service request to that instance.

In case no such instance is available, policy manager invokes the capability engine (**Q3**) to create a new instances. The later identifies a ranked list of FCNs whose capabilities match the policy constraints for instantiating a new service and handover this list to the life-cycle manager that provisions the service for each fog device. The life-cycle manager may then extend to the policy repository to identify device, service, and network configuration policies while provisioning any new instance.

5.3.3 Distributed Database

It is a distributed, persistent storage to store policies and resource meta-data (capability, performance, etc). It supports high transaction rate update and retrieval. Though complex to implement, it is ideal for augmenting FCN scalability and fault-tolerance. This database is used to store both application data and necessary meta-data to aid in FC service orchestration. Sample meta-data may include:

a. FN's hardware and software capabilities to enable service instantiation on a platform with matching capabilities.

b. Health and other state information of FCNs and other running service instances for load balancing, and generating performance reports.

c. Business policies that should be enforced throughout a service's life cycle such as those related to security, configuration, etc.

5.4 Automated Workflow for Context Awareness and Distributed Intelligence (Q4)

A customized SOSA for FC defines numerous north-bound APIs that applications use to effectively leverage the processing and commutations across FCNs. They may be either data APIs that allow the consumer application to have access to the fog-distributed database (defined in **Q3**), or control APIs that define the protocols for how to deploy the consumer applications over the FC platform. For illustration, here we provide some governing API instances that can be defined to leverage the execution of a Vehicle-to-Fog (V2F)-based xEV charging framework.

5.4.1 PutStore()
To store/delete/update attributes, data and meta-data related to vehicle dynamics (speed, geo-location, driving profiles, SOC of xEV battery, EVRA parameters, etc.) into the fog-distributed data store.

5.4.2 GetStore()
To retrieve/fetch attributes, data, and meta-data related to vehicle dynamics (speed, geo-location, driving profiles, SOC of xEV battery, EVRA parameters, etc.) into the fog-distributed data store.

5.4.3 CallService()
To request for a service/utility instance that satisfies application-specific constraints. For the V2F use-case, the criteria may be of minimum charging tariff, shortest traveling distance, and minimum queuing delay in decreasing degree of criticality, etc.

5.4.4 CreateService()
To create/setup new service instances satisfying application-specific criteria similar to *CallService()*.

5.4.5 DefinePolicy()
Defines application-specific or consumer-centric policy-sets for multiple stakeholders (providers, subscribers etc.) involved in orchestration framework.

5.4.6 InstallPolicy()/UpdatePolicy()
Calls for installing/updating application-specific or consumer-centric policy-sets for multiple stakeholders (providers, subscribers etc.) involved in orchestration framework.

5.4.7 CreateReports()/GenerateStatus()
To create/generate status reports of FCN health, status, and dynamics.

Besides, this quadrant defines control flow across modules that are involved in embedding context-aware intelligence across the FC nodes. It may be a data collector module that uses plug-in and virtual sensors to interface with the data generators in the physical layer or a mobility management module defining inter/intra layer mappings of network components. The mobility can be categorized as physical-to-logical cluster mobility (in layer 1), logical cluster-to-fog instance mobility (data generators (DG) to FCN schema), FCN to data centers (DC) mobility, etc. The context-awareness policies can also be enforced by location-aware, activity–aware, and time-aware modules. The users may combine/aggregate activities identified by activity-aware modules and generate multiple queries. The location-aware modules are capable of tracking when the device enters into or moves away from a certain area while the time-aware modules store the time-stamps corresponding to different actions/transitions of fog devices, FCNs, etc. Context data from such modules may also be aggregated to other sensing parameters, which are successively retrieved by multiple plug-ins and referred in different queries.

6 SUMMARY

In this chapter, we first identified the mission-critical computational requirements of emerging SG applications in the realm of IoT. We then examined the current state of CC platforms in fulfilling those needs. Correspondingly, we also analysed the suitability of FC in accomplishing the shortcomings associated with cloud-based big data treatment for SG services. In essence, we proposed a multi-tier FC framework, tailored to support, store, compute, and process requirements for BDA in SG and provided a synoptic overview of the varying network and device types in SG deployment scenarios. Finally, we provide a service oriented software architecture (SOSA) to explain the operations of FC-based analytics on SG data.

REFERENCES

1. National Institute of Standards and Technology, "Special Publication 1108 NIST Framework and Roadmap for Smart Grid Interoperability Standards", *Nist Spec. Publ.*, pp. 1–90, 2010.
2. J. Gao, Y. Xiao, J. Liu, W. Liang, and C. L. P. Chen, "A Survey of Communication/ Networking in Smart Grids", *Futur. Gener. Comput. Syst.*, vol. 28, no. 2, pp. 391–404, 2012.
3. P. D. Diamantoulakis, V. M. Kapinas, and G. K. Karagiannidis, "Big Data Analytics for Dynamic Energy Management in Smart Grids", *Big Data Res.*, vol. 2, no. 3, pp. 94–101, 2015.
4. DOE, "Smart Grid Research & Development – Multi-Year Program Plan (MYPP)", *U.S. Dep. Energy – Off. Electr. Delivery Energy Reliab.*, March, p. 83, 2010.
5. S. Bera, S. Misra, and D. Chatterjee, "C2C: Community-Based Cooperative Energy Consumption in Smart Grid", *IEEE Trans. SmartGrid*, vol. 3053, no. c, p. 1, 2017.
6. K. Kaur and N. Kumar, "Smart Grid with Cloud Computing: Architecture, Security Issues and Defense Mechanism", *9th IEEE Int. Conf. Ind. Inf. Syst. ICIIS2014*, 2015.
7. M. M.Hussain, M. S. Alam, and M. M. S. Beg, "Fog Computing for Next Generation Transport – A Battery Swapping System Case Study", *Spr. J. Technol. Econ. Smart Grids Sustain. Energy*, vol. 3, no. 06, 2018.
8. M. H. Toukhy, "Data Mining Techniques for Smart Grid Load Forecasting", Master Thesis, Masdar Institute of Science and Technology, 2012.

9. Y. Saleem, S. Member, N. Crespi, S. Member, M. H. Rehmani, and R. Copeland, "Internet of Things-aided Smart Grid: Technologies, Architectures, Applications, Prototypes, and Future Research Directions", pp. 1–30, arXiv:1704.08977 (Preprint).

10. M. M. Hussain, M. S. Alam, and M. M. S. Beg, "Fog Assisted Cloud Models for Smart Grid Architectures – Comparison Study and Optimal Deployment", pp. 1–27, arXiv:1805.09254 (Preprint).

11. H. Daki, A. El Hannani, A. Aqqal, A. Haidine, and A. Dahbi, "Big Data Management in Smart Grid: Concepts, Requirements and Implementation", *J. Big Data*, Vol. 4, no. 13, pp. 1–19,

12. B. X. Yu, F. Ieee, Y. Xue, and M. Ieee, "Smart Grids: A Cyber – Physical Systems Perspective," *Proc. IEEE*, Vol. 105, no. 5, pp. 1–13, 2016.

13. D. A. Chekired and L. Khoukhi, "Smart Grid Solution for Charging and Discharging Services Based on Cloud Computing Scheduling", *IEEE Trans. Ind. Informatics*, vol. 3203, no. ICD, pp. 1–9, 2017.

14. A. Zanella, N. Bui, A. Castellani, L. Vangelista, and M. Zorzi, "Internet of Things for Smart Cities", *IEEE Internet Things J.*, vol. 1, no. 1, pp. 22–32, 2014.

15. A. Al-Fuqaha, S. Member, M. Guizani, M. Mohammadi, and S. Member, "Internet of Things: A Survey on Enabling", *IEEE Commun. Surveys Tutorials*, vol. 17, no. 4, pp. 2347–2376, 2015.

16. O. Vermesan and P. Friess (eds.), *Internet of Things – From Research and Innovation to Market Development*, River Publishers Series in Communication, 2014.

17. M. M. Hussain, M. S. Alam, M. M. S. Beg, O. Smart, and C. Toscs, "EAI Endorsed Transactions Federated Cloud Analytics Frameworks in Next Generation Transport", *EAI Endorsed Trans.*, vol. 2, no. 7, 2018.

18. R. Aburukba, "Role of Internet of Things in the Smart Grid Technology", *J. Comp. Commun.*, vol. 3, pp. 229–233, 2015.

19. S. Asri and B. Pranggono, "Impact of Distributed Denial-of-Service Attack on Advanced Metering Infrastructure", *Wirel. Pers. Commun.*, vol. 83, no. 3, pp. 2211–2223, 2015.

20. Z. Fan, Q. Chen, G. Kalogridis, S. Tan, and D. Kaleshi, "The Power of Data: Data Analytics for M2M and Smart Grid," *2012 3rd IEEE PES Innov. Smart Grid Technol. Eur. (ISGT Eur.)*, pp. 1–8, 2012.

21. Q. Wang, X. Liu, J. Du, and F. Kong, "Smart Charging for Electric Vehicles: A Survey from the Algorithmic Perspective", *IEEE Commun. Surv. Tutorials*, vol. 18, no. 2, pp. 1500–1517, 2016.

22. P. Porambage, J. Okwuibe, M. Liyanage, M. Ylianttila, and T. Taleb, "Survey on Multi-Access Edge Computing for Internet of Things Realization", pp. 1–31, 2018.

23. D. E. Bakken et al., "Smart Generation and Transmission with Coherent, Real-Time Data 1", pp. 1–62, 2010.

24. M. M. Hussain, M. S. Alam, M. M. S. Beg, and M. Asaad "Viability of Fog Methodologies in IoT Aware Smart Grid Architectures", *Proc. 1st EAI Int. Conf. Smart Grid Assisted Internet Things*. Springer.

25. M. Scarpiniti et al. "Fog of Everything: Energy-efficient Networked Computing Architectures, Research Challenges, and a Case Study", no. IEEE Access, May, 2017 DOI: 10.1109/ACCESS.2017.2702013.

26. S. Bera, S. Misra, and J. J. P. C. Rodrigues, "Cloud Computing Applications for Smart Grid: A Survey", *IEEE Trans. Parallel Distrib. Syst.*, vol. 26, no. 5, pp. 1477–1494, 2015.

27. K. Birman, L. Ganesh, and R. Renesse, "Running Smart Grid Control Software on Cloud Computing Architectures", *In Proc. Work. Comput. Needs Next Gener. Electr. Grid, pp. 1–28, 2011, Cornel University*.

28. S. Yang, J. Yao, T. Kang, and X. Zhu, "Dynamic Operation Model of the Battery Swapping Station for EV (Electric Vehicle) in Electricity Market", *Energy*, vol. 65, pp. 544–549, 2014.

29. "Global EV Outlook 2017: Two millions and counting", 2017, Whitepaper, International Energy Agency, Australia
30. M. Saqib, M. M. Hussain, M. S. Alam, M. M. S. Beg, and A. Sawant, "Smart Electric Vehicle Charging Through Cloud Monitoring and Management", *Technol. Econ. Smart Grids Sustain. Energy*, vol. 2, no. 1, p. 18, 2017.
31. M. Díaz, C. Martín, and B. Rubio, "State-of-the-Art, Challenges, and Open Issues in the Integration of Internet of Things and Cloud Computing," *J. Netw. Comput. Appl.*, Elsevier, vol. 67, May 2016, pp. 99–117.
32. M. Yigit, V. C. Gungor, and S. Baktir, "Cloud Computing for Smart Grid Applications", *Comput. Networks*, vol. 70, pp. 312–329, 2014.
33. M. M. Hussain, M. S. Alam, and M. M. S. Beg, "A FOG Computing Based Battery Swapping Model for Next Generation Transport", *Proc. 2nd Int. Conf. Commun. Comput. Network. Lecture Notes Netw. Syst.*, vol. 46, pp. 957–968
34. D. T. Hoang, P. Wang, D. Niyato, and E. Hossain, "Charging and Discharging of Plug-in Electric Vehicles (PEVs) in Vehicle-to-Grid (V2G) Systems: A Cyber Insurance-Based Model", *IEEE Access*, vol. 5, pp. 732–754, 2017.
35. F. Y. Okay and S. Ozdemir, "A Fog Computing Based Smart Grid Model", *2016 ISNCC*, vol. 10, no. 6, pp. 1–6, 2016.
36. F. Bonomi, "The Smart and Connected Vehicle and the Internet of Things", *Synchronization Telecommun.* WSTS-2013, San Jose, US, 2013.
37. X. Hou, Y. Li, M. Chen, D. Wu, D. Jin, and S. Chen, "Vehicular Fog Computing: A Viewpoint of Vehicles as the Infrastructures", *IEEE Trans. Veh. Technol.*, vol. 65, no. 6, pp. 3860–3873, 2016.
38. C. Wang, X. Li, Y. Liu, and H. Wang, "The Research on Development", in *I. Direction and Points in IoT in China Power Grid, E. and E. E.- Conference on Information Science and Engineering (ISEEE)*, pp. 245–248, vol. 1, 2014.
39. Y. F. Wang, W. M. Lin, T. Zhang, Y. Y. Ma, "Research on application and security protection of Internet of Things in Smart Grid", *IET International Conference on Information Science and Control Engineering 2012 (ICISCE 2012)*, pp. 1–5
40. L.-E. Spano, L. Niccolini, S. Di Pascoli, and G. Iannacconeluca. "No Title", *Trans. Smart Grid*, vol. 6, no.1, pp. 468–476.
41. S. Mohanty, B. N. Panda, and B. S. Pattnaik, "Implementation of a Web of Things based Smart Grid to Remotely Monitor and Control Renewable Energy Sources," in *Students' Conference on Electrical, Electronics and Computer Science (SCEECS)*, pp. 1–5, 2014.
42. E. Simmon, K. Kim, R. Lee, F. De Vaulx, and K. Kim, "NISTIR 7951: A Vision of Cyber-Physical Cloud Computing for Smart Networked Systems."
43. OpenFog Consortium Architecture Working Group, "OpenFog Reference Architecture for Fog Computing", *OpenFog Consortium*, February, pp. 1–162, 2017.
44. M. M. Hussain, M. S. Alam, and M. M. S. Beg, "Fog Computing in IoT Aided Smart Grid Transition – Requirements, Prospects, Status Quos and Challenges", arxiv.org/abs/1802.01818

CHAPTER 15

When Big Data and Data Science Prefigured Ambient Intelligence

Christophe Thovex

DATA2B R & D - 35510 Cesson-Sevigné, France French-Mexican Laboratory on Computer Science and Control LAFMIA, UMI CNRS 3175 Universidad de Las Americas, Puebla, Mexico

CONTENTS

From antiquity to future generations, data analysis adds value, provides power, and raises knowledge within civilizations. Reading and counting prefigured the fundamental operations to be theoretically automated before running a Turing's machine or a quantum computer. So then, studies of founding theories for Data Science and of theoretical models for Big Data ignoring these primitive foundations might easily mislead, steering attention away from the main observable results and perspectives.

The chapter presents an insight into founding theories for Data Science and theoretical models for Big Data, based on the historical development of sciences and computer science towards Artificial Intelligence (AI). It proposes a state-of-the-art, driven by the chronological evolution of data analysis in sciences and society, as a prospective tool for the exploration of perspectives in Data Science, Big Data, Artificial Intelligence and their business applications.

1 INTRODUCTION

Recalling the theoretical foundations of data processing sets the focus on the way data analysis currently converges with cognitive processes, resulting in mainstream trends such as Artificial Intelligence (AI), biomimetics, neurosciences or applications in robotics and computational linguistics. Following the historical time-line, the combination of current methods for predictive analysis, machine learning, computational intelligence with the Internet of Things (IoT) and Linked Data (Semantic Web) might determine the next steps in Big Data and Data Science, towards ambient intelligence and smart data distributed through the ubiquitous Web (Web of Data).

Following the historical development of sciences towards ambient intelligence, an overview of the origins of Data Science and Big Data is first presented in Section 2. Then, Section 3 provides a panorama of the founding theories and trends for data science and/or Big Data. It also sets the focus on multidisciplinary trends, definitely essential in AI and in current tracks for the future of data science. As a consequence, ambient intelligence and smart data distributed through the ubiquitous Web might prefigure a logical paradigm for the forecasting of future needs and trends, steering the theoretical evolution of Data Science and Big Data. Section 4 proposes to explore ambient intelligence based on such a paradigm, before to sum up the main conclusions and perspectives closing this chapter in Section 5.

2 ORIGINS OF DATA SCIENCE AND BIG DATA

The History of Science is commonly admitted as starting in ancient times with agronomy – 6000 BC in southern Mexico – oral tradition, then astronomy, mathematics, medicine (Egypt, around 3500 BC), philosophy (Greece), physics, chemistry, biology, sociology, and so on until computer science and neurosciences.[1]

Thanks to the development of the World Wide Web, scientific knowledge in science is now digitized, readable and shareable, being news, facts, personal videos or industrial and business processes. Such diversity and volume form Big Data. Everyone finds value in Big Data, entailing data analysis to turn into a structured and multidisciplinary science called Data Science.

Computer science and data science stem on primitive operations inherited from human cognitive processes: reading, writing, counting. Reading is the interpretation of a code represented by symbols. Counting is an abstract operation coding items, quantities and occurrences/ranks into mathematical symbols. Digital data is a code symbolized by (1) alphanumeric symbols for texts, numbers, operators, (2) pixels for pictures, and (3) streams for audio, video and not human-readable data streams. As we know, in computing processes digital data are transcoded into bits (binary digits), for primary operations such

---

[1] Earlier scientific knowledge could be lost as "legendary" due to natural or societal phenomena causing the disintegration or destruction of historical evidences – *e.g.* erosion, seisms, oral tradition, colonization and wars.

as reading/writing Inputs/Outputs (I/O) and counting. Primary operations for computing machinery are basically similar to human primary operations. These are the underlying fundamentals of AI prefigured by Turing's machine and games-solving algorithms [1,2].

At the opposite of primary operations in a hypothetical hierarchy of cognition, there could be heuristics and paradigms as complex objects lying upon primary operations. Heuristics provide acceptable solutions to complex problems, to be compared with algorithms in data science and AI [3]. Paradigms define partial but coherent representations of the world, based on observed or presupposed data to be compared with data lakes in Big Data. Heuristics and paradigms can be combined, generating new paradigms and so on. For instance, the human (not machine) writing or reading of this sentence entails a paradigm, thanks to cognitive operations processing sets of previously acquired knowledge, which may include recursive implication as a heuristic method leading to conscience, such as defined in Cartesian metaphysics and philosophy [4,5].

In its early stage, AI still understands nothing but simulates parts of human behavior, mostly based on incomplete mathematical representations as explained in C. O'Neil's awarded nonfiction work [6]. However, based on a set of operations added on top of the primary layer "RWC" (Read/Write/Count) for automatic classification, clustering and optimization, AI provides interesting applications, thanks to massive data processing after-the-fact (offline) and/or in real time (online). It is the general concept of Data Science, although precursor works in AI aimed at computing human reasoning with machines [1].

2.1 From Agronomy to Econometrics

We found archaeological proofs of people organized in small groups living from the culture and development of plants such as teosinte and maize since 6 000 BC in Mexico [7]. We also found evidences, in Mexico and Guatemala, of a system by which native cultivators exploited the heterotic nature of maize to increase their harvests by hydration [8]. Based on empirical data observations, these cultivators experimented the trivial premises of modern agronomy and genetics. Cultivators know when maize needs water, looking at the plant color, but data science enables to use hyperspectral images for predicting accurate water needs depending on the plant phenotype [9].

Aztec and Mesoamerican civilizations are known for their culture in astronomy and cosmology. Studying these later civilizations and the very rare codices saved from the colonial books burning (i.e., "auto-da-fe"), ethnologists found evident relationships in-between astronomy, cosmology, and agronomy. As an example, the Codex Borgia is originated in Puebla-Tlaxcala Valley. It contains a seasonal calendar tied to the Sun, Moon and Venus. Its narrative is in relation to the seasonal cycle, which is also evident in a clear contrast between the rainy and dry seasons in the imagery [10]. Water and mostly rain determined the wealthiness of pre-Columbian civilizations based on agriculture. Receiving water from the sky (rain and dew), it is commonly admitted that they observed astral phenomena so as to better understand meteorological events and to control their society. Dependent on climatic events, they might have defined the universe in a creationist way for this reason. Their observations in astronomy were finally oriented toward the understanding and satisfaction of divinities supposed to provide them rain for agriculture and welfare. They developed cosmological knowledge naturally tied to agronomy by their philosophical culture.

Obviously, human beliefs take a major part in the formulation of hypothesis and conjectures founding research works, along times and across continents as in the history of sciences towards data science. We particularly observe the influence of mythological organizations explaining the universe in the main ancient cultures, according to historical knowledge. As the Sun was a god for ancient Greeks (Helios), Egyptians (Ra) and for Mayas (Kinich Ahau), human beings started to seek for new philosophical understandings, rationally coherent with visible observations rather than with the imaginary. According to [11], during the 5th century BC in Athens, Anaxagoras was legally prosecuted for pretending the Sun was a stone in fusion. Nevertheless, Pythagoras had induced a philosophical movement respecting the mythological version during the previous century, and then defined the bases of geometry and arithmetic. According to the numerous biographic works about him, he probably spent years in the school of Memphis (Egypt) to learn geometry and mathematics, and was obsessed by numbers – "all is numbers" – in his philosophical quest [12].

As a matter of fact, it should remind us how much "Intelligence is not to know but what we do when we do not know.", as stated by the multidisciplinary scientist JEAN PIAGET. We might also notice how many ancient mythologies described the beginning of the Earth as a liquid world preliminary to human life apparition, while the primordial soup theory, tied to the big bang theory, still does not refute such a hypothetical vision – e.g., the Egyptian "Nun", Greek gods Chaos and Ocean and Mayan god Itzamna. According to the authors of [13], abstract structures set into the physical world like RNA unavoidably orient standards, science and technical knowledge from the finding of electricity to the design of components found in actual micro-technologies. They argue that human initiatives ignoring natural paradigms mislead and do not reach optimal results, compared with nature-inspired systems – e.g., 14 incompatible electric outlet standards currently persist after more than a century of public electric power vs. artificial neuronal networks.

The beginnings of algebra are also attributed to Ancient Egypt and Babylonia. Two dated papyrus, the Rhind Papyrus and the Golenishchev Papyrus, show evidences of advanced knowledge in mathematics since 1850 BC, for geometric algebra, and 1550 BC for second-degree equations. Both the historical documents show applied purposes related to current uses in these older times, such as computing the strength of the beer made from volumes of grain[2] or predicting the quantity of food for feeding animals and people. With algebra and mathematics naturally oriented towards collective needs, data and science started to support decision-making from quantitative analysis. These theoretical tools were designed and tuned, thanks to human observations about natural phenomena. Nowadays, trends in data science and AI tend towards the automatic

---

[2] The volumes were given in hekat, 1 hekat corresponding to 4.8 liters.

tuning of parameters and identification of determinants with Convolutional Neural Networks (CNN) and reinforcement learning [14,15].

The oldest written evidences of medicine also come from Ancient Egypt and were tied to current needs of the epoch. We found case of injuries, fractures and tumors in the Edwin Smith Papyrus dated from 1600 BC, mostly for military surgery but also for gynecology and cosmetics. It presents a medicine in which rational science does not conflict with magic. Nowadays, we still observe this duality with a modern medicine largely explained and demonstrated by high technologies, and a modern pharmacopoeia based on empirical knowledge inherited from traditional and shamanic cultures – *e.g.*, anaesthetic, antitussive, antitumor, cardiotonic, diuretic. A plethora of actions in learning benefits of plants for healthiness were developed from ancient to modern times. Colonialism has largely contributed to the diffusion of indigenous medical knowledge and species around the world [16]. Genetic modifications by natural grafts were experimented for adapting plants to soils and climates, from a region to another. Merging plants phenotypes based on natural compatibility and observed results prefigured the basic concept of big data and data science, one step forward the Mesoamerican and natural hybridations [8].

Assyrian, Chinese, Egyptian medicinal plants and traditions continue to gain currency among contemporary healers, while we just start to take care about biopiracy and bioethics in intellectual property for sustainable relationships with ancestral cultures [17]. Geographical and contextual factors are also correlated with medicinal plants growing, in [16], as a first use case of data science in medicine. Currently, big data and data science enable to detect medical recommendations before the actual guidelines could reflect them. It is the case with concomitant options of medication found from a recent study revealing the efficiency of beta blockers and proton pump inhibitors for hypertensive patients, as an example [18]. The antithesis of such promising outcomes is to be checked in a second step, with other machine learning applications, so as to ensure their overall efficiency regarding unexpected effects, and then submitted to experts. Medical protocols remain necessary before to release and prescript new treatments.

According to the historical version, the first known elements of natural science and physics were discovered in Archaic Greece with Thales, contemporary with Pythagoras (about 600 BC). Thales was the first to refuse supernatural, religious or mythological explanations of natural observations and to defend the idea of natural cause for all phenomena. However, it is commonly admitted that he recognized water as the first basic element. It seems that the first physical explanation of the Universe was expressed a century later, with the theory of atomism. Then, Aristotle defined the notions of gravitational motion as a base of cosmology, studying the four elements – water, air, earth, and fire – and ether (about 350 BC). Aristotle advocated the idea of Earth being the center of the Universe (geocentrism), in opposition with the earliest Pythagoras' beliefs. It was probably known about one century later again (Erathostenes) that Earth is spherical. Ptolemy defended the Aristotelian and very popular theory during the 1st century BC and heliocentrism remained unclear in collective beliefs until the Copernican revolution, as well as the idea of Earth spinning on its poles sounded absurd regarding observation data available in the 15th century. It marks the importance of available data for understanding the most important phenomena.

When Galileo finally set up his astronomical telescope (inspired from a Dutch terrestrial telescope) and observed the space, the indubitable data collected triggered a historical controversy involving royal and scientific authorities in Rome, Italy and Europa (17th century). The quantitative physics of Galileo, based on rational observations, suffered successive attacks from the supporters of Aristotle qualitative physics, based on religious and popular interpretations sometimes derived from holy writings existing in the epoch – *e.g.*, Tanakh. Quantitative physics stated that ice floats because it is lighter than water, while qualitative physics declared that ice floats due to its state. Truth is not so conflictual, as the solidification of water in the atmosphere makes it lighter than water. It finally results from data collection and cooperation, a fundamental principle for big data and data science. Nevertheless, it appears relevant to notice how long polemics were standing and sustained on the simple basis of Aristotle status and popularity.

Nowadays, cosmology is one of the most characteristic applications of big data and data science. Huge volumes of data are generated by various telescopes in various spectra, most of them being out of human perception (*e.g.*, radio, infrared) and requiring high-performance computing (HPC). Heavy processing is necessary to define and run sequences of complex models in order to provide observable and accurate results to astronomers. Common algorithms concern inverse problem solving and regularization, sparse signal decomposition, blind source separation, in-painting, multiscale geometric transforms for three-dimensional data (data cubes), data on the sphere (geolocated data), or dictionary learning, for instance [19].

At a glance to Figure 15.1, we can guess and wonder how much the beforehand understanding of celestial mechanics might have inspired the first works in mechanical research and engineering.[3]

FIGURE 15.1   Mechanical representation of Newtonian mechanics.

---

[3] Picture from https://jimnicar.com/tag/ernest-keller/

Since the 18th century, agrarian and handicraft economy started evolving towards machine manufacturing and industry. Then, the Industrial Revolution has changed the face of the world. It coincides with the first applications of electricity and telecommunications. Possible application of chemical electricity[4] for analgesia could have existed in the 1st century AD [20]. However, the modern use of electricity and electromagnetism started with M. Faraday (1791–1867) and the dynamo, then J. Maxwell (1831–1879). After drums, pigeons, smoke signals, and optical semaphores, modern applications in telecommunications appeared in the same years with the first telegraphic line (1792), an electrical semaphore built by C. Chappe, France. It was a memorable invention, prefiguring digital networks with the first known *readable data* transfer in a solid body (metal) and long distance (230 kilometers).

Based on mechanics and communication technologies, the industrial revolution brought significant improvements in economy and society. It has fostered the development of human collaboration. Social sciences became important to understand and guide the development of numerous and large groups of people at work, in cities, for business and for international economy [21–23]. Social data and statistics were beginning to add a significant value to the modern world. As a result, Social Networks Analysis and Mining (SNAM) from the social and semantic Web became crucial for the economical and industrial paradigms of the 21th century, which are user-oriented and replace older ones mostly product-oriented [24,25].

As in ancient times, mathematics, statistics, and probabilistic theories are developed for social and economical purposes (*e.g.*, Econometrics) but processed on huge volumes of Heterogeneous data daily generated all over the world [26–28]. Digital revolution enables the Industry 4.0 to supply products customized in shape, colors and features in order to match with the long tail distribution of e-business sales. While markets were looking for best-sellers since the beginning of industrial revolution (19th century), e-business no longer relies on selling more of a few products but on selling a few of each of the millions of products that meet with billions of customers' expectations [29]. Merging set theory, graph theory, knowledge discovery, natural language processing (NLP) and signal processing for big data, data science provides an evolving tool-kit necessary to the guidance of digital revolution and societal progress, from business process management, medias and knowledge economy to healthcare and education [30,31].

2.2 Computer Science, Big Data and Data Science

Computer science aims at automatizing abstract operations. Low-level functions are Reading, Writing, and Counting, based on binary operations directly enabled by hardware components – *e.g.*, Arithmetic and Logic Unit (ALU), registers, memories and storage. High-level functions such as man–machine interactions, decision support or artificial

---

[4] Baghdad/Parthian Battery, set of artifacts found together and supposed to constitute a battery.

intelligence require various algorithms, implemented upon low-level functions and interfaces (*e.g.*, network interface, computer numerical command interface, video interface). As for human intelligence, artificial intelligence and data science require basic operations – reading, writing, counting. These operations are parallelly repeated extremely fastly in complex algorithms, for detecting and tracking faces into video streams, for instance [32].

Big Data is trivially defined in the "5Vs" rule: Volume, Variety, Velocity, Veracity and Value. Big data is a generic expression for data sets which are very large in volume and/or diversity, and may also be time-constrained such as real-time data streams from the IoT and the Internet of Data.

The Internet of Data is close to Linked Open Data (LOD), a W3C[5] initiative which tends to link open data from different databases through the Web, thanks to common labels representing metadata. This concept for knowledge management is generalized by the Resource Definition Framework (RDF), an XML-based standard enabling to link entities with triples such as <London> "is a" <city>. RDF datasets represent conceptual networks usually named ontologies [33]. There exist various ontologies on the Web for linking data such as DBPedia, the semantic database subjacent to Wikipedia.

Thanks to semantic databases for generic knowledge (DBPedia), geographical knowledge (Geonames, CIA world facts book), named entities extracted from DBPedia (GlobalAtlas, YAGO), medical knowledge (Bioportal) or media (Google Knowledge Graph), the Semantic Web enables to link the huge and multilingual volume of text stored on the Web in order to provide a common structure to unstructured data [24]. Such a structure is queried thanks to SPARQL, a W3C protocol and query language for RDF stores. So we can retrieve pictures, songs and videos qualified by labels/tags tied by conceptual relations through the social and semantic Web. The Open Archive Initiative[6] (OAI) also provides a protocol for databases harvesting through the Web based on the Dublin Core metadata.[7]

The cloud of LOD is constantly evolving. In Figure 15.2, the core of the cloud is DBPedia and the red cluster represents the Bioportal ontologies.

Big data first concerned the Web before to concern industries, groups, then small and medium enterprises. With the development of IoT, smart cities also started to manage big data for security, transportation, energy management and urban planning. Sensors and Intranet of Things take an important part in the Industry 4.0, in which big data flows control robots and cobots along the production process and foster just-in-time supply chain, lean management and customized production or enable data science for quality control, predictive maintenance or energy saving – *e.g.*, optimization, machine learning.

Tied to industry and manufacturing, marketing and services providers take advantage on big data for logistic organization, sales previsions and promotion, as a continuity of

---

[5] W3C: acronym for World Wide Web Consortium.
[6] www.openarchives.org/
[7] http://dublincore.org/

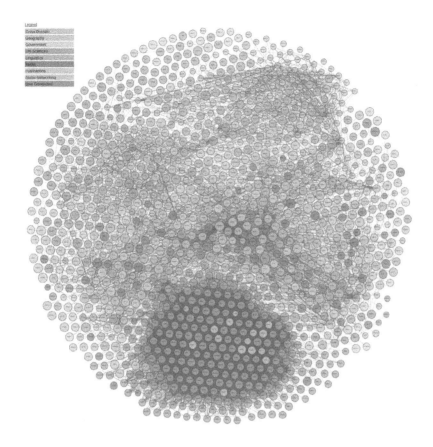

FIGURE 15.2   Linked Open Data 2018: https://lod-cloud.net

econometrics. Banks, insurances, communication and media operators commonly optimize their business exploiting the large databases, histories and data lakes that result
from their activities. The wide diversity of data sources, application domains and use-
cases involved by data lakes and big data entails the permanent research and development of big data systems and data science techniques, orienting the digital revolution
and socioeconomic progress.

Succeeding to the main stream inspired by the Web and due to observed bias such as
acquisition and exploitation costs that result from processing large and noisy datasets,
we observe marginal trends yet – *e.g.*, small data. Small data are oriented data selected
by human intuition/analysis from big data [34]. As with sampling methods in statistics,
with a set of a thousand variables and according to domain experts or using correlation
networks it is possible to first select the most relevant 10 variables to get the same results
at reduced execution cost than processing the whole data set.

Big data and data lakes remain useless without adapted techniques and algorithms of
analytic intelligence, outcomes from data science research and development. The cost-
effectiveness of big data mostly depends on the efficiency of data science. At the lowest

level, computer science supports data science with distributed databases and parallel software systems adequate for big data storage and management. Software architectures for big data separate reading and/or writing operations into asynchronous and parallel tasks managed by processes executed on hardware clusters – *e.g.*, Hadoop, Spark. Indexing operations are massively run on heterogeneous datasets, mostly declared as texts in specific file systems such as Parquet or Hadoop Distributed File System (HDFS). Big data indexing and querying software implement Map/Reduce, a parallel model inspired from full text indexing methods and mapping the whole data partition before to aggregate (reduce) entries into a distributed and shared index [35]. The environment defined by computer science for big data so provides convenient foundations to perform research and development of data science applications.

Data science might be defined as the sum of analytic methods for knowledge extraction from (big) data, aimed at smart software applications. The theoretical and multidisciplinary foundations of data science are computer science, mathematics, statistics, signal processing, NLP, knowledge engineering, biology, physics and economy. Data Science may include other disciplines such as sociology and psychology for applications based on Social Networks Analysis (SNA) and game theory, for instance [36,37].

Due to the network structure of the Web and the numerous data representations requiring networks and graph structures for modeling and analysis, Network Science, a graph-oriented branch of data science, was defined in 2005 by the National Research Council of the USA [38]. According to the definition, network science is the study of network representations of physical, biological and social phenomena leading to predictive models of these phenomena. Algorithms for transportation in operational research or community discovery in SNAM are parts of network science, with hierarchical graph structures defined for deep learning – *e.g.*, Graph Transformer Network [14].

2.3 Intermediate Conclusion

Historical applications of data analysis prefigured data science in their purposes and conceptual similarities, since the beginning of written tradition in ancient civilizations. Archaeological vestiges bring evidences of the premises of data science in agronomy, astronomy, medicine, and economy in antiquity with the development of geometry, algebra, mathematics, or physics.

Reading, writing and counting are primary operations common to human intelligence and AI. Computer science now allows to repeat and multiply these operations extremely fast in complex models for huge and heterogeneous data sets – structured/unstructured data. Modern applications of big data and data science are based on the Web of data and enterprise data, driving the digital revolution towards massive analysis and collective intelligence. They are multidisciplinary and tend to merge theoretical foundations from domains as distinct as NLP, physics, biology or sociology/psychology. The next section presents these theoretical foundations and trends.

3 THEORETICAL TOOLS, MODELS AND CURRENT TRENDS

Basically, data science aims at making value from knowledge.[8] It defines multiple methods for knowledge extraction and mining from digital data, commonly shared in scientific conferences and publications – *e.g.*, conference Knowledge Discovery and Data (KDD).

Topics in data science might be categorized in top domains: knowledge engineering, statistics and probabilities, signal processing. Below these domains, many sub-domains are identified but not necessarily separated, as certain methods present conceptual similarities common to multiple domains. Figure 15.3 proposes a map of the main topics in data science with generalization/specialization relations in-between topics. Such a representation remains subjective; either it results from algorithms and/or from manual design, but it offers an overall understanding of the main theoretical tools and their lineage with the foundations of data science (top-level concept in Figure 15.3). Terms are sized depending on their page-rank value within the illustrated network [39].

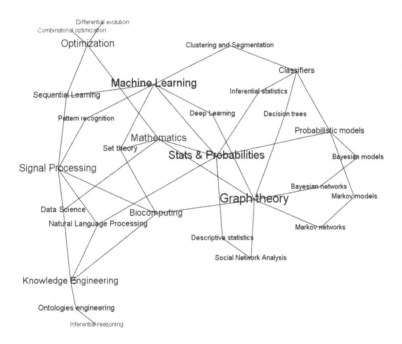

FIGURE 15.3   Main topics map in data science (2018).

Data science being multidisciplinary in essence and based on computer science, it resorts to various sub-domains tied to big data such as genomics or geomatics, depending on expected use cases and applications out of our current scope. Only main topics are detailed next.

---

[8] Added value is immaterial (computed information, stock market) and materialized, thanks to business processes (*e.g.*, production, sales, deliveries, management) generating monetized products or services.

3.1 Founding Theories and Trends for Data Science

Historically, mathematics and particularly statistics appear in the early beginning of computer science applications for econometrics and large data sets. Econometrics is tied to RAGNAR FRISCH, co-winner of the first Nobel Prize in Economic Sciences in 1969. In 1933, his definition of econometrics prefigured yet the paradigm of big data and data science [40].

> Thus, econometrics is by no means the same as economic statistics [...] economic theory [...] application of mathematics to economics. Experience has shown that each of these three viewpoints is [...] not [...] sufficient [...]. It is the unification of all three that is powerful. And it is this unification that constitutes econometrics.
>
> R. Frisch
> Editor of Econometrica 1933–1954, The Econometric Society

Theoretical unification and data conjunctions generate the power of data science and big data. More than before, no data or model alone generates high value but convenient sets of models and data are the key to get value from big data and data science.

Data scientists manage data sets, from big data to small data and choose relevant models from the state-of-the-art for each use case and application. They regularly have to define new composite algorithms, combining well-known models and/or new ones specifically researched and developed so as to provide the expected outcomes. Furthermore, for execution costs reasons some algorithms must first be abstracted for catching their concept and to be implemented in trivial ways, or to merge together several abstractions into a single and cost-efficient algorithm. As an example, merging theoretical foundations from decision trees, sampling layers and gradient descent enabled to define convolutional networks for deep learning [14]. Knowledge extraction from big data with long and complex processes enables to get smart data – *i.e.*, valuable data explicitly representing the results from facts and/or phenomena.

Data science for big data extends the abstraction defined behind the notion of econometrics by R. FRISCH, aiming at the automatic generation of smart data. Multidisciplinary approaches open wider perspectives in data science with models resulting from the unification of physics, sociology, and/or computer science, for instance. Commonly accepted measures in social networks integrate well-known laws of current distribution in solid circuits [41,42]. Such a theoretical assumption unifying conceptually separated disciplines was theoretically formalized and demonstrated with KRIPKE logic in [43], clarifying a philosophical trouble [44]. Thus, data science requires a permanent quest of research grounded on the wide and basic knowledge of its main theoretical foundations, detailed next.

Statistics and probabilities. Statistics are commonly qualified as descriptive or inferential. Descriptive statistics describe oriented facts from known data, mostly thanks to quantitative methods and theoretical tools named estimators. Data are generally named populations. For large populations, numerous works on sampling methods and estimation of the samples significance enable to get relevant results from a small subset of the studied population. It particularly helps in large data sets processing, preparing small data sets for big data analysis. Well-known sampling methods such as Gibbs, Monte–Carlo simulation, or more exotic ones such as annealing are widely described in the literature [45].

The applications of descriptive statistics can help sales managers to know consumers profiles according to products in socioeconomic and demographic terms, for instance. Estimators are generally based on operations such as harmonic/geometric mean, median, standard deviation, variance and kurtosis.[9]

Inferential statistics mostly predict facts from known data, thanks to quantitative or qualitative methods and theoretical tools named classifiers and predictors. Classifiers are methods for classifying variables into predefined categories. When categories are not previously known, classifying methods belong to segmentation and clustering models. For instance, given the qualitative variable *energyclass* with modalities A, B, C, D, E, F, G and a population of domestic devices represented with a set of attributes in a table *devicetable*, (1) classification enables to set the energy class of each device according to a given scoring equation, (2) segmentation enables to separate devices having the same score, thanks to external variables, and (3) clustering enables to find clusters of devices having similar attribute values so as to infer categories from these clusters. Decision trees such as random forests are inferential classifiers, and the R software documentation gives access to numerous models for classification, clustering and segmentation [46].

Smart data requires data scientists to be able to catch the concept behind models and algorithms, in order to define smart implementations for big data applications. Otherwise, they could not bring certain expected results to users, may be due to missing data or to the execution costs of algorithms. The abstraction ability of human intelligence fosters the constant adaptation of the state-of-the-art to new requirements. As an example, the abstraction of *k-means*, clustering algorithm based on distances like *k-nearest neighbors*, is largely declined in graph models or signal processing, although it is commonly attributed to inferential statistics [47].

In a multidisciplinary context tending to theoretical unification, the border between inferential statistics tools and probabilistic tools or machine learning is permeable. Without multidisciplinary approach, statistical learning emerges from complex models using clustering algorithms to compute classes as categories for classification algorithms [48]. Machine learning is named supervised or unsupervised learning, depending on the way algorithms necessitate input parameters to be set by human or not, and on the facts they need training data sets or not.

Decision-support algorithms for real-world problems necessitate sometimes to resort to fuzzy criterion. For instance, to classify birds according to genre is easy because genre is a clear variable with two disjoint modalities – male or female – for birds. To classify birds by size in two classes – small or big – is not so simple as the size value separating specimens may vary according to genre for each species and to geographical zones for

---

[9] The kurtosis is the acuity coefficient of a variable distribution.

a species. In such a case, the separation threshold must be statistically computed based on implication rules and considered as a fuzzy variable. Implicative statistics embed statistical learning, fuzzy logic, probabilistic classification and knowledge representation in a unified approach so as to provide theoretical tools for solving and/or optimizing complex problems from the real world implying human knowledge from various fields [49].

Merging data and heuristics from various domains, implicative statistics enable to get smart data from big data for smarter recommendations, taking complex interactions into account while classical statistics provide solutions for locally identified problems, mathematically separated from external implications. Although solutions to locally identified problems are useful to data scientists, for real-world applications of data science and big data, it is crucial to notice how much local and incomplete mathematical representations can be dangerous for the social and economical consequences of AI on the digital revolution, and how frequent they are too easily accepted as trustworthy and smart for decision-support systems [6].

Probabilistic models stem on the theory of probabilities, which integrates hazardous phenomena and uncertainty into statistics. They are mostly based on Bayes theorem, allowing to define inferential chains and probabilistic decision trees. Equation 1 symbolizes the Bayes theorem. It defines $P(A \mid B)$ the probability of an event A knowing $P(B)$, probability of an event B, such as:

$$P(A \mid B) = \frac{P(B \mid A) \cdot P(A)}{P(M \mid A) \cdot P(A) + P(M \mid B) \cdot P(B)} \tag{1}$$

As an example with two populations A, B of 100 individuals such as $P(A) = 0.5$ and $P(B) = 0.5$, 30 males in $A : P(M \mid A) = 0.30$ and 60 males in $B : P(M \mid B) = 0.60$, the probability to find a male in A is $1/3 \approx 33,33\%$.

Equation 1 typically introduces inferential chains propitious to large and/or deep network structures for multivariate and combinatorial analysis. We retrieve such a kind of structures in Bayesian networks, Markov networks, random forest trees and deep neural networks.

Bayesian networks enable to process inferential abductions, instead of deductions commonly produced in inferential statistics, studying beliefs networks for instance [50]. Mixing Markov chains with big data is significantly faster using graphs as interpolating structures [51]. Hidden Markov Models (HMM) and the Markovian paradigm were already compared with Artificial Neural Networks (ANN) in 1998, at the early beginnings of deep learning and convolutional networks [14,52]. As with ANN, Bayesian networks enable to produce reinforcement learning models, enhancing their own training sets (and performance) after each pass of the learning algorithms [15].

Random forest trees generally resort to gradient boosting methods for classification [53]. Gradient descent is also an efficient method for learning features in pictures in order to recognize visual patterns with Convolutional NN [14]. There exists numerous works combining CNN with classifiers such as Support Vector Machines (SVM), Conditional Random Fields (CRF) or kernel methods such as K-means [47]. Deep network structures for machine learning such as graph transformer networks, memory NN, recurrent NN, energy trellis or Generative Adversarial Networks (GAN) require classifiers for local or global optimization within their separation layers [54]. These structures specifically resort to rectifiers such as ReLU for reducing the noise of input or sub-sampling layers [55]. They find applications in numerous fields such as computer vision, automatic translation, or power systems management [56].

Offline and Online applications. The topics illustrated in Section 3 and models presented above are mostly efficient in offline applications, *i.e.*, analysis and results after-the-facts, requiring sometimes long training periods and differed execution times. As an example, the CNN LeNet-5 requires about 20 passes on a training set of 60 000 patterns before to reach a stable performance of recognition [14]. Applications such as autonomous driving, and basically all applications computing smart data based on real-time events, require online process of analysis – *i.e.*, algorithm providing real-time or short-time indications/recommendations taking immediate information about the context into account. Online analysis becomes a recurrent need for paradigms such as IoT, Smart Cities, or the Industry 4.0.

The GAFAs' vocal assistants show how online and offline analyses cooperate with online algorithms for speech-to-text/text-to-speech and offline algorithms for computing answers to questions/queries. However, online and offline solutions to a given problem may require very different approaches. Online object tracking in video streams will not need the same execution costs at all with a CNN model rather than a HOG model [57]. Detecting credit card frauds offline is possible but online detection requires to lower the performance expectations with similar algorithm, or to resort to parallel architectures for Big Data such as Spark clusters [28,58].

Sequential learning is a particular branch of machine learning for online analysis based on the study of temporal changes to classify and predict real-time events in stochastic phenomena. It offers an alternative to deep learning for cost-efficient applications and signal processing, with common models such as time-series or wavelets for real-time /short-time applications from big data [59]. Inverse problems and convex problems for game optimization are typically mathematical approaches of sequential learning [60]. It finds online interests for auctions or high-frequency trading applications, and offline interests for bioinformatics too with genetic algorithms and connate applications such as access network selection for radio-telecommunications [61].

Finally, there exist certain marginal and recent tracks to be exploited for computing smart data. Evolutionary computation and differential evolution supply theoretical foundations for global optimization with very large statistical populations. They are powerful tools for generating smart data from big data, thanks to predictive clustering and, in general terms, for optimized future choices [62,63]. SNA and NLP are now integrated as main streams in research works and also tied to knowledge representation and management, but the unification of these three domains has just started [64,65]. As with econometrics, multidisciplinarity is at the core of data science. Multidisciplinary trends are explored next.

3.2 Multidisciplinary Trends in Data Science

We found the idea of AI in the Vaucanson automaton (18th century), but the premises of thinking machines appear with computing machinery and the imitation of human thought, from mathematicians such as C. Babbage (1791–1871), Ada of Lovelace (1815–1852) and A. Turing [1].

ANN and deep learning were first inspired from biology and neurology, such as reminded in the literature [14,66]. SNA integrates physics with the unification of Ohm's laws with Kirchhoff's laws for SNA, which is theoretically demonstrated [41–43]. Multidisciplinarity enables attempts such as simulating waves interferences in a finite data space and time-reversal in a propagation and back-propagation method for big data [67,68]. Such an approach was experimented with large data sets from real-world processes and paves the way for future alternatives inspired from deep networks and natural observations [68].

The observation of life and nature is a major inspiration for science in biomimetics. However, this trend is much more developed in medicine and science of materials than in computer science [69]. No general trends appear in biomimetics for smart data, except certain projects merging neurosciences and AI – e.g., Deep Mind (Oxford University, UK), Human Brain Project (EPFL, Switzerland).

Deep neural networks supply solutions to various problems based on patterns and distances but found limitations with other classes of problems, such as global optimization of heterogeneous data or machine reasoning. Currently, the major limitation to data science and AI for big data is the lack of truly learning machine. Machine learning mostly classifies patterns among large data much faster than human. It is more Analytic Intelligence than AI. Even though an oriented AI does better than human with inferences and brute force, it is still far from reproducing human learning such as do junior students with scholar readings [70]. In upcoming years, it could bring us back to the sources of AI with attempts in self-programming software and rules-generative algorithms, such as that introduced since 1990 by precursor researchers in truly learning machines [71] – "thinking machine" [1].

Based on the Web structure and on the massive development of ANN-based models, network science should remain important for smart data [38]. Deep and complex networks unifying ANN, NLP, knowledge representation and social sciences might appear, pulled by raising markets for smart assistants, cobots and autonomous transports.

4 AMBIENT INTELLIGENCE AND SMART DATA

Tied to advances in robotics, the conjunction of the Web of data (LOD), IoT, parallel computing in the cloud (GPUs), and distributed databases for big data (Map/Reduce) with advances in data science or IA let foresee a global paradigm of ambient intelligence based on smart data. Ambient intelligence pulls data from IoT, LOD and Web services to push smart data within our daily environment. It provides smart data improving our decision-making in professional environments (plants, offices, outlets) or personal environments (home, smart cities, transports), through connected devices such as smartphones and mobile or stationary dashboards, converging together for communicating information.

Ambient intelligence is close to the notion of ubiquitous Web, allowed by a permanent access to the Web wherever we are and whenever we want. However, while the ubiquitous Web only ensures the ability to permanently share and access information through the Web, ambient intelligence entails the computation of smart data and the access to user-oriented information through the ubiquitous Web and through environment-integrated devices. A trivial example of ambient intelligence is visible on certain highways equipped with digital signalization screens that display automatic warnings regarding open or closed lanes for the next road sections depending on the traffic quantified from cameras networks and computer vision software. Navigation systems embedded in the digital dashboards of connected cars with vocal command also prefigure the generalization of ambient intelligence.

Wearable devices such as watches, glasses or new connected clothes participate in the IoT, the ubiquitous Web, and ambient intelligence, providing big data and receiving smart data through augmented/mixed reality systems and other audio/visual interfaces. As with econometrics, big data and data science for smart data, it is the unification of all advances in electronics and cognitive sciences that is powerful and that constitutes ambient intelligence as a global trend and a paradigm for the future. Based on the historical evolution of data and algorithms in human civilizations, forecasting the future needs and trends steering the theoretical evolution of data science and smart data might stem on this paradigm like multivariate predictions stem on previously known data and polynomial equations.

Computational intelligence prefigures a base component of ambient intelligence, interfacing faceted subsets of big data and data science with natural language queries for various knowledge domains – e.g., mathematics, chemistry, political geography, history, finance, entertainment. Computational intelligence engines only begin to be reliable for certain domains (e.g., WolframAlpha), but related works are pulled by significant social and economical stakes [72].

Meta-learning represents another base component for ambient intelligence. Meta-learning could be thought as a renewal of interest for the theoretical foundations of AI after they were abandoned for cost-efficient methods, oriented towards brute force and large databases for classification and optimization [71]. It aims at building meta models on top of collections of machine learning algorithms, in order to globally optimize their learning phases and parameters and to process meta-knowledge [73]. Meta-knowledge is defined as the future of AI since 1999 by J. PITRAT [74].

Based on middle-ware components unifying the latest advances in electronics and cognitive sciences, ambient intelligence represents the most powerful paradigm imagined by human civilizations since antiquity. As a consequence, knowing that information processing and cryptography were yet determining weapons during the Second World War and before, the digital revolution as well as smart data and data science for big data might bring unprecedented change in the history of civilizations. The Singularity, symbolic point to which computational machinery will use more neurons than the human brain, could as well produce no special consequence as to start irreversible change of the possible futures [75]. Basically, according to the well-known law of entropy similarly observed in physics by L. BOLTZMANN and in information theory by C. SHANNON, the singularity should result in a stronger but not better intelligence than the one of mankind having it created. Standing on neutral positions, we can consider extreme hypothesis as fictions but a rational analysis, based on recurrent and leading factors observed in the long-term evolution of humanity, introduces a beginning of likely answer to this philosophical interrogation regarding societal benefits and issues in [76]. Anyway, global surveillance and social networks represent yet a major concern with ambient intelligence, governance and ethics [23,76]. Finally, observing the A. AVANESSIAN's time complex, we ought to pay attention to the influence of language and expression on our own world, while speculative logic can open the field of possibles as well as it could deprive us of the best possible future [77].

5 CONCLUSIONS AND PERSPECTIVES

Smart data results from the application of data science to big data. Since antiquity, humans write, read, count data and discover methods of data processing that produce valuable results. Following the history of data and science, we retrieve the premises of genetics in agronomy, then the origins of astronomy, philosophy, mathematics, physics, chemistry, biology, sociology, and so on until computer science and neuroscience. Paying attention to recurrent abstractions, we follow the long evolution of human intelligence towards artificial intelligence in which latest advances in data science and multidisciplinary research prefigure the future of ambient intelligence.

Along the interactions between human beliefs and science, we discover the origins of data science and the conditions of its development, tied to computer science and deeply anchored onto the primitive tools of human cognition – reading, writing, counting. Nevertheless, the state-of-the-art in AI reveals how much A. TURING was conscious about the challenge of building a thinking machine: the most sophisticated AI is still far from reading to acquire knowledge [70]. Learning machines might have been abandoned for machine learning when brute force became more cost-effective than hardly understandable self-programming software and rules-generative algorithms. Singularity could be much more far from a neurons count than we can imagine, but does it really matter while we already take advantage on smart data and ambient intelligence through the ubiquitous Web?

Exploring theoretical foundations for big data and data science towards the major tracks in knowledge engineering, signal processing, adversary learning or evolutionary computation, we find hope to retrieve hidden knowledge from data lakes like crowds retrieve wisdom from collective games [78]. Then, larger components such as meta-learning and computational intelligence emerge from the knowledge graph of data science, reproducing the multidisciplinary abstraction in econometrics once again as the infinite loop of a fractal function.

As human likely started to speak before to read, write and count, NLP could be considered as the mother science of AI, among the multiple disciplines of data science. Anyway, smart data resulting from data science algorithms constitutes the combustible in the paradigm of ambient intelligence steering in return the evolution of data science and smart data, as an evolution cycle. The entropy in such a recurrent transformation is still undefined but, paying attention to ethics and Avanessian's speculative logic, we should be able to keep on converging towards the best possible future, not losing our own languages.

6 GLOSSARY

Biopiracy: Actions and facts of declaring intellectual property (patents) on biological objects and knowledge which belongs first to indigenous people or traditional cultures.

Biomimetics: Biomimetics picks out research hypothesis from the observation of nature and life to foster scientific discovery.

Cobot: Contraction for collaborative robot. A cobot learns gestures and actions from human interactions.

Codex Borgia: Pre-Columbian manuscript of 38 pages (leather) discovered in Center Mexico during the 16th century and first conserved by the cardinal S. Borgia in Italy. Its age is unknown (at least 600 years) and it is commonly attributed to the mixtec civilization (about year 1000 BC to 14th century).

Cosmology: Study of the universe, its origin, evolution and eventual fate.

Data lake: A data lake is a heterogeneous and large data storage permanently filled with data streams incoming from various data sources.

Econometrics: The quantitative analysis of actual economic phenomena based on the concurrent development of theory and observation, related by appropriate methods of inference [79].

Edwin Smith Papyrus: It is unique among the four principal medical papyri in existence that survive today because it presents rational and scientific approach while the other ones are solely based on magic. It is conserved at the New York Academy of Medicine.

Entropy: Principle related to the unpredictability of changes in the matter constituting the Universe and to constant energy and initial matter losses/transformations from a state to another.

Golenishchev Papyrus: Ancient Egyptian mathematical papyrus, dated from 1850 BC area of a hemisphere (problem 10) and finding the volume of a truncated pyramid. It presents other class of problems and belongs to the collection of the Pushkin State Museum of Fine Arts in Moscow.

Heuristic: Heuristic are human strategies relying on using readily accessible, though loosely applicable, information to control problem solving in human beings, machines and abstract issues.

Heterotic Nature: Nature submitted to a phenomenon resulting from hybridization, in which offspring display greater vigor, size, resistance, etc. than the parents.

Hyperspectral imaging: Methods for collecting and processing information from across the electromagnetic spectrum in order to make it human-visible.

Nun: In Egyptian mythology, the primordial ocean is named the Nun. It is an ocean which made life and will make death, surrounding the world.

Rhind Papyrus: Ancient Egyptian mathematical papyrus, dated from 1550 BC and describing algebraic problems from defining fractions to computing linear and second-degree equations. It belongs to the collection of the British Museum in London.

RNA: Acronym for ribonucleic acid, a macromolecule essential for all known forms of life such as DNA, lipids, proteins and carbohydrates. Some RNA molecules play an active role within cells by catalyzing biological reactions, controlling gene expression, or sensing and communicating responses to cellular signals.

Stochastic: Events are said stochastic when they randomly change along time without appearing strictly submitted to a random distribution.

Tanakh: Acronym for the three parts of the Hebraic Bible as known before Christ, Torah–Nevi'im–Ketouvim. The new testament was written after Christ.

Teosinte: Ancient cereal variety similar to maize but less productive and more robust.

Theory of atomism: This theory might have started during the 5th century BC, stating that everything is composed of indivisible elements called atoms.

BIBLIOGRAPHY

1. A. M. Turing. Computing machinery and intelligence. *Mind*, 59(236):433–460, 1950.
2. R. Banerji and G. Ernst. Strategy construction using homomorphisms between games. *Artificial Intelligence*, 3:223–249, 1972.
3. J. Pearl. *Heuristics: Intelligent Search Strategies for Computer Problem Solving.* Addison-Wesley Longman Publishing Co., Inc., Boston, MA, 1984.
4. R. Descartes. *Discourse on the Method, Optics, Geometry and Meteorology.* Hackett, 2001, tr. Olscamp P.J., revised edition, Indianapolis edition 1637, Indianapolis IN, USA.
5. R. Descartes. *Meditations on First Philosophy.* Cambridge University Press, 1996, tr. Cottingham, J., Cambridge edition, UK, 1641.
6. C. O'Neil. *Weapons of Maths Destruction.* Crown Books, Danvers, MA, USA, 2016.
7. B. F. Benz. Archaeological evidence of teosinte domestication from Guila Naquitz, Oaxaca. *Proceedings of the National Academy of Science of USA*, 98:2104–2106, 2001.
8. H. G. Wllkes. Hybridization of maize and teosinte, in mexico and guatemala and the improvement of maize. *Economic Botany*, 31(3):254–293, Jul 1977.
9. Y. Ge, G. Bai, V. Stoerger, and J. C. Schnable. Temporal dynamics of maize plant growth, water use, and leaf water content using automated high throughput rgb and hyperspectral imaging. *Computers and Electronics in Agriculture*, 127(C):625–632, september 2016.
10. S. Milbrath. *Cosmology, Calendars, and Horizon-Based Astronomy in Ancient Mesoamerica*, A Seasonal Calendar in the Codex Borgia, pages 139–162. University Press of Colorado, 01, Boulder CO, USA, 2015.
11. L. Bruit-Zaidman and P. Schmitt-Pantel. *La religion grecque.* Armand Colin, Paris, 1989.
12. K. S. Guthrie. *The Pythagorean Sourcebook and Library: An Anthology of Ancient Writings Which Relate to Pythagoras and Pythagorean Philosophy.* Red Wheel/ Weiser, Newburyport, MA, USA, January 1987.
13. A. Wagner, S. Ortman, and R. Maxfield. From the primordial soup to self-driving cars: Standards and their role in natural and technological innovation. *Journal of the Royal Society Interface*, 13(115), 1–9, February 2016.
14. Y. Lecun, L. Bottou, Y. Bengio, and P. Haffner. Gradient-based learning applied to document recognition. In *Proceedings of the IEEE*, pages 2278–2324, 1998.
15. C. Dimitrakakis and C. A. RothkopfBayesian multitask inverse reinforcement learning. In M. Hutter and S. Sanner, editor, *Recent Advances inReinforcement Learning. EWRL*

2011., volume 7188 of *Lecture Notes in Computer Science*, 273–284 Springer, Berlin, Heidelberg, 2012.

16. R. Voeks. Disturbance Pharmacopoeias: Medicine and Myth from the Humid Tropics. *Annals of the Association of American Geographers*, 4:868–888, 2004.

17. R. S. King, T. J. Carlson, and K. Moran. Biological diversity, indigenous knowledge, drug discovery and intellectual property rights: Creating reciprocity and maintaining relationships. *Journal of Ethnopharmacology*, 51(1):45–57, 1996. The American Society of Pharmacognosy Interim Annual Meeting Intellectual Property Rights, Naturally Derived Bioactive Compounds and Resource Conservation.

18. G. Koren, G. Nordon, K. Radinsky, and V. Shalev. Machine learning of big data in gaining insight into successful treatment of hypertension. *Pharmacology Research & Perspectives*, 6 (3):e00396, 2018.

19. J.-L. Starck, F. Murtagh, and J. Fadili*Sparse Image and Signal Processing: Wavelets and Related Geometric Multiscale Analysis*. Cambridge University Press, Cambridge (GB), 2015.

20. P. T. Keyser. The Purpose of the Parthian Galvanic Cells: A First-Century A.D. Electric Battery Used for Analgesia. *Journal of Near Eastern Studies*, 52(2):81–98, 1993.

21. J. L. Moreno. *Who Shall Survive: A New Approach to the Problem of Human Interrelations*. Nervous and Mental Disease Publishing Co., Washington, DC, USA, 1934.

22. G. W. Allport. *Handbook of Social Psychology*, volume 1, The Historical Background of Modern Social Psychology, pages 3–56. Addison-Wesley., Reading, MA, 1954.

23. N. Chomsky and Z. Herman. *Manufacturing Consent: The Political Economy of the Mass Media*. Pantheon Books, New York, NY, USA, 1988.

24. T. Berners-Lee, J. Hendler, and O. Lassila. The semantic web. *Scientific American Magazine*, May 2001.

25. T. R. Gruber. Collective knowledge systems: Where the social web meets the semantic web. *Web Semantics: Science, Services and Agents on the World Wide Web*, 6(1):4–13, February 2008.

26. C. C. Aggarwal and P. S. Yu. Online analysis of community evolution in data streams. In *Proceedings of the2005 SIAM International Conference on Data Mining*, pages 56–67. SIAM, 2005.

27. V. D. Blondel, J. L. Guillaume, R. Lambiotte, and E. Lefebvre. Fast Unfolding of Communities in Large Networks. *Journal of Statistical Mechanics: Theory and Experiment*, 10: 10008, 2008.

28. R. Brause, T. Langsdorf, and M. Hepp. Neural data mining for credit card fraud detection. In *Proceedings of the 11th IEEE International Conference on Tools with Artificial Intelligence*, ICTAI '99, page 103, Washington, DC, 1999. IEEE Computer Society.

29. C. Anderson. *The Long Tail: Why the Future of Business Is Selling Less of More*. Hyperion, New York, NY, USA, 2006.

30. R. F. Hunter, H. McAneney, M. Davis, M. A. Tully, T. W. Valente, and F. Kee. "Hidden" social networks in behavior change interventions. *American Journal of Public Health*, 105, 2015.

31. A. Yessad, C. Faron, R. Dieng, and T. Laskri. Ontology-driven adaptive course generation for web-based education. In *ED-MEDIA 2008 (World Conference on Educational Multimedia, Hypermedia and Telecommunications, Vienna, Austria, June 30–July 4, 2008)*, 2008.

32. C. P. Passarinho, E. O. T. Salles, and M. Sarcinelli-Filho. Detection and tracking faces in unconstrained color video streams. In G. Bebis, R. Boyle, B. Parvin, D. Koracin, S. Wang, K. Kyungnam, B. Benes, K. Moreland, C. Borst, S. DiVerdi, C. Yi-Jen and J. Ming, editors, *Advances in Visual Computing*, pages 466–475, Springer, Berlin, Heidelberg, 2011.

33. T. R. Gruber. A translation approach to portable ontology specifications. *Knowledge Acquisition*, 5(2):199–220, June 1993.

34. M. Lindstrom. *Small Data: The Tiny Clues That Uncover Huge Trends*. Hodder & Stoughton, London, UK, 2016.

35. J. Dean and S. Ghemawat. MapReduce: simplified data processing on large clusters. In *OSDI 04: Proceedings of The 6th Conference on Symposium on Operating Systems Design and Implementation*. USENIX Association, 2004.

36. D. Knoke. *Emerging Trends in Social Network Analysis of Terrorism and Counterterrorism*. John Wiley & Sons, Inc., Hoboken, NJ, USA, 2015.

37. J. Von Neumann. *Theory of Games and Economic Behavior*. Princeton University Press, Princeton, NJ, USA, 1944.

38. National Research Council. *Network Science*. The National Academies Press, Washington, DC, 2005.

39. S. Brin and L. Page. The anatomy of a large-scale hypertextual web search engine. In *Proceedings of the seventh International Conference on the World Wide Web (WWW1998)*, pages 107–117, 1998.

40. R. Frisch. Editor's note. *Econometrica*, 1(1):1–4, 1933.

41. U. Brandes and D. Fleischer. Centrality Measures Based on Current Flow. In *22nd Symp. Theoretical Aspects of Computer Science (STACS 05)*, number 3404 in LNCS, pages 533–544. Springer Verlag, 2005.

42. M. E. J. Newman. A measure of betweenness centrality based on random walks. *Social Networks*, 27(1):39–54, 2005.

43. C. Thovex and F. Trichet. An Epistemic Equivalence for Predictive Social Networks Analysis. In *Web Information Systems Engineering - WISE 2011 and 2012 Workshops, Sydney, Australia and Paphos, Cyprus, volume 7652 of Lecture Notes in Computer Sciences (LNCS)*, pages 201–214. Springer-Verlag, Berlin Heidelberg, 2013.

44. S. A. Kripke. *Philosophical Troubles: Collected Papers, Volume 1*, volume 1. Oxford University Press, Oxford, UK, 2011.

45. W. A. Fuller. *Sampling Statistics*. John Wiley & Sons, Inc., Hoboken, NJ, USA, 2009.

46. C. Chapman and E. M. Feit. *R for Marketing Research and Analytics*, Segmentation: Clustering and Classification, pages 299–338. Springer, New York NY, USA, Use R! 2015.

47. I. Dhillon, Y. Guan, and B. Kulis. *A unified view of kernel k-means, spectral clustering and graph cuts*. Technical report, University of Texas at Austin, Department of Computer Sciences Austin, TX 78712, 2005.

48. T. Hastie, R. Tibshirani, and J. Friedman. *The Elements of Statistical Learning: Data Mining, Inference, and Prediction*. Second Edition. Springer, New York NY, USA, 2009.

49. R. Gras, E. Suzuki, F. Guillet, and F. Spagnolo. *Statistical Implicative Analysis, Theory and Applications*, volume 127 of *Studies in Computational Intelligence*. Springer Verlag, Berlin, Germany, 2008.

50. L. M. De Campos, J. A. Gomez, and S. Moral. Partial abductive inference in bayesian belief networks by simulated annealing. *International Journal of Approximate Reasoning*, 27 (3):263–283, 2001.

51. S. Boyd, P. Diaconis, and L. Xiao. Fastest mixing Markov chain on a graph. *SIAM Review*, 46:667–689, 2003.

52. P. Wilinski, B. Solaiman, A. Hillion, and W. Czarnecki. Toward the Border Between Neural and Markovian Paradigms. *IEEE Transactions on Systems, Man, and Cybernetics, Part B*, 28 (2):146–159, 1998.

53. L. Breiman. Random Forests. *Machine Learning*, 45(1):5–32, 2001.

54. Z. Yao, M. S. Andrew, S. A. Madhu, and A. L. Alpha. Energy-entropy competition and the effectiveness of stochastic gradient descent in machine learning. *Computing Research Repository, CoRR*, abs/1803.01927: 1–8, 2018.

55. A. Krizhevsky, I. Sutskever, and G. E. Hinton. ImageNet Classification with Deep Convolutional Neural Networks. In *Advances in Neural Information Processing Systems 25: 26th Annual Conference on Neural Information Processing Systems 2012. Lake Tahoe, Nevada, United States*, pages 1106–1114, 2012.

56. Q. Wang. Artificial neural network and hidden space svm for fault detection in power system. In *ISNN2009:Proceedings of the 6th International Symposium on Neural Networks*. Springer Verlag, 2009.

57. M. Pedersoli and T. Tuytelaars. A scalable 3d hog model for fast object detection and viewpoint estimation. In *20142nd International Conference on 3D Vision*, volume 1, pages 163–170, Dec 2014.

58. Y. Dai, J. Yan, X. Tang, H. Zhao, and M. Guo. Online credit card fraud detection: A hybrid framework with big data technologies. In *2016 IEEE Trustcom/BigDataSE/ISPA*, pages 1644–1651, Aug 2016.

59. M. Devaine, P. Gaillard, Y. Goude, and G. Stoltz. Forecasting electricity consumption by aggregating specialized experts. *Machine Learning*, 90(2):231–260, 2013. 33 pages.

60. S. Bubeck and R. Eldan. Multi-scale exploration of convex functions and bandit convex optimization. In *Conference On Learning Theory - COLT*, 2016.

61. M. Alkhawlani and A. Ayesh. Access network selection based on fuzzy logic and genetic algorithms. *Advance in Artificial Intellgence*, 8(1):1, 1-1:12, January 2008.

62. D. Chakrabarti, R. Kumar, and A. Tomkins. Evolutionary clustering. In *Proceedings of the 12th ACM SIGKDD International Conference on Knowledge Discovery and Data Mining*, pages 554–560. ACM, 2006.

63. V. Feoktistov. *Differential Evolution: In Search of Solutions*. 2006.

64. H. Putnam. *Mind, Language and Reality*. Cambridge University Press, Cambridge, UK 1975.

65. C. Thovex, B. Le Grand, O. Cervantes, A. J. Sanchez, and F. Trichet. *Encyclopedia of Social Network Analysis and Mining*, Semantic Social Networks Analysis, pages 1–12. Springer New York, New York, NY, 2017.

66. D. Hubel and T. Wiesel. Receptive fields, binocular interaction and functional architecture in the cat's visual cortex. *Journal of Physiology (London)*, 1(160):106–154, 1962.

67. M. Fink. Time reversal of ultrasonic fields. I. Basic principles. *IEEE Transactions on Ultrasonics, Ferroelectrics, and Frequency Control*, 39(5):555–566, 9, 1992.

68. C. Thovex. Deep probabilistic learning in hidden social networks and facsimile detection. In *The 2018 IEEE/ACM International Conference on Advances in Social Networks Analysis and Mining, ASONAM2018, Barcelona, Spain*, pages 731–735. IEEE Computer Society, 2018.

69. J. Hwang, Y. Jeong, J. M. Park, K. H. Lee, J. W. Hong, and J. Choi. Biomimetics: forecasting the future of science, engineering, and medicine. *International Journal of Nanomedicine*, 10:5701–5713, 2015.

70. N. H. Arai, N. Todo, T. Arai, K. Bunji, S. Sugawara, M. Inuzuka, T. Matsuzaki, and K. Ozaki. Reading skill test to diagnose basic language skills in comparison to machines. In *CogSci*, 2017.

71. J. Pitrat. *Artificial Beings: The Conscience of a Conscious Machine*. ISTE. Wiley, London, UK, 2010.

72. H. K. Lam, S. S. H. Ling, and H. T. Nguyen. *Computational Intelligence and Its Applications: Evolutionary Computation, Fuzzy Logic, Neural Network and Support Vector Machine Techniques*. Imperial College Press, London, UK, 2011.

73. P. Brazdil, C. Giraud-Carrier, C. Soares, and R. Vilalta. *Metalearning: Applications to Data Mining*. Springer Publishing Company Incorporated, Heidelberg, Germany, 1st edition 2008.

74. J. Pitrat. *Metaconnaissance: Futur de l'intelligence artificielle*. Hermes, 1990.

75. R. Kurzweil. *The Singularity Is Near: When Humans Transcend Biology*. Penguin (Non-Classics), London, UK, 2006.

76. C. Thovex. *Social Networks and Surveillance for Society*, We Shall Not Only Survive To The Future of Social Networks, pages 101–113. Ö-zyer, T. and Bakshi, S. and, Alhajj, R., Springer, Heidelberg, Germany, 2018.

77. A. Avanessian, A. Hennig, and L. R. Bryant. *Metanoia: A Speculative Ontology of Language, Thinking, and the Brain.* Bloomsbury Publishing, New York NY, USA, 2017.

78. J. Surowiecki. *The Wisdom of Crowds.* Anchor Books, New York, NY, USA, 2005.

79. P. A. Samuelson, T. C. Koopmans, and J. R. N. Stone. Report of the evaluative committee for econometrica. *Econometrica*, 22(2):141–146, 1954.

CHAPTER 16

Ethical Issues and Considerations of Big Data

Edward T. Chen

University of Massachusetts Lowell, Lowell, MA, USA

CONTENTS

1 INTRODUCTION

"Big Data" is a popular phrase that has been spread widely on the media and among the common public in the last few years. It talks about extremely large and highly heterogeneous datasets that may be explored computationally to uncover "patterns, trends, and associations," specifically relating to behaviors and interactions of humans. The novelty of Big Data encloses ethical problems which are not new.

At the Netherlands, one of a 16-year-old girl's birthday was celebrated in her town and more than 3,000 people came to the party after she had by mistake, on Facebook, posted her birthday invitation (BBC, 2012). We may think that the significant ethical challenge that the current technology is posing concerns primarily youngsters. It appears that way, however, specifically with the advent of Big Data, and thus, traditional ethical concepts have to be re-evaluated by the ethicists (Zwitter, 2014).

Ethics refers to standards of right and wrong that direct what we have to do, typically guided by duties, rights, costs, and benefits. Ethical issues are commonly well known and be aware of, and are also broadly debated often in the media. For instance, they come up in the context of the Snowden leaks and the corresponding inquiries by *The Guardian*, concerned with the abilities of intelligence bureau (Scheuerman, 2014; The Guardian, 2013).

Another scenario is, police predictive software produces probability reports on criminality and assures us that by using this software program, societies will reduce crime. Other programs are looking for patterns from Big Data that would help us predict a terrorist attack. Criminal justice systems are using a technological solution to predict future crimes of those applying for bail or those to be sent on a parole. However, it leads to a series of ethical challenges relating to privacy, discrimination, and presumption of innocence (Mayer-Schönberger & Cukier, 2014).

Big Data uprising creates a set of ethical problems mainly associated with the following concerns:

- Privacy and group privacy
- Confidentiality
- Transparency
- Identity
- Propensity
- Research ethics
- Inference attack

The purpose of this paper is to find, describe, and assess some of the key Big Data ethical issues and to put forward ideas and ways in which some of them may be tackled. It further directs and guides scientists and organizations to rethink on policymaking and research strategies while handling Big Data.

2 BIG DATA

A radical change which makes the Big Data more valuable to businesses is the ability to bring together and measure both structured and unstructured data speedily. Structured data denotes a well-organized data model, for example, rows and columns on a Relational Data Base Management Systems (RDBMS). Unstructured data denotes to a data lake, which contains pre-organized data like text, digital pictures, social media conversations, etc. (Brinkmann, 2013).

Big Data is frequently created through automation, which is less expensive than the manual process. For example, web logs, transaction data, point-of-sale scanners, and Radio Frequency Identification (RFID) tags are generated automatically. The beginning of "digital communication and social media" has opened a door to generate and gather an enormous amount of digital contents like text and images (Forbes, 2017). For example, sensors what we use in our homes and cars and even in our bodies such as Smartwatch generate Big Data in a sub-second from multiple streams. Digital devices are data generation machines (Dias & Paulo Silva Cunha, 2018; Koshy et al., 2018). They can routinely produce records of our activities, from browsing on the web and through Mobile Apps like RunKeeper. Data has been generated widely using low-cost data generation technologies, which means Big Data can grow to terabytes and petabytes (1,000 terabytes) very quickly. McKinsey assessed in 2011 that the volume of digital content on the Web is expected to rise by 44 times by 2020, at an annual growth rate of 40% (Manyika, Chui, Brown, Bughin, Dobbs, Roxburgh, & Byers, 2011). Let us review some Big Data-related topics and concepts in this section, which are going to be useful to understand the issues and solutions related to Big Data ethics further in this article.

2.1 Datafication

"A set of collective tools, technologies, and processes used to transform an organization to a data-driven enterprise" is called datafication. It is also called Datafy. A firm that carries out datafication is called datafied.

2.2 Data Stewardship

Providing easily accessible high-quality data to the business users in a consistent manner by properly managing the data assets of an organization is called Data Stewardship.

2.3 Upstream and Downstream

"Upstream" sources of data and "Downstream" uses of data are part of "information supply chain" within the Big Data industry. The examples of "Upstream" sources are

1. Quality: Level of data accuracy

2. Biases: Race; Ethnicity; Gender; Geography

3. Privacy: Violation of confidentiality agreement

The examples of "Downstream" uses are

1. Consequences to Consumers: Value created or destroyed by using customer data for analytics

2. Level of Treating Consumers: Individuals respected

2.4 Negative Externality

When a transaction happens between producer and consumer, it means it is between first and second parties respectively. But a cost of pain experienced by a third party as a result of that business transaction is usually not considered by first and second parties. That cost is called Negative Externality. For example, if a company produces steel and that creates pollution. Then, the company gets a business contract with a customer and sells steel. But that business transaction does not consider the cost of pollution incurred by the business. This is an example of Negative Externality. That means a resource or an individual indirectly affected by a transaction. Another example is long-term impact to individuals due to excessive data gathering by an organization with no short-term impact to the organization.

2.5 Procedural Data Due Process

Instead of setting up regulations on personal data collection, use, or disclosure, it regulates the process to run analytical processes of Big Data fairly with regard to how data scientists use the personal data of an individual in any "adjudicative" process. It is a process that identifies attributes or traits of an individual (Barocas & Nissenbaum, 2014; Ferguson, 2013).

2.6 Internet of Things

Internet of Things (IoT) is a concept which allows disparate electronic devices to perform data transfer. For example, the heart rate of a person can be monitored wirelessly by a mobile pacemaker and the data can be sent to the doctor and hospital for further diagnosis and action (Tarakji, Vives, Patel, Fagan, Sims, & Varma, 2018). Another example is that some smartphone applications can sense your location and physical movement (Chan et al., 2018). RunKeeper app collects the data for your use or for your doctor's perusal during physical checkup or emergency. With the wide spread of Internet access hot spots, IoT is becoming a major part of human life (Porambage,Ylianttila, Schmitt, Kumar, Gurtov, & Vasilakos, 2016). Mario Morales estimated that the revenue opportunity through IoT will become a $4 trillion-dollar industry by 2020 (Gonzalez, 2015).

2.7 Big Data Analytics

By using collected data that recorded your past actions, Big Data analytics can find out what you will do before even you think of to do it. It is very powerful to study consumer online behavior patterns and bring value to the marketers such as market demand, consumer awareness, intention to purchase, etc. This will assist marketers to send promotions and incentives to entice the consumers and gain more market share on their products (Bibri & Krogstie, 2017; Tsai, Lai, Chao, &Vasilakos, 2015).

2.8 Data Scientists

Data scientists are people who can analyze and interpret complex and heterogeneous data to help an organization to take an appropriate decision-making in their business. Data scientists use both statistical methods and machine learning techniques to recognize the patterns and understand the meanings behind the data structure. In fact, data scientists use software tools alike to those of statisticians, data miners, and predictive modelers (Tractenberg, Russell, Morgan, Fitzgerald, Collmann, Vinsel, Steinmann, & Dolling, 2015).

One of "news" websites called IncredibleAd (actual name has been changed) is sustained purely by advertising revenue. To prove its value to advertisers, IncredibleAd supplies statistics of how often readers click on the banner ads. Data scientists at IncredibleAd have discovered a new way to increase revenue. If they place a vertical banner ad on the right side of the browser such that all but an edge of the banner is hidden, then the number of "clicks" doubles—an outcome that has been proved beyond any statistical doubt in repeated experiments. It is surmised that readers accidentally click on the advertisement section while using the scrollbar (Fung, 2016).

Even today, many data scientists think this kind of data manipulation is not against Big Data ethics. This example is one of the several ethical dilemmas being faced by real-world data scientists (Fung, 2015, 2016; Tractenberg et al., 2015).

2.9 Big Data Breaches

Breachlevelindex.com shows more than 1.9 billion data breaches happened in the first half of 2017. As we all know, the personal data like Social Security Number (SSN) stored in

Government offices is more valuable than any other industry. Unfortunately, more records are breached in Government offices with a whopping 21%. In 2017, identity theft was the leading type of data breach based on the number of incidents (74%) and nuisance is all-time high based on the number of breached records. In the first half of 2017, the number of breaches by identity theft jumped 49% from the previous six months when the total was 456. The number of records stolen by the type of identity theft during the first half of 2017 is dramatically increased compared with previous six months, rising 255% from 78 million to 275 million (Gemalto, 2017). Breachlevelindex.com reported that 1.90 billion data records are compromised globally in the first half of 2017. Despite the fact that many organizations are focused on detecting and stopping threats from outsiders, the internal threats like malicious intruders, accidental loss, and other negligence are considered as low risk (Ahmed,Latif, Latif, Abbas, & Khan, 2018; Gemalto, 2017).

To breach data privacy, by exploiting software and hardware design flaws in the Big Data platform infrastructure, intruders inject false data into the raw data or steal large sensitive datasets. They access already analyzed datasets to snip the business intelligence stored on those datasets, which was generated by the data scientists using BI algorithms from the original data (Illingworth, 2015). The identity of a person and inferred data can be compromised through Big Data breach. Therefore, while companies reap the benefits of Big Data, they should focus on challenges that include preventing security risks and attacks aimed at the Big Data platform infrastructure where sensitive raw data and inferred knowledge are stored (Simo, 2015).

3 BIG DATA ETHICS AND RELATED ISSUES

3.1 Privacy

The ability of an individual or a group to separate themselves or isolate the information about themselves is called Privacy. Thus, they can reveal themselves selectively. It does not mean that the information must always be kept secret. Confirming privacy of data is a matter of outlining and imposing information rules, not just setting up rules for collecting data. But, it is applicable to usage and retention of data as well (Davis, 2012). The general public must have the ability to handle the flow of their personal information through massive analytical systems owned by an institution. It is not an easy task to keep privacy alive using latest technologies. For example, a software developed by Raytheon using Rapid Information Overlay Technology (RIOT) consumes social networks data that is accessible freely and information linked with an IP address, cookies, etc. to create a profile of an individual and make people to fully see-through the day-to-day activities of that person (Gallagher, 2013).

3.2 Shared Private Information Can Still Be Confidential

It is unrealistic to group the information can be treated as either secret or shared, entirely public or private. Usually, by the design of the trusted services, some data is shared or created such as address books, global positioning systems, cellphone towers, and mobile trackers. But, there is no implicit meaning that we allow to share or create information with no rules, particularly data connected to our medical records, finance, home address, current location, etc. (Richards & King, 2014; Zimmer, 2010).

3.3 Big Data Entails Transparency

Big Data is a weapon to produce new predictions and inferences from a dataset. Even though the data was collected for the business purpose over and over again without our approval, the data is shared in many ways to the third-party vendors, which we do not want. The people who handle the data like data scientist need to have a crystal-clear view of how the data is being used in their analytical process and shared with third-party vendors.

3.4 Big Data Can Compromise Identity

No more we can expect full protections against privacy. By allowing institutional surveillance to moderate, the identity of a person can be compromised through Big Data analytics. Even it determines who we are before we make up our own minds. We should be very cautious about what kind of data we will allow and what we should not; based on how it can aid someone to predict and inference about us (King & Richards, 2014; Tsai et al., 2015).

3.5 Group Privacy

The data of location, religion, gender, age, and other information, that is used for statistical analysis relevant for the belongingness to a group, relates to the issue of group privacy. For example, knowing that a particular group prefers soccer game and most of the people on that group has a condition like "which party to vote for is being undecided." One can offer soccer game ticket to this group to react in a particular way by creating a conditionality such as if one votes to a specific "Party" gets a soccer game ticket. Even though this is a typical party politics, we cannot deny that Big Data analytics increase the proficiency to discover buried associations. That will in turn increase the capability of data scientists to create incentives whose purposes are opaque (Tsai et al., 2015).

3.6 Propensity

It is a visualization of upcoming, which predicts about what a person was likely to do could lead to his/her imprisonment with no act has been committed. For example, results from Big Data analytics could point to a certain dangerous location, criminal groups, or innocent individuals such as a divorced mom or dad living in a community with no job, who probably would commit a crime, so that police have them watched with more vigilance for prevention of potential crimes (Mayer-Schönberger & Cukier, 2014).

3.7 Research Ethics

Ethics of planning, conducting, and reporting of research, a researcher could accidentally reveal uncomfortable information about a group (Swazey & Bird, 1997; Tikly & Bond, 2013). For example, data scientists who use Twitter might share uncomfortable facts about particular groups, possibly with negative effects on the examined group (Elson, Yeung, Roshan, Bohandy, & Nader, 2012).

3.8 Inference Attack

The opponent or competitor takes a published dataset possibly with some background knowledge as input and tries to deduce some personal information regarding individuals exposed in the dataset.

4 IMPLICATIONS OF BIG DATA ETHICS

4.1 Data Breaches or Breaches in Ethics?

If we focus only on data security and compliance, the behavior of an employee might be observed but certainly cannot be controlled easily. Every firm is built with different kinds of human resources like full-time employees, contractors, and business partners. Each resource is going to have its own weaknesses and problems that cannot be recorded and stored in company scorecard (McChesney, 2015). Preventing data breaches using tools and techniques is more effective to monitor and prohibit employees from unauthorized data transfer or data modification. But, it cannot totally prevent irrational or criminal activities of employees who work in an enterprise. Therefore, both data breaches and breaches in ethics should be addressed at the same time (Lieberman, 2011).

To address the breaches in ethics, the company has to create a set of rules and train its employees to enforce the ethical behaviors with good management, sensing, and dosage of fear in workplace (McChesney, 2015; White, Ariyachandra, & White, 2017).

4.2 Big Data Ethical Examples and Impacts

The following are some real-life examples that would help to understand the importance of Big Data ethics:

- Privacy notice has not been conveyed when personal information is gathered by an institution.

- The specific type of data that can put the organization in danger is being used and is not gauged by the organization.

- Preventive measures have not been taken by an organization to mitigate the risks related to Big Data ethics such as data access control and penalties for misuse.

- Vigilant analysis was not done by the firm when sharing or acquiring data from third parties.

The following are the organizational impacts as a result of abovementioned ethical breakings:

- Losing tens of thousands of customers like Facebook.

- Brand reputation damage like Sony, Ashley Madison, Barclays, TJ Maxx, and Carphone Warehouse.

- Paying penalties like Equifax, TransUnion, and Experian.

- Negative impact on revenue like Macy's, Adidas, Delta, and Best Buy.

4.3 Future Implications

- By 2018, 50% of business ethics abuses will be related to data ().

- Impact humanity and environment severely.

- Opens a door for "Indirect Discrimination."

5 RECOMMENDED SOLUTIONS

5.1 The Consumer Privacy Bill of Rights Framework

In recent years, Big Data has been expanded tremendously and, in consequence, the potential threat of security breaches and data mismanagement has also been raised incredibly, as discussed in detail in above three sections.

In 2012, while presenting "The Consumer Privacy Bill of Rights" to the Congress, President Obama stated that "One thing should be clear, even though we live in a world in which we share personal information more freely than in the past, we must reject the conclusion that privacy is an outmoded value." This bill is one kind of framework for protecting consumers' shared data and the firm's collected data (McChesney, 2015). A similar bill must be passed by every country, not only the United States. Most importantly, the framework should be strictly implemented and followed by every institution to protect consumer data and citizen information. The key principles of this framework are:

5.1.1 Individual Control
Customers are authorized to do data share as they wish. Based on the function of the firm, consumers can publicize or hold up the data. The firm must provide *clear* information on what the data will be used for and how it will be used.

5.1.2 Transparency
Consumers have rights to be aware of the privacy threats related to sharing their Personally Identifiable Information (PII).

5.1.3 Context
The PII provided by each person must be used for the purposes by which individuals consented to. If a firm would like to consume the PII for another purpose, it must get permission from the consumer, with "clear distinction for the purpose of use."

5.1.4 Safeguard
PII must be protected with cutting-edge security platform and data exposure to cyber-attack or degradation must be prevented (Fuller, 2017). The best practices on safeguarding customer data should be openly revealed by the organizations.

5.1.5 Data Access and Accuracy

The consumer has rights to correct their PII data. It is the accountability of the firm to keep proper and accurate information. Once the companies set up a facility for the consumers to access and modify their incorrect PII data, then the consumer is legally responsible to the data inaccuracy.

5.1.6 Focused Collection

Organizations should use collected consumer data only to attain company objectives. This principle concurs with the abovementioned "Context" principle, as organizations are only permitted to gather information what is required. When the objective of the company is achieved, the data must be removed permanently, or the individual's file must be indicated as "unidentified material."

5.1.7 Liability

Organizations are compelled to observe to the "Consumer Privacy Bill of Rights" and will be held responsible for any infringements against the mishandling of any consumer information.

5.2 General Guidelines to Organizations

The following are the general guidelines to organizations to be away from Big Data ethical issues:

- Being able to reap the benefits of Big Data by not only safeguarding the privacy of individuals, but also by ensuring that they remain in control of their digital lives. Companies must enforce regulatory methods to let users examine and correct the information collected about them.

- Appoint a Chief Data Officer (CDO) to strictly observe business ethics.

- Safeguard privacy

  ○ Chief Privacy Officer (CPO) has to establish and enforce processes and practices to meet privacy concerns of customers, employees, and vendors.

- Organizations must use appropriate security measures, technologies, and tools.

- Data scientists must apply more prescriptive analytics into business analytics applications.

- CIO must allocate enough fund to increase staffing and for adequate infrastructure to follow the abovementioned recommendations (Pearlson, Saunders, & Galletta, 2016).

5.3 Possible Solutions for Information Supply Chain Industry Ethical Issues

The information supply chain starts from an individual's personal data and ends with a customer. Guidelines to solve ethical issues for a sustainable Big Data supply chain industry are discussed in this section. We will apply the abovementioned concepts of Data Stewardship, Data Due Process, Upstream and Downstream, and Negative Externality. These concepts will help us to understand the below-recommended solutions vividly. There are three major ethics problems we are trying to solve in this section as listed in the Table 5.1.

1. Supply chain sourcing and use issues: For example, retailing company Target sent a congratulatory letter to a girl's house when it identified she was pregnant based on her purchase history. Her parents were unaware of her pregnancy and that created a chaos in the family (Martin, 2015).

2. Surveillance as Negative Externality: Surveillance affects not only the individuals who are being watched, it also affects who are not actually being watched. Because they believe and act as though they are under surveillance. For example, prisons are designed to watch a set of prisoners. But the prisoners do not know exactly who is being watched by the guards at a given point of time.

3. The issues arise from reselling consumer's data to the secondary market of Big Data.

Martin (2015) recommends solutions to directly address these three common Big Data ethical issues. Martin provides guidelines to "CIOs" and "CDOs" to resolve these problems. Despite Big Data supply chain industry has potential to create harm, it has more potential to be a force for good (Martin, 2015). Therefore, by solving Big Data ethics problems as described below would create more value for all stakeholders.

5.4 Ethical Principles for Data Scientists

To build a successful business by an organization using Big Data platforms, the data scientists who are also called "Big Data analysts" need to abide by the following principles of ethics (Kassner, 2017).

5.4.1 Beneficial

The Big Data should deliver great value to both the individuals who did data generation and the institution that gathers and analyzes it. For example, one of the Senior VP of Caesars Entertainment, Joshua Kanter, mentioned "Before conducting any new analysis, we ask ourselves whether it will bring benefit to customers in addition to the company. If it does not, we will not do it" (Kassner, 2017).

5.4.2 Progressive

There should be a culture of continuous improvement and innovation from the organization to achieve anticipated improvements with less data-intensive processing. The data scientists should guide the business team to use a minimal amount of necessary data to meet their desired goal with an understanding that minimal use of data helps more sustainable analysis with fewer risks.

TABLE 16.1 Information supply chain recommended solutions (Martin, 2015).

Problem	Root Cause	Possible Solution	Action Items for "CIOs" and "CDOs"
Supply Chain Sourcing and Use Issues	**Data Stewardship**		
	Supply chain not noticeable	Make data stewardship practices of supply chain noticeable	Do not enter into confidentiality agreements that preclude explaining your data partners, either upstream sources or downstream uses
	Organizations are not responsible for conduct of upstream sources and downstream customers	Explain the role of the organization in large supply chain. Create machine readable notification of supply chain info for "policymakers, reports and privacy advocates"	Identify and take ownership of upstream sources and downstream customers/uses of data. Making sure information about data stewardship practices is open to experts and novices
Surveillance as Negative Externality	**Data Due Process**		
	Harm to others not captured by firms collecting, storing, or using PII	Reduce surveillance	Make tracking known to consumer
		Internalize cost of surveillance with increased data due process	Require additional data due process for firms acquiring and retaining PII
Harmful Demand for PII	**Data Integrity**		
	Secondary market of data trading has lower quality needs than primary consumer-focused market	Use a data integrity professional when handling or selling PII	Get data integrity professional or board of projects partnering with Big Data sources and customers
	Secondary market is not visible to primary market (consumers)	Make activity in secondary market visible to regulators and consumers	Account for and communicate additional risk from partnering in secondary market for Big Data through disclosure

5.4.3 Sustainable

When data scientists use Big Data in a production system, sustainable value should be provided over a reasonable time frame. We need to consider the following three categories to maintain sustainability.

Data Sustainability: It is related to what kind of data access an organization does have to do with various social data sets. For example, it may cause havoc when both public and private sources are combined during a data set creation. The issue of sourcing like inconsistency in sample file size or approaches would shake the integrity of the data. Also, it could impact the sustainability of the algorithm.

Algorithmic Sustainability: Algorithm's longevity is really critical. It will be affected by the way the data has been generated, collected, and analyzed.

Device/Manufacturer-Based Sustainability: The lifetime of the data being gathered should be considered. For instance, if a device that collects the data has been discontinued or the data is auctioned off to a vendor, what would happen?

5.4.4 Respectful

Data scientists should be more cognizant of the data belongs to whom, company that creates the data, company that rollups the data, and those who regulate the data in various ways. Individual who provides the data will be affected mostly by Big Data analytical process done by the data scientists, especially when they make private and semi-private data to the public. The executives of the company should ask themselves "Have we been transparent and comprehensive?"

5.4.5 Fair

Even though US government's law disallows the discrimination based on gender, race, and age, data processes developed by the data scientists can predict all of those traits by not looking the fields labeled age, gender, and race. Before releasing the sensitive and personal information of consumers, the top-level executives of the company and data scientists should think about how people would react if those details are released openly. Will it threaten customer relationship and loyalty or strengthen them?

6 CONCLUSION

As far as Big Data Ethics is concerned, it is not an overemphasis to say that, Big Data has a solid impact on assumptions about the power distributions across Big Data collectors, Big Data utilizers, and Big Data generators, and individual responsibility. In the long run, ethicists have to bring the topics like "how people can live in a *datafied* world and what are all Big Data abuse preventing measures?" to their table.

There is a considerable amount of work to do in transforming the above-recommended solutions and discussed principles into laws and references into rules that will produce clear standards in the ethical handling of Big Data. And certainly, more principles need to be developed as we continuously build more efficient Big Data ecosystem. Any person involved in managing Big Data should express their concerns or opinions in the ethical discussion concerning how Big Data should be used. Data scientists, developers, and data administrators are on the front lines of the whole issue.

Even though the law is a powerful weapon for Big Data Ethics, it is far from handling many use-cases and nuanced scenarios that surface. Enforcing the following regulations are also vital to an organization:

1. Institutional statements of ethics like rules, norms, and strategies.

2. Organizational principles of handling big data.

3. Self-policing of potential breaches and hacks.

4. Any additional forms of ethical guidance such as professional codes of conduct.

Technology itself can be an instrument to intelligently track how our data is being used. It can help us decide on whether we allow the analysis to use the data that takes place beyond our control and spheres of awareness or not. We also need well-defined fundamental default rules to allow certain processing of personal data and to accept only certain decisions based on personal data when they have an emotional impact on people's lives.

Eventually, Big Data ethical issues will be solved and corrected more and more when organizations continue to put more focus and effort on the need of security measures to safeguard individuals as well as their organization. Let us keep in mind that each and every one of us has an obligation to preserve data. We must be accountable for the data what we hold on and share with. Big Data ethics, what we discussed and recommended in this chapter, is for everyone who is a responsible data user.

REFERENCES

Ahmed, A., Latif, R., Latif, S., Abbas, H., & Khan, F.A. (2018). Malicious insiders attack in IoT based multi-cloud e-healthcare environment: a systematic literature review. *Multimedia Tools and Applications, 77*(17), 21947–21965.

Barocas, S., & Nissenbaum, H. (2014). Computing ethics: big data's end run around procedural privacy protections. *Communications of the ACM, 57*(11), 31–33.

BBC. (2012). Facebook party invite sparks riot in Haren, Netherlands. *BBC News.* Retrieved January 10, 2018 from www.bbc.co.uk/news/world-europe-19684708

Bibri, S.E., & Krogstie, J. (2017). The core enabling technologies of big data analytics and context-aware computing for smart sustainable cities: a review and synthesis. *Journal of Big Data, 4*(1), 1–50. doi:10.1186/s40537-017-0091-6

Brinkmann, P. (2013). Whybig data is a big deal. *InsuranceERM,* Milliman. Retrieved December 20, 2017 from www.milliman.com/insight/2013/Why-big-data-is-a-big-deal/

Chan, Y.Y., Bot, B.M., Zweig, M., Tignor, N., Ma, W., Suver, C., Cedeno, R., Scott, E.R., Hershman, S.G., Schadt, E.E., & Wang, P. (2018). The asthma mobile health study, smartphone data collected using ResearchKit. *Scientific Data, 5,* 1–11.

Davis, K. (2012). *Ethics of Big Data: Balancing Risk and Innovation.* Sebastopol, CA: O'Reilly Media Inc.

Dias, D., & Paulo Silva Cunha, J. (2018). Wearable health devices-vital sign monitoring, systems and technologies. *Sensors, 18*(8), 2414–2441. doi:10.3390/s18082414.

Elson, S.B., Yeung, D., Roshan, P., Bohandy, S.R., & Nader, A. (2012). *Using Social Media to Gauge Iranian Public Opinion and Mood after the 2009 Election.* RAND Corporation. Retrieved January 10, 2018 from www.rand.org/pubs/technical_reports/TR1161.html

Ferguson, R.B. (2013). Why predictive analytics needs due process. *MIT Sloan Management Review.* Retrieved December 17, 2017 from https://sloanreview.mit.edu/article/why-predictive-analytics-needs-due-process/

Forbes, D. (2017). Professional online presence and learning networks: educating for ethical use of social media. *International Review of Research in Open and Distance Learning, 18*(7), Retrieved December 18, 2017 from www.irrodl.org/index.php/irrodl/article/view/2826/4438

Fuller, M. (2017). Big data, ethics and religion: new questions from a new science. *Religions, 8*(5), 88–98. doi:10.3390/rel8050088.

Fung, K. (2015). The ethics conversation we're not having about data. *Harvard Business Review.* Retrieved January 10, 2018 from https://hbr.org/2015/11/the-ethics-conversation-were-not-having-about-data

Fung, K. (2016), Ethical dilemmas in data science and analytics. Retrieved January 8, 2018 from http://junkcharts.typepad.com/numbersruleyourworld/2016/07/ethical-dilemmas-in-data-science-and-analytics.html

Gallagher, R. (2013). Software that tracks people on social media created by defense firm. *The Guardian*. Retrieved January 15, 2018 from www.theguardian.com/world/2013/feb/10/soft ware-tracks-social-media-defence

Gemalto. (2017). 2017 poor internal security practices take a toll: findings from the first half of 2017, breach level index. *Gemalto*. Retrieved December 20, 2017 from https://cdn.securityledger.com/wp-content/uploads/2017/09/Breach_Level_Index_Report_H1_2017_Gemalto_FINAL.pdf

Gonzalez, N. (2015). The moral and ethics surrounding big data. *Aponia*. Retrieved December 20, 2017 from http://aponia.co/moral-ethics-surrounding-big-data/

Illingworth, A.J. (2015). Big data in I-O psychology: privacy considerations and discriminatory algorithms. *Industrial and Organizational Psychology*, 8(4), 567–575. doi:10.1017/iop.2015.85.

Kassner, M. (2017). 5 ethics principles big data analysts must follow. *Tech Republic*. Retrieved January 8, 2018 from www.techrepublic.com/article/5-ethics-principles-big-data-analysts-must-follow/

King, J.H., & Richards, R.M. (2014). What's up with big data ethics? *Forbes*. Retrieved January 10, 2018 from www.forbes.com/sites/oreillymedia/2014/03/28/whats-up-with-big-data-ethics/#3cc470793591

Koshy, A.N., Sajeev, J.K., Nerlekar, N., Brown, A.J., Rajakariar, K., Zureik, M., Wong, M.C., Roberts, L., Street, M., Cooke, J., & Te, A.W. (2018). Smart watches for heart rate assessment in atrial arrhythmias. *International journal of cardiology*, 266, 124–127.

Lieberman, D. (2011). Data breaches or breaches in ethics?*Infosec Island*. Retrieved January 10, 2018 from www.infosecisland.com/blogview/14520-Data-Breaches-or-Breaches-in-Ethics.html

Manyika, J., Chui, M., Brown, B., Bughin, J., Dobbs, R., Roxburgh, C., & Byers, A.H. (2011). Big data: the next frontier for innovation, competition, and productivity. *McKinsey Global Institute*. Retrieved January 8, 2018 from www.mckinsey.com/business-functions/digital-mckinsey/our-insights/big-data-the-next-frontier-for-innovation

Martin, K. (2015). Ethical issues in big data industry. *MIS Quarterly Executive*, 14(2), 67–85.

Mayer-Schönberger, V., & Cukier, K. (2014). *Big Data: A Revolution That Will Transform How We Live, Work, and Think*. Boston, MA: Houghton Mifflin Harcourt.

McChesney, A.P. (2015). *The Case for a Consumer Privacy Bill of Rights: A Study of Online Behavioral Advertising and Mobile Device Tracking*. Senior Theses, Trinity College, Hartford, CT. Retrieved December 20, 2017 from https://digitalrepository.trincoll.edu/cgi/viewcontent.cgi?article=1475&context=theses

Pearlson, K.E., Saunders, C., & Galletta, D.F. (2016). *Managing and Using Information Systems: A Strategic Approach*. 6th Edition Hoboken, NJ: John Wiley & Sons.

Porambage, P., Ylianttila, M., Schmitt, C., Kumar, P., Gurtov, A., & Vasilakos, A.V. (2016). The quest for privacy in the Internet of things. *IEEE Cloud Computing*, 3(2), 36–45.

Richards, N.M., & King, J.H. (2014). Big data ethics. *Wake Forest Law Review*, 40, 393–432. Retrieved December 20, 2017 from www.informatica.uniroma2.it/upload/2017/IA2/RIchards%20and%20King%20BigDataEthics.pdf

Scheuerman, W.E. (2014). Snowden and the ethics of whistle blowing. *Boston Review*, May 21. Retrieved January 10, 2018 from www.bostonreview.net.umasslowell.idm.oclc.org/books-ideas/scheuerman-snowden-greenwald-harding-sagar

Simo, H. (2015). *Big Data: Opportunities and Privacy Challenges*. Darmstadt, Germany: Fraunhofer Institute for Secure Information Technology. Retrieved January 8, 2018 from https://arxiv.org/ftp/arxiv/papers/1502/1502.00823.pdf

Swazey, J.P., & Bird, S.J. (1997). Teaching and learning research ethics. In D. Elliott & J.E. Stern (Eds.), *Research Ethics: A Reader* (pp. 1–19). Hanover, NH: University Press of New England.

Tarakji, K.G., Vives, C.A., Patel, A.S., Fagan, D.H., Sims, J., & Varma, N. (2018). Success of pacemaker remote monitoring using app based technology: does patient age matter? *Pacing and Clinical Electrophysiology: PACE*, *41*(10), 1329–1335. doi:10.1111/pace.13461.

The Guardian. (2013). NSA files: decoded. What the revelations mean for you. *The Guardian.* Retrieved January 12, 2018 from www.theguardian.com/world/interactive/2013/nov/01/snowden-nsa-files-surveillance-revelations-decoded

Tikly, L., & Bond, T. (2013). Towards a postcolonial research ethics in comparative and international education. *Compare*, *43*(4), 422–442.

Tractenberg, R.E., Russell, A.J., Morgan, G.J., Fitzgerald, K.T., Collmann, J., Vinsel, L., Steinmann, M., & Dolling, L.M. (2015). Using ethical reasoning to amplify the reach and resonance of professional codes of conduct in training big data scientists. *Science and Engineering Ethics*, *21*(6), 1485–1507. doi:10.1007/s11948-014-9613-1.

Tsai, C.W., Lai, C.F., Chao, H.C., & Vasilakos, A.V. (2015). Big data analytics: a survey. *Journal of Big Data*, *2*(21), 1–32. doi:10.1186/s40537-015-0030-3.

White, G., Ariyachandra, T., & White, D. (2017). Big data, ethics, and social impact theory – a conceptual framework. *Journal of Management & Engineering Integration*, *10*(1), 22–28.

Zimmer, M. (2010). But the data is already public: on the ethics of research in Facebook. *Ethics and Information Technology*, *12*(4), 313–325.

Zwitter, A. (2014). Big data ethics. *Big Data & Society*, *1*(2), 1–6.

CHAPTER 17

Data Protection by Design in Smart Data Environments[1]

Paolo Balboni

CONTENTS

---

[1] All websites were last visited on 31 August 2018.

1 INTRODUCTION

1.1 Welcome to the Data Gold Rush!

Data is frequently called "the oil of the 21st century" or "the fuel of the digital economy," and the era we live in has often been referred to as the "data gold rush."[2] The European Data Protection Authorities, in the general assembly, denominated Article 29 Working Party (which was renamed European Data Protection Board[3] on 25 May 2018, when Regulation 679/2016[4] became directly applicable in all member states of the European Union), defined big data as "the exponential growth both in the availability and in the automated use of information: it refers to gigantic digital datasets held by corporations, governments and other large organizations, which are then extensively analysed using computer algorithms." This definition regards big data as a phenomenon composed of both the process of collecting information and the subsequent step of analysing it. Storing and owning a massive amount of data is meaningless, as the key point is to identify, locate, and extract valuable knowledge from large datasets to enable enhanced insights, inform decision-making, and process automation. Such extracted valuable knowledge is usually referred to as "Smart Data" which is vital in providing suitable decisions in highly on-demand business, science, and engineering applications.

1.2 Topic and Aim

This chapter aims to provide a sound legal methodology to lawfully generate Smart Data from big data and harness value in massive datasets through the correct application of the data protection by design approach. In fact, Smart Data cannot be produced if the data are not lawfully collected in a way that enables their analysis. Legal compliance should therefore be regarded as one of the main enablers of Smart Data.

While big data does not always consist of personal data and could, for example, relate to technical information or to information about objects or natural phenomena, the European Data Protection Supervisor[5] pointed out in its Opinion 7/2015 that "one of the greatest values of big data for businesses and governments is derived from the monitoring of human behaviour, collectively and individually."[6] Analysing and predicting human behavior enables decision-makers in diverse areas to make decisions that are increasingly accurate, consistent, and economical, thereby potentially enhancing the efficiency of society as a whole. A few fields of application that immediately come to mind when

---

[2] European Commission – Press Release – Speech: The Data Gold Rush. 2014. Europa.Eu.http://europa.eu/rapid/press-release_SPEECH-14-229_en.htm.

[3] https://edpb.europa.eu/.

[4] Regulation (Eu) 2016/679 of the European Parliament and of the Council of 27 April 2016 on the protection of natural persons with regard to the processing of personal data and on the free movement of such data, and repealing Directive 95/46/EC (General Data Protection Regulation), *Official Journal of the European Union*, L 119/3, 4/5/2016. Available at: https://eur-lex.europa.eu/legal-content/EN/TXT/HTML/?uri=CELEX:32016R0679&from=IT.

[5] https://edps.europa.eu/edps-homepage_en.

[6] European Data Protection Supervisor. 2015. Opinion 7/2015 – Meeting The Challenges Of Big Data: A Call For Transparency, User Control, Data Protection By Design And Accountability. Available at: https://secure.edps.europa.eu/EDPSWEB/webdav/site/mySite/shared/Documents/Consultation/Opinions/2015/15-11-19_Big_Data_EN.pdf.

thinking of big data analytics based on personal data are university admissions, job recruitment, customer profiling, targeted marketing, and health services. Analysing the information about millions of previous applicants, candidates, customers, or patients makes it easy to establish common threads and to predict all sorts of things, such as whether a specific person is fit for a position, or if an individual is likely to develop a certain disease in the future.[7]

In 2014, the European Data Protection Supervisor warned that "[c]ompanies may consider most of their data to be non-personal data sets, but in reality it is now rare for data generated by user activity to be completely and irreversibly anonymised."[8] For this reason, the availability of massive amounts of data from different sources combined with the desire to learn more about people's habits poses a serious challenge regarding the right to privacy of the individual and requires that the data protection principles are carefully taken into consideration.

1.3 Structure, Arguments, and Methodology

As to the structure of the present chapter, first, data protection by design as a means to comply with the fundamental principles of data protection will be presented (Section 2). The reader must, in fact, understand the main rules to be respected in dealing with (big) data from the start. Specific attention will be dedicated to the principles of fairness and data quality which are particularly relevant in Smart Data Environments. The essential question: *what is personal data?* will then be addressed (Section 3). In the same section, anonymization and pseudonymization techniques will be presented together with recommendations of how to use them in a way that best preserves the privacy of individuals and mitigates possible risks of not complying with applicable personal data protection rules. The roles of the parties involved in the processing of personal data will be presented: controller, processor, and joint-controller, together with practical impli- cations in terms of obligations, responsibilities, and ways to regulate them by contractual arrangements (Section 4). A practical methodology to design processing activities in line with the core principles of personal data protection will be offered in Section 5. The chapter will then go on to conclude that it is not possible to lawfully generate Smart Data in the absence of the application of a data protection by design approach (Section 6).

---

[7] For more information on big data, technique to analyse them, and possible applications of the generated knowledge, see the following two studies produced by the Obama administration: Big Data: Seizing Opportunities, Preserving Values. Available at: https://obamawhitehouse.archives.gov/sites/default/files/docs/big_data_privacy_report_may_1_2014.pdf. Report To The President Big Data And Privacy: A Technological Perspective. Available at: https://obamawhitehouse. archives.gov/sites/default/files/microsites/ostp/PCAST/pcast_big_data_and_privacy_-_may_2014.pdf.

[8] European Data Protection Supervisor. 2014. Preliminary Opinion Of The European Data Protection Supervisor Privacy And Competitiveness In The Age Of Big Data: The Interplay Between Data Protection, Competition Law And Consumer Protection In The Digital Economy. https://secure.edps.europa.eu/EDPSWEB/webdav/site/mySite/ shared/Documents/Consultation/Opinions/2014/14-03-26_competitition_law_big_data_EN.pdf.

Concerning the chosen methodology, observations made throughout the chapter are based on European Union personal data protection legal sources to leverage the research conducted by regulatory and advisory bodies in combination with the empirical research and practical experience of the author. European Union data protection legislation embeds all the core international data protection principles. The arguments and the conclusions reached in this work can also very well be extended beyond the European Union, being generally valid on an international level.

2 DATA PROTECTION BY DESIGN AS A MEANS TO ACHIEVE COMPLIANCE WITH DATA PROTECTION PRINCIPLES

In one of the most recent opinions on topics related to big data issued by the European Data Protection Supervisor, the Supervisor observed that "we need to protect more dynamically our fundamental rights in the world of big data."[9] It was argued that the "traditional" data protection principles (i.e., those established before the era of big data) such as transparency, proportionality, and purpose limitation have to be modernized and strengthened, but also complemented by "new principles" that have been developed more recently in response to the challenges brought about by big data itself—accountability, privacy by design, and privacy by default. In the opinion of the author, data protection by design, more than a principle, can be regarded as a dynamic means which can be used to comply with the fundamental privacy principles and the related obligations, so to protect fundamental rights in the world of Smart Data. This notion is also coherent with what is stated in Recital 4 of Regulation 679/2016: "[t]he processing of personal data should be designed to serve mankind."[10]

Article 25 of the Regulation 679/2016 defines Data protection by design and by default as follows:

1. *Taking into account the state of the art, the cost of implementation and the nature, scope, context and purposes of processing as well as the risks of varying likelihood and severity for rights and freedoms of natural persons posed by the processing, the controller shall, both at the time of the determination of the means for processing and at the time of the processing itself, implement appropriate technical and organisational measures, such as pseudonymisation, which are designed to implement data-protection principles, such as data minimisation, in an effective manner and to integrate the necessary safeguards into the*

[9] European Data Protection Supervisor. 2015. Opinion 7/2015 – Meeting The Challenges Of Big Data: A Call For Transparency, User Control, Data Protection By Design And Accountability, p. 4. Available at: https://secure.edps.europa.eu/EDPSWEB/webdav/site/mySite/shared/Documents/Consultation/Opinions/2015/15-11-19_Big_Data_EN.pdf.

[10] Recital 4, Regulation (Eu) 2016/679 of the European Parliament and of the Council of 27 April 2016 on the protection of natural persons with regard to the processing of personal data and on the free movement of such data, and repealing Directive 95/46/EC (General Data Protection Regulation), *Official Journal of the European Union*, L 119/3, 4/5/2016. Available at: https://eur-lex.europa.eu/legal-content/EN/TXT/HTML/?uri=CELEX:32016R0679&from=IT.

processing in order to meet the requirements of this Regulation and protect the rights of data subjects.

2. *The controller shall implement appropriate technical and organisational measures for ensuring that, by default, only personal data which are necessary for each specific purpose of the processing are processed. That obligation applies to the amount of personal data collected, the extent of their processing, the period of their storage and their accessibility. In particular, such measures shall ensure that by default personal data are not made accessible without the individual's intervention to an indefinite number of natural persons. (...)*

Compliance with the data protection principles[11] can thus be regarded as the goal to be achieved through the correct application of the data protection by design approach.[12] It is therefore important to understand the content of the core and internationally recognized fundamental privacy principles, such as those of the General Data Protection Regulation and also those outlined in Figure 17.1 from the United Nations Conference on Trade and Development.[13]

2.1 Openness

Data controllers must be open about their personal data processing (developments, practices, and policies with respect to personal data). Individuals should be able to obtain information without unreasonable effort (in terms of time, knowledge, cost, etc.) about the existence and nature of personal data, and the main purposes of their processing as well as the identity and contact details of the data controller. The openness principle is a prerequisite for the access and correction principle. In general, openness can be achieved through provisions of the relevant information concerning the processing of personal data by data controllers, e.g., publication of privacy policies on websites and applications. Data subjects whose data are collected and processed should be aware of any processing of their data, including the details of the data controller and of the processing activities being carried out, whether/how their data will be shared with other entities or transferred different countries, and should have the choice to object to such activities. Data controllers must inform data subjects before the processing of their data takes place. Unless specifically permitted by law, there must be no secret and covert processing of personal data. Processing

[11] Such principles are set out in Article 5 of the Regulation (Eu) 2016/679 of the European Parliament and of the Council of 27 April 2016 on the protection of natural persons with regard to the processing of personal data and on the free movement of such data, and repealing Directive 95/46/EC (General Data Protection Regulation), *Official Journal of the European Union*, L 119/3, 4/5/2016. Available at: https://eur-lex.europa.eu/legal-content/EN/TXT/HTML/?uri=CELEX:32016R0679&from=IT.

[12] The European Data Protection Supervisor reflected the same view in its Opinion 5/2018, Preliminary Opinion on privacy by design, p. 6. Available at: https://edps.europa.eu/sites/edp/files/publication/18-05-31_preliminary_opinion_on_privacy_by_design_en_0.pdf.

[13] See Article 5 of the Regulation (Eu) 2016/679 of the European Parliament and of the Council of 27 April 2016 on the protection of natural persons with regard to the processing of personal data and on the free movement of such data, and repealing Directive 95/46/EC (General Data Protection Regulation), *Official Journal of the European Union*, L 119/3, 4/5/2016. Available at: https://eur-lex.europa.eu/legal-content/EN/TXT/HTML/?uri=CELEX:32016R0679&from=IT.

FIGURE 17.1   International Data Protection Core Principles.[14]

operations must be explained to the data subjects in an easily accessible way which ensures that they understand what will happen to their data. Openness is an extremely important principle to keep in mind in Smart Data environments where many data processing activities (including profiling[15] which is very invasive for the privacy of the individuals) tend to take place in the background, without the data subjects being effectively informed and without having the possibility to notice them.

2.2 Collection Limitation: Lawfulness and Fairness

There should be limits to the collection of personal data, e.g., data should be obtained by lawful and fair means, with the knowledge and, where appropriate, the consent of the data

---

[14] Source: United Nations Conference on Trade and Development (UNCTAD) http://unctad.org/en/pages/newsdetails. aspx?OriginalVersionID=1237.

[15] Profiling is defined as:

> any form of automated processing of personal data consisting of the use of personal data to evaluate certain personal aspects relating to a natural person, in particular to analyse or predict aspects concerning that natural person's performance at work, economic situation, health, personal preferences, interests, reliability, behaviour, location or movements

Article 4(4) of the Regulation (Eu) 2016/679 of the European Parliament and of the Council of 27 April 2016 on the protection of natural persons with regard to the processing of personal data and on the free movement of such data, and repealing Directive 95/46/EC (General Data Protection Regulation), *Official Journal of the European Union*, L 119/3, 4/5/ 2016. Available at: https://eur-lex.europa.eu/legal-content/EN/TXT/HTML/?uri=CELEX:32016R0679&from=IT.

subject. This principle aims to limit indiscriminate data collection. This is very relevant in Smart Data environments where many companies tend to collect as many data as possible. Specific limits in various legal instruments often relate to the purposes and the grounds for the data processing, sensitivity of data, the data quality aspects, etc.

Lawfulness means that data controller may only be allowed to process personal data based on a lawful basis,[16] e.g., one of the following grounds:

- consent (which typically needs to be freely given, specific, unambiguous, explicit, informed, and revocable);

- contractual purposes (e.g., processing of data for billing purposes or in order to take steps at the request of the data subject prior to entering into a contract);

- compliance with a legal obligation (e.g., when a customer's personal data are given to the police on the basis of a legal ground, or data related to transactions are retained by companies to comply with relevant book keeping and administrative legal obligation);

- protection of vital interests of data subject (this only applies in severe cases, e.g., of life and death);

- task of public interest (this mainly applies to public bodies);

- legitimate interests of the data controller or third parties (this ground for processing has to be carefully assessed on a case-by-case basis and it is valid when the interests of the data controller outweigh the privacy and data protection right of the data subject, e.g., fraud prevention, but it may also apply to IT security).

Fairness relates to balanced and proportionate data processing. In line with this principle, data controllers should take into account the interests and reasonable expectations of privacy of data subjects. The processing of personal data should not unreasonably intrude upon the privacy, autonomy, and integrity of data subjects, and data controllers should not exert pressure on data subjects to provide personal data. Fairness, as explained below, is highly pertinent in Smart Data environments and goes beyond what is strictly prescribed by the law, also taking an ethical dimension into consideration. The relationship between ethics and data protection can be successfully illustrated through the example of the Cambridge Analytica[17] case in which the original purposes for the profiling system developed by the Psychometrics Centre of Cambridge University had the potential capability of leading to

---

[16] See Articles 6, 9, and 10 of the Regulation (Eu) 2016/679 of the European Parliament and of the Council of 27 April 2016 on the protection of natural persons with regard to the processing of personal data and on the free movement of such data, and repealing Directive 95/46/EC (General Data Protection Regulation), *Official Journal of the European Union*, L 119/3, 4/5/2016. Available at: https://eur-lex.europa.eu/legal-content/EN/TXT/HTML/?uri=CELEX:32016 R0679&from=IT.

[17] See extensively on this the Information Commissioner's Office "Investigation into the use of data analytics in political campaigns Investigation update" 2018 report that provides details with respect to the office of Information Commissioner Elizabeth Denham's investigation of the widespread use of data analytics in electoral campaigns. Available at: https://ico.org.uk/media/action-weve-taken/2259371/investigation-into-data-analytics-for-political-purposes-update.pdf.

useful academic, societal, and business insights concerning psychological targeting as a tool to influence behavior, something that is undoubtedly important to understand. Such technology and specifically, algorithms, however, also present significant risks as they have effectively been transformed into a means to influence democratic processes, essentially hampering the fundamental principles of democratic society which must be protected.

Technology is neither good, bad, or neutral as Melvin Kranzberg, wisely pointed out.[18] It is now possible to create an algorithm that is capable of predicting individual's behavior, and the logical consequence of this technology is improved regulation on the part of legislators and responsibility on the part of governments and businesses. However, such incredible technologies should be used in a fair way, so to respect fundamental rights and freedoms and to grant dignity to the digital society. Accordingly, fairness should also be built into the very design of data processing activities, whether they be products, services, or applications, and—most importantly—the algorithms that underpin the information/ data processing should be designed and developed in a way that is compatible with the concept of "fairness by design."

The collection limitation principle also relates to restrictions imposed on the processing of predefined categories of personal data due to their nature. Many national and international instruments define a set of data which are regarded as sensitive for data subjects and provide for more stringent processing requirements than the ones applicable to other types of data. Sensitive data are often defined as personal data revealing racial or ethnic origin, political opinions, religious or philosophical beliefs, or trade union membership, and the processing of genetic data, biometric data for the purpose of uniquely identifying a natural person, data concerning health, or data concerning a person's natural sex life or sexual orientation. The processing of sensitive data may in principle be forbidden, unless, e.g., when the data subject has given explicit consent, the processing is necessary to comply with legal obligations, or in order to protect the vital interests of the data subject.

Legislation usually also restricts the collection and use of personal data related to children. Processing of the personal data of a child may be lawful only where the child is at least 16 years old. Where the child is below the age of 16 years, such processing can be subject to the prior consent given by the holder of parental responsibility over the child. Some restrictions might also apply in relation to the processing of personal data relating to criminal convictions and offences.

2.3 Purpose Specification

The purposes for which personal data are collected should be specified before or at the time of collection and the subsequent processing should be limited to the fulfilment of those purposes or other compatible ones. The purpose specification (or alternatively termed finality or purpose limitation) principle typically has three separate components: the purposes for which data are collected should be specified/defined, lawful/

---

[18] Melvin Kranzberg, Technology and History: "Kranzberg's Laws", in *Technology and Culture*, Vol. 27, No. 3 (Jul., 1986), pp. 544–560.

legitimate, and should not be incompatible with the purposes for which the data were first collected. This principle is closely related to the data quality principle and the use limitation principle. Processing for undefined and/or unlimited purposes is not compliant with this principle.

The purpose must have been specified and made manifest by the data controller before the processing of data takes place. Every new purpose for processing data must have its own specific legal basis and cannot rely on the fact that the data were initially acquired or processed for another legitimate purpose, unless the second purpose for which data are further processed is compatible with the former. This principle becomes extremely relevant in the context of Smart Data because, very frequently, large datasets that are analysed were originally collected for other different purposes (e.g., data collected in the context of the purchasing of goods or services, which companies then want to analyse in order to better understand the preferences of their customers). When considering the scope and limits of a particular purpose, the concept of compatibility is adopted: the use of data for compatible purposes is allowed on the ground of the initial legal basis. To ascertain whether the processing is compatible with the purpose for which the personal data are initially collected, account should be taken of, *inter alia*, elements including:

a) any link between the purposes for which the personal data have been collected and the purposes of the intended further processing;

b) the context in which the personal data have been collected, in particular regarding the relationship between data subjects and the data controller;

c) the nature of the personal data, in particular whether special categories of personal data are processed (e.g., sensitive and judicial data);

d) the possible consequences of the intended further processing for data subjects;

e) the existence of appropriate safeguards.

The purpose specification principle also closely relates to data minimization. The set of data to be collected must be minimal and identified based on the purposes of processing. Data should not be retained for any longer than strictly necessary to achieve the intended scope of the processing.

2.4 Use Limitation

Personal data should not be disclosed to third parties, made available, or otherwise used for purposes other than those that were initially specified or compatible purposes (see also Purpose Specification Principle). This principle is especially relevant in Smart Data environments where the companies/organizations that analyse large data sets often tend to share such knowledge (which may include personal data) with other companies/organizations.

Exceptions from this principle may include disclosure with the consent of the data subject or with the authorization granted by Data Protection Supervisory Authorities. The principle of use limitation is not always expressed in data protection instruments in the same way. It is not always specifically addressed but instead covered under the conditions for processing personal data, such as fair and lawful processing, and purpose specification.

2.5 Security

Personal data should be protected by reasonable security safeguards against such risks as loss or unauthorized access, destruction, use, modification, or disclosure of data. Security safeguards include physical measures (e.g., locked doors, identification cards), organizational measures (e.g., authorizations to access personal data, confidentiality obligations on personnel processing personal data), and technological measures (e.g., encryption and pseudonymization of personal data, strict identity management and access control to preserve data confidentiality, other technical measures to ensure integrity, availability, and resilience of data processing systems). Security becomes very relevant when processing large datasets, especially if sensitive data are included. Moreover, unauthorized/unlawful use of Smart Data (i.e., the knowledge produced by analysing large datasets) may pose very high risks to the rights and freedoms of the related individuals.

In principle, data protection legislation requires data controllers and processors to implement (reasonably) feasible security measures to prevent risks of unlawful processing, unauthorized access, loss, and alteration of personal data. Elements to be taken into considerations by data controllers and processors may be the technological state of the art, the costs of implementation, the nature, scope, context, purposes of processing as well as the risk of varying likelihood, and severity for the rights and freedoms of natural persons (data subjects). Some legislation or Data Protection Supervisory Authorities identify specific mandatory security measures as baseline.

2.6 Data Quality

Personal data should be relevant to the purposes for which they are to be used, and should be accurate, complete, and kept up-to-date. The obligation to ensure accuracy of data must be seen in the context of the purpose of data processing. In fact, there may also be cases where updating stored data is legally prohibited, because the purpose of storing the data is primarily to document events (e.g., a medical operation protocol). In such circumstances, only additions to the remarks in the protocol may be made, as long as they are clearly marked as contributions made at a later stage. Historical data, data related to social research, and the activities of archives may also often be subject to specific regulations which coherently specify and/or limit the application of the Principle of Data Quality. Concurrently, there are situations where regular checking of the accuracy of data, including updating, is an absolute necessity because of the potential damage that may be caused to the data subject if such data were to remain inaccurate (e.g., relationships with banking institutions).

The Data Quality principle often includes other principles, such as:

- The data relevancy and data minimization principles—Only such data shall be processed as are adequate, relevant, and limited to what is necessary in relation to the purposes for which they are processed. The categories of data chosen for processing must be necessary in order to achieve the declared overall aim of the processing operations, and a data controller should strictly limit the collection of data to such information as is directly relevant for the specific purpose pursued by the processing.

- The data accuracy principle—A data controller holding personal information shall not use information without taking steps to ensure with reasonable certainty that the data are accurate and up to date. Every reasonable step must be taken to ensure that personal data that are inaccurate, having regard to the purposes for which they are processed, are erased or rectified without delay.

- The limited retention of data principle—Personal data should be kept in a form which permits the identification of data subjects for no longer than is necessary for the purposes for which the data were collected or for which they are further processed. In principle, the data must therefore be erased or anonymized when those purposes have been served, unless otherwise provided by the applicable laws. Retention of data should be proportionate in relation to the purpose of collection and limited in time. The time limitation for storing personal data applies, however, only to data kept in a form which permits the identification of data subjects (in this regard, anonymized data are therefore excluded).

The principle of data quality assumes high relevance in Smart Data environments. In fact, a fundamental part of big data analytics is that the raw data must be accurate in order to lead to accurate results. Massive quantities of inaccurate data can lead to skewed results and poor decision-making. Bruce Schneier, an internationally renowned security technologist, refers to this as the "pollution problem of the information age."[19] Data quality is therefore not only a legal compliance obligation but is instead paramount to ensuring that algorithms and analytical procedures are carried out successfully and that the predicted results correspond with reality.

2.7 Access and Correction

The right of individuals to access and correct their personal data is generally regarded as one of the most important privacy protection safeguards. According to this principle, an individual should have the right:

a) to obtain from a data controller a confirmation of whether or not the data controller has data relating to him or her;

b) to have his/her personal data communicated to him/her within a reasonable time at a non-excessive (if any) charge, in a reasonable manner, and in an intelligible form;

---

[19] Schneier, Bruce. 2015. Data And Goliath. New York: W.W. Norton.

   c) to be given reasons if a request to access personal data is denied, and to be able to challenge such denial; and

   d) to challenge data relating to him/her and, if the challenge is successful, to have the data erased, rectified, completed, or amended.

The right to access should be easy to exercise, e.g., it should not involve any legal process or similar measures. In some cases, intermediate access to personal data can be provided (e.g., through Data Protection Supervisory Authorities). The right to challenge should include the possibility to challenge the denial of access to personal data at the level of the data controller and subsequently in courts, administrative bodies, or other institutions.

The right of access is not unconditional and the obligations of data controllers to respond to a data subject's access request may be restricted as a result of the overriding legal interests of others. Overriding legal interests may involve public interests such as national security, public security, and the prosecuting of criminal offences, as well as private interests which are more compelling than data protection interests. For example, when data are processed solely for the purpose of scientific research or for statistical purposes, access rights may be restricted if adequate legal safeguards are in place.

The right of access often includes additional rights for the data subjects, e.g., to know the source from which data have been obtained, for what purposes such data were collected and how they are being processed, to request that the personal data relating to them are extracted and made available in an intelligible format, that such data are updated, rectified, supplemented, or to block the processing activities if the data are not being processed in accordance with the applicable legislation. New rights for the data subjects were recently introduced as a further extension of the right of access, such as the right to restriction of processing (e.g., where the accuracy of the personal data is contested by the data subject, for a period enabling the controller to verify the accuracy of the personal data; or where the processing is unlawful and the data subject opposes the erasure of the personal data and instead requests the restriction of their use) and the right to data portability (the right for the data subject to receive the personal data concerning him or her, which he or she has provided to a controller, in a structured, commonly used and machine-readable format and the right to transmit those data to another controller without hindrance from the first controller to which the personal data have been provided).

Companies and organizations operating Smart Data environments should carefully assess the application of the principle of access and correction to the relevant data processing activities that they carry out, and in principle, such entitles must be ready to provide data subjects with access to and the possibility to correct their personal data.

2.8 Accountability

Accountability requires the active implementation of measures by data controllers to promote and safeguard data protection in their processing activities. Moreover, at any time, data controllers should be able, autonomously or with the assistance of data processors, to demonstrate compliance with data protection provisions to data subjects, to the general public and to Data Protection Supervisory Authorities. The essence of accountability is the data controller's obligation to:

- put in place measures which would—under normal circumstances—guarantee that data protection rules are adhered to in the context of processing operations; and

- have documentation ready which demonstrates to data subjects and to Data Protection Supervisory Authorities what measures have been taken to achieve adherence to the data protection rules (including adherence to approved data protection codes of conduct and certification mechanisms).

Coherently, data controllers and data processors may be required to maintain a record of processing activities under their responsibility, to be made available to the Data Protection Supervisory Authorities on request. In other words, data processing activities carried out in Smart Data environments need to be documented together with the relevant information in order to demonstrate that they have been carried out in full compliance with the relevant applicable legal provisions (i.e., in compliance with all the principles mentioned above).

3 PERSONAL DATA, PSEUDONYMIZED DATA, ANONYMOUS DATA

An organization dealing with large datasets needs to clearly understand what personal data are. The consequences are highly significant because data protection law only applies to personal data and not anonymous data. Pseudonymized data will also be subject to data protection legal provisions, despite the fact that pseudonymization is very often mistakenly considered an anonymization, when it is, in fact, a very useful security measure that can be applied to personal data.

3.1 Personal Data

The concept of personal data is defined in Article 4(1) of Regulation 679/2016 as

any information relating to an identified or identifiable natural person ('data subject'); an identifiable natural person is one who can be identified, directly or indirectly, in particular by reference to an identifier such as a name, an identification number, location data, an online identifier or to one or more factors specific to the physical, physiological, genetic, mental, economic, cultural or social identity of that natural person.[20]

Moreover, in Recital 26 of Regulation 679/2016 it is explained that:

---

[20] Article 4(1), Regulation (Eu) 2016/679 of the European Parliament and of the Council of 27 April 2016 on the protection of natural persons with regard to the processing of personal data and on the free movement of such data, and repealing Directive 95/46/EC (General Data Protection Regulation), *Official Journal of the European Union*, L 119/3, 4/5/2016. Available at: https://eur-lex.europa.eu/legal-content/EN/TXT/HTML/?uri=CELEX:32016R0679&from=IT.

the principles of data protection should apply to any information concerning an identified or identifiable natural person. Personal data which have undergone pseudonymisation, which could be attributed to a natural person by the use of additional information should be considered to be information on an identifiable natural person. To determine whether a natural person is identifiable, account should be taken of all the means reasonably likely to be used, such as singling out, either by the controller or by another person to identify the natural person directly or indirectly. To ascertain whether means are reasonably likely to be used to identify the natural person, account should be taken of all objective factors, such as the costs of and the amount of time required for identification, taking into consideration the available technology at the time of the processing and technological developments. The principles of data protection should therefore not apply to anonymous information, namely information which does not relate to an identified or identifiable natural person or to personal data rendered anonymous in such a manner that the data subject is not or no longer identifiable. This Regulation does not therefore concern the processing of such anonymous information, including for statistical or research purposes.[21]

While the list of factors specific to the identity of the person has been enriched from the previous definition of personal data that was contained in Directive 95/46/EC,[22] the main elements remain the same. These elements have been discussed and elaborated by the Article 29 Working Party in its Opinion 4/2007, which establishes that there are four fundamental elements to establish whether information is to be considered personal data.[23]

According to the Opinion, these elements are: "any information," "relating to," "identified or identifiable," and "natural person."

3.1.1 Any Information

All information relevant to a person is included, regardless of the "position or capacity of those persons (as consumer, patient, employee, customer, etc.)."[24] In this case, the information can be objective or subjective and does not necessarily have to be true or proven. The words "any information" also imply information of any form, audio, text, video, images, etc. Importantly, the manner in which the information is stored is irrelevant. The Article 29 Working Party expressly mentions biometric data as a special

---

[21] Recital 26, Regulation (Eu) 2016/679 of the European Parliament and of the Council of 27 April 2016 on the protection of natural persons with regard to the processing of personal data and on the free movement of such data, and repealing Directive 95/46/EC (General Data Protection Regulation), *Official Journal of the European Union*, L 119/3, 4/5/2016. Available at: https://eur-lex.europa.eu/legal-content/EN/TXT/HTML/?uri=CELEX:32016R0679&from=IT.

[22] Directive 95/46/EC of the European Parliament and of the Council of 24 October 1995 on the protection of individuals with regard to the processing of personal data and on the free movement of such data. Available at: https://eur-lex.europa. eu/legal-content/EN/ALL/?uri=celex:31995L0046.

[23] Article 29 Data Protection Working Party. 2007. Opinion 4/2007 On The Concept Of Personal Data. Available at: http:// ec.europa.eu/justice/article-29/documentation/opinion-recommendation/index_en.htm.

[24] Article 29 Data Protection Working Party. 2007. Opinion 4/2007 On The Concept Of Personal Data, p.7. Available at: http://ec.europa.eu/justice/article-29/documentation/opinion-recommendation/index_en.htm.

case,[25] as such data can be considered as information content as well as a link between the individual and the information. Because biometric data are unique to an individual, they can also be used as an identifier.

3.1.2 Relating To

Information related to an individual is information about that individual. The relationship between data and an individual is often self-evident, an example of which is when the data are stored in an individual employee files or in a medical record. This is, however, not always the case, especially when the information regards objects. Such objects belong to individuals, but additional meanings or information is required to create the link to the individual.[26]

At least one of the following three elements should be present in order to consider information to be related to an individual: "content", "purpose," or "result". An element of "content" is present when the information is in reference to an individual, regardless of the (intended) use of the information. The "purpose" element instead refers to whether the information is used or is likely to be used "with the purpose to evaluate, treat in a certain way or influence the status or behavior of an individual."[27] A "result" element is present when the use of the data is likely to have an impact on a certain person's rights and interests.[28] These elements are alternatives and are not cumulative, implying that one piece of data can relate to different individuals based on diverse elements.

3.1.3 Identified or Identifiable

"A natural person can be 'identified' when, within a group of persons, he or she is 'distinguished' from all other members of the group."[29] When identification has not occurred but is possible, the individual is considered to be "identifiable." In order to determine whether those with access to the data are able to identify the individual, all reasonable means likely to be used either by the controller or by any other person should be taken into consideration.[30] The cost of identification, the intended purpose, the way the

---

[25] Article 29 Data Protection Working Party. 2007. Opinion 4/2007 On The Concept Of Personal Data, p.8. Available at: http://ec.europa.eu/justice/article-29/documentation/opinion-recommendation/index_en.htm.

[26] Article 29 Data Protection Working Party. 2007. Opinion 4/2007 On The Concept Of Personal Data, p.9. Available at: http://ec.europa.eu/justice/article-29/documentation/opinion-recommendation/index_en.htm.

[27] Article 29 Data Protection Working Party. 2007. Opinion 4/2007 On The Concept Of Personal Data, p.10. Available at: http://ec.europa.eu/justice/article-29/documentation/opinion-recommendation/index_en.htm.

[28] Article 29 Data Protection Working Party. 2007. Opinion 4/2007 On The Concept Of Personal Data, p.11. Available at: http://ec.europa.eu/justice/article-29/documentation/opinion-recommendation/index_en.htm.

[29] Article 29 Data Protection Working Party. 2007. Opinion 4/2007 On The Concept Of Personal Data, p.12. Available at: http://ec.europa.eu/justice/article-29/documentation/opinion-recommendation/index_en.htm.

[30] On this point the following example may contribute to a better understanding:

> (...) if an organisation collects data on individual travel movements, the individual travel patterns at event level would still qualify as personal data for any party, as long as the data controller (or any other party) still has access to the original raw data, even if direct identifiers have been removed from the set provided to third parties. But if the data controller would delete the raw data, and only provide aggregate statistics to third parties on a high level, such as 'on Mondays on trajectory X there are 160% more passengers than on Tuesdays', that would qualify as anonymous data.

Article 29 Working Party, Opinion 05/2014 on Anonymisation Techniques, p.9. Available at: http://ec.europa.eu/justice/article-29/documentation/opinion-recommendation/index_en.htm.

processing is structured, the advantage expected by the data controller, the interest at stake for the data subjects, and the risk of organizational dysfunctions and technical failures should be taken into account in the evaluation.[31]

On this point, it is important to notice that according to Recital 30 of Regulation 679/2016

> [n]atural persons may be associated with online identifiers provided by their devices, applications, tools and protocols, such as internet protocol addresses, cookie identifiers or other identifiers such as radio frequency identification tags. This may leave traces which, in particular when combined with unique identifiers and other information received by the servers, may be used to create profiles of the natural persons and identify them.[32]

3.1.4 Natural Person

Regulation 679/2016 is applicable to the personal data of natural persons, a broad concept which calls for protection wholly independent from the residence or nationality of the data subject. The concept of personality is understood as "the capacity to be the subject of legal relations, starting with the birth of the individual and ending with his death."[33] Personal data thus relate to identified or identifiable living individuals. Data concerning deceased persons or unborn children in principle falls outside the application of personal data protection legislation. When the data relate to other living persons, or when a data controller makes no differentiation in their documentation between living and deceased persons, it may not be possible to ascertain whether the person the data relates to is living or deceased. Legal persons are excluded from the protection provided under Regulation (EU) 679/2016). It is possible to conclude that in some cases, the data may not be personal in nature, but may become personal data as a result of cross-referencing it with other sources and databases containing information about specific users, therefore shrinking the circle of potential persons to "identifiable persons" and ultimately even to specifically identified individuals.

3.2 Pseudonymized Data

Pseudonymization is defined in Article 4(5) of Regulation (EU) 679/2016 as

> the processing of personal data in such a manner that the personal data can no longer be attributed to a specific data subject without the use of additional

---

[31] Article 29 Data Protection Working Party, Opinion 4/2007 On The Concept Of Personal Data, p. 15. Available at: http://ec.europa.eu/justice/article-29/documentation/opinion-recommendation/index_en.htm.

[32] Recital 30, Regulation (Eu) 2016/679 of the European Parliament and of the Council of 27 April 2016 on the protection of natural persons with regard to the processing of personal data and on the free movement of such data, and repealing Directive 95/46/EC (General Data Protection Regulation), *Official Journal of the European Union*, L 119/3, 4/5/2016. Available at: https://eur-lex.europa.eu/legal-content/EN/TXT/HTML/?uri=CELEX:32016R0679&from=IT.

[33] Article 29 Data Protection Working Party, Opinion 4/2007 On The Concept Of Personal Data, p. 22. Available at: http://ec.europa.eu/justice/article-29/documentation/opinion-recommendation/index_en.htm.

information, provided that such additional information is kept separately and is subject to technical and organisational measures to ensure that the personal data are not attributed to an identified or identifiable natural person.

As it was maintained by the Article 29 Working Party, it is important to clarify immediately that pseudonymization is not to be considered as anonymization, and that pseudonymization is only capable of limiting the likelihood that specific data can be traced back to the data subject.[34] This is largely because by way of linking between diverse data sets, it may be possible to identify an individual.

The Information Commissioner's Office clarifies that

[p]seudonymisation may involve replacing names or other identifiers which are easily attributed to individuals with, for example, a reference number. Whilst you can tie that reference number back to the individual if you have access to the relevant information, you put technical and organisational measures in place to ensure that this additional information is held separately. Pseudony-mising personal data can reduce the risks to the data subjects and help you meet your data protection obligations. However, pseudonymisation is effec-tively only a security measure. It does not change the status of the data as personal data.[35]

Accordingly, Recital 28 of Regulation 679/2016 clarifies that

---

[34] Article 29 Working Party, Opinion 05/2014 on Anonymisation Techniques, p. 3 and p. 10. Available at: http://ec.europa.eu/justice/article-29/documentation/opinion-recommendation/index_en.htm. As an example of linkability, the Article 29 Working Party referred the

> well-known 'AOL (America On Line) incident'. In 2006, a database containing twenty million search keywords for over 650,000 users over a 3-month period was publicly released, with the only privacy preserving measure consisting in replacing AOL user ID by a numerical attribute. This led to the public identification and location of some of them. Pseudonymised search engine query strings, especially if coupled with other attributes, such as IP addresses or other client configuration parameters, possess a very high power of identification. p. 11

[35] Information Commissioner's Office, Guide to the General Data Protection Regulation (GDPR). Available at: https://ico.org.uk/for-organisations/guide-to-the-general-data-protection-regulation-gdpr/what-is-personal-data/what-is-personal-data/. An example of pseudonymization provided by the Information Commissioner's Office is the following:

> [a] courier firm processes personal data about its drivers' mileage, journeys and driving frequency. It holds this personal data for two purposes: (i) to process expenses claims for mileage; and (ii) to charge their customers for the service. For both of these, identifying the individual couriers is crucial. However, a second team within the organization also uses the data to optimize the efficiency of the courier fleet. For this, the identification of the individual is unnecessary. Therefore, the firm ensures that the second team can only access the data in a form that makes it not possible to identify the individual couriers. It pseudonymizes this data by replacing identifiers (names, job titles, location data and driving history) with a non-identifying equivalent such as a reference number which, on its own, has no meaning. The members of this second team can only access this pseudonymised information. While the second team cannot identify any individual, the organization itself can, as the controller, link that material back to the identified individuals. This represents good practice under the GDPR.

[t]he application of pseudonymisation to personal data can reduce the risks to the data subjects concerned and help controllers and processors to meet their data-protection obligations. The explicit introduction of 'pseudonymisation' in this Regulation is not intended to preclude any other measures of data protection.[36]

Recital 29 of the Regulation 679/2016 specified further that

[i]n order to create incentives to apply pseudonymisation when processing personal data, measures of pseudonymisation should, whilst allowing general analysis, be possible within the same controller when that controller has taken technical and organisational measures necessary to ensure, for the processing concerned, that this Regulation is implemented, and that additional information for attributing the personal data to a specific data subject is kept separately. The controller processing the personal data should indicate the authorised persons within the same controller.[37]

It is noteworthy that pseudonymization is also referred to as a possible means to consider in order to satisfy the principle of data protection by design, and, more precisely, it can be used as a technical and organizational measure to implement principles of data protection including but not limited to data minimization, thus allowing for adequate protection of the data subject in line with the data protection legislation.[38] Effectively, pseudonymization can be seen as a means to increase privacy. It prevents direct identification without losing likability to the individual, making pseudonymization a useful security measure.

More practically,

the result of pseudonymisation can be independent of the initial value (as is the case of a random number generated by the controller or a surname chosen by the

---

[36] Recital 28, Regulation (Eu) 2016/679 of the European Parliament and of the Council of 27 April 2016 on the protection of natural persons with regard to the processing of personal data and on the free movement of such data, and repealing Directive 95/46/EC (General Data Protection Regulation), *Official Journal of the European Union*, L 119/3, 4/5/2016. Available at: https://eur-lex.europa.eu/legal-content/EN/TXT/HTML/?uri=CELEX:32016R0679&from=IT.

[37] Recital 29, Regulation (Eu) 2016/679 of the European Parliament and of the Council of 27 April 2016 on the protection of natural persons with regard to the processing of personal data and on the free movement of such data, and repealing Directive 95/46/EC (General Data Protection Regulation), *Official Journal of the European Union*, L 119/3, 4/5/2016. Available at: https://eur-lex.europa.eu/legal-content/EN/TXT/HTML/?uri=CELEX:32016R0679&from=IT.

[38] See Article 25, Regulation (Eu) 2016/679 of the European Parliament and of the Council of 27 April 2016 on the protection of natural persons with regard to the processing of personal data and on the free movement of such data, and repealing Directive 95/46/EC (General Data Protection Regulation), *Official Journal of the European Union*, L 119/3, 4/5/ 2016. Available at: https://eur-lex.europa.eu/legal-content/EN/TXT/HTML/?uri=CELEX:32016R0679&from=IT.

   Taking into account the state of the art, the cost of implementation and the nature, scope, context and purposes of processing as well as the risks of varying likelihood and severity for rights and freedoms of natural persons posed by the processing, the controller shall, both at the time of the determination of the means for processing and at the time of the processing itself, implement appropriate technical and organisational measures, such as pseudonymisation, which are designed to implement data-protection principles, such as data minimisation, in an effective manner and to integrate the necessary safeguards into the processing in order to meet the requirements of this Regulation and protect the rights of data subjects.

data subject) or it can be derived from the original values of an attribute or set of attributes e.g. a hash function or encryption scheme.[39]

In 2014, the Article 29 Working Party offered a very useful description of the most used pseudonymization techniques in the light of the applicable data protection compliance legal framework:

- *Encryption with secret key: in this case, the holder of the key can trivially re-identify each data subject through decryption of the dataset because the personal data are still contained in the dataset, albeit in an encrypted form. Assuming that a state-of-the-art encryption scheme was applied, decryption can only be possible with the knowledge of the key.*

- *Hash function: this corresponds to a function which returns a fixed size output from an input of any size (the input may be a single attribute or a set of attributes) and cannot be reversed; this means that the reversal risk seen with encryption no longer exists. However, if the range of input values [and] the hash function are known they can be replayed through the hash function in order to derive the correct value for a particular record. For instance, if a dataset was pseudonymised by hashing the national identification number, then this can be derived simply by hashing all possible input values and comparing the result with those values in the dataset. (…)[40]*

- *Keyed-hash function with stored key: this corresponds to a particular hash function which uses a secret key as an additional input (this differs from a salted hash function as the salt is commonly not secret). A data controller can replay the function on the attribute using the secret key, but it is much more difficult for an attacker to replay the function without knowing the key as the number of possibilities to be tested is sufficiently large as to be impractical.*

- *Deterministic encryption or keyed-hash function with deletion of the key: this technique may be equated to selecting a random number as a pseudonym for each attribute in the database and then deleting the correspondence table. This solution allows diminishing the risk of linkability between the personal data in the dataset and those relating to the same individual in another dataset where a different*

---

[39] Article 29 Working Party, Opinion 05/2014 on Anonymisation Techniques, p.20. Available at: http://ec.europa.eu/justice/article-29/documentation/opinion-recommendation/index_en.htm.

[40]
Hash functions are usually designed to be relatively fast to compute, and are subject to brute force attacks. Pre-computed tables can also be created to allow for the bulk reversal of a large set of hash values. The use of a salted-hash function (where a random value, known as the 'salt', is added to the attribute being hashed) can reduce the likelihood of deriving the input value but nevertheless, calculating the original attribute value hidden behind the result of a salted hash function may still be feasible with reasonable means.

Article 29 Working Party, Opinion 05/2014 on Anonymisation Techniques, p.20. Available at: http://ec.europa.eu/justice/article-29/documentation/opinion-recommendation/index_en.htm.

pseudonym is used. Considering a state-of-the-art algorithm, it will be computation-ally hard for an attacker to decrypt or replay the function, as it would imply testing every possible key, given that the key is not available.

- *Tokenization: this technique is typically applied in (even if it is not limited to) the financial sector to replace card ID numbers by values that have reduced usefulness for an attacker. It is derived from the previous ones being typically based on the application of one-way encryption mechanisms or the assignment, through an index function, of a sequence number or a randomly generated number that is not mathematically derived from the original data.*[41]

3.3 Anonymous Data

It is clearly stated in Recital 26 of Regulation 679/2016 that

[t]he principles of data protection should (...) not apply to anonymous information, namely information which does not relate to an identified or identifiable natural person or to personal data rendered anonymous in such a manner that the data subject is not or no longer identifiable. This Regulation does not therefore concern the processing of such anonymous information, including for statistical or research purposes.

In 2013, the MIT Technology Review raised the question of whether big data has made anonymity impossible, arguing that the exponential "expansion" of data most definitely "carries someone's digital fingerprints."[42] It should be noted that big *personal* data is becoming more and more than norm, rather than the exception, calling for the adoption of specific safeguarding measures with regard to the individual's right to privacy.

Simply speaking, to obtain genuine anonymization in the sense of the GDPR, the individual must in no way be identifiable from his/her personal data. This means that in the case that it is indeed possible to identify the individual in any way through the use of available technology, the data shall be considered as merely pseudonymized as opposed to anonymized and therefore constitute personal data which is subject to relevant legislation.[43] Going further into a European legal perspective, it is relevant to highlight four key features when discussing anonymization:

[1] Anonymization can be a result of processing personal data with the aim of irreversibly preventing identification of the data subject.

---

[41] Article 29 Working Party, Opinion 05/2014 on Anonymisation Techniques, pp. 20–21. Available at: http://ec.europa.eu/justice/article-29/documentation/opinion-recommendation/index_en.htm.

[42] MIT Technology Review. 2013. Big Data Gets Personal. www.technologyreview.com/business-report/big-data-gets-personal/.

[43] Information Commissioner's Office, Guide to the General Data Protection Regulation (GDPR). Available at: https://ico.org.uk/for-organisations/guide-to-the-general-data-protection-regulation-gdpr/what-is-personal-data/what-is-personal-data/.

[2] Several anonymization techniques may be envisaged, and there is no prescriptive standard in EU legislation.

[3] Importance should be attached to contextual elements: account must be taken of "all" the means "likely reasonably" to be used for identification by the controller and third parties, paying special attention to what has lately become, in the current state of technology, "likely reasonably" (given the increase in computational power and tools available).

[4] A risk factor is inherent to anonymization: this risk factor is to be considered in assessing the validity of any anonymization technique—including the possible uses of any data that is "anonymized" by way of such technique—and severity and likelihood of this risk should be assessed.[44]

With respect to anonymization techniques, randomization and generalization have been extensively considered by Article 29 Working Party in the context of the European legislation. Randomization is contemplated within a group of techniques that effectively eliminate the connection between the individual and his/her data, emphasizing that

If the data are sufficiently uncertain then they can no longer be referred to a specific individual. Randomization by itself will not reduce the singularity of each record as each record will still be derived from a single data subject but may protect against inference attacks/risks and can be combined with generalization techniques to provide stronger privacy guarantees. Additional techniques may be required to ensure that a record cannot identify a single individual.[45]

The Article 29 Working Party groups generalization into what it terms a "second family of anonymization techniques",[46] which

consists of generalizing, or diluting, the attributes of data subjects by modifying the respective scale or order of magnitude (i.e. a region rather than a city, a month rather than a week). Whilst generalization can be effective to prevent singling out, it does not allow effective anonymisation in all cases; in particular, it requires specific and sophisticated quantitative approaches to prevent linkability and inference.[47]

Last but not least, as Article 29 Working Party wisely reminded,

[44] Article 29 Working Party, Opinion 05/2014 on Anonymisation Techniques, pp. 6–7. Available at: http://ec.europa.eu/justice/article-29/documentation/opinion-recommendation/index_en.htm.

[45] Article 29 Working Party, Opinion 05/2014 on Anonymisation Techniques, p. 12. Available at: http://ec.europa.eu/justice/article-29/documentation/opinion-recommendation/index_en.htm.

[46] Article 29 Working Party, Opinion 05/2014 on Anonymisation Techniques, p. 16. Available at: http://ec.europa.eu/justice/article-29/documentation/opinion-recommendation/index_en.htm.

[47] Article 29 Working Party, Opinion 05/2014 on Anonymisation Techniques, p. 16. Available at: http://ec.europa.eu/justice/article-29/documentation/opinion-recommendation/index_en.htm.

data controllers should consider that an anonymised dataset can still present residual risks to data subjects. Indeed, on the one hand, anonymisation and re-identification are active fields of research and new discoveries are regularly published, and on the other hand even anonymised data, like statistics, may be used to enrich existing profiles of individuals, thus creating new data protection issues. Thus, anonymisation should not be regarded as a one-off exercise and the attending risks should be reassessed regularly by data controllers.[48]

Organizations handling data in Smart Data environments should first consider whether the goals that they aim to achieve can nonetheless be pursued by analysing anonymized information, instead of personal data. This will avoid the application of the personal data protection legal framework and fully protect the privacy of individuals. If it is not possible to obtain the desired results by processing anonymized information, then pseudonymization should be considered as a useful security measure that can be applied to personal data in order to improve legal compliance and mitigate the risks on individuals. The processing of personal data should indeed be the last option that companies and organizations consider.

4 CONTROLLER, PROCESSOR, AND JOINT-CONTROLLERSHIP

The traditional data protection roles of controller and processor are significantly challenged in a Smart Data environment where a high volume of data is processed by algorithms and potentially transferred between machines. Determining the controller and the processor of data is of fundamental importance in order to correctly allocate compliance duties, obligations, and responsibilities between the parties. In principle, data controllers bear more duties, obligations, and responsibilities than data processors. However, it is note-worthy that under EU data protection law, the controller and processor are under a regime of joint and several liability with respect to individual rights to compensation.[49]

---

[48] Article 29 Working Party, Opinion 05/2014 on Anonymisation Techniques, p. 4. Available at: http://ec.europa.eu/justice/article-29/documentation/opinion-recommendation/index_en.htm.

[49] See Article 82 of the Regulation (Eu) 2016/679 of the European Parliament and of the Council of 27 April 2016 on the protection of natural persons with regard to the processing of personal data and on the free movement of such data, and repealing Directive 95/46/EC (General Data Protection Regulation), *Official Journal of the European Union*, L 119/3, 4/5/2016. Available at: https://eur-lex.europa.eu/legal-content/EN/TXT/HTML/?uri=CELEX:32016R0679&from=IT.

> Right to compensation and liability. 1. Any person who has suffered material or non-material damage as a result of an infringement of this Regulation shall have the right to receive compensation from the controller or processor for the damage suffered. 2. Any controller involved in processing shall be liable for the damage caused by processing which infringes this Regulation. A processor shall be liable for the damage caused by processing only where it has not complied with obligations of this Regulation specifically directed to processors or where it has acted outside or contrary to lawful instructions of the controller. 3. A controller or processor shall be exempt from liability under paragraph 2 if it proves that it is not in any way responsible for the event giving rise to the damage. 4. Where more than one controller or processor, or both a controller and a processor, are involved in the same processing and where they are, under paragraphs 2 and 3, responsible for any damage caused by processing, each controller or processor shall be held liable for the entire damage in order to ensure effective compensation of the data subject. 5. Where a controller or processor has, in accordance with paragraph 4, paid full compensation for the damage suffered, that controller or processor shall be entitled to claim back from the other controllers or

The data controller can be defined as the natural or legal person who determines (alone or with others) the purposes and means of the processing of personal data.[50] Generally speaking, this is the entity that collects, or for which data are collected. Since it makes the most important decisions, the responsibilities for compliance rest on its shoulders. The data processor is regarded as the natural or legal person that actually collects and processes personal data upon instructions, on behalf and under the supervision of the data controller.[51]

"Purpose" can be typically defined as "an anticipated outcome that is intended or that guides your planned actions" (*WHY*) and "means" as "how a result is obtained or an end is achieved" (*HOW*).[52] To understand who decides/determines the purposes, the relevant questions are "why is this processing taking place? Who initiated it?"[53] It is worth pointing out that the level of influence on the "why" is greater than the one on the "how" to qualify a controller. On this point, the Article 29 Working Party specified that

> while determining the purpose of the processing would in any case trigger the qualification as controller, determining the means would imply control only when the determination concerns the essential elements of the means. In this perspective, it is well possible that the technical and organizational means are determined exclusively by the data processor.[54]

Moreover, Article 29 Working Party further explained that "the crucial challenge is thus to provide sufficient clarity to allow and ensure effective application and compliance in practice. In case of doubt, the solution that is most likely to promote such effects may well be the preferred option."[55]

Practically speaking, analysis on large datasets is typically outsourced to companies which have developed sophisticated algorithms and methodologies and it is difficult to fit such relationship into client–controller and service provider–processor. In

processors involved in the same processing that part of the compensation corresponding to their part of responsibility for the damage, in accordance with the conditions set out in paragraph 2.

6. Court proceedings for exercising the right to receive compensation shall be brought before the courts competent under the law of the Member State referred to in Article 79(2)."

[50] See Articles 4(7) and 24 of the Regulation (Eu) 2016/679 of the European Parliament and of the Council of 27 April 2016 on the protection of natural persons with regard to the processing of personal data and on the free movement of such data, and repealing Directive 95/46/EC (General Data Protection Regulation), *Official Journal of the European Union*, L 119/3, 4/5/2016. Available at: https://eur-lex.europa.eu/legal-content/EN/TXT/HTML/?uri=CELEX:32016R0679&from=IT.

[51] See Articles 4(8) and 28 of the Regulation (Eu) 2016/679 of the European Parliament and of the Council of 27 April 2016 on the protection of natural persons with regard to the processing of personal data and on the free movement of such data, and repealing Directive 95/46/EC (General Data Protection Regulation), *Official Journal of the European Union*, L 119/3, 4/5/2016. Available at: https://eur-lex.europa.eu/legal-content/EN/TXT/HTML/?uri=CELEX:32016R0679&from=IT.

[52] See Article 29 Data Protection Working Party. 2010. Opinion 1/2010 on the concepts of "controller" and "processor", p. 13. Available at: http://ec.europa.eu/justice/article-29/documentation/opinion-recommendation/index_en.htm.

[53] See Article 29 Data Protection Working Party. 2010. Opinion 1/2010 on the concepts of "controller" and "processor", p. 8. Available at: http://ec.europa.eu/justice/article-29/documentation/opinion-recommendation/index_en.htm.

[54] Article 29 Data Protection Working Party. 2010. Opinion 1/2010 on the concepts of "controller" and "processor", p. 14. Available at: http://ec.europa.eu/justice/article-29/documentation/opinion-recommendation/index_en.htm.

[55] Article 29 Data Protection Working Party. 2010. Opinion 1/2010 on the concepts of "controller" and "processor", p. 7. Available at: http://ec.europa.eu/justice/article-29/documentation/opinion-recommendation/index_en.htm.

a situation where Company A has collected a database and Company B is requested to analyse it on behalf of Company A, one would say that Company A is the controller and Company B is the processor. However, Smart Data environments are far more complex than this example. First, data are often analysed in almost real time, e.g., consider analytic cookies and similar tracking technologies. Leveraging the roles from the previous example, in this case, the database is subject to analysis initiated by both Company A and Company B. Moreover, Company B provides the same services to a number of other companies and sometimes shares knowledge derived from the analysis of data collected by different companies. In this case, one may consider the functioning of data management platforms (DMPs) typically used for collecting and managing data, mainly for digital marketing purposes.[56] In Smart Data environments, therefore, the data protection role of Company B is often progressively transformed into a controller—or a joint-controller—instead of being a mere processor.

Article 26 of Regulation 679/2016 states that "[w]here two or more controllers jointly determine the purposes and means of processing, they shall be joint controllers."[57] It is reasonable to maintain that joint-controllership will become increasingly applicable to Smart Data environments as an effect of a recent decision of the Court of Justice of the European Union (the "Court"), which makes it necessary to profoundly re-think the allocation of data protection roles. On 5 June 2018, in the landmark decision involving Wirtschaftsakademie Schleswig-Holstein GmbH and Unabhängiges Landeszentrum für Datenschutz Schleswig-Holstein,[58] the Court ruled that administrators of fan pages on social networks may be considered as "joint controllers", along with the companies responsible for those social networks, regarding the processing of personal data of social network users which may be carried out via those pages.

Though based on the now repealed Directive 95/46/EC, the similarities between the provisions, the Directive assessed, and those found in Regulation 679/2016 signify that the decision maintains relevance in the current framework. More precisely, the administrators of fan pages on Facebook are able to obtain anonymous statistical information on fan page visitors—whether or not these visitors have a Facebook account—by means of the "Facebook Insights" service. This service automatically places "cookies" (i.e., small text files) onto the devices used by visitors, containing a unique user code, which can be read and matched to users by Facebook. The resulting information (which is considered personal data) is used to provide

---

[56] See the Wikipedia definition here: https://en.wikipedia.org/wiki/Data_management_platform.

[57] Article 26, Regulation (Eu) 2016/679 of the European Parliament and of the Council of 27 April 2016 on the protection of natural persons with regard to the processing of personal data and on the free movement of such data, and repealing Directive 95/46/EC (General Data Protection Regulation), *Official Journal of the European Union*, L 119/3, 4/5/2016. Available at: https://eur-lex.europa.eu/legal-content/EN/TXT/HTML/?uri=CELEX:32016 R0679&from=IT.

[58] Case C-210/16. Available at: http://curia.europa.eu/juris/document/document.jsf;jsessionid=9ea7d0f130daa5580c707a0 b4ee09cb787cc77515c22.e34KaxiLc3eQc40LaxqMbN4Pb3iPe0?text=&docid=202543&pageIndex=0&doclang= EN&mode=lst&dir=&occ=first&part=1&cid=325138.

aggregated statistics to fan page administrators, and also to enable Facebook to improve its ability to target advertisements over its network.

The Court's decision results from the actions of the German supervisory authority for the Region of Schleswig-Holstein, which issued an order against Wirtschaftsakademie Schleswig-Holstein GmbH—an administrator of a Facebook fan page—to deactivate the fan page. The reasoning for this order was that neither the administrator nor Facebook informed visitors that such processing would occur. The administrator contested this, essentially maintaining that it should not be considered a controller in relation to processing carried out solely by Facebook. The matter was brought before the German courts, culminating in a referral to the Court of Justice of the European Union. In his Opinion, Advocate-General Bot stated that the decision to create and operate a fan page on Facebook is what triggers this data processing, and that administrators can decisively influence the termination of processing by deactivating a fan page. The Court noted that merely making use of a social network would not suffice to render the user a joint controller regarding the processing of personal data by the network. However, by creating a fan page and relying on "Facebook Insights," the administrator effectively enables Facebook's ability to place cookies on visitors' devices.

Additionally, "Facebook Insights" allows administrators to define abstract criteria regarding the "target audience" of their fan page, based upon which information will be collected and the statistics that will be generated (e.g., age, sex, occupation, purchasing habits). As such, the Court held that administrators contribute to determining the purposes of processing of personal data on these visitors, even though they actually receive no "personal data" (but only anonymized, aggregated statistical reports)—this is because, as the Court clarifies, "Directive 95/46 does not, where several operators are jointly responsible for the same processing, require each of them to have access to the personal data concerned [in order to be considered data controllers]."

In its conclusion, the Court stressed that relying on a social network in order to benefit from associated services will not exempt fan page administrators from compliance with their obligations regarding the processing of personal data—in particular, providing adequate information to data subjects.

The Court's decision highlights that companies may be found to be joint-controllers regarding the processing of personal data which is carried out over social networks if they somehow enable or contribute to that processing.

Aside from the specific context (i.e., social media), the decision clearly paves the way to a very extensive interpretation of the joint-controllership relationship. The Court effectively *de facto* argued that even an "indirect" and "partial" determination of the purposes and the means of the data processing activities may configure a joint-controllership between the parties involved. Art. 26 of Regulation 679/2016 requires joint controllers to establish an arrangement, determining their respective responsibilities for compliance with the Regulation 679/2016. Therefore, duties, obligations, and respective responsibilities will be allocated on the relevant parties participating in the data processing activities by means of contractual arrangements and should be given particular attention.

5 METHODOLOGY TO DESIGN PROCESSING ACTIVITIES IN LINE WITH THE DATA PROTECTION PRINCIPLES

Now that the core principles of data protection have been explained, the concept of personal data analysed in depth, and the roles of controller and processor clarified, it is possible to discuss a practical methodology to design processing activities in compliance with the relevant legal rules.

In order to correctly apply the approach of data protection by design, a thorough analysis of the relevant data processing activities that an organization would like to carry out is necessary. In this respect, the so-called data protection impact assessment (DPIA)[59] can be seen as an integral part of the data protection by design approach. Despite the fact that according to European Union data protection legislation a DPIA is only required in certain circumstances, such as where the processing is likely to result in a risk to rights and freedoms, it is a sound practice to undertake a DPIA regarding any type of processing activities an organization is considering carrying out. This is even more relevant for organizations that handle personal data in Smart Data environments, which usually involve a large amount of personal data, present a high level of complexity, and a potentially high risk for the involved data subjects. In fact, a DPIA can be regarded as a tool that can be used to understand the relevant data processing in depth and to identify and reduce the data protection risks of processing activities by helping organizations to design processes for handling personal data not only in compliance with legal requirements but that are also more efficient and effective.[60]

A DPIA typically contains:

(a) a systematic description of the envisaged processing operations and the purposes of the processing, including, where applicable, the legitimate interest pursued by the controller;

(b) an assessment of the necessity and proportionality of the processing operations in relation to the purposes;

(c) an assessment of the risks to the rights and freedoms of data subjects (...); and

---

[59] See on the data protection impact assessment Article 35 of the Regulation (Eu) 2016/679 of the European Parliament and of the Council of 27 April 2016 on the protection of natural persons with regard to the processing of personal data and on the free movement of such data, and repealing Directive 95/46/EC (General Data Protection Regulation), *Official Journal of the European Union*, L 119/3, 4/5/2016.Available at: https://eur-lex.europa.eu/legal-content/EN/TXT/HTML/?uri=CE LEX:32016R0679&from=IT. Further information on the data protection impact assessment and the related methodology to correctly carry it out can also be found in the Article 29 Working Party's Guidelines on Data Protection Impact Assessment (DPIA) (wp248rev.01). Available at: http://ec.europa.eu/newsroom/article29/item-detail.cfm? item_id=611236.

[60] This view is also confirmed by the Information Commissioner's Office Guide to the General Data Protection Regulation (GDPR). Available at: https://ico.org.uk/for-organisations/guide-to-the-general-data-protection-regulation-gdpr/ accountability-and-governance/data-protection-by-design-and-default/.

(d) the measures envisaged to address the risks, including safeguards, security measures, and mechanisms to ensure the protection of personal data and to demonstrate compliance (…) taking into account the rights and legitimate interests of data subjects and other persons concerned.[61]

By means of a systematic and rigorous DPIA, organizations active in Smart Data environments can practically determine the type of technical and organizational measures they need to adopt in order to ensure that processing complies with the core data protection principles indicated above and, in a nutshell, ensure:

- *Openness*—data subjects are correctly and exhaustively informed about the data processing activities carried out in Smart Data environments, with special attention to profiling activities which can be very intrusive to the privacy of the individuals. When data is collected responsibly, consumer trust can improve, and users may therefore provide more accurate data. In a recent survey by SDL, 79% of respondents said they are more likely to provide personal information to brands that they "trust."[62] Having an adequate, transparent, and easy-to-understand privacy policy is the first step in that direction, as it would contribute to balancing out the information asymmetry between companies and consumers.[63]

---

[61] Article 35.7 of the Regulation (Eu) 2016/679 of the European Parliament and of the Council of 27 April 2016 on the protection of natural persons with regard to the processing of personal data and on the free movement of such data, and repealing Directive 95/46/EC (General Data Protection Regulation), *Official Journal of the European Union*, L 119/3, 4/5/2016. Available at: https://eur-lex.europa.eu/legal-content/EN/TXT/HTML/?uri=CELEX:32016R0679&from=IT.

[62] SDL. 2014. New Privacy Study Finds 79% Of Customers Are Willing To Provide Personal Information To A "Trusted Brand". www.sdl.com/about/news-media/press/2014/new-privacy-study-finds-customers-are-willing-to-provide-perso nal-information-to-trusted-brands.html.

[63] Too often, privacy policies consist of texts written in "legalese" that are not understood by users. A study conducted by Pew Research Center found that 52% of respondents did not know what a privacy policy was, erroneously believing that it meant an assurance that their data would be kept confidential by the company. This could also be the result of the fact that privacy policies are often long and complex texts that would simply take too much time to read carefully. According to a study carried out by two researchers from Carnegie Mellon, it would take a person an average of 76 work days to read the privacy policy of every website visited throughout a year (Cranor, Lorrie Faith and Aleecia McDonald. 2008. Reading The Privacy Policies You Encounter In A Year Would Take 76 Work Days. Available at: www.theatlantic.com/technology/archive/2012/03/reading-the-privacy-policies-you-encounter-in-a-year-would-take-76-work-days/253851/). The study was conducted in 2008 and, considering the dynamic expansion of the use of internet, it may well be that nowadays an individual would not even have enough time in a year to read all the privacy policies of the websites visited within that same year.

Privacy policies are, at the moment, the main tool that is considered to ensure transparency and yet, they are inefficient at achieving that purpose. Some options for improving privacy policies were suggested by a group of professors from Carnegie Mellon at PrivacyCon held in January 2016 (2016. PrivacyCon Organised By The Federal Trade Commission. Expecting the Unexpected: Understanding Mismatched Privacy Expectations Online. Available at: www.ftc.gov/system/files/documents/videos/privacycon-part-2/part_2_privacycon_slides.pdf). These ideas could help users decipher the privacy policies and understand how their data is being used, increasing transparency and contributing to balancing out the information asymmetry between data controllers and data subjects. The author supports these suggestions and agrees with the idea that visually enhanced privacy policies would be more effective and would transmit information quickly, grabbing users' attention. Using different colours to identify the privacy level compliance would render the privacy policy, as a tool, more efficient in communicating the information. As a positive side effect, easier to understand privacy policies would enhance user trust in the data

- *Collection limitation: lawfulness and fairness*—the data processed are relevant, proportionate, and not excessive, avoiding indiscriminate data collection, obtained and further processed on a lawful legal ground (with the knowledge and, where appropriate, the consent of the data subject). Moreover, considering fairness, the processing of personal data should not unreasonably intrude upon the data subjects' privacy, autonomy, and integrity, and data controllers should not exert pressure on data subjects to provide personal data. Technologies should be used in a fair way, so to respect fundamental rights and freedoms and to grant dignity to the digital society. Accordingly, fairness should also be built into the very design of data processing activities, whether they be products, services, or applications and—most importantly—the algorithms that underpin the information/data processing should be designed and developed in a way that is compatible with the concept of "fairness by design."

- *Purpose specification*—the large datasets to be analysed are collected for such purpose, or if the data were collected for other different purposes, the controller will have to preventively ascertain whether the processing is compatible with the purpose for which the personal data were initially collected.[64]

---

controller and contribute to data quality, as users tend to provide more accurate data about themselves when they trust the company that is the controller of that data.

[64] To ascertain whether the processing is compatible with the purpose for which the personal data are initially collected, account should be taken of, inter alia, to elements like: a) any link between the purposes for which the personal data have been collected and the purposes of the intended further processing; b) the context in which the personal data have been collected, in particular regarding the relationship between data subjects and the data controller; c) the nature of the personal data, in particular whether special categories of personal data are processed (e.g., sensitive and judicial data); d) the possible consequences of the intended further processing for data subjects; e) the existence of appropriate safeguards. In addition, it is noteworthy that Article 29 Data Protection Working Party (in its Opinion 03/2013 on purpose limitation Adopted on 2 April 2013. Available at: http://ec.europa.eu/justice/article-29/documentation/opinion-recommendation/index_en.htm) specified that, in order to lawfully process big data, in addition to the key factors of the compatibility assessment to be fulfilled, additional safeguards must be assessed to ensure fair processing and to prevent any undue impact. Article 29 Working Party considered two scenarios to identify such additional safeguards:

> 1. [i]n the first one, the organizations processing the data want to detect trends and correlations in the information. 2. In the second one, the organizations are interested in individuals (...) [as they specifically want] to analyse or predict personal preferences, behaviour and attitudes of individual customers, which will subsequently inform 'measures or decisions' that are taken with regard to those customers.

In the first scenario, so-called "functional separation" plays a major role in deciding whether further use of data may be considered compatible. Examples of "functional separation" are: "full or partial anonymisation, pseudonymization, or aggregation of the data, privacy enhancing technologies, as well as other measures to ensure that the data cannot be used to take decisions or other actions with respect to individuals".

In the second scenario, prior customers/data subjects' consent (i.e., free, specific, informed and unambiguous "opt-in") would be required for further use to be considered compatible. In this respect, Article 29 Data Protection Working Party specifies that "such consent should be required, for example, for tracking and profiling for purposes of direct marketing, behavioural advertisement, data-brokering, location-based advertising or tracking-based digital market research." Furthermore, access for data subjects: (i) to their "profiles", (ii) to the algorithm which develops the profiles, and (iii) to the source of data that let to the creation of the profiles is regarded as pre-requisite for consent to be informed and to ensure transparency. Moreover, data subjects should be effectively granted the right to correct or update their profiles. Last but not least, Article 29 Data Protection Working Party recommends allowing "data portability":

- *Use limitation*—personal data are not disclosed to third parties (e.g., share knowledge—which may include personal data—generated by the analysis of large datasets with other companies/organizations) without having a lawful ground for doing so; made available or otherwise used for purposes other than those that were initially specified or compatible purposes (see also Purpose Specification Principle).

- *Security*—personal data are protected by reasonable security safeguards against such risks as loss or unauthorized access, destruction, use, modification, or disclosure of data (e.g., by using encryption and pseudonymization techniques—see also Section 3 above, strict identity management and access control to preserve data confidentiality, other technical measures to ensure integrity, availability, and resilience of data processing systems). Given that unauthorized/unlawful use of Smart Data (i.e., the knowledge produced by analysing large datasets) may pose a very high risk to the rights and freedoms of the related individuals, security is of paramount importance when processing large datasets, especially if sensitive data are involved.

- *Data quality*—the personal data collected and further processed are relevant to the purposes for which they are to be used, accurate, complete, and effectively kept up-to-date. In this respect, it is important to keep in mind that data quality is not only a legal compliance obligation, but it is paramount to ensuring that algorithms and analytical procedures are carried out successfully and that the predicted results correspond with the reality. Contrariwise, massive quantities of inaccurate data can lead to skewed results and poor decision-making. In this respect, the implementation of regular reviewing procedures aimed at identifying the data that is still relevant, rectifying the data that is out of use or incorrect, and deleting the data that is no longer of use is helpful. It would also constitute an opportunity to periodically "clean up" the database in order to ensure that there is no "dead data" from the so-called "zombie accounts."[65]

- *Access and correction*—the extent of applicability of the principle of access and correction is carefully evaluated with respect to large datasets and/or to a specific portion of them. Accordingly, data subjects should be effectively provided with access to their personal data and the possibility to correct them, where this principle applies without restrictions. Moreover, organizations should keep in mind that new rights for data subjects were recently introduced as a further extension of the right

---

safeguards such as allowing data subjects/customers to have access to their data in a portable, user-friendly and machine readable format [as a way] to enable businesses and data-subjects/consumers to maximise the benefit of big data in a more balanced and transparent way.

[65] European Data Protection Supervisor. 2014. Report Of Workshop Of Privacy, Consumers, Competition And Big Data. https://secure.edps.europa.eu/EDPSWEB/webdav/site/mySite/shared/Documents/Consultation/Big%20data/14-07-11_EDPS_Report_Workshop_Big_data_EN.pdf.

of access, such as the right to restriction of processing (e.g., where the accuracy of the personal data is contested by the data subject, for a period enabling the controller to verify the accuracy of the personal data; or where the processing is unlawful and the data subject opposes the erasure of the personal data and instead requests the restriction of their use) and the right to data portability (the right for the data subject to receive the personal data concerning him or her, which he or she has provided to a controller, in a structured, commonly used, and machine-readable format and have the right to transmit those data to another controller without hindrance from the controller to which the personal data have been provided).

Such new rights actually empower users in the control of their own data. Importantly, the European Data Protection Supervisor recently spoke of the "featurization" of personal data in Opinion 7/2015 on Big Data, arguing that the degree of control over one's data can be construed as a feature of the service provided to the user.[66] Data controllers, argues the European Data Protection Supervisor, should "share the wealth" created by the processing of the personal data with those persons whose data is being processed. At the moment, users do not usually have easy access to the type of data stored about them by a specific company and most data controllers give users the possibility to contact them via email or telephone in order to enquire about their data. Alternatively, users can be provided with easy access to their data, for example, by logging into a control panel section on a website, along with the possibility of modifying it or changing the permissions to process it. Users who have control of their data are likely to trust the data controller more and, potentially, to collaborate for various projects by volunteering their data or agreeing to participate in case studies. The European Data Protection Supervisor speaks of "personal data spaces" ("data stores" or "data vaults") as "user-centric, safe and secure places to store and possibly trade personal data."[67] A (highly positive) side effect would be the granting to users of more control over their data which would in turn contribute to increasing data quality, which, as suggested earlier may significantly impact the relevance of the processing and the decisions made as a result of it.

- *Accountability*—data processing activities carried out in Smart Data environments are documented together with the relevant information in order to demonstrate that they have been carried out in full compliance with the relevant applicable legal provisions. Accountability is related not only to how the data is processed (how transparent the procedures are, how much access the data subject has to his/her own data, etc.) but also to issues of algorithmic decision-making, which is the direct result of big personal

[66] European Data Protection Supervisor. 2015. Opinion 7/2015 – Meeting The Challenges Of Big Data: A Call For Transparency, User Control, Data Protection By Design And Accountability. Available at: https://secure.edps.europa.eu/EDPSWEB/webdav/site/mySite/shared/Documents/Consultation/Opinions/2015/15-11-19_Big_Data_EN.pdf.

[67] European Data Protection Supervisor. 2015. Opinion 7/2015 – Meeting The Challenges Of Big Data: A Call For Transparency, User Control, Data Protection By Design And Accountability. Available at: https://secure.edps.europa.eu/EDPSWEB/webdav/site/mySite/shared/Documents/Consultation/Opinions/2015/15-11-19_Big_Data_EN.pdf.

data processing in the 21st century.[68] Processing personal data at a high level is only a means to an end, the final purpose being reaching the ability to make informed decisions on a high scale based on the information collected and stored in big databases. As the European Data Protection Supervisor underlined in Opinion 7/2015, "one of the most powerful uses of big data is to make predictions about what is likely to happen but has not yet happened."[69] Proactive steps, such as disclosing the logic involved in big data analytics or giving clear and easily understandable information notices to data subjects, are necessary to establish accountability. This is especially true since the information contained in the datasets is not always collected directly from the concerned individual—data can be "volunteered, observed or inferred, or collected from public sources."[70] Apart from disclosing the logic involved in decision-making based on big data analytics and ensuring that data subjects have access to their own data, as well as to information as to how it is processed, companies should also develop policies for the regular verification of data accuracy, data quality, and compliance with relevant legislation. In this respect, the European Data Protection Supervisor pointed out that "accountability is not a one-off exercise."[71]

6 CONCLUSIONS

In Smart Data environments, large volume of data will be processed by numerous entities at a very high speed. It was explained in the chapter that such intensive processing activities potentially expose individuals to risks. An effective protection of individuals' rights to privacy and data protection is needed. Data protection by design has been presented as the means to dynamically achieve compliance with privacy principles—granting dynamic proception to the involved individuals—and structure processes which will return more meaningful results to organizations.

More precisely, this chapter has explored the concept of data protection by design as a means of compliance with the principles of data protection, making use of high-level European Union regulations and legal opinions in combination with the empirical research and experience of the author. European Union data protection legislation has been used as a point of reference due to the international applicability of its principles and the high standard of protection that it offers data subjects. EU privacy legislation indeed embeds all the core international data protection principles and is in fact being used as a point of reference in forthcoming legislation in other parts of the world. The arguments and the

---

[68] Kubler, Kyle. 2016. "The Black Box Society: The Secret Algorithms That Control Money And Information". Information, Communication & Society, 1–2. doi:10.1080/1369118x.2016. 1160142.

[69] European Data Protection Supervisor. 2015. Opinion 7/2015 – Meeting The Challenges Of Big Data: A Call For Transparency, User Control, Data Protection By Design And Accountability. Available at: https://secure.edps.europa.eu/EDPSWEB/webdav/site/mySite/shared/Documents/Consultation/Opinions/2015/15-11-19_Big_Data_EN.pdf.

[70] European Data Protection Supervisor. 2015. Opinion 7/2015 – Meeting The Challenges Of Big Data: A Call For Transparency, User Control, Data Protection By Design And Accountability. Available at: https://secure.edps.europa.eu/EDPSWEB/webdav/site/mySite/shared/Documents/Consultation/Opinions/2015/15-11-19_Big_Data_EN.pdf.

[71] European Data Protection Supervisor. 2015. Opinion 7/2015 – Meeting The Challenges Of Big Data: A Call For Transparency, User Control, Data Protection By Design And Accountability. Available at: https://secure.edps.europa.eu/EDPSWEB/webdav/site/mySite/shared/Documents/Consultation/Opinions/2015/15-11-19_Big_Data_EN.pdf.

conclusions reached in this chapter can therefore very well be extended beyond European boarders.

The chapter commenced by providing the reader with a general understanding of the fundamental data protection principles, focusing especially on the concepts of fairness and data quality within the Smart Data Environment. Particular attention was then given to answering the essential question of what constitutes personal data while at the same time addressing anonymization and pseudonymization techniques alongside best practices for compliance that both protect data subjects and help companies and organizations to make more informed and accurate decisions. Subsequently, in the chapter, the concepts of controller, processor, and joint-controller were analyzed also using the very recent example of the Court of Justice of the European Union's Opinion in the Wirtschaftsakademie Schleswig-Holstein GmbH case, providing a practical understanding of the different roles and responsibilities of each actor. Finally, a practical methodology, which also leverages the highly relevant tool known as the data protection impact assessment, for designing processing activities in compliance with the relevant legal rules was considered.

The chapter concludes that the integration and application of data protection by design is a necessary prerequisite for the lawful generation of Smart Data, stressing its use as an instrument for allowing companies to comply with relevant legislation while possibly increasing trust from customer and therefore allowing for further business insights while at the same time benefiting data subjects.

Index